Conflict and Peace Building i Divided Societies

CW00797376

This groundbreaking book provides an integrated account of ethnic, nationality and sectarian conflicts in the contemporary world, the causes of civil war and insurgencies. It explains how collective myths and threat propaganda promote violence and block conciliation, shows the dilemmas of counterinsurgency in the Occupied Territories, Balkan wars, Afghanistan, Iraq, highlights the shortcomings of humanitarian intervention (Rwanda, Bosnia and Darfur) and showcases peace negotiations and their implementation. Oberschall analyzes:

- peace building through constitutional design
- power sharing governance
- disarming combatants, post-accord security and refugee return
- transitional justice (truth and reconciliation commissions, war crimes tribunals)
- economic and social reconstruction in a multiethnic society

In addition to many examples from the last two decades, Oberschall provides a comprehensive overview of the conflict and peace processes for Bosnia, Northern Ireland, and Israel–Palestinians. He argues that insurgency creates contentious issues over and above the original root causes of the conflict, that the internal divisions within the adversaries trigger conflicts that jeopardize peace processes, and that security and rebuilding a failed state are a precondition for lasting peace and a democratic polity.

This book will be essential reading for undergraduate and postgraduate students, researchers and academics interested in the fields of peace studies, war and conflict studies, ethnic studies and political sociology.

Anthony Oberschall was educated at Harvard and earned a PhD in sociology at Columbia in 1962. He has taught at UCLA, Yale and since 1980 at the University of North Carolina, where he is now Emeritus Professor. He has been a Guggenheim fellow and a New Century Scholar in the Fulbright program. He has taught and researched in East and Central Africa, the People's Republic of China, Germany, France, Hungary, Bosnia, and Northern Ireland. Among his books are *Social Conflict and Social Movements* (1973) and *Social Movements: Ideologies, Interests, and Identities* (1993). Since the late 1980s, he has studied, lectured and written on conflict and conflict management in divided societies.

Conflict and Peace Building in Divided Societies

Responses to ethnic violence

Anthony Oberschall

LONDON AND NEW YORK

First published 2007
by Routledge
2 Park Square, Milton Park, Abingdon, Oxon OX14 4RN

Simultaneously published in the USA and Canada
by Routledge
270 Madison Ave, New York, NY 10016

Routledge is an imprint of the Taylor & Francis Group, an informa business

© 2007 Anthony Oberschall

Typeset in Sabon
by Keystroke, 28 High Street, Tettenhall, Wolverhampton
Printed and bound in Great Britain
by Antony Rowe Ltd, Chippenham, Wiltshire

British Library Cataloguing in Publication Data
A catalogue record for this book is available from the British Library

Library of Congress Cataloging in Publication Data
A catalog record for this book has been requested

ISBN10: 0–415–41161–0 (pbk)
ISBN10: 0–415–41160–2 (hbk)

ISBN13: 978–0–415–41161–5 (pbk)
ISBN13: 978–0–415–41160–8 (hbk)

Contents

Maps

Preface

I started writing this book in my mind when Yugoslavia was breaking up in 1991–2. I had studied and written about the by-and-large peaceful change in Eastern Europe from communism to democracy, and I had also written about the failed democracy movement in China in 1989. The different courses and outcomes required an explanation. When peace implementation got under way after Dayton, the travails of the peace process in the Balkans and elsewhere focused my attention on peace building. Excellent books and publications on international conflict management and ethnic conflicts had been written and more were published every month. I learned a lot reading them; nevertheless I believe the link between the conflict side and the peace building side of the whole story had been downplayed, and that is how I developed the "conflict and conciliation dynamic" which serves as my unifying theme throughout.

I owe a debt to a 1998 grant from the National Science Foundation for research on "Cooperation and conflict: encounters between Europeans and non-Europeans" and from the United States Institute of Peace in 1998 to study "Ethno-national conflict and its prevention." I am also thankful for having gotten a Fulbright fellowship in the New Century Scholars Program in 2002–3 whose theme was "Addressing sectarian, ethnic, and cultural conflicts." I am a firm believer in field work for complementing other modes of social science research. These grants enabled me to travel, observe, and interview in Serbia, Bosnia, and Croatia in the summer of 1998 and in Ireland, north and south, in the summer of 2003. I am very much indebted to the academics, political leaders, media professionals, and just ordinary people that I interviewed and consulted during these research trips. Unfortunately plans for field work in the West Bank in association with Israeli and Palestinian scholars fell through when the al-Aqsa intifada erupted in the fall of 2000.

I thank Professor Mari Fitzduff at INCORE at the University of Ulster in Derry (now at Brandeis University), who kindly hosted me in Northern Ireland, and Professor Boldizar Jaksic and Ivana Spasic at the Institute for Philosophy and Social Theory, who hosted me in Belgrade and helped arrange interviews. Professor Ivana Vuletic at my university was indispensable for a content analysis of news stories on ethnic conflict in Bosnia.

I am grateful to Louis Kendall Palmer III, who was researching for a PhD dissertation on the peace process in both Bosnia and Northern Ireland and kept providing useful data from the field, and valuable criticism for the Bosnia and Northern Ireland chapters. I was supervisor of Ken's dissertation "Power Sharing Extended: Policing and Education Reform in Bosnia-Hercegovina and Northern Ireland," which he completed in 2005.

Many individuals and groups helped in one way or another. I had the benefit of having some wonderfully alert students from around the world enrolled in short courses on ethnic conflict and peace building that I taught at UNC and Duke, Brno and Nürnberg. I thank the UNC University Center for International Studies and the Duke Center for International Development for that opportunity, and Rotary International, who funded the UNC–Duke Center for International Studies in Peace and Conflict Resolution. At the University of Nürnberg–Erlangen, I thank Professor Henrik Kreutz for inviting me, and at Thomas Masaryk University in Brno the dean of the social science faculty Ladislav Rabusic. I benefited a great deal from discussions with fellow New Century Scholars Edward Tiryakian, James Peacock, John Darby, Pierre du Toit, and Bruno Coppieters. Other friends who may not even know that I kept learning from them during many conversations over the years are Donald Horowitz, Robert Jenkins, Fatos Tarifa, Niki Harsanyi, Michael Seidman, and Norbert Kerzman. None of those mentioned here are responsible for my shortcomings.

I owe a debt to the International Association of Genocide Scholars, whose member I have been, for organizing conferences and meetings during which, in addition to hearing academics from many disciplines and countries, we all had a chance to hear and converse with diplomats, UN officials, military officers in peacekeeping operations, constitutional lawyers, international tribunal prosecutors, humanitarian aid workers, human rights advocates, media professionals, and others, who provided a continuous commentary and analysis on conflicts and peace operations around the world which they had participated in. The Association is a valuable repository of human capital on international conflict management. I also wish to thank Laura Oaks for the painstaking editing job of getting my text into publishable format.

This book is dedicated to my wife Aida who was the first to know everything about its contents and the first to advise me on how I was doing and where I was headed. Aida helped me interviewing informants in Northern Ireland and in London and improved my writing style with her red pen.

1 The dynamics of ethnic conflict

Ethnic conflict

In a wide-ranging review of US foreign policy for the twenty-first century, David Callahan writes that:

> Ethnic conflict and quests for self-determination around the world are likely to be the most important factors . . . in the next decades . . . this phenomenon should not be seen as separate from other global problems such as terrorism, failed states, rivalry among the great powers, access to natural resources, and clashes between the modern and the traditional, or between the rich and the poor.
>
> (2002: 02)

Most states are multiethnic. "Nation state" is a frequently misused or loosely used term for states in which a single nationality is dominant. A survey of 132 entities considered states as of 1971 showed that only 12 states (9 percent) can be justifiably termed "nation states" (i.e. with a very small minority distinct from the dominant nationality, as e.g. Japan). In 30 percent the largest nationality accounts for less than half the population, and in another 23 percent the largest is between half and three-quarters (O'Connor 1978). Twenty years later, there were about 180 states and "fewer than twenty are ethnically homogeneous, in the sense that ethnic minorities account for less than 5 percent of the population" (Welsh 1993: 45). What state an ethnic group is located in, whether it is large rather than small in relation to other groups, whether it is a majority or minority, and whether it is integrated or excluded, dominating or subordinate in mainstream institutions, are complex results of empire building and break-up, war, conquest, migration, forced expulsion, genocide, epidemics and environmental degradation, nationalist movements, state formation, assimilation, discrimination, and encapsulation, i.e. the ebb and flow of history. When the relationships of the dominant group to ethnic minorities are hostile rather than cooperative, the society can be described for short as "divided." What determines whether the relations between these groups will be hostile rather than cooperative?

Of an estimated 700 to 800 minority groups of substantial size worldwide, the Minorities at Risk (MAR) project (Quinn and Gurr 2003) identified 285 that were politically active at some time since the 1950s. Of these, about half pursued self-determination goals such as collective rights, political autonomy, or an independent state of their own. Of the 148 that pursued self-determination goals, 78 engaged in conventional, non-violent politics, but 70 have waged some form of armed struggle at one time or another in the past 50 years. Ethnic armed movements stubbornly resist settlement. Of the 70, as of 2003, six had deescalated to conventional or militant but non-violent politics; 26 hostilities had ceased but a peace agreement remained contested (these two together are termed "contained" conflict); 25 had varying modes of violent conflict; and in only 12 cases was the conflict "settled," i.e. there existed an uncontested peace agreement granting regional autonomy to the ethnic challenger or an independent state that is internationally recognized. The five independent states were Bangladesh in 1971, Slovenia and Croatia in 1991, Eritrea in 1993, and East Timor in 2002.

Quantitative analysts of civil wars and major civil strife of all types since World War II, including ethnic conflict, found that various measures of ethnic, linguistic, and religious divisions in a country are correlated with the risk of major violent conflict. The strength of these relationships is disputed because of differences over operationalizing civil wars, ethnic factionalism, and religious divisions. Nevertheless, after a comprehensive review of measurement issues, Nicholas Sambanis wrote that:

> I have shown that there is a very strong relationship between ethnic heterogeneity [in a state] and an aggregate indicator of armed conflict and much less so with civil war. To the extent that violence escalates from minor to higher levels, we should find ethnic factionalism to be significant in a dynamic model of violence escalation.
>
> (2004: 848)

Doyle and Sambanis (2000) found that 64 percent of 124 post-World War II civil wars are ethnic and/or religious; James Fearon (2003: 15) classifies 55 percent of civil wars as "ethnic" and another 17 percent as having an ethnic component. Roy Licklider (1995) found that 69 percent of civil wars are "identity based," i.e. ethnic, religious, or both. Depending on various ways of defining the pivotal variables, several researchers find that between 15 percent and 30 percent only of all civil wars are settled in negotiations, the vast majority ending with unilateral military victory, and that is especially true for ethnic civil wars (King 1997; Walter 1997). Doyle and Sambanis (2000: 786) found that civil war settlements have a 65 percent failure rate, i.e. there is resumption of armed conflict after two or more years of no hostility, and write that "wars with an ethnic or religious overtone are less likely to be resolved" than other civil wars. Licklider (1995) agrees that identity civil wars settled by negotiation are less likely to be stable than those settled by military victory. Fearon (2003: 15) finds that ethnic wars last longer than other civil wars, especially when a minority fights state-sponsored control of indigenous resources by immigration.

From this body of quantitative research one must conclude that, although a majority of ethnic groups have conventional, non-violent, albeit strained, political relations with their governments and other groups, there is a substantial risk that violent forms of contention will occur and that these will escalate to insurgencies and civil war. Once armed fighting starts, ethnic conflict resists negotiated settlement, lasts longer, and has a greater like-lihood of renewed violence. It is therefore important to explain why ethnic groups persist, what makes them susceptible to conflict with dominant groups and one another, and what circumstances cause change from non-violent to violent modes of conflict.

Ethnic groups

"Ethnic group" denotes a large aggregate of people who have a self-defined name, believe they share a common descent, have common historical memories and elements of shared culture (such as religion and language), and have an attachment (even if only historical and sentimental) to a specific territory (Kaufman 2001: 16). Ethnic groups tend to have solidarity and we-feeling; their members experience something of "ourselves" in each other (Horowitz 1985: 155). "Nationality" refers to a large group of people having a common and distinguishing racial, linguistic, and cultural back-ground, and forming a constituent element of a larger group (*Webster's Third New International Dictionary* 1981). The two terms, "ethnic group" and "nationality," overlap; social scientists prefer "ethnic group" because it is more richly descriptive and includes religion as a possible focus of self-defined identity, and because some ethnic groups are marginal rather than a constituent element of a larger group. Because "ethno-national" is more cumbersome than "ethnic," I will simply use "ethnic." Religious groups may not believe they share a common descent, but they share beliefs about the sacred, rituals, and organizations that set them apart from other religious groups, and they have an attachment to specific holy places. In some cases, like the designation Protestant and Catholic in Northern Ireland, the religious categories mask the underlying nationality division and conflict, which is Unionist and Nationalist, i.e. those who want the province to remain in the United Kingdom and those who want it to unite with the Republic of Ireland. Unionists and Nationalist have no conflict over the freedom of religion or matters of religious belief and doctrine. In some other cases where religion divides along lines of ethnicity or nationality, as with Bosniaks, Albanians, Muslims, Serbs, and Croats in the former Yugoslavia, or Greek and Turkish Cypriots, there may have been some peripheral religious issues on top of fundamental territorial sovereignty and minority self-determination conflicts, but freedom of worship was not contested by the adversaries. In these conflicts, religious differences carry the freight of past hostile group relations, and prejudice and justification for superior status are expressed in religious as well as ethnic labels and pejoratives. In still other conflicts – Chechen versus Russian, or Sunni and Shia in Iraq, or the military government and the Islamists in Algeria – religious division plays a more central role, but the fundamental religious issue is between a secular and a religious mode of organizing the state and the laws. Again, because "ethno-religious" is a cumbersome term, I will use "ethnic" unless the context demands more specificity.

Ethnic groups are not a fact of nature, like species, and cannot be defined by objective physiological attributes. They have been socially constructed throughout history, as the French historian Ernest Renan pointed out in his path-breaking lecture on the origin of nations at the Sorbonne in 1882, "Qu'est ce qu'une nation?" (What is a nation?):

> A Frenchman is neither Gaul, nor a Frank, nor a Burgundian. Rather he is what has emerged from the cauldron in which, presided over by the Kings of France, the most diverse elements have together been simmering ... An Englishman is ... neither the Briton of Julius Caesar's time, the Anglo-Saxon of Hengist's time, nor the Dane of Canut's time, nor the Norman of William the Conqueror's time, it is rather the result of all these ... Is Germany an exception? ... That is a complete illusion. The whole of the South was once Gallic; the whole of the east ... Slavic ... What is the defining feature of these states? It is the fusion of their component populations.
>
> ([1882] 1996: 42–6)

What is true for nations is also true for ethnic groups. But just because nations and ethnic groups are a product of historical and social construction does not make them arbitrary or less than real in the hearts and minds of their members and for other groups. Belief systems transform what is socially constructed by human action into eternal verities by invoking God's will and design, ancestors, history, biology, and inheritance. Such beliefs tend to legitimize ethnic differences, separation, and exclusion.

Ethnics derive benefits from group membership. Ethnic identities, solidarities, and boundaries persist because they supply a steady stream of benefits to group members. Research by Tajfel and others on social identity and the sources of group boundaries found that "a positive social identity is achieved by comparing one's own group with other groups to establish a positively valued psychological distinctiveness for the in-group vis-à-vis the outgroup" (Hewstone and Cairns 2001: 321). Self-esteem, a sense of belonging, and an identity (who am I?) are not private acts but produced and validated in group interactions. Individuals seek support for their beliefs and values, especially if these cannot be empirically verified, like religious beliefs and political values, and get it with social validation in like-minded groups. That in turn increases loyalty to the support group (Hinde 1997: 10). Preference for the group one belongs to is caused by these benefits of membership and is not motivated by hostility towards other groups.

Why would a group that confers such psychological benefits be an ethnic group rather than some other group? Why would ethnic groups have an in-group preference for neighboring, for schooling, and for associations of all sorts with their fellow ethnics and, by extension, transacting selectively within rather than across ethnic boundaries? Ethnic groups are composed of people who share more in common with one another, on average, than with other ethnic groups and the population at large. They share (or believe they do) ancestors and history, often language and religion, salient values and beliefs, and lifestyles, and they believe that these attributes distinguish them from other groups. There are benefits, not just emotional we-feeling, from such commonalities in transacting with others.

The theory of collective action (Coleman 1990) has demonstrated the advantages of transacting with partners who expect a long-term relationship over an episodic one, who have much rather than little information about one another, who share overlapping social networks rather than weak links, and who count on third-party assistance for social control, and reciprocity rather than absence of obligation. These attributes of transacting make for cooperation rather than opportunism, long-term investment in relationships and the nurturing of social capital rather than a short-term instrumental stake, open-ended rather than instant reciprocity, and personalized rather than stereotyped interaction. In-group relationships build on trust and also create more trust than stranger interactions. Many ethnic trading communities throughout the world, called middlemen minorities, owe their success to group business organization and a distinctive in-group morality. A classic anthropological study of a Hausa trading community in Ibadan attributes its success to the sectarian boundaries it erected for checking assimilation into Yoruba society, and sums it up thus: "ethnicity . . . is not an archaic survival arrangement carried over into the present by conservative people . . . ethnic groups are . . . interest groupings" (Cohen 1969: 190, 192).

Because of in-group preferences, establishing and maintaining shared institutions with outsiders can be problematic. Thomas Schelling (1984) has demonstrated how micro preferences, i.e. slight in-group preferences for fellow ethnics in mixed institutions, can have unexpected macro consequences in the long run, i.e. totally segregated institutions like neighborhoods and schools. Evidence from studies of black–white residential segregation and school integration in the US support that analysis (Giles 1978; "New Survey" 1979). Schelling's insight is that, without discrimination and with a fair amount of acceptance for group mixing, in-group preference makes stability of mixed institutions problematic.

What rapidly unravels mixed institutions is not in-group preference alone but communal violence and the security concerns it engenders. Meron

Benvenisti (1986: 86–8) recalls that during his youth there was no residential segregation in Jerusalem. Then came the Arab riots of 1929 and later the Arab revolt of 1936–9 against the British mandate and the Jewish presence. Jews fled to Jewish districts and the result was almost total segregation: "segregation is a mechanism for coping with physical threat . . . for preserving group identity from alien influences, and to conserve cultural heritage and life-styles." Studies of increasing Catholic–Protestant segregation in Belfast from 1840 on show that the sectarian riots of 1857 and 1886, the civil strife in the early 1920s, and the sectarian rioting followed by paramilitary violence in 1969 led to sharp, discrete jumps in residential segregation (Boal 2002). Nor did public policy in housing reverse the trend. The Northern Ireland Housing Executive had a policy of color-blind allocation, but the residents "reproduced Belfast sectarian geography by self-selection" into green and orange housing estates ("green" for Irish and "orange" for British) "such that public sector housing became more segregated than private sector housing" (Bollens 1998: 97–8). In a wide-ranging analysis of communal riots, Donald Horowitz concluded that they reduce ethnic heterogeneity and lead to separation and sharper ethnic boundaries (2001: 424).

Ethnic groups and collective goods

Well-being depends not only on person-to-person transactions but on collective goods. Mancur Olson (1976) reflected on what would be an optimum social unit whose members would satisfy each other's wants and preferences through interpersonal exchange and sharing collective goods. The answer turns out to be a social unit composed of people who have similar preferences for collective goods but are diverse in their preferences for individual goods and in their talents and capacities. Consensus on collective goods (e.g. language, group identity, collective symbols of shared values and group dignity as expressed in the celebration of holidays, the naming of streets and public monuments, the role of religion in public life) reduces contentious conflicts in politics and makes for low-cost governance. Variety in private tastes, resources, and talents allows for beneficial exchange in fulfilling individual wants. Ethnic groups satisfy the two Olson dimensions of a viable social unit that deliver well-being to members.

Social movement theory and research have shown that ethnic groups are capable and willing to undertake collective action in defense of their interests and way of life. Ethnic groups tend to have a viable communal organization with dense interpersonal networking and cultural, social, and religious associations embedded in the ethnic community. Political mobilization of ethnic groups does not start from scratch. Ethnic activists redirect a pre-existing robust ethnic infrastructure of associations and networks to political pursuits, adapting ethnic symbols and loyalties to political goals. This mode of political mobilization bypasses cumbersome recruitment of individuals a few at a time by recruiting pre-existing groups, termed "bloc mobilization," and overcomes the cost of organization by federation of the blocs into an overarching organization. It is a rapid, low-cost mode of mobilization (Oberschall 1993: chapter 1). Because the blocs are small face-to-face groups, solidarity and internal networking overcome the usual free-rider tendencies in large groups against collective good attainment. Last but not least, solidarity and we-feeling create a "multiplier effect" for grievances: wrongs and injustices to some members of the ethnic group are framed and experienced by others as wrongs and as injustice.

The conclusion of a substantial body of social science is that ethnic groups are viable social units that benefit their members, that they provide advantages for maintaining boundaries and separation with other groups, and that they have high capacity for collective action. Avoidance of other groups in "live and let live" arrangements does not necessarily follow from ethnicity, but tends to be the legacy from past inter-ethnic violence. What might weaken the viability of ethnic groups?

Ethnic groups and social change

In conventional wisdom, social change erodes ethnic groups and boundaries. Social changes produce internal differentiation from migration, work, and education, and ultimately intermarriage between ethnic groups. In the labor force, one has no choice of work mate, but has to accept the employers' assignments. In industries, mines, offices, laboratories, sports teams, armies, and other pursuits, members of various ethnic groups learn cooperation and develop shared interests across ethnic groups, such as trade union or professional association. In time, the more affluent and the less affluent, the more and the less educated, and the religious-minded and the secular will form identities and relationships that breach ethnic encapsulation. In Olson's analysis, internal differentiation produces new wants and preferences for collective goods, e.g. collective bargaining for all workers in an industry. Individual wants, goods, services, and transaction partners can be satisfied just as well or better by associating with outsiders as within one's ethnic group. When ethnic barriers weaken, the pool for associates, friends, and spouses expands. Social psychologists have shown that integration works best when the groups interact as equals and when the contribution of each group is necessary to achieve goals that benefit all (Sherif 1966).

Ethnic majorities and minorities typically resulted from conquest and colonization, labor migration, trading opportunities for immigrants, the diffusion of religions, wars and forced population movements, the formation of states, and the drawing and redrawing of international boundaries. In these processes, relationships of domination and subordination, of superior to inferior, prevailed over ethnic equality. Charles Wagley and Marvin Harris put it thus:

Numerous underprivileged groups of people, ineptly called minorities .
. . are singled out by their societies in which they reside and . . . are
subjected to economic exploitation, segregation, and discrimination . . .
[they] are disliked and ridiculed because they speak a different tongue,
practice a different religion, or because their skin is a different color,
their hair a different texture, or simply because their ancestors emigrated
from a different country.

(1958: 1)

Unless public policy is opposed, ethnic relations of domination and subordination, privilege and exclusion, attraction and rejection in ethnic
relations will reproduce along historical and cultural fault lines.

The pre-modern state built on the viability of ethnic groups and on
ethnic and religious separation. An ancient principle of empires was that
laws and rights were not territorial but group based, each group maintaining their separate institutions, though accepting the overall authority of
the imperial rulers. Thus monogamy and polygamy (and more broadly
different family law) could coexist in the same city, but practiced in separate
religious communities, as in Indian cities for Hindus and Muslims, and in
Jerusalem for Muslims and Jews. When empire, colonial rule, and the dynas-
tic principle for state and government were successfully challenged with
the democratic principle of government by the people and the right to self-
determination of peoples, states had to deal with ethnicity and nationality in
their constitutional design. After the Bolshevik Revolution, the Soviet state's
constitution was anchored in both the territorial and the ethnic principle.
According to Ronald Suny,

the new Soviet state was both federative . . . and based on ethnic
political units. Indeed, for more than a decade following the civil war,
nationalities, like Jews and Armenians, and the Ukrainians in Russia,
enjoyed extra territorial privileges, with their own schools and soviets
operating in republics of other nationalities . . . Rather than a melting
pot, the Soviet Union became the incubator of new nations.

(1993: 57)

When European states in the nineteenth century modernized with rail-
roads, primary education, industries, and expanded state institutions, they
awakened national and ethnic sentiments among groups who wanted their
language, their identity, and their dignity recognized.

Writing about Austro-Hungary, Oscar Jaszi observed that:

the process of national awakening was initiated by the Habsburgs
themselves though indirectly and unintentionally . . . [with] a system
of elementary education in the mother tongue . . . the educational and
the cultural policy of enlightened absolutism aroused in all parts of the

monarchy a certain amount of national consciousness among the backward peoples.

(1961: 252–3)

In Cyprus, before the British occupation in 1878, Greek and Turkish Cypriots spoke a unified Cyprus dialect and were tolerant of religious differences. The British introduced a separate education system which led to separation (Rotchild 1981: 95). With census categories and classifications, policies, and laws that discriminated against particular groups, states legitimize ethnic identities and increase ethnic competition for scarce resources. The modernizing state has had a dual record of ethnic integration and separation. Anthony Smith summarizes a great deal of history when he writes that "the growing interventionism of the modern state simply reinforced ethnic solidarity and exacerbated ethnic differences" (1993: 33).

Like the state, religion has been a great agent of social change, but it too has a checkered record on ethnic mixing. The world religions strove to unite all people into a single brotherhood of believers who share religious beliefs and doctrines, sacred texts, rituals, and lifestyles, under a single authority. Religion has the capacity for shaping both the private values and goals and the collective goods preferences of its adherents, which breaks down ethnic and other inherited barriers to transacting. But the truth value of religious beliefs and doctrines does not rest on experiences common to all humans. It is a matter of social construction and faith, thus vulnerable to dispute and conflict. The history of religions has been as much a history of sects, factions, heresies, and wars as a history of brotherhood and unity. Religious prohibition against intermarriage or the requirement of conversion of one of the spouses and, in a more secular context, the social barriers and inhibitions that persist on religious intermarriage impede ethno-religious integration.

Many religious disputes and sects have mirrored pre-existing divisions based on ethnicity, nationality, and language. When the medieval Catholic Church converted and incorporated pagan Slavs, the converts demanded that they be able to communicate with their priests in their own native languages rather than in German. "In these regions," writes Bartlett, "where Christian peoples of different law and language intermingled, the Church itself became an arena of ethnic competition" (1993: 221). Centuries later, as Christianity spread in Southern Africa, many African converts formed their own breakaway independent sects (Sundkler 1961). As with other processes of socio-economic and political change, religious conversion and diffusion was not a meeting of equals, but of dominant and subordinate, and reproduced existing cleavages. Church congregations in the United States are among the most race-segregated institutions.

Although internal differentiation slowly erodes ethnicity under conditions of equality and of cross-cutting ties, economic change keeps generating inequalities that coincide with ethnic separation and distinctiveness. States and religions have accommodated and made concessions to the logic of ethnicity. Social discrimination and obstacles to integration by dominant groups against minorities maintain ethnic boundaries, and such practices are often encouraged or tacitly condoned by the state authorities and religious organizations. Despite some acculturation and assimilation and some melting together, despite the slow growth of overarching and shared identities, such as citizenship and professions, many ethnic groups have persisted in the contemporary world.

Core issues posed by ethnicity

As the MAR research has documented, about half of politically active minorities have pursued self-determination goals such as an independent state, political autonomy, or collective rights at some time since the 1950s. Societies deeply divided on religion, language, nationality, and ethnicity – ethnicity for short – have to resolve the issue of stateness through constitutional design. According to Juan Linz and Alfred Stepan, "A 'stateness' problem may be said to exist when a significant proportion of the population does not accept the boundaries of the territorial state . . . as a legitimate political unit to which they owe obedience" (1992: 123). The constitutional design and democratic governance for divided societies is problematic. For Donald Horowitz, "some part of the problem of ethnic conflict is a matter of finding ways around the stumbling block of contemporary conceptions of sovereignty" (1990: 453). Ethno-national identity and sentiments are embedded in sovereignty of a territory – a homeland. Control of territory, preferably a state of one's own, provides ultimate security and protection: we are secure here with our own people; our fundamental rights and interests are protected. A state is also a source of pride. One's nationality is recognized by other states, international agencies, the Olympic Games, and so on. It means that "we are somebody," and can be located on the world's map. These emotional attachments are expressed in "blood and soil" and "kinship" metaphors, as in "mother tongue" and "fatherland." Religion and language are face to face and spatial. Lacking critical ethnic mass in a territory, these institutions will languish and those of another ethnic group will prevail.

A variety of constitutional designs and governance institutions have been tried for accommodating ethnic political aspirations in a democratic state, from federation and regional autonomy to political power sharing (Sisk 1996). All face obstacles because the principle of self-determination of peoples is incompatible with the principle of the territorial integrity of states, and because the self-determination claims of different peoples inhabiting the same territory are in conflict. Each group prefers being a majority in their own state to being a minority in another's state, and the same applies for municipalities, cantons, electoral districts, and other political units.

There is no consensus on how best to accommodate to self-determination claims in multiethnic states. Largely on the basis of the same instances of multiethnic states and conflicts, Chaim Kaufmann argues that, after ethnic civil wars, "the international community must abandon attempts to restore war-torn multi-ethnic states" (1996: 137), whereas Timothy Sisk believes that federalism, "the territorial division of powers," is a good design for ethnic conflict management (1996: 49–53). Jack Snyder argues that ethno-federalism, "territorial subunits within the state whose boundaries are designed to coincide with ethnolinguistic concentrations," has "a terrible track record . . . [it] is frequently a recipe for subsequent partition" (2000: 327–8). John McGarry and Brendan O'Leary "offer a more balanced and nuanced assessment of the value and durability of multinational federations than put forward by critics of ethno-federalism" (2005: 287). State sovereignty, state territory and boundaries, and the boundaries of jurisdictions within states are intertwined in complex fashion with minority and majority status of ethnic groups, the history of majority–minority relations in specific contexts, their international relations ramifications, and much else, making generalizations problematic. How the stateness issue was negotiated in peace settlements will be described for Bosnia, Israelis–Palestinians, and Northern Ireland in Chapters 4, 5 and 6.

Theories of ethnic conflict

There is no shortage of theories about the causes of these conflicts. Each suggests a particular mode of ethnic conflict management. Ancient hatred (AH) assumes that ethnic identities and group membership are primordial, sharply distinct, resilient to change, salient across all institutions and activities, and present high risk for repeated destructive conflicts (Kaplan 1994). Ethnic groups resist assimilation and erosion despite education, secularization, and modernization. Ethnic relations are burdened with collective myths, fears, and hostile emotions. Embedded in culture and socialization, their histories highlight past conflicts and threats from other groups. Even during periods of peaceful cooperation, incidents can spark hostilities that escalate rapidly to destructive conflicts. AH is pessimistic about ethnic conflict management and about establishing lasting peace. Only separation will ensure lasting ethnic peace. Mixing or remixing (after ethnic cleansing) the ethnic groups in the same territory invites renewed violent conflict.

Manipulative elites (ME) assumes social construction of ethnic identities rather than primordial origins (Gagnon 1994/5). Ethnic elites contend for power by manipulating ethnic divisions and blowing them out of proportion with fear and hate propaganda, and with aggressive crisis mobilization and politics. Conciliation becomes difficult when rival leaders demonize ethnic opponents who can never be trusted and must therefore be dominated or defeated. Internal conflict management does not work; in all likelihood, external states should intervene to stop the manipulative elites at early stages of conflict with a mix of incentives and sanctions to halt an ethnic crisis.

Identity politics (IP) holds that divisive ethnic myths, symbols and stereo-types, and fears are embedded in folk culture, socialization, and institutions of divided societies (Kaufman 2001). These become activated for aggression at the onset of ethnic conflict, and resonate with ordinary folk. Conflict management consists of building overarching, shared identities and symbols, and providing political institutions that organize interest and divisions that cut across ethnic lines.

Security dilemma (also referred to as the spiral of insecurity) holds that, under conditions of state failure and breakdown (approaching anarchy), all groups fear for their life and property, and some ethnic groups mobilize for their own defense against rivals they view as threatening, including by arming, which in turn is threatening to other groups, who in turn arm, which leaves all more insecure and stimulates further mobilization and counter-mobilization, as in an arms race between states (Posen 1993). The process can be modeled as a Prisoner's Dilemma. Unlike a nuclear weapons arms race that may lead to stable deterrence, in ethnic conflict there are incentives for preemptive strikes justified by past hostile relations. What drives the conflict is not hatred, as in AH, but mistrust and fear. Conflict management will consist of credible assurances of security from external sources, such as interposing a powerful external military force to prevent armed conflict.

Economic roots (ER) disputes that ethnic divisions are at the root of major contemporary internal armed conflicts (Collier *et al.* 2003). Instead, ER holds that the root causes of such conflicts are poverty, economic stag-nation, unemployment, corruption, and a failed state on the demand side, and warlords organizing unemployed young men into armed bands, opportunities for making a living by aggression and robbery, trafficking in narcotics, controlling revenues from natural resources such as oil and diamonds, and favorable terrain for insurgency on the supply side. Conflict management in the short run is to interdict the resources for waging the conflict and economic development in the long run.

These theories have their proponents and critics, and an abundance of case studies and quantitative analyses has made for conflicting results and interpretations that have not been sorted out. All theories could be true, in some conflicts more so than others, yet that is not decisive for peace making. Whether or not ancient hatred is a root cause, ethnic groups that managed to cooperate for decades before armed conflict will come to hate, fear, and mistrust one another as a consequence of destructive conflict. Whether or not manipulative elites instigated the conflict, during armed conflict conciliatory leaders are likely to become eclipsed by manipulative extremists. Whether or not divisive ethnic myths, symbols, and identities preceded the conflict, during confrontation and in its aftermath they become widely believed and accepted at the expense of shared identities and unifying symbols and institutions. Whether or not the spiral of insecurity led to civil war, it surely is the case that, after hostilities cease, disarming the combatants and putting in place institutions that assure the security of the adversaries are necessary for keeping the peace. Whether or not poverty and unemployment are a root cause, protracted violent conflict destroys the economy and the material underpinnings of life and of institutions. The dynamics of the conflict changes the adversaries, adds new issues to the original ones, and calls forth new strategies of contention. Violent conflict fuels ethnic hatred, brings to power manipulative elites, creates fear and insecurity, is responsible for economic ruin, and fosters exclusive identities and divisive symbols. Conflict managers and peace makers must deal with these consequences of conflict, whatever the *status quo ante*. In Chaim Kaufmann's words, "solutions to ethnic wars do not depend on their causes" (1996: 137). Highlighting the root causes of ethnic conflict, at the expense of the changes that take place during the conflict, risks underestimating and misunderstanding the complexities of peace making.

These theories lack specificity and context. Long-standing enmity might exist between two ethnic groups, but violent conflict is episodic, not permanent. Manipulative elites are quite common, but they displace more conciliatory leaders from power only under particular circumstances. Poverty, lack of development, and other components of ER are widespread, but armed ethnic conflict is not. An ethnic group might attack an adversary not because it feels insecure but because it is strong and confident of winning.

The contexts of ethnic conflict

Ethnic groups in conflict are often a majority privileged by the state dominating a minority. They inhabit a society not as equals but as a landlord dealing with weak tenants. There are benefits to domination which the privileged group is opposed to giving up. Exploitation and unequal treatment do not rest on power and coercion alone. Domination is justified by a mixture of folk beliefs and intellectual discourse that the majority accept as truths. The ideology of domination is routinely transmitted by parents and peers, schools, and religious bodies. Conforming to these beliefs, prejudices, and stereotypes gets one accepted in the group; doubting or rejecting them gets one marginalized. The privileged believe that their good fortune is deserved and that exclusion of the minority is justified. The justification is especially robust when the dominant and the excluded group greatly differ on physical appearance, language, religion, customs, and lifestyles. Three circumstances increase the likelihood of violent confrontation between majority and minority:

1   When members of the minority seek relief from domination by assimilation into the dominant group, they are excluded or marginalized. Denied the "exit" option, the minority resort to collective "voice" to press for reforms, equality, and down the road even self-determination. They find justification for the goals and rights denied to them in the legal and moral discourse legitimizing equality, the right to self-determination

of a people, and human rights, enshrined in political philosophy, conventions and treaties, and international charters. To obtain a benefit from someone, one might try persuasion, exchange something of value with the other, or coercion. The dominant group firmly adheres to its ideology justifying domination, and is not persuaded. The subordinate group, the challenger, does not have anything of value to offer in exchange for reforms. What remains is coercion. That does not mean armed struggle, not at the start, but protest, strikes, non-cooperation, and public defiance. Even when non-violent, such confrontation makes trouble by disrupting daily routines and business as usual. The message is clear: we, the minority, stop making trouble when you, the dominant group, make concessions on our justified demands. The dominant group has another option: punishing the troublemakers and repressing others in the minority by way of deterrence. Some challengers then respond in violent confrontation. Alternately, a conciliatory leadership team in the dominant group agrees to some reforms, but these are sabotaged by opponents, or don't provide the expected benefits. The challenger group loses faith in peaceful change, and some within it start violent confrontations.

2   Confrontation is initiated by the dominant group when it perceives a threat from an ethnic minority. When a rapid numerical increase of subordinate groups relative to the size of the dominant group occurs, it is framed as a threat to its favored position and way of life. These changing demographics might be due to differential birth rates, to immigration and internal migration, or both, as was true for Kosovo, which changed from 67 percent Albanian and 24 percent Serb in 1961 to 82 percent Albanian and 10 percent Serb in 1991 (Mertus 1999: 316). In the nineteenth and early twentieth centuries, large-scale immigration to the US, of Irish to East Coast cities in the 1840s, of Japanese and Chinese to the West Coast, of Southern and Eastern European immigrants in the 1890s to 1920s, of black migrants from the South to northern cities in World War I, triggered hostility, xenophobia, race riots, and calls for limiting immigration through legislation, initiated by the majority (Graham and Gurr 1969; Olzak 1966). Influx of ethnic groups increased competition in labor markets, in politics and for living space, often aggravated by manipulative elites who schemed against emerging labor unions by pitting low-wage immigrant workers against higher-wage natives, and hiring strike breakers from ethnic minorities. But the concerns and fears of the dominant group go beyond the effects of competition to more diffuse anxieties of ordinary folk about losing control over institutions that have served them well and about changes alien to their way of life. The perception of threat from changing numbers and the relative size of ethnic groups has been a frequent and predictable source of ethnic conflict initiated by the dominant group.

3   The third circumstance is the waning days of a once stable structure of rule when groups stake out competing claims to power, as at the end of colonial rule, of a communist regime, or of a military strong-man regime. A study of the incidence and causes of internal wars found that the "often violent demise of colonial rule around the world removed a major driver of war from the international system." However, this change did not reduce the number of civil wars because "in many newly independent countries the struggle against colonialism was replaced by wars over who should control the post-colonial state" (Human Security Centre 2005: 151). These changes can set off a free-for-all contention for power by a variety of groups, many of them ethnic, over territorial authority, a new constitutional order, and control of institutions, resources, and symbolic capital. Elections become an ethnic census and a public demonstration of numerical strength. State institutions like the army, the police, the courts, and other institutions on which the stability of the social order rested become internally divided or partisan. Some groups do not trust them to remain impartial or effective. Amidst growing uncertainty, people turn for security of life and property to viable ethnic groups. No group wants to end up a minority in a territory if it can become a majority by redrawing boundaries or by expelling other groups. There are many scenarios of the violent breakup of a stable structure of power. Even when some stability is reached through a succession of armed conflicts and state formation, a legacy of unresolved conflicts remains, as in Kashmir, in Chechnya, in Palestine, and in Cyprus.

Mobilization for armed conflict

For understanding the dynamics of the confrontation, the adversaries have to be further fleshed out: what their constituent units are, how they mobilize their supporters, what opportunities and constraints determine strategies of confrontation, and what changes they undergo as a result of the conflict.

One adversary is the regime. Most likely it is an authoritarian regime: there may be competitive elections for a legislature but it exercises limited control and accountability over the executive. Its human rights record is weak. Monty Marshall (2003: 20) found that, for 1955–91, authoritarian regimes are five to six times more likely to experience armed conflicts and adverse regime change than either autocratic or democratic regimes. In an authoritarian regime, the dominant ethnic majority forms the majority of leaders and officials and controls the security apparatus. But the regime is not a unitary actor. It may have an internal opposition faction. The military, the bureaucracy, the professions, and the media have their own interests, and the top leadership has to rule with these agents. It also needs the support of ordinary citizens to hold power. The relationships between leaders, internal opposition, agents, and the citizenry have to be understood.

The leaders may be divided between moderates and hardliners, between those who consider concessions to an adversary and those who favor ruling coercively. The regime controls the state and its institutions, most importantly the army, police, and other security forces. It controls the state-owned media, industries, pensions, public housing, and employment, and it appoints judges. Nevertheless regime policies and strategy are somewhat constrained by laws, the opposition, the professionalism of its agents, and public opinion. Public perception of threat in a developing ethnic crisis weakens those constraints. Exaggerating the threat boosts public support for emergency measures that authorize the regime to move aggressively against opponents and ethnic adversaries.

The adversary is an ethnic minority. Its challenge is conditioned by grievances, mobilization capacity, ideology, and opportunity (Oberschall 1993: chapter 1). On grievances, David Quinn and Ted Robert Gurr (2003: 34–5) found that, of 285 ethnic minorities, as many as 161 sought greater autonomy or self-determination in 1990–2000. Those that did were more likely to have lost autonomy in the recent past. On mobilization capacity, not surprisingly ethnic minorities are well organized, cohesive, and territorially concentrated, all attributes of viable ethnic groups. As for opportunity, ethnic groups that experience low levels of political discrimination and obtain external support are more likely to become challengers. Ideology was not measured in the research, probably because it was assumed that human rights and self-determination discourse is widely available in the contemporary world. According to Joseph Rotchild, "Out of the reality of the multiethnic state and the principle of self-determination [of peoples] for legitimate state formation came the politics of ethnonationalism" (1981: 14). Like the regime, the challenger may also be split between a conciliatory faction advocating conventional political means and a radical faction favoring coercive means and armed struggle. Its strategy of confrontation is constrained by resources and by the regime response to its challenge. Opportunities for militant strategies increase with external assistance for manpower, weapons, resources, safe haven, and diplomatic backing. Neither the challenger nor the regime is a unitary actor, and both keep changing during the conflict.

In addition to the regime and the challenger, new players enter the conflict: diplomatic initiatives are undertaken by other states; humanitarian agencies for relief of civilians volunteer their services; UN peacekeepers may be deployed; foreign fighters and mercenaries may be recruited by the adversaries. Some interveners want to help end the fighting but others are partisan. The presence of interveners will influence the strategies of the adversaries: a two-player conflict expands into a more complex multi-actor mix of conflict possessing a different dynamic:

1   Real issues in ethnic relations exist such as an impending shift in political power. The issue is threatening because ethnic violence in similar crises has occurred episodically in the past. But there is also a history of non-

violent coexistence between the dominant and subordinate groups and there are institutions for cooperation and sharing. Institutions and popular culture embody both traditions and both realities in ethnic relations, from periods of ethnic violence and from peaceful times.

2   Political leaders make choices in dealing with ethnic crises. Some draw on the conciliatory traditions and institutions for conflict management. Others manipulate the divisions and tensions, magnify the crisis, and are willing to risk collective violence. There is no inevitable linkage between tensions in ethnic relations and collective violence. Brazil and the West Indies did not have lynching after slavery was abolished, but the US South did (Tolnay and Beck 1995). Some Indian cities with mixed Hindu/Muslim populations do not have communal riots, but in others they are frequent (Varshney 2002). Rwanda had a genocide but ethnic war in South Africa was avoided when political leaders from all races and political factions stopped a low-level civil war and implemented a new constitutional design that revolutionized race and ethnic politics.

3   Studies of the effects of communication have found that raising the anxiety level of individuals with threat messages makes them susceptible to persuasion, i.e. accepting the threat as true. Fear-arousing appeals are particularly persuasive and create a public demand for actions to reduce the threat (Hovland *et al.* 1963). A textbook on mass persuasion asserts that:

> Experimental data overwhelmingly suggest that all other things being equal, the more frightened a person is by a communication, the more likely he or she is to take positive preventive action . . . Given the power of fear to motivate and direct our thoughts, there is much potential for abuse. Illegitimate fears can always be invented for any given propaganda purpose.
>
> (Pratkanis and Aronson 2001: 210, 215)

The political scientist J.-P. Derrienic observed that the most common discourse of nationalist leaders is "You are threatened and you therefore need me as your leader" (2002: 102). The Nazi leader Hermann Goering gave his view of threat propaganda at the Nürnberg war crimes trial in the following words:

> The people can always be brought to do the bidding of the leaders. That is easy. All you have to do is tell them they are being attacked and denounce the pacifists for lack of patriotism and exposing the country to great danger. It works the same way in any country.
>
> (quoted in Carruthers 2000: 76)

Political leaders manipulate the public with an ethnic threat discourse.

4   Non-conciliatory political leaders win the contest against their more moderate rivals by promoting crisis discourse and aggressive policies and actions against ethnic adversaries. These leaders and their supporters vilify and dehumanize their ethnic adversaries, spread falsehoods, magnify threats, amplify fears, and provide moral justifications for aggression and violence. The crisis discourse resonates with segments of the public because it is anchored in the collective memory of previous ethnic crises and wars. Persuaded by the threats, bystander publics vote and keep voting for extremist leaders who thus acquire control of the police, the courts, the armed forces, the state mass media, and other state institutions. In turn, the regime uses them for staying in power, for promoting the crisis discourse, and for aggressive policies against ethnic adversaries and internal opponents. Moderates are intimidated and silenced.

5   Backed by the army, the security forces, regime paramilitaries, and other regime agents, the regime implements aggressive policies against ethnic adversaries. The ethnic minority resists, countering coercion with armed resistance. Ethnic conflict turns violent. Insurgency has begun.

The ordinary man thesis

Few obstacles stand in the way of regime aggression against unarmed civilians. The ordinary man thesis explains why (Cohen 2001: chapter 4).

Research on collective violence, civil war, and mass killings found that they cannot be blamed on bloodthirsty and psychopathic perpetrators. Rather, as Ervin Staub (1989) argues, given the right circumstances most people have the capacity for extreme violence and the destruction of human life. Obedience to authority, peer pressure, a perception of threat to one's group survival (real or amplified by the regime), ethnic loyalty, public justification for violence against adversaries, lack of accountability, supplemented for some by opportunities for enrichment through crime, are the most usual circumstances. Stanford University social psychologist Albert Bandura agrees: "Over the centuries much destructive conduct has been perpetuated by ordinary, decent people in the name of righteous ideologies, religious principles, and nationalist imperatives . . . it requires conducive social conditions rather than monstrous people to produce heinous deeds" (2004: 5, 24).

An interviewer who probed paramilitaries in Bosnia on their reasons for ethnic cleansing of civilians got them to articulate a web of justifications for killing (Block 1993):

•   Collective guilt. "They" act in unison; children grow into adults; women give birth to future warriors; even old people stab you from behind; "they" will never change.
•   Danger and survival. These are extraordinary times; one's entire nationality is threatened, and extreme measures are justified.

- Revenge and retaliation. "They" massacred us in the past, and are about to do it again; in fact they have already started. A settling of scores, an eye for an eye, is justified.
- Deterrence and first strike. Disable them before they strike, which they are about to do, despite appearances, because they are secretive and treacherous.
- Legitimacy. The constituted authorities have not come to the defense of our people; we have to do it.

These justifications were not the inventions of the killers. They were articulated in the crisis discourse promoted in the mass media and were embedded in the crisis frame that resonated with the public. Political leaders determined on ethnic violence get ordinary young men to do their bidding.

Teenagers and young men recruited and organized into regime bands, like the Hitler Jugend and the SA Brownshirts, and Mao's Red Guards, enjoying special privileges, wearing uniforms or distinctive clothing with insignia marking them off as special, get indoctrinated into believing they are on a vital mission to save their country, receive weapons training, and learn justifications for aggression against non-threatening civilians. Encapsulation in the organization and peer pressures dampen the influence of parents and other non-regime adults. Other recruitment modes follow bloc mobilization. The largest paramilitary in Serbia, Arkan's Tigers, was recruited from the Red Star fan club in Belgrade. Many were soccer hooligans who had engaged in violent clashes with other rival fan clubs at soccer games. One of their chants mirrored the political discourse of Serb nationalism: "We are the fans of proud Serbia, Slobo [Milosevic] you Serb, Serbia stands behind you, come out on the benches, greet the Serbian race, from Kosovo to Knin, Serb is united with Serb" (Colovic 1998: 279). The Tigers set up a military training camp and became notorious ethnic cleansers. With the recruitment of regime agents eager for violence against ethnic adversaries, regime mobilization for armed conflict is complete.

According to the Final Report of the UN Commission of Experts (Bassiouni Report) that investigated war crimes and crimes against humanity in the Yugoslav wars (UN Security Council S/1994/674 27 May 1994, paragraphs 121, 134, 136, 139, and Annex IIIA, paragraph 80):

> There are 45 reported special forces, which usually operate under the command of a named individual and apparently with substantial autonomy . . . The special forces are supplied and often trained by their respective Governments . . . Among the most notorious of the special forces are Arkan's "Tigers" and Seselj's "Chetniks" . . . These special forces frequently carry out "ethnic cleansing" . . . [They] have committed some of the worst violations of international humanitarian law . . . The coercive means used to remove the civilian populations . . . include: mass murder, torture, rape and other forms of sexual assault

... severe physical injury to civilians ... widespread destruction of villages by systematically burning them to the ground and blowing up all the houses and structures ... including cultural and religious monuments and symbols ... Most of the paramilitary units sustained themselves through looting, theft, ransom, and trafficking contraband.

Framing: how collective myths become persuasive

Public debate takes place not in a vacuum but in an already existing political discourse embedded in culture, history, and political loyalties the public takes for granted. According to William Gamson and André Modigliani,

> Every policy is contested in the political arena ... Advocates' ... weapons are metaphors, catchphrases and other condensing symbols that frame the issue in a particular fashion ... A frame is a central organizing idea or story line that provides meaning to an unfolding strip of events, weaving a connection among them. The frame suggests what the controversy is about, the essence of the issue.
>
> (1987: 143)

Any information system, be it a computer or the human brain, is composed of symbolic elements that are selected, sorted, redirected, joined, processed, and stored according to a structure. Herbert Simon (1969) has shown that perception, cognition, and communication are not possible without structure. The human brain imposes a structure on sense perceptions and transforms them into emotions and cognitions. The mind's structure is a "frame" and the mind's activity is "framing." Framing confers order and meaning to beliefs and other components of culture.

How is the truth or falsity, i.e. the truth value, of beliefs and opinions arrived at? Starting in the sixteenth century, the natural sciences developed the experimental method and statistical inference based on probability theory for establishing the truth value of hypotheses. These methods are transparent and public. Independent replication by many scientists has to confirm the work of pioneers before truth value is accepted. In matters of justice, i.e. whether a person accused of a crime is guilty or not guilty, an adversarial method for establishing truth and falsehood has been institutionalized (with some variations) over the centuries. Both the accuser (the prosecution) and the accused (the defense) make the strongest possible case, under the same rules, and with an equal chance to question and rebut each other's evidence and arguments, before a neutral third party (jury or judges) that decides the truth value of the accusation.

On political issues there is no legitimate, unbiased, proven method of establishing the truth and falsity of beliefs, facts, and opinions that enter political choice and decisions. In the "court of public opinion," adversaries use techniques of persuasion that range from the art of rhetoric to crude propaganda. The purpose of political debate is not to establish truth and falsehood, as in science and justice, but to create a consensus (or at the least majority support) for a position, principle, and policy and the facts and assertions that support them, regardless of their truth value. Unlike science and justice where the method of establishing truth value is designed to extract truth from a jumble of often obscure and contradictory evidence (and, in the case of science, counterintuitive from the viewpoint of everyday experience), political leaders often try to obscure and confuse the issues with spin, misinformation, secrecy, and outright lies. Even in democracies the primary goal of public debate is to forge majority support for a point of view, and only secondarily to establish its truth value before an impartial and attentive public.

When a society faces a crisis – a war or some other grave threat – political leaders call on the people to suspend their differences and unite behind a common purpose. They appeal to the most fundamental values and principles the people share, which in normal times remain unarticulated because they are taken for granted. Robert Bellah (1967) refers to these fundamental values and principles that legitimize institutions and public morality as "civil religion" because it fuses secular with sacred symbols and values. I prefer the term "collective myth" because it puts the accent on the cultural dimension. Collective myths possess greater authority in the hearts and minds of the public than political philosophy or ideology (on which there are legitimate disagreements) and religion (for which there exists a diversity of creeds and religious bodies). Collective myths embody the most widely shared consensus-building symbols, stories, icons, and metaphors from the wider culture. They exhibit surprising persistence and stability. Like language and many customs, they are the social construction of a multitude of past and present anonymous promoters and believers. The collective myths we live by are verities we accept as "self-evident," without reflecting on the fact that myths were made by our predecessors and keep being nurtured by us. And we are offended, or at least troubled, but at times also outraged, when myths are doubted.

One may well ask whether a people, state, or organized entity could just as well get its business done without collective myths, be they religious, nationalist, or civil in character. Although an organized social entity can function with a combination of shared interests, emotional attraction, and coercion, it is likely to be more stable when its institutions are experienced as legitimate. According to Hans Kelsen:

> To justify subjective value judgments . . . man tries to present them as objective principles by transferring to them the dignity of truth, to make them of the same order as statements about reality. Hence he pretends to deduce them from reality, which implies that value is immanent in reality . . . an inference [can thus be] made from "is" to "ought."
> (1957: 159)

The moral order becomes a social fact and is experienced as part of the natural order that is not subject to dispute: who would want to dispute the force of gravity or the changing seasons of the year? Collective myths legitimize our ideals, values, and moral codes, and make them compelling for us.

Most of what we know and want to know about public affairs is not, or only in part, personally experienced. Charles Lindblom observed that:

> I take it as undeniable that what people think about the social world . . . derive[s] from social interchange far more than from direct observation . . . you depend almost entirely on other people, including acquaintances, journalists, and other people who reach you through press and broadcasting. Most of the social world is too far away for anyone to observe much of it.
>
> (1990: 78–9)

There are five common modes of truth validation:

1   We believe trusted authorities and experts, and do not expect them to mislead us.
2   We accept prevailing views in the small groups and social circles we belong to. Conforming to their beliefs and values affirms our membership; dissent marginalizes us. Social psychologists have found that:

> a frequent important aspect of group membership stems from that fact that individuals need to find support for their beliefs, and this may be obtained from those who share those beliefs . . . especially if the convictions, such as religious beliefs, are otherwise unverifiable.
>
> (Byrne *et al.* 1966: 102)

3   We are impressed by the views of a large majority, assuming that so many cannot be mistaken and wrong. *Vox populi, vox dei.* Public rituals, monuments, ceremonial speeches, public holidays, flags, icons, and other symbols are the physical embodiment of our beliefs and values, and these are respected and publicly acknowledged.
4   Because actions speak louder than words, we are influenced by the commitment and sacrifices some make on behalf of a belief or cause. If they are willing to die for it, it must have truth value, or else they are madmen, which surely they are not.
5   We accept as true what fits our cognitive frame, and we reject as false what is discordant. Our frame is a social construction promoted by trusted authorities, taken for granted in our intimate social circles, publicly affirmed by the large groups we identify with, and sanctified through sacrifice. The frame transforms the arbitrary, the uncertain, the unfamiliar, and the questionable into values, beliefs, and opinions that are certain and beyond question. Framing produces truth value.

In probing for truth value, we do not process bits of information as they impact our minds discretely and sequentially. We actively screen information, sort it, and fit it into an existing cognitive and moral frame that makes sense and confers meaning, which we share with our trusted authorities and our social circles. When information does not fit the familiar frame, we tend to be skeptical, ignore it, or explain it away rather than doubt our trusted authorities and question the sound judgments of our intimates. We stretch the frame rather than change it.

How the process of framing and social validation for political truths operates in US election campaigns was researched and described by Paul Lazarsfeld and his associates (Berelson *et al.* 1966). A political party has a distinct set of values, public policies, and positions on issues organized into a frame. During the campaign, party professionals, candidates for office, and the news media fit current issues into the inherited political frame and explain them to the voters. Framing simplifies enormously the variety and range of political information directed at the electorate, or, as the authors put it, the campaign is a "system of organizing disagreement" for political discourse. The voters, on their part, further reduce the uncertainties of political choice through selective exposure to those political commentators and partisan media they trust: they probe "the world outside" selectively, omitting, even distorting, information that does not fit a coherent image of politics, the "picture in their heads." As well, voters look for social validation and confirmation of their political interpretations and provisional choices by conversations with opinion leaders and intimates in trusted micro environments. The social influence process aligns one's political choices with those in one's social milieu and creates "harmony among people." Framing, probing, and social influence thus create political certainty for the voters (Berelson *et al.* 1966: 183, 230–2, 285).

In ethnically divided societies, members of each ethnic group trust their separate authorities, tend to live in segregated social circles, look for guidance to their own community, and admire heroes who sacrificed themselves for their group. Each group possesses its distinct frame and collective myths about ethnic relations, and these will become more distinct in a crisis. A collective myth is the collective memory of a people about their past which shapes their view of the social world they inhabit. Meron Benvenisti writes that:

> Myths are not illusions, they are a jumble of real and legendary events . . . the minute they are absorbed, they become truer than reality itself . . . to force people to confront objective truth cannot succeed because it amounts to an attack on the collective self-identity. It is therefore met with anger.
>
> (1995: 200)

Events impacting on ethnic relations will be interpreted and experienced very differently in distinct ethnic frames.

After researching the divergent interpretations by Serbs and Albanians in Kosovo of the same political events with in-depth probing of informants, sometimes individuals who had personally experienced the same events but from opposite sides, Julie Mertus concluded that "what matters is not what is factually true but what people believe to be 'Truth' . . . the opposite of Truth is not necessarily a lie; rather it is a competing Truth" (1999: 10). Both Palestinians and Israelis have incorporated Jerusalem into their collective myths (Benvenisti 1995: 200). Zionism created the myth that there was plenty of land in Palestine for two peoples, that the Arabs wouldn't be harmed and dispossessed by the influx of Jews, that unlike other white-settler colonies the Jews would return to their "homeland" and create an egalitarian society by taming "nature" and not its Arab inhabitants, and that Arabs belonged to some 20 sovereign states, not to Palestine, where they were recent arrivals. The Palestinian myth is a denial of Israel's permanence: Palestinians will return to villages and houses they fled that no longer exist. The national myths of Israelis and Palestinians deny Jerusalem to the other. Parallel research by Israeli and Palestinian social scientists on Jerusalem found that 92 percent of Palestinians say that Jerusalem is very important to them personally, but 86 percent do not believe Jerusalem is important to Israelis as their national capital. Palestinians deny that there was ever a Jewish Temple (of Solomon) at the Temple Mount, which they call Haram al Sharif (Noble Sanctuary). Conversely, 80 percent of Israelis believe that the Palestinian claim to East Jerusalem as their capital is not justified, and 70 percent will not accept the Temple Mount under Muslim control in a peace settlement (Segal *et al.* 2000). Many Israeli Jews believe that, when Jews started immigrating to Palestine at the turn of the nineteenth century, there were hardly any Arabs living there. "They came to find work when we [Jews] built cities. There was nothing before that," Prime Minister Netanyahu's wife told an astonished Queen Noor of Jordan in 1996 (quoted in *NYRB*, May 29, 2003, 7). The majority of Palestinians and Israelis inhabit different worlds on the question of Palestine and of Jerusalem.

To be sure, in pre-war Bosnia the urban population lived in mixed neighborhoods and there were cross-ethnic friendships among neighbors, class mates, and work mates, some going back to childhood years. One would expect that, in these settings, crude nationalist propaganda would be disbelieved and discounted. Mass communications research has found that people check media messages against the beliefs and opinions in their social milieus in non-partisan interpersonal encounters and conversations (Wright 1959). Ethnic crisis politics breaks down meaningful cross-ethnic political communication. Research in Vukovar and Mostar in Bosnia on pre-war Muslim–Serb and Muslim–Croat friendships found that, when politics became contentious, it strained friendships. Either one avoided discussing public affairs and politics with a friend in order to retain the friendship, or one stopped being friends, and discussed public affairs with a fellow ethnic with whom agreement was likely. In either case, exchange of political views across ethnic boundaries is impoverished. Each group becomes encapsulated: dialogue and understanding cease. The authors conclude that:

> As ethnic relations deteriorated in Vukovar, many residents realized something was terribly wrong in their community and among their friends. Even so they never discussed these perceptions with their friends from other ethnic groups; they felt that discussing such issues would make matters worse . . . the lack of discussion opened up a large space for cognitive distortions.
>
> (Ajdukovic and Corkalo 2004: 291)

Victims and deniers

Ethnic frames diverge during insurgency and civil war, and framing theory explains what blocks a shared political discourse for mending divisions after the fighting stops. Two related issues are particularly contentious: the *double victim syndrome* holds that each group believes it was or is the principal victim; and the *denial syndrome* states that each group denies that their group was responsible for war crimes and atrocities. In Northern Ireland, both the Catholics and the Protestants feel and act like beleaguered minorities: the Catholics, because they are a minority in Northern Ireland; the Protestants, because they fear becoming a minority in a united Ireland. As for Israelis and Palestinians, Benvenisti notes that, "as in Northern Ireland, both sides act and feel like threatened minorities" (1995: 103). The Israelis are victims of terrorist violence and obsessed with security and their vulnerability in the large Arab world around them, and the Palestinians feel they are victims because they have been dispossessed of their lands. Moreover, each group denies that the other is also a victim deserving of justice. Research on the reaction to perceptions of suffering by others documented four common responses (Lerner 1980): helping the victim and eliminating the suffering; ignoring the suffering; persuading oneself that the victim deserves the suffering; and persuading oneself the victim is less than human. In adversary ethnic relations, the last three responses dominate. The researchers who studied ethnic relations in Vukovar and Mostar after the Yugoslav wars concluded that "all national groups felt victimized by the war . . . they felt their national group to be the greatest victim" (Corkalo *et al.* 2004: 146). The Croats who returned to Vukovar "were deeply hurt and offended that their former Serb friends were unable or unwilling to recognize the extent of their families' suffering during the war . . . they longed for some kind of acknowledgement or apology . . . they did not get it" (2004: 296). The Serbs for their part felt that, before the siege started when the newly elected hard-line Croat authorities and armed bands harassed them, broke into their homes for arms searches, bombed their shops, and abducted prominent Serbs, their Croat friends did not assist them, nor even acknowledge the persecution. The researchers found that

Croats and Serbs had a totally different interpretive frame about the war and the same events they both lived through, be it the causes and start of the war, what happened during the siege, the Serb occupation, the return of some Croats after the war's end, or the aftermath of war.

Denial of responsibility for war crimes and atrocities, like victimization, is also a matter of truth and justice. Without a public admission of responsibility for the killing of innocent victims by the perpetrators, i.e. without truth and justice, one lives in a social world stripped of moral meaning, and that is profoundly unsettling. Justice Richard Goldstone wrote that "It is my belief that when nations ignore the victims' call for justice, they are condemning their people to the terrible consequences of ongoing hatred and revenge" (2000: 60). Yet adversaries tend to deny, or minimize, atrocities and war crimes committed by their own group, and highlight and exaggerate those alleged to have been committed by the others.

The self-image of ethnic groups and nations is positive: its members derive dignity from it, and seek public recognition for it. Atrocities and war crimes reflect poorly on self-image and dignity. Even if one did not personally participate in these crimes, accusations and war crime trials are experienced as an attack against the entire group because they lower the image and dignity of all. Group self-deception is a common response to preserving self-image and dignity under assault. The response is downplaying the extent of the crimes, justifying them, holding a few "bad apples" responsible, and outright denial. Collective denial is made easier when one's leaders and trusted authorities deny, when the media support a denial discourse, when one's ethnic frame expresses "victimization" ("the others did it to us"), and when one's circle of intimates is firm in denial, which is often the case.

The reaction to war crimes is demonstrated in the aftermath of the My Lai massacre in the Vietnam war. On March 16, 1968, about 500 unarmed Vietnamese civilians, many of them women and children, were killed point-blank by a platoon of US soldiers led by Lieutenant William Calley. There were US witnesses, among them an army photographer and a helicopter pilot and crew. When the incident was brought to the attention of the army command, it immediately tried to cover it up. Later it transpired that 28 officers helped in the cover-up. Several internal investigations were started, and eventually information started leaking out to the public, including color photos of victims in *Life* magazine and cover stories in *Time* and *Newsweek*, yet the chair of the House Armed Services Committee, L. Mendel Rivers, stated bluntly: "There was no massacre." Others called for an independent inquiry. The Army Criminal Investigation Division investigated 46 soldiers for the war crimes at My Lai, charges were brought against 13 men, but only Lt. Calley was convicted, on November 12, 1970, for premeditated murder and sentenced to hard labor for life. Opinion polls showed that a majority of the public (58 percent in one national poll, 78 percent in another) disapproved of the verdict, and that 51 percent thought President Nixon should free Lt. Calley. In the event, he only served four years before he was paroled (Linder 2006).

According to a report by the Serbian Helsinki Committee on Human Rights (2001), opinion polls in 2001 in Serbia showed that:

> over 50 percent of Serb citizens could not cite any crimes committed by the Serbian military forces in recent wars, but all of them were quite knowledgeable about crimes committed against Serbs. The majority of respondents were convinced of the veracity of reports about Serb suffering and casualties, but only a few believed that Serbs committed any crimes.

The majority praised Karadzic, Mladic, Milosevic and other Serb leaders indicted for war crimes by the UN International Criminal Tribunal for the Former Yugoslavia (ICTY) as "the greatest defenders of Serbhood." Four years later, after many victims' bodies had been dug up in mass graves at Srebrenica out of an estimated 7,000 Muslim victims, after confessions made by Serb officers who carried out some of the executions, after some survivors had told their stories in the Serb media and to the ICTY as witnesses in war crimes trials, after a video showing Serb paramilitaries called the Scorpions executing six Muslims at Srebrenica was shown on Serb national television, and after the president of the Republika Srpska called the massacre "a black stain on the history of the Serb people," a poll in Serbia found that one-third of the public believed that the video was a fake (Institute for War and Peace Reporting 2005). No matter how strong and abundant the evidence, a large segment of the Serb public persists in denial.

When there cannot be denial of fact because the atrocities were personally witnessed, there may be moral denial: the atrocities were justified. This happened in Ahmici, where on April 16, 1993 one of the most savage ethnic cleansings during the Bosnian war occurred. Armed Croat troops killed 116 unarmed Muslim civilians, including women, children, and old men, and almost all 180 Muslim houses in the village were destroyed and damaged, including two mosque minarets that were dynamited. The ICTY convened four trials with a dozen Bosnian Croat defendants, some already convicted by the time displaced Muslims started returning to Ahmici. Yet the Croat residents refused to acknowledge any responsibility for the massacres that they witnessed. In defiance, they symbolically affirmed the legitimacy of the ethnic cleansing by erecting a huge neon cross at the entrance of the village, with a plaque memorializing Croats who died in the war, without listing a single Muslim who perished in the massacre (Stover 2004: 116; pictures of the neon cross and the dynamited mosques are shown on a website that can be accessed through Google under Ahmici).

Collective myths are the enemy of truth and justice. Ethnic conflict management and peace building are hampered by crisis framing, the victim syndrome, and denial.

Conflict and conciliation dynamics (CCD)

Peace making is but a phase of a longer process of changing relationships among adversaries and third parties. There are relatively stable periods when the conflict lies dormant. Events initiated by either adversary result in an unstable peace that may escalate into a confrontation-crisis mode during which a variety of conflict modes and conflict management practices coexist in changing configurations and intensities, aptly termed "turbulent peace" (Crocker *et al.* 2001). A useful conceptualization of the changing configuration of conflict and conciliation comes from the Minorities at Risk project (Marshall and Gurr 2003: 27–8), which distinguishes several phases of conflict and peace making: conventional politics, militant politics, armed confrontation (of varying intensity and character), talk/fight, ceasefire, peace agreement (contested to varying degrees), and implementation, with a lot of reversing and recycling over these phases until a stable, self-sustaining peace or some other outcome is achieved. Some conciliation may take place even at the height of armed struggle; some spoiler violence may keep disrupting implementation after a peace accord. There are no clear-cut boundaries between phases and the process is not unidirectional. Some armed conflicts persist for decades and become a way of life for combatants. Some conflicts end after peace accords are implemented, others when one adversary imposes a winner's peace unilaterally, and still others when an external team of states assumes responsibility for imposing and implementing a peace. These processes I refer to as "conciliation and conflict dynamics," CCD for short.

In CCD, the salient issues, the key players, and the players' strategies change, and may be quite different during conventional politics, armed struggle, negotiations for a peace accord, and implementation. The cast of *players* changes: some bystanders and neutrals get to be active participants, moderates become extremists, adversaries split into rival factions, new alliances form and old ones are broken, some players get destroyed or exit as refugees, and external players (states, international organizations, humanitarian NGOs, transnational terrorists) intervene with diplomacy, mediation, humanitarian aid, and peacekeepers or on the contrary with weapons for combatants. *Issues* also change. At the start the core issues are minority rights, autonomy, self-determination, and stateness. Winding down an armed conflict and negotiating for peace bring up additional issues such as disarming the fighters, the status of combatants and prisoners, dealing with a culture of violence, and other security concerns; the return and compensation of refugees and internally displaced persons; justice for perpetrators and victims of war crimes and crimes against humanity; and physical and economic reconstruction. *Strategies* of conflict change from conventional politics to armed warfare to negotiations and conciliation, and within each mode choices are made about specific tactics, such as the type of warfare and counterinsurgency.

CCD models the dynamics of contention viewed as strategic interaction among adversaries and interveners. A fully articulated dynamic theory of conflict does not exist, but segments of it that are robust and empirically supported can be assembled and tested, despite gaps that remain. I refer to these segments as "dilemmas" or "paradoxes." How CCD explains the paradox of participation in risky opposition to an authoritarian regime will clarify their meaning.

A very general proposition states that conflict with other groups increases solidarity and unity within the group (Coser 1956). A second fundamental idea is that a wrong suffered by a group becomes a grievance that stimulates protest. A third proposition is that, as group solidarity increases, injuries suffered by some members of the group are experienced as wrongs by other group members who did not themselves suffer them. This is referred to as the "multiplier effect" in so far as such individual wrongs get multiplied by group members into a collective grievance (Oberschall 1993: 25). For instance, when police handle non-violent protesters brutally, bystander publics get angered by "police brutality." A fourth idea is that, as the perception of success increases, more will participate in opposition and, as more join, their perception of success increases. Safety in numbers decreases expected costs of challenge, and heightened perception of success increases expected benefits. Together they result in a "bandwagon" effect (1993: chapter 8). These four ideas or propositions have a stimulating effect on challenge.

Other propositions explain impediments to challenge. According to Mancur Olson (1968), in large groups there is a tendency to be a free rider (not to participate) for achieving collective goods, such as regime change. Second, increasing the cost of an activity, such as responding to opposition with negative sanctions, is a disincentive for opposition. Third, the "erosion of authority" accounts for the speed of anti-regime activity (Oberschall 1989). A social control apparatus is hierarchic, each link of the edifice supporting the others. The regime leaders order a crackdown, the police arrest, the prosecutors prosecute, and the courts convict. Weaken one or more links, and social control weakens, which stimulates more opposition. Suppose that the future of the regime becomes uncertain because of mounting opposition. Some regime agents become reluctant to repress because they want to save their necks from a successor regime. In a typical Prisoner's Dilemma, all agents would be better off if they all repressed and saved the regime and themselves, but each has an individual interest in earning good will with regime opponents. In short order regime authority unravels, to the astonishment of observers, challengers, and the regime itself.

The seven propositions are salient for explaining the mechanisms underlying the confrontations between regime and opponents: repression both suppresses opposition and increases it. The propositions unpack the paradox. Each mechanism or proposition has some empirical and theoretic backing. Unfortunately, we don't know as a rule the magnitudes and interactions of these effects *ex ante,* and thus an overall outcome cannot be predicted, though the propositions can explain *ex post* how the outcome came about. These are the limitations of the current state of a dynamic theory. Participants and observers, not just theorists, live with this uncertainty, as everyone is astonished at how seemingly powerful regime-states such as those of communist East Germany and Czechoslovakia caved in to mounting non-violent demonstrations in 1989, whereas similar protest movements in China in the same year and in 1991 in Belgrade against the Milosevic government ended with regime victories. Nevertheless, the seven propositions provide a coherent explanation even though they do not constitute a predictive theory. Absent such a comprehensive theory, CCD focuses on specific mechanisms that drive issues, players, and strategies in a conflict process to outcomes. These mechanisms are issue accumulation, the mobilization dilemma, the security dilemma, the coercion paradox, the escalation trap, the uncertainty dilemma, and the paradox of peace making.

Issue accumulation explains the protracted character of conflict and conciliation. The conflict starts over long-standing *core* issues such as inequality and self-determination. When unconventional confrontations take place, be they non-violent or coercive, a new set of *derivative* issues (so-called because they derive from the confrontation) surface over the actions of the adversaries: whether the challengers initiated violence; whether the police used unnecessary force against peaceful demonstrators; whether those arrested were given a fair trial, and the like. There will be calls for investigations and reform of the police and security forces. Bystander publics not engaged on core issues may become partisans on derivative issues; thus new players join the adversaries. In these confrontations, the actions and statements of the adversaries diminish trust between them, e.g. both sides blame one another for the violence, charging that it was a unilateral provocation despite previous assurances of non-violence. *Trust* becomes a casualty, and with lack of trust conciliation is more problematic. From core issues at the start there are now derivative issues and diminishing trust.

When the adversaries attempt conciliation, a new set of *procedural* issues arise: Are there preconditions to peace talks? Are there non-negotiable issues? Are the negotiations conducted in secret or in the open? The *recognition issue* arises when one or both sides are unwilling to negotiate with leaders and groups who have committed atrocities and who refuse to renounce violence. Of these procedural issues, recognition is the most critical since without compromise or concession about it no negotiations will take place at all. Israeli Prime Minister Rabin put it thus in 1993 when he explained why he was negotiating with Yassir Arafat, the chairman of the PLO: "Peace is not made with friends. Peace is made with enemies, some of whom – I won't name names – I loathe very much." *Security* issues keep upsetting conciliation. The adversaries are not unitary entities. Negotiation leaders and organizations seldom control all the activists and organizations that adhere to their cause. Rejectionists want continued armed struggle instead of a peace settlement and engage in spoiler violence. On the authorities' side, hardliners and death squads want to torpedo the conciliation process and continue killings. Thus spoiler and state violence may continue during peace making, and the capacity of the peace makers to deliver security and peace may be in doubt.

There are further *implementation* issues concerning disarmament, demobilization, and reconstruction (DDR for short), and rebuilding a failed state after civil war. Security issues get tangled up with prisoner release, amnesty for political crimes, weapons' decommissioning, and combatant demobilization. There may be an entire cohort of young men whose only skill is handling weapons, drug trafficking, and criminal activities. A pivotal implementation problem is how functions of government exercised by warlords and ethno-political organizations during armed conflict are restored to the courts, the civil service, and democratically elected legislators.

Finally, there are *legitimation* issues after a peace agreement is signed by political leaders. How is the consent of the people expressed and achieved? Is the public prepared for the mutual concessions that a peace accord and implementation require?

What at the start was a conflict over *core issues* becomes entwined during the conflict and the peace process with further issues: *derivative issues, procedures, recognition, security, implementation,* and *legitimation.* Peace making can break down over any one or several of them, and each breakdown jeopardizes peace making. Core issues started the conflict, but accumulated issues have to be dealt with as well for success in peace making.

During confrontation there is a *mobilization paradox* for leaders and activists. An effective mobilization strategy is to exaggerate grievances and threats, raise fears, stereotype adversaries, sharpen distinctive and exclusive identities, and promote collective myths and ethnic solidarities. Such a strategy will be met with a matching strategy of propaganda, falsehood, and fear. Polarization in discourse makes the relationship between adversaries more hostile and more violent. Conciliation and peace making will be more difficult with adversaries one has successfully labeled hostile, untrustworthy, amoral, and barbaric. The paradox is that the more success an adversary has mobilizing its constituency, the more difficult and uncertain conciliation and peace making become subsequently.

Ordinary people initially may not be engaged partisans on the core issues, but the *security dilemma* they face during conflict makes partisans out of bystanders even when most people, on both sides, would prefer to live in peace with one another. A security dilemma occurs when people find themselves responsible for their own (and their families') security in conditions of emerging anarchy. As social polarization deepens and the conflict becomes more violent, conditions approximating anarchy are reached at the grass roots. Men of military service age cannot avoid choosing sides, though they prefer living in peace. They are aware of how much pressure they themselves and their peers in all groups are under for choosing sides and taking up arms.

If others do arm, and one does not, one becomes a defenseless victim, the worst possible outcome in anarchy. Therefore men choose sides and arm, and that makes civil war more likely, though most agree that they would have been better off had they all refused to arm and to fight.

Asked whether there would be war in Bosnia a week before its outbreak, a Serb taxi driver explained his security dilemma to the German ambassador:

> My Muslim friends and I don't want to fight one another. But they know that, if I don't take up arms, my fellow Serbs will kill me, and I know that, if they don't take up arms, their fellow Muslims will kill them. So we will all take up arms, and we will fight each other.
>
> (author interview with a German Malteser in Banja Luka, June 1998)

"Killing" could be literally true, but other modes of coercion are just as likely: becoming marginalized in one's peer group, or one's family being harassed by neighbors and by the authorities. Is there no exit from the dilemma? Some young men manage to escape the draft or recruitment into paramilitaries by hiding or fleeing abroad, but most cannot. Even for the non-combatant population, there is no avoidance strategy for escaping social polarization. In ordinary times it is possible to bridge deep social divisions with multiple identities, but not in an ethnic crisis. Can a Catholic in Belfast unilaterally declare that from now on he is neither Irish, nor British, but simply a "human being" minding his own peaceful business, and everyone take note? Can a Palestinian do it in East Jerusalem, or a Muslim in Republika Srpska? Could a Jew have done so in Nazi Germany? The security dilemma forces an ethnic straightjacket on ordinary people and, tragically, even people who are at bottom peace minded, decent and well meaning end up making choices that are mutually harmful when they become combatants.

Coercion is a common strategy in ethnic conflict, either by itself or as part of a "carrot and stick" response to challenge. Incumbents choose coercion because it is cheaper than making concessions on core issues, because they have the responsibility to maintain law and order, and because they have pre-existing social control agencies for that purpose. Challengers choose it because other means of goal attainment have not worked. Though coercion raises the cost of contention to one's adversary and is expected to inhibit conflict, it may at the same time stimulate conflict among bystander publics by offending and outraging them. Much repression in civil wars collectively punishes an entire group: combatants, activists, sympathizers, and innocent civilians alike are targeted. The *coercion paradox* is that though coercion is intended to suppress opposition it also stimulates more of it. As I have argued in an earlier section, it is hard to tell *ex ante* whether on balance coercion will suppress and inhibit or, on the contrary, stimulate and increase opposition. Coercion contributes to issue accumulation with derivative issues, e.g. when suspects in an insurgency are rounded up and detained in prison they frequently go on hunger strikes, and the handling of the strike may then become a new issue.

When both adversaries engage in a coercive strategy, they generate a spiral of tit-for-tat retaliations, increasing the amounts of tit-for-tat punishment with each move, both players paying a higher and higher price for a continuing standoff. I refer to it as an *escalation trap*. Each side views the conflict as a contest for domination and hopes for a unilateral win outcome. Usually, the greater the cost of a good or an outcome, the less one is likely to choose it, compared to alternatives, because the cost of a good or service is set by market forces and not by the psychology of the consumer. The trap of conflict escalation is that the greater the cost and sacrifice expended in the conflict, the more valuable winning becomes, and the less likely one is to change course, i.e. value of the goal is not constant but grows with the cost expended on obtaining it. As an example, it is more difficult for political leaders to cede territory or compromise on a principle after hundreds of lives have been sacrificed to defend it than before the lives were lost. Beyond the original value of the territory or principle, its value has been augmented by those lost lives. How can a leader justify the sacrifice to the families of the fallen and to the public if he yields that territory or principle on the cheap? For adversaries caught in the escalation trap, the stakes become higher as value and commitment increase, and concessions and compromise more costly.

Because both adversaries are likely to have rejectionists and moderates, there will be internal disagreement over the mix of coercion and conciliation in the conflict. Because these groups or factions continue to mobilize for and against peace making in rivalry with one another during all stages of conflict and peace making, the two principal adversaries in the original conflict grow into six adversaries waging three simultaneous conflicts: the two conflicts between rejectionists and moderates within each adversary are added to the main conflict between the two adversaries. Among Palestinians, Hamas and other jihadi rejectionists of an Israeli state confront the PLO and the Palestine Authority over negotiating a final status peace treaty with Israel. In Israel, much of the Likud and the nationalist and religious parties favor settlement expansion and annexation of the occupied territories to Israel and oppose the Labor party and peace movement over establishing a viable Palestinian state with a peace agreement. The *paradox of peace making* is that the internal conflict dynamics within each adversary can come to dominate the peace process.

For a peace settlement to be accepted and implemented in good faith, each side must be convinced that the other is willing and capable of abiding by its terms and enforcing them. Internal factions create *uncertainty* about that willingness and capacity. During the fighting and during peace making, the rejectionists keep undermining the peace process. Who is to say that the moderates who achieved the peace settlement will prevail over the rejectionists in the future? If, as in the Dayton agreement, external states impose a peace settlement on the hardliners, the political leaders who were responsible for war remain in power and become responsible for peace making. They are tempted to salvage what they lost in battle and in negotiations by obstructing the implementation of the peace settlement. So long as the hardliners are responsible for implementing the peace settlement or else retain sufficient power to undermine the moderates' peace building, uncertainty surrounds peace building even after the armed fighting has ceased.

These dilemmas and paradoxes are derived from the literature on group conflict. They seek to explain how a conflict moves back and forth over various stages to an eventual outcome, with a changing cast of players, issues, and strategies. CCD is less than a fully articulated theory of ethnic conflict yet more than an elaborate descriptive account with *ex post* plausible explanations. It does not assume permanent, homogeneous ethnic categories, as "ancient hatreds" does. To the contrary it is mindful of internal factions and shifting coalitions, of bystanders joining the conflict as issues accumulate, and of ordinary men recruited because of the security dilemma rather than because of hate. It recognizes the importance of agency and of leaders, as does "manipulative elites," yet it conceptualizes mobilization, the security dilemma, the coercion paradox, and legitimation as a two-way influence process between leaders and followers. CCD, like "identity politics," highlights the emotional attachment to ethnic symbols and collective myths, but it does not slight interest, calculation, and coercion for explaining participation, partisanship, and group formation. "Economic roots" focuses on the insurgents and on opportunities for revolt; CCD unpacks the dynamics between regime leaders and their agents, and between them and the population. CCD is mindful of the original core issues in the conflict but supplements them with derivative issues that grow out of confrontation and peace making. CCD clarifies and explains the causes, courses, and outcomes of conflict.

In summary, for CCD, the causes of ethnic conflict only partially shed light on the course and outcome of ethnic insurgency and civil war, and on peace making and peace implementation. The conflict dynamic creates further obstacles to conflict management and peace making because contentious issues keep getting generated during conflict and accumulate. Peace making generates divisive issues that may become as contentious as the original core issues. Trust is in free fall. Adversaries internally change in ways that make peace more problematic: hardliners gain over moderates; rejectionists of peace accords actively undermine negotiations; bystander publics become polarized and encapsulated in mutually hostile subcultures. A crisis mentality and collective myths justify aggression. Adversaries continue living in the same society but their relationship has become more mistrustful, hostile, and uncooperative during the armed conflict. After the fighting stops, political leaders continue divisive mobilization in elections and in politics against both internal rivals and their main ethnic adversaries. Resources and energies needed for peace implementation are spent on contentious ethnic politics. In short, the polity, the economy, and the society change during armed conflict. War-making institutions and capabilities strengthen, and peace-making institutions and capabilities weaken.

Negotiations

CCD can be thought of as a sequence of choices and moves by the adversaries and by external interveners which are strategic in as much as the choices of party A are meant to influence the choices of party B, and vice versa. The simplest way of describing the choices is to distinguish conciliatory or cooperative moves from coercive or hostile moves. Moves are verbal or actual events. Verbal communications affirm the position of leaders on the core issues. Adversaries will test the opportunities for conciliation by expressing willingness to talk to each other and floating proposals aimed at their own constituency, the adversary, and interested third parties. Verbal moves are accompanied by actions: protests, demonstrations, strikes, boycotts, riots, armed fighting, intimidation of civilians, robbery for getting resources, and terrorist acts, too numerous to list, and by countermoves such as emergency laws, surveillance of opponents, detention and incarceration, banning organizations, closing borders, sanctions, collective punishment of populations suspected of harboring rebels, targeted assassination, and many more. Even while generating a steady stream of coercion, both players may also engage in conciliation, some unilateral and some bilateral: release of prisoners, recognizing the adversary, agreeing to meet and talk, engaging in preliminary talks, eventually participating in negotiations for reaching a peace agreement, changing hard-line leaders and military commanders for more conciliatory ones, accepting third-party mediators, and the like. When third parties enter the conflict as mediators and conciliators, they generate conciliatory actions: mediation, fact finding, commissions of inquiry, election monitoring, humanitarian assistance, ceasefire observation, technical support and advice in negotiations, and guarantees for enforcement of peace implementation (Gurr and Khosla 2000).

An example based on the Oslo peace process in Chapter 5 will clarify the methodology of CCD. During the Oslo peace process from 1993 to 2001, the main conflict was between the Israeli government and the Palestinians represented by the Palestine Liberation Organization, the PLO, and later the Palestine Authority (PA). The Israeli government is a coalition of parties challenged by rival parties that wanted to become the government. The PLO is also challenged by its rivals, Hamas and other militant groups, for control of the Palestinian movement. Advancing the peace process with conciliatory moves gets derailed when the two main adversaries both keep making hostile moves they believe are necessary for staying in power against internal rivals. The game between the Israeli government and the

PA becomes an interconnected set of games between them, between them and their internal rivals, and between the governments and the militant rejectionists on the opposite side.

The main game is "Land for Peace." The Israeli government (IG) offers control of land in the occupied West Bank in return for peace by the PA, which is the Oslo peace process deal. The status quo is no land and no peace, i.e. the pre-Oslo violent conflict. Land for peace benefits both, and they agree to it. However, if the IG builds more Jewish settlements, which undermines the commitment to more "land," the PA argues it will not be able to curb militant violence against Israeli targets. For the IG, violence by militants undermines the expectation of peace.

The second game is the "Coalition Game" played by the IG with its right-wing coalition partners who want to build more settlements. The partners support the IG but only if more settlements are built, or else they will oust the government by withholding Knesset majority. Because the IG wants to stay in power, it agrees to settlement expansion.

In response to settlement expansion, the Palestinian militants attack settlers and organize suicide bombings in Israel. The IG tells the PA to crack down on the militants or else it will suspend the peace process and will crack down on the militants.

This sets off the third game between the PA and the militants. If the PA cracks down on the militants, it risks civil strife among Palestinians and losing to the militants. If it does not crack down, it jeopardizes the peace process, but stays in power. The militants prefer confrontation with the IG rather than the PA. The PA chooses not to crack down, which risks more violent attacks against Israel.

The fourth game is between the IG and the Palestinian militants. Although both prefer no violence and no more settlements, that choice by the IG will upset the coalition game it is playing with its right-wing partners. The IG prefers risking violence over facing new elections and being ousted from power. Thus it opts for cracking down on the militants and for settlement expansion.

The outcome of game four then recycles to the main game, but, unlike the post-Oslo choice of land for peace, one ends up with no land and no peace. More precisely, since these games are sequential and repeated over and over again during 1993–2001, land/peace conciliation keeps getting trumped by fight/talk conflict. This is but a simplified representation of the Oslo process, which is described in greater detail in Chapter 5. It demonstrates that a two-player representation of the conflict does not capture the actual conflict dynamic.

The fact that peace negotiations tend to be more than two-party complicates its dynamics because, as Steven Brams and Alan Taylor point out, "When there are three or more parties with distinct interests, the coalition possibilities and cleavages increase rapidly, making a possible settlement not only more complicated but also less amenable to a procedural solution" (1999: 9), by which they mean the application of simple fairness rules in bargaining like proportionality.

Entering and staying in negotiations can be viewed from the cost side of the conflict. According to William Zartman (2001: 4), when the adversaries come to realize that neither can impose a unilateral outcome by winning through coercion alone, they reach a "mutually hurting stalemate" and will start conciliation. The notion of a tipping point in the conflict process due to mutually hurting stalemate is useful, though objective criteria *ex ante* for what is a hurting threshold are hard to pin down. In the Kosovo war, NATO estimated that Serbian President Milosevic would cave in after a few days (the Serbs' "hurting" threshold), but it turned out to be 87 days. Moreover, it was not only mounting costs from bombing that changed Milosevic's mind, but Russia's refusal to help Serbia militarily and diplomatically (Judah 2000: 228, 272). NATO *ex ante* very much underestimated Milosevic's "hurting" point, whereas Milosevic miscalculated his own when he called NATO's bluff and chose war.

One might also look at the tipping point between coercion and conciliation from the benefit side of achieving an agreement on core issues as well as from the cost side. If such agreement is likely at an acceptable cost, one will pursue a conciliatory strategy. If agreement is unlikely, then a hostile strategy is chosen with an expectation that coercion will force the adversary to adopt outcomes in the acceptable range. On the cost side, the choice of coercion depends on viability, in an extreme case on survival itself. In the Oslo process, both the Israeli government and the Palestine Authority refused to risk their status as incumbents by choosing conciliation consistently rather than episodically. Because estimation of benefits, costs, and probabilities of success and failure for strategies depends on perceptions and commitments conveyed in flawed communications between adversaries, the players probe and test one another with a variety of moves over a period of time until they lock in on conciliation. Testing and probing account for the cycles that repeatedly move through insurgency to "fight and talk" and conflict cessation, and then back to "fight and talk."

Outcomes should be feasible, acceptable, and final

Issues differ on obstacles to resolution (Oberschall 1973: 49–64). Issues whose outcomes are *divisible* and *reversible* are more easily resolved than indivisible and irreversible issues. Divisibility makes for give-and-take bargaining; reversible outcomes might be renegotiated at a later time. Stateness is recognition of a political entity in the international system of states and control of a legitimate government in a territory, including the protection of sovereignty in the international system and the legitimate exercise of the use of force in the state. It has permanence and an all-or-nothing quality. It is not divisible and unlikely to be reversed. Conflicts over resources (such as budgetary allocations or revenues from a natural resource) tend to be more divisible and reversible and subject to give-and-take bargaining. Unlike stateness itself, state borders can be altered and chunks of territory swapped. State territory is divisible though not readily reversible.

Conflicts over basic values, principles, and symbols are more intense and contentious than conflicts over resources (Coser 1956). Symbols are collective representations expressing a people's moral worth and dignity, identity, and equality with other people. Though symbols are socially constructed and subject to manipulation, they are not arbitrary, embedded as they are in the history and culture of a people. Jerusalem is not simply a piece of Middle Eastern real estate, and the Western Wall and the al-Aqsa Mosque are not just any physical structures in Jerusalem.

In contemporary international negotiations, no one argues simply that "might is right," as the Athenian emissaries told the Melians: "we will not make a long and unconvincing speech, full of fine phrases . . . that we are attacking you because you have wronged us . . . the strong do what they can, and the weak submit" (Thucydides 1960: 402). In today's international relations, writes Roger Fisher:

> The position which a country takes in a particular controversy is usually not an *ad hoc* position applicable only to those circumstances; it generally reflects broad political and moral principles of wide applicability. A major difficulty in settling a dispute lies in the fact that it is often seen in terms of principle, and on matters of principle countries are usually unwilling to yield.
>
> (1971: 162)

This is just as true for ethnic adversaries who both present themselves as victims of aggression deserving of justice, and for third parties that justify their intervention in the conflict on human rights and on humanitarian grounds. Bargaining is constrained by a great deal of moral baggage. The opposite of a moral principle is not amorality but another moral principle.

Negotiated outcomes must possess certainty. Uncertainty of outcomes can be due to doubtful feasibility, problematic acceptability, or lack of finality. The more uncertain an outcome, the less likely it will be agreed to. If an adversary is split or factionalized and there is a likelihood that a rejectionist group will come to power and refuse to implement the agreement, the settlement is fraught with uncertainty and the incentive to settle is much diminished. A settlement that does not settle an issue is after all not a settlement but a gamble.

Grassroots acceptance of an agreement negotiated by leaders is another source of uncertainty. The agreement may have to be submitted to a referendum or a vote in the legislature, with hardliners and rejectionists opposed. Some leaders fear, with good reason, that, if they compromise on some issues in a peace agreement, they are putting their leadership position at risk. If the commitment of leaders to an agreement is lukewarm and fraught with reservations, what is the agreement worth? In fact, a mobilized public does not wait for an agreement to be signed before registering its opposition; it organizes mass demonstrations and strikes to signal its opposition and bind the hands of its leaders, as so often happened in Northern Ireland. One reason for secret talks between adversaries is to avoid premature popular opposition.

The decision by the adversaries to engage in coercive or conciliatory strategies entails complex assessments, a mixture of guesses and calculations amid a great deal of uncertainty. The choice of a conciliatory strategy for conflict resolution raises several questions. Can an issue be compromised at all, e.g. can security and independence for an ethnic group be reframed from "stateness" to local autonomy, minority rights, and power sharing? Will the compromise be implemented or subverted, i.e. is a settlement entered in good faith and finality by both sides, or are negotiations a lull for an adversary to gather strength for a resumption of coercive moves? Will it be accepted by the rank-and-file citizenry? Will the leaders who agreed to compromise continue in leadership or will they be displaced by rivals? When the choice is a coercive strategy, is it likely to pressure the adversary to negotiate an acceptable settlement, or will it prolong and escalate the conflict? These are matters of feasibility, acceptance, and finality.

To break out of a tit-for-tat coercion sequence, a conciliatory move by one of the adversaries has to be reciprocated. Christopher Gelpi found that in international crisis negotiations "norms emerge out of the interactions of the bargaining states themselves" (2003: 20). Signaling, however, is ambiguous because an adversary often makes simultaneous conciliatory and hostile moves, as was true for the Oslo process in as much as the adversaries pursued several games at the same time. An adversary reaffirms commitment to insurgency to quiet internal critics even as he signals willingness to conciliate. It takes diplomatic skills and much testing and probing to sort out ambiguous signaling between adversaries and lock in on conciliatory moves that build confidence. When conciliation is consistently responded to with conciliation, a norm of reciprocity backed by publics and external stakeholders strikes roots in the peace process. Those who disrupt the process are labeled "spoilers" and are condemned.

It will be recalled that violence against an adversary is justified by both sides who present themselves as the victim in the conflict, and aggression is framed as "self-defense." A single conciliatory move by an adversary is not sufficient to cancel the accumulated injuries from the past. The conflict has a history, and that history is different for the adversaries. In a television interview, Senator George Mitchell (2002) observed about his experience as mediator in ethnic conflict that "There is a fixation and obsession with the past that hampers the ability to look at the future . . . unless people . . . look at the future, they are going to continue and relive the past with all the negatives that brings." For a full-fledged peace process, all the parties in the peace process must shift from coercion to conciliation: not just the principal leaders and organizations, but the lesser factions and organizations that together with the principals make up an adversary. This seldom happens because some factions, the rejectionists, refuse going along with the principals, as was true for the Oslo peace process. For all these reasons, negotiations for peace are messy and complex.

2 Insurgency, terrorism, human rights, and the laws of war

When ethnic warfare breaks out in divided societies, it tends to be a mix of conventional war, guerilla war, terrorism, banditry, and organized crime. Martin van Creveld put it thus: "In the future war will not be waged by armies but by . . . terrorists, guerillas, bandits, and robbers" (1991: 197). Though exaggerating, he pointed to an important change in warfare. Mary Kaldor (2001: chapter 1) refers to "new wars" that blur the distinction between violence between states (the original meaning of war), organized crime for private economic gain, and large-scale violation of human rights when the state and armed groups turn violently on civilians. Unless restrained, regular armies in counterinsurgency become like their adversaries in the mode of fighting, and civilians become the principal casualties and victims.

In conventional war, the treaties and conventions that bind adversaries are symmetrical and reciprocal, as for the treatment of prisoners and the protection of civilians. Both sides benefit from compliance. Non-compliance is deterred by reciprocal non-compliance, as was the case in World War II for the non-use of toxic chemicals following their disastrous use in the first one. In wars between states and insurgents, there is no such symmetry and reciprocity. Unconventional warfare is an unsettling experience for professional armies trained to fight other professional armies. The killing of their comrades by snipers, concealed landmines and roadside bombs, fighters disguised as civilians or using them as cover, and atrocities against captured soldiers and against the civilians it is their mission to protect destroy morale and discipline and put tremendous pressure on armies and the authorities to protect soldiers and civilians. What may well result is tit-for-tat escalation of brutalities, atrocities, and outrages. There is a disjunction between the rules of war and the realistic situations faced by human agents responsible for fighting, e.g. soldiers ordered to root out insurgents who use civilians in buildings as a cover, police targeted by snipers from within hostile crowds, soldiers manning checkpoints at risk of suicide bombings, insurgents using ambulances and religious buildings for the transportation and hiding of explosives and weapons, and the like. A military analyst who studied unconventional urban warfare has concluded that:

> The central question confronting today's political and military leaders is . . . reconciling a restrictive legal and moral framework with what is known about the nature of urban war . . . urban operations take place in what is by far the most complex of all environments in which the military operate.
>
> (Hills 2004: 222)

If restraints on human rights violations weaken on the government side, they are even weaker on the insurgent side. The insurgents claim that their cause is legitimate and their adversary oppressive, and therefore violent means justify their ends. The insurgents' goal is to make the war so costly that the adversary will eventually give up and settle for a political solution or, better yet, make unilateral concessions. They hope that human victims, financial costs, disruption of normal routines and institutions, and international criticism and pressures, among others, will turn the government and the public against a military solution to an insurgency. The insurgents' restraint on violence against civilians is strategic rather than principled: they do not want to turn the population whose support they need against the insurgency. But moderates opposed to violence, bystanders who do not commit to the insurgency, and especially those who side with the authorities – the "collaborators" – are intimidated and often ruthlessly killed. The insurgents create a security dilemma for the bystanders. With the authorities unable to protect them, many will cooperate with the insurgency and refuse to assist the authorities in counterinsurgency out of fear.

Unconventional warfare possesses a "dirty warfare" dynamic

1   The insurgents choose guerilla warfare and terrorism because it works best for achieving their goals. Outgunned and outmanned, it would be suicidal to engage the government forces in conventional battle. Insurgents require the cooperation of the population for manpower, resources, information, and cover. When appeals and persuasion fail, they will use intimidation, fear, and violence. The insurgents kill officials, moderates, innocent bystanders, and "traitors" who side with the adversary. The number of such victims can exceed the casualties they inflict on the security forces.
2   Frustrated by the inability to tell insurgents from ordinary people and by lack of cooperation for identifying and locating the insurgents, the security forces resort to collective punishment, mass arrests and detentions, coercive interrogation and torture, internment, forced population movement from contested war zones to fortified camps or villages, and other security measures. However effective these may be, they will at the same time antagonize bystanders some of whom will support and join the insurgency.

3   When the government no longer ensures security of life and property, the livelihood of people becomes uncertain. The number of socially dislocated people increases. Armed groups and criminal gangs, some loosely tied to the combatants and others autonomous, make a living by robbery, extortion, hostage taking, drug trading, smuggling, and preying on civilians and humanitarian relief workers. The pre-war economy becomes subverted by an economy of predation. The World Bank study of 59 especially lethal insurgencies and civil wars, many in Africa, found that:

> Most entrepreneurs of violence have essentially political objectives, and presumably undertake criminal activities only as a grim necessity to raise finances. However, over time the daily tasks involved in running criminal business may tend to develop a momentum of their own ... Loot is not usually the root motivation for conflict, but it may become critical for its perpetuation.
>
> (Collier *et al.* 2003: 79)

In one notorious instance, the police chief in Prijedor in the Republika Srpska told Judah (1997: 204) that the assets of 50,000 Muslims and Croats who had been ethnically cleansed in his district amounted to millions of Deutschmarks which were expropriated by private individuals or had been transferred to Serbia. Vojislav Seselj, leader of the paramilitary Chetniks, boasted in a Radio Valjevo interview on November 11, 1993 that "War booty was pulled out on trailer trucks [from Bosnia]. Convoys of trailer trucks ... everything that was looted was looted with the consent of the authorities ... or directly organized by the authorities" (Seselj 1991–2001: 131–2).

4   Both adversaries escalate the violence and commit atrocities and war crimes. Fear and hate displace more moderate views of the adversaries. Propaganda, accusations, exaggerations, and falsehood come to dominate public discourse. The restraints on "dirty warfare" from within the professional armed forces and from domestic institutions and public opinion weaken as security becomes an obsession with the government and the public. Nevertheless, even with weakened restraints, though the security forces win important battles they are not likely to win the war itself. Two experts on counterinsurgency summarize the historical record in a single sentence: "the history of counterinsurgency warfare is a tale of failure" (Press and Valentino 2004).

5   Agreeing with Clausewitz, Charles Garraway writes that "the art of warfare goes beyond the simple task of winning conflict: it goes to setting the basis for winning the peace" (2002: 953). Because unconventional warfare loosens restraints on violence, it makes a negotiated termination of the conflict problematic. A political solution necessitates two adversaries who commit to stable peace and political compromise, and who

are capable and willing to control the extremists within their camp. If adversaries cannot or will not control their own extremists, they lose credibility because the most persuasive commitment to peace is restraint on violence. Absent such credibility, the adversaries will seek military victory.

Unconventional warfare and the laws of war

The Geneva Conventions protect civilians in war and affirm the rights of combatants. The Conventions ban torture, hostage taking, summary executions, deportations, and the wanton destruction of civilian property. They limit the modes of warfare that put civilians at risk, such as excessive collateral civilian damage in military operations, and for limiting civilian casualties require proportionate response to armed attack. Combatants and members of an armed force must wear a uniform, carry arms openly, and be subject to an organization that enforces compliance with the rules of war. When captured, they become prisoners of war and are required to give only their name, rank, and date of birth, and may not be subject to physical or mental torture. They may be tried only by a military court. They must be released and repatriated at the end of the hostilities. Combatants are only those who take an active part in hostilities.

Whether and to what extent fighters in clandestine organizations, be they insurgents, guerillas, or terrorists, meet these criteria for combatants and should benefit from these protections is a matter of controversy (Anderson 2003; Roth 2004). The same is true for the legal status of those who hide, transport, supply, finance, provide explosives and weapons, act as lookouts, and spy for such insurgents. Governments and security forces have found that the laws of war framework in unconventional war denies adequate protection for soldiers and the civilian population and hinders reasonable military operations against insurgents.

Consider the following typical situation in counterinsurgency. Is it justified under the laws of war to destroy a moving vehicle that carries insurgents when it may carry civilians as well? In a realistic scenario, it is highly unlikely that the security forces will encounter these and other insurgents without a proximate civilian presence, e.g. in the desert. The choice is between destroying the vehicle at that moment and assaulting the same insurgents later when they are in a building in which civilians are also trapped. From a laws of war perspective every precaution should be exercised to avoid civilian casualties, and it is hard to find fault with the values and sentiments expressed in the precaution. For the security forces, the choice is which set of civilians will become at risk when they fight it out with the insurgents.

Consider another typical situation. Soldiers are conducting house-to-house searches for insurgents and weapons in a hostile neighborhood where previously buildings had been booby-trapped and some soldiers were killed. When the soldiers forcefully enter a house, the residents refuse to tell them anything about a weapons cache, an ambush, booby traps, or anything else. Taking a hostage and using a human shield is outlawed by the Geneva Conventions. The soldiers nonetheless force a resident to precede them during the house search rather than risk being blown up. The residents could avoid risking death by telling the soldiers about a trap or an ambush, but do not. From a moral and practical point of view, the situation differs from civilian bystanders used as a shield by soldiers in a firefight with insurgents when the civilians are innocent bystanders. Anderson (2003: 9) calls for realism on "raising the standards ever higher for protecting the civilian population when the burden effectively falls on the attacking forces."

The sanitized legal debate on *jus in bello* should be anchored in the real world of soldiering. In an erudite analysis of the rules of war in counter-insurgency, Roth (2004) examines the case of a senior al Qaeda official who had been allegedly involved in the October 2000 bombing of the USS *Cole* and who was killed, together with five companions, by a drone-fired missile while driving in a remote part of Yemen in 2002. In Roth's view, whether the missile strike is justified depends on whether the terrorist suspect is a civilian or a combatant. Under the laws of war, attacking current com-batants, but not past ones, is justified. Participation in the 2000 terrorist attack on the *Cole*, writes Roth, does not necessarily make the official a combatant two years later because he could have subsequently withdrawn from al Qaeda and reverted to civilian! If such a categorical distinction has to be established during counterterrorism before an attack on terrorists, it is highly unlikely that such an attack can ever be lawful because such groups purposely and secretively blur the combatant–civilian distinc-tion. The lawful alternative is to attempt the arrest of the terrorist suspect by pursuing him into the Yemeni hinterland and determining whether he is still a terrorist, an event that has a zero probability of taking place in the real world.

Arresting and prosecuting members of insurgent and terrorist organiza-tions under the criminal law is problematic. The peacetime legal machinery is ill suited for prosecuting insurgents when juries and witnesses are threatened and rules of discovery expose information sources for combating a hidden adversary. Deterrence through the criminal law and justice system and prosecution after a crime has taken place do not work. Counter-insurgency, it has been argued, necessitates prevention, i.e. identification and arrest of terrorists before an attack, and preemption, i.e. killing or destroying terrorists when there is imminent risk of attack. Faced with insurgency and terrorism, governments are under pressure from a fearful public to suspend legal restrictions on surveillance, arrest, detention, and prosecution of suspects and offenders. Rather than lifting all legal and constitutional restraints on security and social control, democratic governments enact emergency powers for fighting insurgents and terrorists.

Anti-terrorist legislation and emergency powers authorize surveillance, search, arrest, and detention of suspects, their isolation from legal counsel, coercive interrogation and acceptance of confession under duress as evidence, hearsay and uncorroborated evidence from informers, and non-public trials with protected witnesses and juries or in special military courts. The legality of emergency powers derives from the derogation principle that gives a government the right to suspend international treaties and conventions in an emergency when the state itself is threatened. Emergency and anti-terrorist legislation create a high risk of abuse by the executive branch, the military, and the security forces because it restricts accountability and transparency to the public, the news media, the legislature, and the judiciary. For these reasons, Michael Ignatieff argues for limits to derogation: "actions which violate foundational commitments to justice and dignity – torture, illegal detention, unlawful assassination – should be beyond the pale . . . emergency derogations . . . should be temporary, publicly justified, and deployed as a last resort" (2004: xiv).

There is a fundamental incompatibility between respect for human rights and counterinsurgency. Human rights and the criminal law assume innocence until guilt is proven. Counterinsurgency rests on suspicion of complicity and guilt with a low probability that innocence can be proven. The justice system is intentionally structured to produce few false positives (guilty verdict when in fact not guilty) at the risk of many false negatives (verdict of not guilty when in fact guilty). Counterinsurgency by contrast is the opposite: many innocent people are caught in the net for the sake of catching a few who are terrorists or insurgents, i.e. many false positives. They remain in detention or under surveillance for a long time without correction of the errors that misclassified them. "Murky intelligence" drives many terrorist investigations, and the government, citing security reasons, conceals the sources of information on which its case is based (Roth 2004: 3–4).

It is understandable that human rights advocates voice misgivings on giving the government such emergency powers. International human rights law was developed in the context of safeguarding individual liberties against a tyrannical state where human rights are the last and often the only obstacle to an oppressive government. Weakening the international support for human rights is a blow to hundreds of millions of ordinary people trapped in these undemocratic regimes. The context for justifying emergency powers is the defense of democracy and individual liberties against violent attackers of democracy and individual liberties and not the protection of citizens against an authoritarian regime.

Democracy under attack cannot avoid balancing security concerns against the liberties of its citizens. Political leaders are bound by an ethic of responsibility, as Max Weber argued:

> "Thou shalt resist evil by force" or else you are responsible for the evil winning out . . . No ethics in the world can dodge the fact that in numerous instances for attainment of "good" ends . . . one must be willing to pay the price of using morally dubious means . . . This is not

to say . . . that an ethic of responsibility is identical with unprincipled opportunism.

(1958: 119)

Ruti Teitel poses a rhetorical question: "Given a fifty year forward march of international human rights norms, how can we explain the seemingly unending perpetration of war crimes and atrocities?" (1999: 110). Debate about emergency powers in unconventional warfare should not be limited to analyzing the body of international human rights law and the laws of war from a legal angle. One needs a critical examination of the actual practices of democratic states when they battle insurgents and terrorists in the realistic context of armed conflict. The case studies of unconventional warfare in Malaya, Northern Ireland, Palestine, and the US "global war on terror" serve this purpose.

Detention in the US global war on terror

To provide an empirical foundation for the analysis, I first review detention and coercive interrogation as practiced in the Bush administration under emergency powers after the 9/11 terrorism attacks. The review will show that the emergency measures are ineffective and subject to abuse, yet they persist. A registration program of legal immigrants from Arab countries considered breeding grounds for terrorism yielded 83,000 names and several thousand who were in the US illegally. Of these, 768 aliens were arrested as "special interest" detainees, and subsequently 531 were deported, but only two were directly linked to a terrorist organization (*9/11 Commission Report* 2004: 327–8). A top official was not surprised by this result, nor should anyone else be, because it is highly unlikely that a terrorist would register himself for investigation by the government ("Program's Value in Dispute as a Tool to Fight Terrorism," *NYT*, December 21, 2004). A massive electronics and wiretap surveillance program of suspects instituted by the National Security Agency (NSA) evaded the Foreign Intelligence Surveillance Act and monitoring by a federal court where "probable cause" had to be established. How many thousands or tens of thousands of investigations were opened under the program has still not been revealed. The FBI complained that "it required hundreds of agents to check out thousands of tips a month, but virtually all of them . . . led to dead ends or innocent Americans" (*NYT*, January 17, 2006). In answer to critics, General Hayden, the head of the NSA, argued that accountability should not be public for such security operations:

> this program has given us information that we would not otherwise have been able to get. *It is impossible for me to talk about this any more in public without alerting our enemies to our tactics or what we have learned. I can't give details without increasing the danger to Americans.*

A private research group tracking Justice Department prosecutions for "international terrorism" found that, for September 11, 2001 to May 31, 2006, of 6,472 cases opened, 3,581 were closed without prosecution. Of the remaining cases, there were 1,329 convictions – often on lesser charges like immigration violations or fraud. The median sentence was 20–28 days, with many receiving no jail time at all, suggesting that the vast majority of these cases were not about terrorism, as that term is commonly used ("Study Finds Sharp Drop in the Number of Terrorism Cases Prosecuted," *NYT*, September 4, 2006).

These programs were casting a very wide net, and one expects many false positives. What surprises is how small the number of true positives they have yielded. What of presumably more focused insurgency control measures? According to US military intelligence, between 70 percent and 90 percent of Iraqis arrested in the aftermath of the Iraqi war were misidentified as insurgents, and an estimated 85 percent to 90 percent of the prisoners at Abu Ghraib had "no intelligence value" (Danner 2005). How did they end up in detention? Lacking information about the growing insurgency in Iraq in 2003, American combat troops rounded up large numbers of Iraqis who happened to be near a military engagement against insurgents in "cordon and capture" operations. Abu Ghraib quickly filled up with prisoners who had no connection with the insurgency nor had any intelligence value. They were not released because there was no way of identifying the few among them who were insurgents. In effect, the net meant to catch insurgents became preventive detention for thousands of ordinary Iraqis.

A more tightly drawn net on insurgents and terrorists is the detainees in Guantanamo Bay (Gitmo), whom Defense Secretary Rumsfeld referred to as "the most dangerous, best trained, vicious killers on the face of the earth." These detainees were more carefully screened by the CIA as well as military intelligence, before being transferred from Afghan and other foreign sites as "enemy combatants." Because the Department of Defense was successfully sued by attorneys representing detainees, it released documents and military tribunal transcripts on some of the prisoners. Several hundred have been released or transferred elsewhere, but the US was holding about 500 detainees there in early 2006. Forty-five percent of the detainees have been charged with a hostile act against the US, but only 8 percent have been classified as al Qaeda fighters (*NYT*, February 17, 2006). An in-depth analysis of 132 cases indicates that a majority were not picked up by US forces in Afghanistan (where the war took place) but by the Pakistani authorities in Pakistan, nor are they accused of hostilities against the US. Corinne Hegland concluded that:

> Many [of the enemy combatants held at Guantanamo] are accused of hostility against the United States and its allies. Most, when captured, were innocent of terrorist activity, were Taliban foot soldiers at worst, and were often far less than that. And some, perhaps many, are guilty

of being foreigners in Afghanistan and Pakistan at the wrong time. And much of the evidence, even the classified evidence, gathered by the Defense Department is flimsy . . . largely based on admissions by the detainees themselves, or on coerced, or worse, interrogation of their fellow inmates, some of whom have been proved liars.

(2006: 2)

Another analysis of the same released documents reports that:

several of those whose cases were detailed in the documents appeared to have close ties to senior Al Qaeda leaders . . . Other captives appear to have been low-level fighters caught on the battlefields in Afghanistan . . . One detainee, for instance, was challenged to explain why he was found in possession of a certain model Casio wristwatch. That model watch "has been used in bombings that have been linked to al Qaeda," a tribune official said. "I did not know that watch was for terrorists," the detainee, a Yemeni, replied. "I saw a lot of American people wearing the same watch. Does that mean we are all terrorists?"

(Miller *et al.* 2006)

Even in the select group of Gitmo detainees, there are many false positives. Whether they will get a chance to contest their status as "enemy combatants" according to accepted norms of justice remains to be seen. Whatever intelligence on terrorist organizations and activities the detainees who were terrorists or affiliated with such groups may have had at the time of capture, the value of it several years after capture is nil. As of the spring of 2006, the Gitmo program has become preventive detention and an international embarrassment to the US. How to make these emergency measures more effective and how to prevent abuses have become a major political and human rights issue.

Coercive interrogation and torture

Information obtained in interrogation of insurgents, terrorists, and suspects is central to successful counterinsurgency. What modes of interrogation can be justified under emergency laws, and when do they become "coercive" and "torture"? Mark Bowden (2003) interviewed experienced (retired) interrogators of insurgents and terrorists from the CIA and the Israeli security agencies. Most believe that coercive interrogation that falls short of torture, i.e. sleep and sensory deprivation, moderate physical pressure (slapping, shaking), and psychological pressure (especially inducing fear), is useful and sometimes the only means of obtaining information. These methods are deemed to be "cruel and inhumane" and illegal according to the International Covenant against Torture and Other Cruel, Inhuman or Degrading Treatment or Punishment and the International Covenant on

Civil and Political Rights, both of which allow for no exceptions during periods of emergency and internal political instability. Under the Geneva Convention, combatants must distinguish themselves from civilians by a uniform or some other distinguishable markers recognizable at a distance. They have a right to be treated as POWs and are required only to give their name, rank, date of birth, and equivalent information. Additional Protocol I (1977):

> grants combatant rights including the vital right to be treated as a P.O.W. on the basis of certain motives for fighting, referring specifically to those who fight against "racist regimes" (as in South Africa under apartheid) or "alien occupation" (as in the West Bank of Palestine) . . . the protocol grants legal combatant status even to guerrillas who conceal themselves and their weapons among the civilian population, as long as the fighters reveal themselves to the adversary "preceding the launching of an attack."
>
> (Anderson 2003)

Captured insurgents are barred from being questioned, e.g. those captured in an attack cannot be lawfully questioned in battlefield interrogations on whether there are more pending attacks by other insurgents, let alone threatened, beaten, or otherwise made to talk by their captors. No responsible government will conform to such rules that put its soldiery and civilians at risk. It is somewhat disingenuous to expect only one adversary to be bound by laws and norms that "tie its hands." Bowden recognizes a huge dilemma:

> How does a country best regulate behavior in its dark and distant corners, in prisons, on battlefields, and in interrogation rooms . . . How can we ensure that the practice does not become commonplace – not just a tool for extracting vital, life saving information in rare cases, but a routine of oppression?
>
> (2003: 74)

Nor is this a novelty, for colonial wars in earlier centuries tended to be unconventional. During the French colonial war in North Africa, a dispatch in 1833 lamented that "We have surpassed in barbarity the barbarians we came to civilize" (quoted in Winik 2003).

Terrorists, spies, and other criminal groups change their codes, plans, hiding places, and operations when a member of their team has been captured because they assume that the captors will force them to talk. As a former resistance fighter against the Germans in World War II stated, "we protected ourselves with small cells and rapid communications so that we were warned when somebody who knew our address was caught" (Ligthart 2005: 43). An insurgency is decentralized. The rank-and-file participants will know very little of the entire operation: an arms cache, a few names, a safe house or hiding place. Only the very top people can tell about the command structure and high-level strategy. Artful interrogation of many captured suspects by skilled interrogators might weave together a more accurate understanding of the insurgent organization from bits of information, if they can be triangulated with information from communications intercepts, cell phones, captured notebooks, and computer hard discs.

The most important argument for coercive interrogation of insurgent and terrorist suspects is the claim that it is the only way to make them talk when there is imminent danger of attack that cannot be prevented in some other manner. There is surprisingly little published evidence on whether what prisoners and detainees actually tell their captors under coercive interrogation – sleep deprivation, rough treatment, isolation, hooding, shackling, sensory deprivation, exposure to hot and cold, deafening noise, painful position, waterboarding – is truthful and of any intelligence value, or more truthful and valuable than what is obtained in non-coercive interrogation. The conventional wisdom is expressed by a critic who writes that:

> Almost anyone, given the right circumstances, can be persuaded to confess to a crime they did not commit . . . intelligence officers in search of information can easily make detention and questioning so intolerable that their subjects will say anything for a way out.
>
> ("Being Made to Confess to Something, Anything," www.NewScientist.com, November 20, 2004)

The CIA manual on interrogations, released to the *Baltimore Sun* under the Freedom of Information Act, states that "Intense pain is quite likely to produce false confessions, concocted as a means of escaping from distress" (www.parascope.com/articles/0397/Kubark01.htm, 93). More recently, Porter Goss, director of central intelligence, testified that "I know for a fact that torture is not productive. This is not professional interrogation. We do not torture" (*NYT*, March 8, 2005). In a lengthy Department of Defense Working Group Report on Detainee Interrogation in the Global War on Terrorism issued on April 4, 2004, just about every aspect of interrogations is reviewed, including coercive interrogation (e.g. what is pain, what is torture), except its effectiveness. It may be that security and military organizations have researched the truthfulness and usefulness of information extracted under various modes of interrogation, but if that is the case they have kept such knowledge secret. Academic research on such topics is interesting but has limited applicability to counterinsurgency (Gudjousson 1999).

Democracies have regularly and repeatedly used torture in counterinsurgency and counterterrorism – the French in Algeria, the Israelis against the Palestinians, the British in Kenya, Malaya, and Northern Ireland, and the United States since the 9/11 "global war on terror" in Afghanistan and in

Iraq. Top security chiefs and lower-level interrogators must believe that coercive interrogation and torture have value under some circumstances (Danner 2004b). Do democracies limit torture and coercive interrogation, how do they do it, and what are the consequences for fighting insurgents and terrorists?

Malaya: birth of the theory of counterinsurgency

Based on his experiences in Malaya, Robert Thompson (1966), the practitioner and theoretician of counterinsurgency, believes that a democratic government can both achieve a military victory and reach a democratic political solution with an appropriate military and social control strategy that avoids brutal and violent repression against the population in which insurgents are embedded. In the aftermath of World War II, Malaya was a British colony when communist insurgents started an anti-colonial guerilla campaign in 1948 against the authorities, drawing most of their support from rural ethnic Chinese. With selective murders, abductions, and torture of village officials and their families and other prominent locals, whom they accused of corruption, the insurgents frightened the villagers, who became too scared to provide intelligence to the authorities. For lack of witnesses willing to testify and juries that would convict, the peacetime legal process for arrest and prosecution proved inoperable.

In the 12 years of the Emergency from 1948 to 1960, there were 3,283 civilian murders by the insurgents and 1,865 security forces killed. Large-scale military operations found few insurgents because the guerillas dispersed and later returned when the troops left the area. Security forces were ambushed; roads were mined; casualties increased. Women, children, and old people were too scared to talk. Frustrated soldiers stole pigs and chickens, beat up and tortured bystanders for information, and alienated the people. The insurgency grew.

The government switched to a two-pronged strategy for defeating the insurgency. On the political side, the British announced their intention of creating a free, independent, and democratic Federation of Malaysia in which the 30 percent Chinese ethnic population would be a full partner. That goal was achieved in 1957 with the assumption of power by the Alliance Party made up of leading Malay, Chinese, and Indian political associations. A purely military response would have unleashed an Islamic religious war against the Chinese and would have united the Chinese behind the insurgency. On the military side, the authorities replaced large sweeps and "search and destroy" operations with smaller military actions that cleared a limited area of insurgents but then held it, providing security for villagers in strategic hamlets, and then gradually expanding the "clear and held" areas. They expanded intelligence capabilities from captured documents and insurgents, and were mindful that "the government must function in accordance with the law."

The authorities implemented very tough emergency legislation, within a lawful framework, and enforced it on the insurgents, on the population, and, more important, on the security forces: strict curfews, life imprisonment for providing supplies to insurgents, the death penalty for carrying weapons, and restricted residence, banishment, or detention for suspected terrorists and supporters. But the authorities stopped collective punishment, such as fines on an entire village; punished torture and executions of suspects by soldiers; and brought suspects to trial in regular rather than military courts. As Thompson advised, if the state does not observe lawful restraints the conflict becomes civil war and not an insurgency. These strategies paid off. Thompson noted that:

> Well treated and carefully interrogated, some over a long period, [suspects] reveal a tremendous amount of information . . . Any later individual who is captured or surrenders can then be interrogated on the basis of information already available . . . This shocks the truth out of him more effectively than torture.
>
> (1966: 87)

Lastly, the government's psychological warfare avoided a hate and misinformation campaign against insurgents: "Adherence to truth is a precious asset of the government," as it seeks to gain trust and legitimacy, and it makes post-violence cooperation with the adversaries for peace and reconstruction more likely. Thompson's analysis of counterinsurgency became an oft-cited model, yet it was not adhered to.

Unconventional warfare in Northern Ireland

In the Northern Ireland insurgency from the late 1960s to the late 1990s, the British authorities deployed a formidable security apparatus and measures against the insurgents, mostly the Provisional Irish Republican Army (a.k.a. PIRA, "Provos," or simply IRA). During the worst year of the "Troubles" in 1972, there were 12,000 terrorist incidents, 467 deaths and about 5,000 injuries, and 21,000 British Army deployed without counting police and other security forces. In 1973, 75,000 homes were searched for weapons and explosives, and about 2,000 IRA suspects were detained. Despite the death toll and injuries, many to civilians, the adversaries in the "Troubles" observed limits to violence. The army and police did not indiscriminately fire into hostile crowds, though it was alleged in the incident known as Bloody Sunday when 13 people were shot dead (which is the subject of a long trial in Derry), they did not torture detainees by means of electric shock, and they did not summarily execute prisoners and detainees. The battle of Algiers by far exceeded in horror the battle for Belfast. On their part the PIRA did not commit atrocities, such as mutilating the bodies of victims, and some bombings in civilian areas were preceded by warnings to the media.

This said, though the conflict was tempered "dirty warfare," it nevertheless was "dirty."

The principal adversary and target of the security forces was PIRA, which fought the army and police with sniper shootings and with bombs. Massive border surveillance was mounted at the Eire border with observation posts, helicopters and infrared sensors to interdict movement of terrorists, arms, and explosives. Undercover teams of the Special Branch (SAS) were deployed to observe bars, taverns, houses, and farmsteads suspected of PIRA links. The core of the counterinsurgency effort was the arrest, interrogation, detention, and internment – later the detention, trial, and incarceration – of PIRA members and suspects. A set of tough emergency laws and orders were enacted: the Special Powers Act, the Emergency Provisions Act, the Detention of Terrorists Order, the Prevention of Terrorist Act, the Diplock courts, and several modifications and amendments to these, some in response to legal and political objections. What started in 1971 as wide powers of arrest, interrogation, detention, and internment came gradually under increased judicial supervision and accountability. The non-jury Diplock courts were created for trials in terrorist offenses because of juror and witness intimidation, and replaced internment without trial. Because of allegations of ill-treatment and torture during interrogation, which were investigated by a succession of commissions, legal safeguards on interrogations and other aspects of the emergency laws were instituted, e.g. arrest on "reasonable suspicion" replaced arrest on suspicion alone. What is important is that the emergency measures were lawful and their operation was made accountable to Parliament, the British judiciary, and the European Court.

The purpose of these legal and security measures was to obtain information on PIRA terrorists and supporters and to remove as many as possible from the PIRA network and Republican population by confinement. Given the character of urban insurgency and scant information for distinguishing hard-core PIRA from sympathizers who were not breaking any laws and from bystanders who were intimidated or simply conforming to community sentiment, many of those arrested were never charged with crimes and were later released. Thousands of house searches for weapons, ammunition, and explosives were conducted in homes where none were hidden (altogether 360,000 house searches over 30 years). Absent an alternative for policing Republican areas, many people experienced the heavy hand of the emergency legislation (Ellison and Smyth 2000: chapter 6).

The investigations of ill-treatment in detention identified wall standing, hooding, subjection to noise, sleep deprivation, and food and drink deprivation as the most common practices. A European Court of Human Rights judgment (Ireland versus United Kingdom, December 13, 1977, paragraph 167) termed them inhumane or degrading treatment, but not torture, the distinction being based on a "difference in intensity of the suffering inflicted." Critics and advocates of coercive interrogation agree that they were successful in obtaining important information. Ellison and Smyth (2000) report that, during 1976, over 2,000 suspects charged with PIRA-related incidents were convicted in Diplock courts. Most confessed within two days and were convicted on the basis of their confession alone. The confessions also implicated others who were in turn arrested and convicted. In a 12-month period in 1977–8, 2,800 were arrested under the three-day detention power, of whom 35 percent were later charged as a result of confession under interrogation. The European Court of Human Rights (December 13, 1977, paragraph 98) found that the five inhuman and degrading techniques of interrogation led to a considerable quantity of intelligence information leading to the identification of 700 PIRA members and discovery of individual responsibility for 85 unexplained shootings.

The authorities did investigate complaints of ill-treatment and assault brought against the police and army, but the convictions and punishment against the security forces were few and mild. In the midst of insurgency, the authorities could not afford to demoralize the security forces with punishment. More than £300,000 was paid in compensation in 473 civil claims for wrongful arrest, false imprisonment, and assault. Thus there existed some civil and criminal mechanisms for restraining abuses.

Despite these successes, the emergency laws and counterinsurgency measures backfired by alienating the Catholic community and increased support for the Republicans. The initial 1971 internment was followed by a huge escalation of violence with 143 killings, 729 explosions, and 1,437 shooting incidents for the balance of the year. The PIRA reorganized from a military to a small, clandestine cell structure more difficult to penetrate, trained its members to resist interrogation, increased its bomb-making capabilities and tactics as an addition to shooting, became more successful in raising funds from Irish Americans, and obtained more deadly weapons from abroad.

The authorities consistently overestimated the extent to which they had crippled the PIRA. In the 1970s, it was thought that the hard core consisted of 300, with as many as 3,000 active sympathizers who would hijack autos, hide and carry weapons, serve as drivers, and provide lookouts for terrorist acts (Baldy 1987: 56). Another estimate (Elliott and Flackes 1999: 401) put PIRA strength in Northern Ireland at 800. In the 1980s to 1994, persons detained under the Prevention of Terrorism Act fluctuated between 1,000 and 1,500 each year. If these figures are accurate, the authorities held at least one-half and probably even more of the PIRA membership in their prisons. And yet the insurgency continued. Despite arms caches seized and arms shipments intercepted, bombings prevented and explosives defused, the PIRA was never short of weapons and of men. When the Northern Ireland Peace Agreement was signed in 1998, PIRA refused to decommission its arsenal of hidden weapons, which included even flame throwers and anti-aircraft missiles, though it permitted an international commission to inspect them.

British counterinsurgency did manage to decrease the level of violence, as measured by the annual figures for civilian deaths, police deaths, army deaths, deaths attributed to Republican paramilitary shootings, shootings, and explosions; e.g. a per annum average of 2,988 shootings in the 1970s was down to 477 in 1990–4 (Northern Ireland, Statistics on the Operation of the Prevention of Terrorism Acts, and other information from the cain.ulst.ac.uk website). But what is striking is the more dramatic declines due to peace-making political initiatives starting in the mid-1990s. To be sure there was an upsurge of violence around the time of the signing and ratification of the Northern Ireland Peace Agreement in 1998. Shortly, however, both Republican and Loyalist paramilitary groups, with a few exceptions, announced the cessation of military activity, which was a condition for prisoner release. Communal violence continued in connection especially with Orange parades which were held, rerouted, or banned, and criminal and revenge/control violence by paramilitaries against civilians and one another. In sum, one has to agree with Fintin O'Toole, when he wrote that:

> the IRA has been the most effective terrorist organization in the world. A huge apparatus of repression (British troops, electronic surveillance, internment without trial, covert special forces, networks of informants) contained it, but did not defeat it . . . what was not achieved by military and security measures has been achieved by political engagement.
>
> (2002)

Mindful of Thompson's advice, the British government knew it from the start and kept open a credible political settlement for which it enlisted the cooperation of the Irish Republic.

The Palestinians versus Israel

At the conclusion of the 1967 war, Israel held the West Bank and Gaza which under international law were occupied territories, pending a peace treaty. Faced with over 1 million Palestinians in the Occupied Territories (OTs), Israel gradually imposed a civil and military administration. The border with Jordan was sealed against guerilla infiltration and raids. Israeli military installations and roads and settlers who benefited from Palestinian land annexations were entrenched. Through issuing identity cards, documents, and permits (for economic activity, travel, building, working in Israel, etc.), and checkpoints, the Israeli administration established control over the population. The Palestinian economy became a dependent, labor-exporting segment of the Israeli economy with infrastructure and resources – water, electricity grid, telephone service, roads – under firm Israeli control. Though the Palestinian economy benefited, it was at the expense of freedom, human rights, and dignity. The settler population and settlements kept increasing.

The first Palestinian revolt against the Israeli occupation – referred to as 'intifada' – started in December 1987 with demonstrations, roadblocks and barricades, burning tires and other obstacles, and stone throwing and some firebombs against Israeli soldiers. The Israeli Defense Forces (IDF) responded by clearing the roads, dismantling barricades, controlling public spaces, dispersing hostile crowds, and protecting Israeli settlers and movement, which escalated to mass arrests, coercive interrogation to extract confessions, internment, and other dirty war incidents in confrontations with the insurgents. The IDF deployed tens of thousands of soldiers to disperse hostile crowds, enforce curfews, break strikes, close the borders, guard prisoners at detention centers, demolish homes, uproot trees in orchards, and deport suspects (Schiff and Ya'ari 1989: chapter 5; B'tselem 1998). From December 1987 to February 1991, Israeli soldiers killed 750 Palestinians in the OTs, wounded 13,000, demolished 350 homes, placed 40,000 Palestinians in administrative detention, and arrested 60,000. Another 37 were killed by Jewish settlers, and a further 349 were killed in intra-Palestinian turf fights between rival groups and as alleged "collaborators," which might mean anything from actually informing to the Israeli security services to selling land to Israeli organizations or refusing to participate in a strike. The economic losses to Palestinians were an enormous 30 percent to 40 percent drop in their standard of living (Schiff and Ya'ari 1989: 263). On the Israeli side casualties were light: 13 soldiers killed, 13 civilians killed, about 2,500 soldiers and 1,100 civilians wounded mainly because Palestinians threw stones and firebombs but used few firearms, unlike during the second al-Aqsa intifada starting on September 27, 2000 (Lustick 1993: 394–5; Ezrahi 1997: chapter 9).

Despite the top IDF generals' warning that the uprising necessitated a political strategy to complement a military response, as Thompson had also warned, none was developed. The army was caught in a dilemma. It was designed to fight other armies with tanks, artillery, and airstrikes. How cope with an uprising when the militants are embedded in a sea of people including women and children, and hostile crowds that provide a shield? To decrease the lethality of control, the army issued clubs for riot control and plastic and rubber bullets, but that tactic led to hitting and beating of demonstrators by soldiers, injuries and deaths, and Palestinian anger. To restore order and to break the will of the Palestinians, the authorities employed collective punishment to make life unpleasant and to reestablish domination. Roadblocks and checkpoints and searches created long delays that interfered with the routines of life, including work and commerce. Together with curfews, cutting electricity and the telephone service, the Israeli response was experienced by the Palestinians as punitive harassment and an assault on their dignity.

As Thompson noted, intelligence is the key to counterinsurgency. Standard police methods for collecting evidence are not practical in civil strife. The population is either hostile or intimidated from providing information on who the ringleaders are. In a crowd of 15- to 25-year-old males, looking and dressed alike, in a confusing situation, who threw a firebomb is going to be difficult to identify. When soldiers chase a crowd of youths, those who run the slowest, or were closest, or stumbled and fell are the ones who will be caught. House searches and curfews are collective punishments that seldom net specific enough information to lead to the arrest of an activist since the militants hide weapons and documents in homes other than their own. In order to obtain useful information, the Israeli security forces resorted to arrests, detentions, coercive interrogations, trials in military courts where confessions are sufficient to convict, and incarceration, all on a large scale. Because the Israeli military remained in part accountable to the civil courts, the news media, political opponents, and international human rights organizations, a great deal about coercive interrogation and other abuses has become public. The most common abuses were forced standing, hooding, shackling to pipes and rings, sleep deprivation, beatings and kicking, choking, violent shaking, threats, and psychological abuse (Human Rights Watch/Middle East 1994b). Though the Landau Commission (named after Justice Moshe Landau of the Israeli High Court) issued guidelines on interrogation of suspects with many safeguards, supervision, and accountability, enforcement was spotty and criminal prosecutions for ill-treatment were rare. Of 83,321 Palestinians tried in military courts, between 1988 and 1993, only 3.2 percent were acquitted. The vast majority was convicted on the basis of confessions. Many were charged not for insurgent actions but with membership in an illegal organization. Many faced with serious charges languished in detention before being brought to trial. The right of being charged before a judge within 48 hours, consulting a lawyer, contacting family, and having a coerced confession disqualified were rarely granted.

Since 70 percent of the detainees plea-bargained with their captors, the security services must have gotten a great deal of useful information about the insurgency through these coercive methods. The large number of Palestinians killed by other Palestinians for collaboration is also an indicator of the effectiveness of coercive interrogation. Another goal of the repression was preventive detention. By 1992, the intifada had much diminished in intensity, as indicated by the lower level of repression by the IDF. From 1988 to 1991, there were 100 house demolitions per year, but in 1992 only eight. In 1988 and 1989, 290 and 286 Palestinians were killed by the Israeli security forces, in 1990 and 1991, 126 and 96 respectively (calculated from www.btselem.org/English/Statistics).

Investigations into torture document the medical problems sustained by the detainees and other violations of international declarations, covenants, conventions, and law dealing with human rights and torture (Human Rights Watch/Middle East 1994a). It is far more difficult to get data on success in prevention of terrorism against Israeli civilians. In January 1997, in a case of torture brought by a Palestinian against the General Security Service (GSS or Shin Bet) in the Israeli Supreme Court, the GSS argued that violent "shaking" of a detainee, enough to cause death, was necessary for questioning Palestinian detainees who might have information about a planned terrorist attack on Israel. The GSS provided evidence that interrogations of terrorists for the past two years had foiled some 90 terrorist acts in Israel: 10 suicide bombings, 7 car bombings, 15 kidnappings of soldiers and civilians, and some 60 attacks ranging from shootings and stabbings to placing explosives. In the single clear-cut case of a "ticking bomb," Abd al-Halim Belbaysi admitted after denials that he had planned a terrorist attack at Beit Lid on January 22, 1995 at which two suicide bombers blew themselves up and killed two Israelis. He also confessed that three bombs were prepared at his house, which led to seizure of the third bomb from its hiding place before it was used in a planned suicide bombing (paragraphs 24 and 18 of http://home.att.net/~slomansonb/Israel.html).

By 1990, the conflict became a standoff with lower intensity of violence and was perceived as successful containment by many Israelis. The authorities were unable to force total submission, and the Palestinians were unable to force an Israeli withdrawal from the OTs. Just as the IRA had learned from repression and adapted itself to new modes of confrontation – cell organization and terror bombings in Britain instead of Belfast – so did the Palestinian resistance. New underground Islamist organizations (Hamas, Islamic Jihad) spread in the OTs and called for suicide actions instead of stone throwing. Since religious organizations are afforded maximum protection for freedom of worship in democratic states, these organizations and their military wings enjoyed some immunity from counterinsurgency. As in Northern Ireland, mass incarceration of militants had unanticipated consequences: prisoners solidified bonds with one another and became popular heroes. The military feared that, without a political strategy for conflict settlement, the Palestinian population was becoming radicalized: "The time will come when they will be fed up with stones . . . and they will have to move on to the use of rifles" read the minutes of a staff meeting (quoted in Schiff and Ya'ari 1989: 288).

Started under Norwegian auspices as secret face-to-face talks between Israelis and Palestinians, the Oslo peace process got underway with the signing of a Declaration of Principles (DOP) on September 13, 1993. Though the seven-year Oslo process was marred by episodic suicide bombs by Hamas and other Palestinian rejectionist groups, and by Israeli settlement expansion that occasioned violent clashes, confrontations became less lethal: Palestinians killed dropped from 16.3 per month during the intifada to 3.9 per month in the seven years following the DOP. Israeli civilian and soldier deaths in the OTs dropped from 1.3 per month to 0.9; in Israel itself there was a small increase from 1.0 to 1.5 per month owing to the episodic suicide bombing. These figures changed dramatically for all concerned after the Camp David peace talks failed and the second, al-Aqsa, intifada broke out. As the IDF had warned years earlier, insurgents came to possess and used firearms, and suicide bombers regularly penetrated the border for blowing up civilian targets. Deaths in Israel increased to 7.4 per month in the first 16 months of the al-Aqsa intifada, and then to 26.8 per month from February to July 2002; for Palestinian deaths the corresponding figures were 37.9 and 78.6 per month. The death figures do not adequately capture the changing mode of violence calculated to produce fear and outrage by breaching restraints and limits: bombing a school bus and a teenager disco, mob lynching of two soldiers, stoning to death two teenage hikers, targeted assassination with helicopter rocket attacks, infants and children killed in shootings, and the like. There was a corresponding surge in public opinion supporting violence. Eighty percent of Palestinians surveyed were in favor of military attacks, including suicide bombing, against Israelis in November 2000, compared to 44 percent in 1988 and the low 20s in 1996 (*NYT*, November15, 2000). One hundred and thirty-eight suicide bombs were set off from September 29, 2000 to September 15, 2004; two-thirds of the 916 Israeli dead were civilians (*NYT*, October 3, 2000).

Urban fighting and the laws of war

Israeli counterinsurgency needs to be examined in two contexts: hostile crowd and riot control in the al-Aqsa intifada when some insurgents used firearms against soldiers, and preventing suicide bombings before they occur. In the ritualized clashes of the first intifada at checkpoints and other public spaces of Palestinian teenagers and young men hurling stones and occasional firebombs at IDF soldiers from behind burned-out vehicles, the routine was familiar to both sides. First warnings, then tear gas, then rubber bullets fired over the heads, then aimed at legs, and finally aimed at bodies was the predictable sequence. In the background were ambulances; on the side were the news media filming the clash; bystanders all around shouted encouragement to the militants and insults at the soldiers. There were injuries, and occasionally deaths. The soldiers had helmets, shields, and equipment to put out fires. The rules of engagement for the soldiers were clear and conformed to international conventions and rules on the control of hostile crowds: use of firearms only in self-defense or imminent danger of death and injury, exercise of restraint, and use of means of control proportionate to the seriousness of the offense. When insurgents with firearms mingle in hostile crowds and use them as cover to shoot at the soldiers, as in the al-Aqsa intifada, the rules fail to provide guidance. Warnings, tear gas, and rubber bullets don't stop the snipers. How is imminent danger defined in these situations? Does not any crossfire endanger the lives of civilians, and what then is a proportionate response? Is shooting a demonstrator who advances with his hands behind his back as though concealing an explosive legitimate self-defense? Under ideal conditions, perfect visibility and hearing, wide open space between insurgents and soldiers, and no fatigue from lengthy clashes, experienced soldiers may have learned clues on when, who, and where to fire and, more important, not to fire. Fill the space with yelling and moving hostile people, poor visibility, echoes making directionality of bullets uncertain, and exhaustion from lack of sleep, i.e. in the "fog of war," and the rules provide uncertain guidance for proportionate response.

The identification and rooting out of terrorist teams presents many dilemmas for counterinsurgency, as the material from Northern Ireland indicates. To make the discussion concrete, here is an Israeli case of rooting out Palestinian insurgents thought to harbor suicide bombers from the Jenin refugee camp located in the middle of the city. In bitter fighting from April 3 to 12, 2002, 21 Israeli soldiers and 53 Palestinians (22 civilians, 27 insurgents, and four unidentified) lost their lives, according to an investigation by Human Rights Watch (2002) and a *New York Times* report (April 21, 2002), though the Palestinians claimed hundreds of dead. In the previous month, there had been 12 suicide bombings in Israel, and many, including earlier ones (an estimated 23), had originated from the Jenin camp. The suicide bombers were glorified as "martyrs" in the Palestinian media. The camp had 14,000 inhabitants living in dense housing amid twisting alleys with an estimated 80–100 heavily armed insurgents protecting access with bombs and booby traps, and positioned to kill everyone approaching through the alleys.

On April 3, Israeli troops backed by tanks, armored bulldozers, and attack helicopters moved into position around the camp where the fighters were entrenched. Contrary to expectations, the fighters did not melt away or surrender, but stood their ground. Many civilians were caught in the urban battlefield. To enable heavy armor to penetrate, armored bulldozers widened the alleys by shearing off the fronts of buildings. Soldiers knocked holes in walls between buildings for safe interior passage, a practice called "mouseholing," and forced residents to move ahead of them in case the building was booby-trapped. The fighting raged fiercely. In an ambush on April 9, 13 IDF soldiers were killed; thereupon the IDF used helicopter missile strikes for advancing, and some missiles struck houses which sheltered no fighters. It was "dirty warfare" on both sides. On April 11, the remaining 29 fighters contacted an Israeli peace group for mediating a surrender, which happened the next morning. There were immediate charges of deliberate massacre of civilians by the IDF, but investigators found no evidence of it. According to the IDF, civilians were killed by gunfire, missiles, and bulldozers in the midst of fighting. The IDF maintained they did not bomb the entire neighborhood, which would have killed many more civilians, but fought their way into the camp, house by house, to kill or capture the fighters, knowing that it would endanger the lives of some soldiers, which it did. Aerial photos and maps showed 140 completely destroyed buildings. The IDF warned the residents in Arabic to leave. Bulldozers waited to let residents escape before demolition. The IDF also claimed that some residents were helping the fighters and had chosen to remain. Those trapped in their homes later said they were afraid to leave because of the crossfire, and others said they did not hear the warnings.

Questions remained about whether the Palestinian fighters deliberately endangered the civilians by using them as cover, and whether Israeli soldiers used excessive firepower in the presence of civilians. According to Human Rights Watch:

> While there is no doubt that Palestinian fighters . . . had set up obstacles and risks to IDF soldiers . . . many explosives were found and many houses were booby trapped . . . the wholesale leveling of the entire district extended well beyond any conceivable purpose of gaining access to fighters, and was vastly disproportionate to the military objectives presumed.
>
> (2002: 43)

The core of the many recommendations made to both sides by Human Rights Watch (2002: 5–6) is that the means of warfare should conform to international humanitarian law as codified in the Geneva Conventions and its additional protocols, in particular upholding the principle of civilian immunity, taking all feasible precautions to protect civilians, discriminating between military and civilian targets, and refraining from disproportionate use of force.

These are admirable recommendations, but are they realistic, specific guides for unconventional warfare? Under these rules, Israeli foot patrols would have had to move up the alleys for engaging the fighters, which under the Jenin circumstances would have sent them to certain death. The Palestinian fighters would have had to evacuate from their buildings and shoot it out with the IDF, as in eighteenth-century warfare, which would have been a suicide mission. Without the Geneva Conventions, humanitarian law, and restraints on warfare by the military itself, warfare would be more horrible and destructive than it is. They have a moderating influence on unconventional warfare, and they did in Jenin, even though total conformity to them is unrealistic. In the Jenin fighting, of 1,400 inhabitants in the district where the fighters holed up, 52 and not hundreds lost their lives. Many homes were destroyed, but the inhabitants were not forcibly relocated as a collective punishment for harboring the fighters. No hostages were taken. The fighters who surrendered were taken prisoner, and not summarily executed. The target of the operation was the fighters, and not the entire population indiscriminately.

Islamist jihad

The insurgency and counterinsurgency so far analyzed had a well-defined ethnic and territorial focus. The Irish Republican Army had a hard-core base in Belfast. To be sure, it received some support from groups within the Republic of Ireland, raised funds in the United States, had cells elsewhere in Northern Ireland, and exploded bombs in British cities. But Paris metro riders and Air India passengers had nothing to fear from IRA terrorism. The IRA wanted Northern Ireland to become a part of Eire. Its violence targeted the British army and government, and the loyalist paramilitaries. What of transnational terrorism from al Qaeda and radical Islamist groups that has struck targets in North America, Western Europe, the Middle East, South Asia, and North and East Africa? Are there limits on violence by transnational terrorists, and what means of combating them are effective?

The radical Islamist movement is based on an ideology that has and has had many diverse leaders, clerics, and organizations affiliated with it. It predates Osama bin Laden and al Qaeda.

The targets of the radical Islamist movement have been not only the United States and Western governments, but the governments and leaders of Egypt, Jordan, Syria, Saudi Arabia, Algeria, and others in the Arab and Muslim world. The movement has had state sponsors, notably Iran and Saudi Arabia, and Muslim charities and foundations in many countries. Berman observes that "Al Qaeda is not only popular, it is institutionally solid, with a world wide network of clandestine resources . . . This is an organization with ties to the ruling elites in a number of countries" (2005: 26). Governments have manipulated the jihadi movement when it has suited their purpose. Jessica Stern writes that:

> Pakistani militant groups are killing civilians and engaging in terrorism in Indian held Kashmir under the guise of holy war. The government of Islamabad supports the militants and their religious schools as a cheap way to fight India and educate Pakistani youth, but this policy is creating a culture of violence.
>
> (2000: 116)

The Iranian Revolution of 1979 spawned and sponsored radical Islamic movements and groups in the Muslim world, especially among the Shi'ites. Ayatollah Khomeini branded the US as the "Great Satan" responsible for the ills of the Muslim countries, and proclaimed a holy war against the US, Israel, and Arab states such as Saudi Arabia that were allegedly clients and willing agents of the West. According to Khomeini and Arab radicals, the troubles of the Muslim world were many: underdevelopment and poverty, military backwardness and humiliating defeat of Arab armies by Israel, autocrats backed by the West (as the Shah had been), dependence on the West, squandering of oil wealth to favor a few privileged, and much else (Lewis 2002). Arab nationalism under Gamal Abdel Nasser had failed; Baathist socialism in Syria and Iraq had failed; secularism in Turkey was said to have failed. For some the response to failures was not more modernization and Western influence but return to the original Muslim faith, society, and theocratic polity that had existed at the time of Arab and Muslim greatness. Muslim fundamentalists believe the troubles of the Muslim world stem from imposing infidel ways on Muslim peoples. Their goal is to overthrow modernizing rulers and expel their foreign patrons and protectors, and return to purely Islamic ways of life in accord with the principles of Islam. In this vein, Osama bin Laden (*NYT*, October 8, 2001) refers to "our Islamic nation" that has been "tasting humiliation and disgrace, its sons killed and their blood spilled, its sanctities desecrated" for more than 80 years, i.e. when the Middle East was colonized by the West following the fall of the Ottoman empire.

Urged on by Khomeini and backed by the resources of revolutionary Iran and its revolutionary cadres, religious leaders, mosques, schools, and media, the ideology of Islamic revival and crusade (jihad) diffused in the Muslim world, with special resonance among minority Shi'ites. Khomeini proclaimed that "Islam and the teaching of the Koran will prevail all over the world . . . weapons in our hands are used to realize divine and Islamic aspirations" (Wright 2001: 27).

The Iranian religious zealots who captured the US embassy and precipitated the 1979 hostage crisis – a public humiliation of the Great Satan – pioneered in the early 1980s the covert organizational structure that became the model of subsequent Muslim terrorist groups and networks, like al Qaeda. Sponsored by the Association of Militant Clerics in Teheran, the Council for the Islamic Revolution, and the Revolutionary Guard Corps, a call went out throughout the Muslim and Arab world for young men to come to Iran and become holy warriors. They came from Libya, Yemen, Palestine, Egypt, Lebanon, the Gulf States, Saudi Arabia, and other places. At various centers and training camps, they were subjected to religious indoctrination, weapons training, and other studies. A select few, the elite for the jihad, became volunteers for martyrdom. They returned to their home countries to start local cells of radical Islamist groups; others were enlisted in the Iran–Iraq war as revolutionary fighters.

The first terrorist campaign of these Iranian-trained holy warriors was against the Sunni-dominated Gulf State rulers and against Saudi Arabia. The aim was to overthrow the rulers and to replace them with an Iranian-style theocracy. The most traumatic terrorist assault against the traditional Arab rulers was the seizure and occupation of the Great Mosque of Mecca, the holiest shrine of Islam, with 40,000 pilgrims trapped inside. On November 20, 1979, a band of at least 200 heavily armed Muslim radicals seized it and fought off the Saudi security forces for ten days (Wright 2001: 146–9). Altogether 255 pilgrims, troops, and terrorists were killed in the retaking of the Mosque, and some 500 were injured. Until 9/11 it was the most destructive terrorist Islamist action, and it was against a 100 percent Muslim target.

The response of the Saudi and Gulf rulers to Islamist radicalism in the Arab world and the Iranian-sponsored hostile propaganda and jihad against them was to become more militantly pious and puritanical than their Islamic critics and adversaries (Rouleau 2002). Building on the austere Wahabism, the state religion of the House of Saud, they enforced the Islamic religious codes (the Sharia) with their religious police. In Arabia as well as in neighboring countries, using religious foundations, the Saudis supported and bankrolled fundamentalist mullahs and mosques, religious schools, and social service and charitable organizations, which, in addition to serving legitimate religious and social purposes, became a religious infrastructure for jihadis and religiously motivated terrorists, including eventually against the Saudis themselves.

The next jihad was against the Soviet army and the communist-backed government in Afghanistan. Using the model created by the Iranian Revolutionary Guards for assembling a jihad and backed by his own and Saudi money, Osama bin Laden in the 1980s established recruitment centers for mujaheddin in the Middle East, North Africa, and Asia. Volunteers flocked to Pakistani camps where they were trained and indoctrinated, and readied for guerilla combat in Afghanistan. The US backed the Afghan resisters, including the mujaheddin, and supplied them sophisticated anti-aircraft missiles. Osama bin Laden later told a journalist:

> To counter these atheist Russians, the Saudis chose me as their repre-sentative in Afghanistan. I settled in Pakistan in the Afghan border region. There I received volunteers from the Saudi Kingdom and from all over the Arab and Muslim countries. I set up my first camp where these volunteers were trained by Pakistani and American officers. The weapons were supplied by the Americans, the money by the Saudis.
> (quoted in Rashid 2001: 132)

The transnational mujaheddin mode of organization was later adapted by Osama bin Laden for al Qaeda in the 1990s. Al Qaeda itself resulted from a merger of three jihadi groups, bin Laden's Arab fighters in Afghanistan, Egyptian Islamic Jihad led by Ayman al Zawahiri, and a lesser Egyptian militant group. Al Qaeda extended the recruitment and funding of terrorists from Arab countries to Western Europe wherever Muslim immigrants had created an encapsulating religious infrastructure of fundamentalist mullahs, mosques, schools, and foundations. Given lax controls on travel, com-munications, financial transactions, foreign study, identification papers, and especially religious activity, it was relatively easy to embed and hide illegal, criminal, and terrorist activities in democratic Western countries.

The war against the Soviets in Afghanistan was won. Then came the Gulf War after Iraq invaded and devastated Kuwait: one Arab state attacked another. The US-led Operation Desert Storm routed the Iraqi invasion and restored the state of Kuwait, yet it became a turning point in Osama bin Laden's radicalism. Half a million foreign soldiers were stationed in Saudi Arabia, infidels in the Muslim heartland, and 20,000 remained after the war in Saudi military bases. He told CNN: "the Saudi regime is but a branch or agent of the US. It has stopped ruling people according to what God revealed" (quoted in Wright 2001: 251). In the 1998 manifesto entitled "The

International Islamic Front for Jihad against Jews and Crusaders," bin Laden denounced the US for:

> occupying the lands of Islam in the holiest places, the Arabian peninsula, plundering its riches, dictating to its rulers, humiliating its people, and terrorizing its neighbors . . . to kill Americans and their allies – civilian and military – is an individual duty for every Muslim, in order to liberate the al-Aqsa mosque [Jerusalem] and the holy mosque [Mecca] from their grip.

After the attack on the World Trade Center and the Pentagon, his message on video broadcast by Al Jazeera called the rulers of the Arabian peninsula "hypocrites" and "apostates" who followed "the wrong path," and called on all Muslims to "remove evil from the peninsula of Mohamed" (*NYT*, October 8, 2001). He called America and its allies the modern world's symbol of paganism. He blamed the US for supporting Israeli repression of the Palestinians. He threatened that "America will not have peace before peace reigns in Palestine and before all the army of infidels depart the land of Mohamed." Among instructions to the suicide skyjackers was the following: "Remember the battle of the Prophet . . . against the infidels, as he went building the Islamic state" (Makiya and Mneimneh 2002: 28).

Some Western commentators are fixated on a poverty–social injustice–exploitation interpretation of discontent and grievance in the Muslim world. They are confused and bewildered by religious crusaders who dedicate their lives to realizing God's will on earth by violence. Nothing quite like it has existed in the Western world since the persecution of heretics and the wars of religion. When bin Laden proclaims that "the world is divided into two camps, the camp of the faithful and the camp of the infidels" it strikes one as alien and archaic. Yet consider some of the actions the Taliban took and the reasons for them. Barring women from work and girls from schooling has nothing whatever to do with ameliorating poverty, realizing social justice, or fighting imperialism. To the contrary these measures create poverty for women and children, many of whom were war widows and orphans in Afghanistan. Stoning women to death when convicted of adultery hardly advances an anti-poverty agenda. A religious police that confiscates video cassettes, prevents children from flying kites, enforces a dress code, and fines people for playing music has a religious, not a secular, explanation. When the Taliban demolished the magnificent and unique Buddha rock statues despite universal pleas and opposition, in a country where Buddhism hadn't existed for centuries and the Buddha was not worshipped by anyone, it was because they were sacrilegious. However much poverty and social injustice exist in the Muslim world, bin Laden and his associates turned on Arab rulers and the US for politico-religious and not for other reasons. Their purpose is to establish Muslim theocracies in the Middle East, and the US presence in the region is a major obstacle.

Al Qaeda

Bin Laden's hostility to the Saudi rulers led to his expulsion from Saudi Arabia in 1991 and loss of citizenship in 1994. After the Soviet–Afghan war, with over 500 mujaheddin, lots of money, and weapons, he moved from Afghanistan to the Sudan and then back to Afghanistan. More importantly, he put into effect a long-term plan to strike within the US. Al Qaeda brought terrorism to the US because the damage it inflicted on US installations in the Middle East was not traumatic enough to change US foreign policy, and because the mindset of US counterintelligence and security organizations, as well as public opinion, ruled out such a strike, as the 9/11 Commission later noted:

> Al Qaeda . . . considered the environment in the United States so hospitable that the 9/11 operatives used America as their staging area for further training and exercises – traveling into, out of, and around the country and complacently using their real names with little fear of capture.
>
> (*9/11 Commission Report*: 366)

At its zenith before the Afghan war, al Qaeda was a low-budget, low-cost, $30-million-a-year operation. It funded salaries for jihadists, training camps, arms, and vehicles, and the development of training manuals. The planning and implementation of the 9/11 air attacks cost only an estimated $400,000 to $500,000. It paid the Taliban $10 million to $20 million a year for safe haven. Most of the funds came from donors and religious charities in the Gulf countries and Saudi Arabia (*9/11 Commission Report*: 170–2). The inner core of al Qaeda consisted of 200 to 300 faithful who had sworn an oath of allegiance to serve bin Laden until death. Several thousand jihadists trained in weaponry and bomb making in its camps and were indoctrinated in the jihadist ideology, as was revealed from captured notebooks of trainees. Some of them were affiliated with other jihadi groups allied to al Qaeda which operated their own training camps (Olcutt and Babajanov 2003: 37). The indoctrination was unambiguous. An Uzbek notebook reads: "Jews, Russians, and Americans are always against Muslims and kill Muslims. And the Muslims are sound asleep." To make sure the message is understood, there is the drawing of four dogs tearing apart a map of Uzbekistan. The dogs are marked Jews, Americans, Russians, and Christians. The central message is that holy war is imperative "for our faith of Islam, to make Allah pleased with us, to eradicate oppression against Muslims, to establish Islamic rule in perpetuity" (Olcutt and Babajanov 2003: 36).

In Western Europe, the Muslim diaspora subculture of alienated young Muslims grown up in Europe sought dignity and identity in the community of Muslim faithful through jihad. The theme of Muslims being victimized by the West and jihadi revenge is widespread among jihadis. In the last message videotaped by a suicide bomber to be broadcast after his death, one of the July 7, 2005 London underground suicide bombers stated: "Your democratically elected government continually perpetuates atrocities against my people, and your support of them makes you directly responsible, just as I am directly responsible for protecting and avenging my Muslim brothers and sisters" (*NYT*, September 2, 2005). Inspired by the same ideology that the West is the enemy of Islam, militants who are not members of al Qaeda itself affiliated with local jihadi groups and have received some weapons training. Travel from these local groups to Afghanistan was common, some of it out of curiosity, some of it to get further terrorist training, and some to fight on the side of the Taliban against the Northern Alliance in the Afghan civil war. US intelligence estimates that 10,000 to 20,000 fighters went through the al Qaeda camps from 1996 to September 2001. At the outer edge of jihadi international is public opinion in Muslim states, an enormously important support for an ideological movement. Zogby International polls in these states show that respondents sympathize with al Qaeda because it stands up for Muslim causes and because it confronts the United States (Benjamin and Simon 2006).

The Afghan war was a US military success if measured against the demise of the Taliban government and military forces, but it was a failure if measured against destroying al Qaeda. The key failure was the escape of bin Laden, senior al Qaeda commanders, and several hundred of the best Arab and Chechen fighters from the Tora Bora cave complex after they had been driven to seek refuge there. According to Philip Smucker (2004), "scant intelligence, poorly chosen allies, and dubious military tactics fumbled a golden opportunity."

The Bush administration created an enormous security apparatus as part of homeland security and the global war on terror. John Negroponte, director of national intelligence, said in an interview (*NYT*, April 21, 2006) that the US now employs 100,000 people "stealing secrets and analyzing information to help protect national security." The budget for all intelligence agencies totaled $44 billion. I have already described the limited results of detaining and prosecuting "enemy combatants" in the Afghan war and in the aftermath of the 9/11 terrorist attacks in the US itself. Negroponte said that the government had made "great progress in capturing or killing several members of the high command of al Qaeda . . . but we haven't yet dealt a knockout blow to Mr. bin Laden himself." He did not say how many of them were actually killed or captured, and whether foreign intelligence agencies or US agencies had been responsible. No official has named a specific terrorist "sleeper cell" that has been neutralized. Tom Ridge told CNN shortly after he resigned as head of homeland security: "Can I tell you today, there are X number of incidents [of terrorism] we were able to thwart and prevent? I cannot" (quoted in Raban 2005: 25). As for Defense Secretary Donald Rumsfeld:

in October 2003, reflecting on progress after two years of waging the global war on terrorism, [he] asked his advisers: "Are we capturing, killing or deterring and dissuading more terrorists every day than the madrassas and radical clerics are recruiting, training and deploying against us? . . . The cost benefit ratio is against us! Our cost is billions against the terrorists' costs of millions."

(quoted in *9/11 Commission Report*: 374–5)

The Iraqi war: US counterinsurgency

The reason for Rumsfeld's puzzle is that the Bush administration followed up the Afghan war with the war on Iraq. The occupation of Iraq by the US military has been a magnet for attracting jihadists from all over the Muslim world and has become a vast training ground for global terrorists. Why the Bush administration decided to topple the Saddam Hussein regime in Iraq by military force and its relation to the global war on terror have not been satisfactorily explained. The fear that a "rogue state" would make weapons of mass destruction (WMDs) for a terrorist group was probably an important, though by no means the only, reason. Before the Iraqi war, President Bush rejected containment and deterrence as strategies for the war against terrorism in several speeches. The National Security Strategy of the United States, issued by the White House in September 2002, justified preventive war against rogue states and terrorists in view of the threat of WMDs falling into the wrong hands: "Given the goals of rogue states and terrorists, the United States can no longer rely on a reactive posture as we have in the past . . . We cannot let our enemies strike first."

To justify the Iraqi war, the Bush administration discounted intelligence on the lack of relations between the Iraqi regime and al Qaeda and inflated uncertain evidence on Iraqi possession of WMDs. Paul Pillar, who was the national intelligence officer in the CIA for the Near East and South Asia from 2000 to 2005, has written that:

> In the wake of the Iraq war, it has become clear that official intelligence analysis was not relied on in making even the most significant national security decisions, that intelligence was misused publicly to justify decisions already made, that damaging ill will developed between policy makers and intelligence officers, and that the intelligence community's own work was politicized . . . intelligence on the Iraq weapons program did not drive the decision to go to war . . . [the administration's] decision to topple Saddam was driven by other factors – namely the desire to shake up the sclerotic power structures of the Middle East and hasten the spread of more liberal politics and economics in the region.
>
> (2006: 15–16)

Regime change in Iraq had been a foreign policy goal of neo-conservatives who would become members of and advisers to the Bush administration.

Installing a pro-Western democratic regime there would stabilize that volatile region, and should be done unilaterally, if necessary. In a January 28, 1998 letter to President Clinton signed by Donald Rumsfeld, Paul Wolfowitz, Richard Armitage, Elliott Abrams, Richard Perle, John Bolton, Robert Kagan, and several others, the signers stated that:

> we may soon face a threat in the Middle East more serious than we have known since the end of the Cold War . . . the only possible strategy is one that eliminated the possibility that Iraq will be able to use or threaten to use weapons of mass destruction.
>
> (www.newamericancentury.org/iraqclintonletter.htm)

John Deutsch, former director of central intelligence, believes that it was "the conviction of some in the [Bush] administration that the U.S. military intervention to topple Saddam would result in a near-spontaneous conversion of Iraq, and with luck, the entire Middle East, to a democratic society" (2005: 33).

US counterinsurgency (COIN) has inflicted much violence on civilians. Force protection for avoiding military casualties has become the overriding objective of the US military. According to Col. Anthony Hartle, "non-combatants in the vicinity of legitimate targets appear to be at severe risk under current American policy in the war against terrorism" (2002: 975). In an urban insurrection environment, that means avoiding hand-to-hand combat with insurgents as much as possible; in its lieu force protection calls for lethal airstrikes and artillery shelling against targets in densely inhabited places. A Johns Hopkins School of Public Health study based on 988 households in 33 neighborhoods compared deaths in the year before the Iraqi war to deaths in the year and a half after the invasion and found that 84 percent of violent deaths were by the coalition forces, and of those deaths 95 percent were due to airstrikes and artillery ("Iran Death Toll Soared Post-war," *BBC News*, October 29, 2004). A Human Rights Watch study (2003) examining civilian casualties attributed to US forces in Baghdad between May 1 and September 30, 2003 found a "pattern of over aggressive tactics, excessive shooting in civilian areas, and hasty reliance on lethal force" during raids, at checkpoints, and after the ambush of convoys. It noted that soldiers are asked to switch from acting as warriors to serving as policemen for which they are not properly trained and equipped. As of April 2006, Iraqi Body Count (IRB) estimated that civilian deaths ranged from 34,511 to 38,660, with about 15 percent of them women and children. IRB estimates that American fire accounted for 37 percent of deaths; sectarian, revenge, and criminal deaths for 36 percent; insurgent attacks for about 10 percent; and "unknown agents" for the remainder. The single most lethal US military operation was in Falluja in April 2004 and claimed between 600 and 1,000 lives. These and other civilian body counts are crude estimates because insurgents and terrorists do not wear uniforms and it is therefore difficult to tell whether men who are killed are insurgents or civilians, unless a weapon is found on them.

What counterinsurgency is like in Iraq at the grass roots has been vividly described by Dexter Filkins on the activities of a battalion (800 soldiers) under the command of Lt. Col. Nathan Sussman in the heart of the Sunni Triangle when insurgents were having a lot of success in 2003. Senior American commanders were stunned and authorized aggressive tactics against the insurgents. Sussman's superior ordered him to "increase lethality." After one of his men was cut in half by a rocket-propelled grenade in violation of what Sussman believed was a truce he had negotiated with local Sunni sheiks, he resorted to tough tactics. The priority became to kill insurgents and punish those who supported them. His soldiers went into hostile villages "to kick down doors," imposed curfews, surrounded a village with barbed wire, issued ID cards, and established checkpoints for controlling movement in and out of the villages and towns. An old man complained that "It's just like a prison now. The Americans do night raids, come into our houses when the women are sleeping." When the insurgents fired a mortar into his compound, Sussman retaliated with 28 artillery shells and 42 mortar rounds and called for two airstrikes, one with a 500 lb. bomb and the other with a 2,000 lb. bomb. "We just didn't get hit after that," said Sussman. The result was non-cooperation and defiance from the population. As US authority eroded, "Sussman took the concept of non-lethal force to its limit." When his men came under fire from a wheat field, he burned down the entire field with phosphorus shells. His men demolished the house of a villager suspected of hijacking trucks with four anti-tank missiles after giving the family 15 minutes' notice to get out. A wounded man suspected of being an insurgent was threatened with no medical treatment unless he informed on the insurgency. These tough-guy methods were condoned by Sussman's superiors. In the end he was forced to retire when he tried to cover up an unintended homicide by soldiers under the command of one of his junior officers (a curfew violator had been forced to jump off a bridge into the Tigris river and drowned). Sussman explained that "There was no way I was going to let them court-martial my men, not after all they had been through." Filkins concludes that:

> The generals wanted body counts, and they wanted the insurgency brought under control, but they left the precise tactics up to soldiers in the field . . . Where is the line that separates nonlethal force that is justified . . . from nonlethal force that is criminal? . . . How much more serious was it to throw an Iraqi civilian into the Tigris, which was not approved, than it was to, say, fire an anti tank missile into an Iraqi civilian's home, which was?
>
> (2005: 108)

COIN (counterinsurgency) produces high civilian casualties. The irony of COIN tactics is that "the more you protect your forces, the less secure you are," according to Conrad Crane (2006). Lethal firepower aimed at distant insurgents in dense urban places saves soldiers' lives at the expense of high civilian casualties, but high civilian casualties motivate ordinary people to join and help the insurgency, which then leads to further military operations in more unsafe areas. COIN backfired because of the paradox of coercion. The military has had second thoughts on its tactics and was rewriting the army and marines' counterinsurgency manual in which they call for "restraining firepower" and "encouraging the military to understand the culture of a country . . . in order to determine how best to fight the enemy" (NPR, April 14, 2006; also *NYT*, May 2, 2006). Except for Special Forces, the US military is not trained, organized, and equipped for COIN. General Anthony Zinni said in an interview that:

> The military . . . became more and more saddled with conflict resolution . . . peace keeping, humanitarian efforts, nation building . . . It can't be dumped on a military that is not trained, equipped, or organized for that mission . . . the military basically has the mission to fight the country's wars. To defend the nation as their role in combat. That takes a lot in this day and age. It takes a lot of time; it takes a lot of training. It is very sophisticated. It is highly technical . . . If we are going to stay in the business of being the world's policemen . . . then we need to add capabilities.
>
> (2003)

Lacking intelligence from the population in a hostile environment on who is and who is not an insurgent and their location, US forces arrest a lot of people who happen to be at or near the site of an ambush, bombing, or shooting, interrogate them coercively, and transfer them to detention camps and prisons for further screening and interrogation. A report by Human Rights Watch (2005) describes detainee abuse by soldiers of the 82nd Airborne Division stationed at Forward Operating Base Mercury near Falluja as follows: "One officer and two non-commissioned officers . . . who witnessed abuse . . . described how their battalion in 2003–2004 routinely used physical and mental torture as a means of intelligence gathering and for stress relief." By torture they meant daily beatings, sleep deprivation for days on end, forced repetitive exercise, sometimes to the point of unconsciousness, and exposure to extremes of heat and cold. These soldiers reported that "the torture and other mistreatment of Iraqis in detention was systematic and was known at varying levels of command."

Had urban warfare and detention provided security from violence, the Iraqi population might have accepted them as a necessary price for normalization and reconstruction. Instead, violence and chaos continue. COIN tactics fly in the face of advice from counterinsurgency experts like Robert Thompson. Before the start of the Iraqi war, experts from within the military warned of an insurgency against a US occupation, the potential for terrorism, the likelihood of suicide bombing, and the danger of civil war in Iraq, and counseled that the first priority in the aftermath of war should be security, but their warnings were dismissed by the civilian leadership in the Pentagon (Crane and Terrill 2003).

Restraints in the global war on terrorism

Restraints in democratic states in national crises have four sources. The most important is professionalism within the military itself. Checks from within the polity are due to the separation of powers, competitive political parties, and commitment to the rule of law. The third source is a vigorous civil society: institutions that promote access to information, free speech, and opposition to the government. These institutions depend on independent news media, professional and scholarly associations, religious organizations, policy institutes and think tanks, and human rights advocacy groups. The final source is sensitivity to international opinion, to the reaction of allies, and commitment to international organizations and treaties that regulate war and international relations. How did these restraints fare after 9/11 with respect to coercive interrogation and torture in US detention facilities?

Torture and coercive interrogation are banned by US criminal law and the Geneva Conventions and laws of war to which the US is a signatory. Such practices of counterterror (CT) are more likely when certain conditions exist: (1) there is a national security crisis; (2) behaviors and practices usually banned are authorized; (3) a category of persons and situations is defined as a legitimate target for CT; (4) accountability for security operations is weakened, e.g. access to information is made difficult by secrecy and the security agents and authorities claim maximum discretion for security reasons; (5) command responsibility is suspended, i.e. every agent in the chain of command claims they are carrying out lawful orders originating with the top authority; (6) public attitudes are supportive of extraordinary emergency measures.

1   No one disputes that the terrorist attacks on the Twin Towers and the Pentagon constituted a national emergency, that other yet unidentified terrorist groups in the US might be ready to strike, and that, in view of the Taliban government's refusal to surrender al Qaeda terrorists responsible for these attacks, the US had the right to invade Afghanistan to kill and capture terrorists.
2   and 3 In anticipation of conducting President Bush's global war on terror, from November 2001 through January 2002 a small group of officials and lawyers in the White House, the Justice Department, and the Pentagon developed a legal strategy for a new military justice system that gave the president and the executive branch the right to bypass the Geneva Conventions by creating a new category of fighters termed "unlawful" or "enemy" combatants, prosecuting them in military

tribunals called "commissions" without specific congressional approval and oversight and lacking constitutional "due process" guarantees, and authorizing extraordinary powers for collecting intelligence.

What is extraordinary about this strategy and these claims in a democratic country is that they were instituted by executive orders and not by Acts of Congress as the Patriot Act on homeland security was. All the anti-terrorism measures of the UK against the IRA were based on Acts of Parliament and judicial oversight – the Special Powers Act, the Emergency Provisions Act, the Diplock courts, the Detention of Terrorists Order. The UK recognized the authority of the European Court of Human Rights, though it sought "temporary derogation" from conventions and treaties for detention, interrogation, and prosecution of terrorist suspects. According to the *New York Times* inquiry, "Senator Patrick J. Leahy, the Vermont Democrat who was then chairman of the Senate Judiciary Committee, was among a handful of legislators who argued that the administration's plan required explicit Congressional authorization." Leahy wanted changes in the operation of the military commissions, such as a presumption of innocence for defendants and appellate review by the Supreme Court, both of which are at the very foundations of the US justice system, but "the Congressional opposition melted in the face of opinion polls showing strong support for the president's measures against terrorism." Institutional checks and balances failed to work as restraints in the face of a nationwide crisis mentality. Because of opposition from within the administration, in particular the Department of State and the Judge Advocate General's corps (JAG), some modifications were made to the military commissions' modus operandi: "[Secretary of Defense] Rumsfeld granted the defendants a presumption of innocence, set 'beyond a reasonable doubt' as a standard for proving guilt, and allowed defendants to hire civilian lawyers though he restricted the lawyers access to case information" (*NYT*, October 24, 2004). In February 2002, President Bush issued a directive for treating detainees "humanely" in a manner consistent with the Geneva Conventions, within the limits of "military necessity."

4   In accordance with these presidential directives, the fighters captured in the Afghan war believed to have a terrorist link were transferred from Afghanistan and Pakistan to the military prison at Guantanamo Bay. From the start, "the Guantanamo Bay prison camp was conceived by the Bush administration as a place operated outside the system of national and international laws that normally govern the treatment of prisoners in U.S. custody" (Mayer 2005: 60). It operated in utmost secrecy from both media and legal scrutiny. Interrogators had difficulty making the detainees provide useful information because they would not cooperate or because they had no useful information. As one interrogator told Jane Mayer, "At the time we didn't even understand what

al Qaeda was. We thought the detainees were all masterminds. It wasn't the case. Most of them were just dirt farmers in Afghanistan." The pressure on interrogators to get results was intense. In October 2002 Guantanamo officials asked the Pentagon for permission to use harsh interrogation techniques on resistant detainees including some that were defined as cruel, inhumane, and degrading, such as prolonged sleep deprivation, prolonged standing, isolation, removal of clothing, exploitation of detainees' fear of dogs, hooding, and others. One list recommended by a working group "for use with unlawful combatants outside the U.S." color-coded each technique on whether it conformed to the "Torture Convention (torture)," "Torture Convention (Cruel, Inhuman, Degrading)" and "U.S. domestic law." The techniques were rated on "contribution to intelligence collection" on a three-category scale (high, medium, low). Secretary of Defense Rumsfeld did not approve "waterboarding" and "threats to harm family members" but approved 16 harsh techniques for use on uncooperative detainees that went beyond what the Army Field Manual authorized for intelligence interrogations (Mayer 2005: 68).

The military lawyers in the JAG became the most persistent internal critics of the Bush administration anti-terrorism techniques at Guantanamo Bay because they were contrary to long-standing US military tradition on proper conduct in war as expressed in the Army Field Manual's rules for intelligence interrogation ("Military Opposition to Harsh Interrogation Is Outlined," *NYT*, July 28, 2005). The FBI interrogators at Gitmo who witnessed "torture techniques" opposed them because they considered them useless, and reported to their superiors in Washington the disagreements they had with Department of Defense officials ("Report Discredits FBI Claims of Abuse at Guantanamo Bay," *NYT*, July 14, 2005). These disagreements did not become public until two years later when emails about the internal conflict were leaked to the *New York Times* ("Two Prosecutors Faulted Trials for Detainees," August 1, 2005). The detailed story was described by Seymour Hersch in two articles (2004a, 2004b). He concluded that:

> The roots of the Abu Ghraib prison scandal lie not in the criminal inclinations of a few Army reservists but in a decision, approved last year [2003] by Defense Secretary Rumsfeld to expand a highly secret operation, which had been focused on the hunt for Al Qaeda, to the interrogation of prisoners in Iraq.
>
> (2004a: 22)

The Abu Ghraib story on the humiliating and coercive treatment of detainees was revealed not as a result of the checks and balances of the US political system, military professionalism, investigative reporting by independent news media, or human rights groups. Within the armed forces and US security agencies, hundreds, if not thousands, witnessed or knew about what was taking place. Many of them believed these measures were useful, necessary, and authorized within the war on terror framework. The media, the Congress, and the public were kept in the dark by a veil of secrecy concealing these programs and abusive actions. Ordinary soldiers engaged in the abuses, and ordinary officers condoned them, or purposely ignored them. And an equally ordinary soldier, in the 372nd Military Police Company whose members were engaged in prisoner abuse and were taking and circulating digital photos of abuse incidents, decided to complain to his superiors and submitted some of the torture photographs to them.

5   The Army Criminal Investigation Division immediately opened an investigation into the mistreatment of prisoners. Shortly a number of other internal investigations were opened, the most informative and transparent by General Taguba. The public first took note of the abuses when the photos were broadcast on CBS's *60 Minutes II* on April 28, 2004, which made the abuses into a worldwide news story. The publicity roused congressional committees out of their "checks and balances" slumber on oversight of the executive branch. They held hearings at which Rumsfeld and top military brass had to testify. The Congressmen (and the public) were stonewalled. In the words of Senator Mark Dayton, a member of the Armed Services Committee:

We've now had fifteen of the highest level officials involved in this operation, from the secretary of defense to the generals in command, and nobody knew that anything was amiss, nobody approved anything amiss, nobody did anything amiss. We have a general acceptance of responsibility, but there is no one to blame, except for the people at the very bottom in one prison.

(quoted in Danner 2004a)

Meanwhile, Joseph Darby, the whistleblower, was put into protective custody because he and his family had received death threats and moved out of their Maryland home in August 2004 (www.jfklibrary.org/profile incourageaward/2005). Another whistleblower, Army Captain James Yee, the Muslim chaplain at Gitmo, suffered a worse fate. When he called the attention of his superiors to prisoner abuse, he was arrested and imprisoned on charges of espionage. He was also accused of adultery and possession of pornography. Later all charges were dropped and he was given an honorable discharge. But the Gitmo administration won: the news story shifted from prisoner abuse to Muslim espionage at Gitmo and Yee's moral character.

6   Concerning restraints on the emergency powers of the state in a democracy, Michael Ignatieff argues that "we keep antiterrorist policy under the bright light of adversarial justification" (2004: ix), by which

he means courtrooms, the free press, legislative hearing rooms, free elections, and especially full judicial review. Many wholeheartedly agree, yet his prescription for restraint assumes an idealized view of the US polity. The main reason that the congressional hearings, military investigations and reports, and the public debate in the "elite" media and forums initially have had little impact on public demand to stop the abuses and to punish those responsible is that the public believes the Bush administration assertions and justifications about detainee abuse: a "few bad apples" are responsible and you always get a few bad apples in a large basket; the detainees are dangerous terrorists who refuse to reveal valuable information, and to make them talk you can't go by the book; and there is a direct link between the war in Iraq and the global war on terror, i.e. if you don't capture and kill them in Iraq, they will kill you in Los Angeles and New York. The Pew Research Center for People and the Press reported from one of its surveys on June 13, 2005 that 54 percent of respondents believed that Guantanamo prisoner mistreatments are isolated incidents, versus 34 percent who believed they form a wider pattern of abuse. Other polls indicated that the public was not much troubled by the Iraqi prisoner abuse photos even though three-quarters of the respondents had seen them. Rush Lindbaugh, the right-wing broadcaster heard on 600 stations, dismissed the abuse shown in the photos as no worse than typical college hazing. In the 2004 television debates for presidential candidates, prisoner abuse was unmentioned. Torture was not an issue because the Democrats did not raise it, and they did not raise it because they believed that any criticism of the military in war would be turned against them as unpatriotic and not "supporting our troops." Prisoner abuse does not fit that frame.

Research on support for war indicates that the public turns against it not for moral reasons but when US casualties mount while public confidence in US victory is eroding (Gelpi 2006). In the end, mounting US casualties and growing public skepticism about the Bush administration's strategy for winning against the insurgency and installing a democratic government in Iraq emboldened the polity and the civil society to assert themselves and to demand restraints on the executive branch in the global war on terrorism. The news media downsized their patriotic journalism and increased critical coverage of the Iraqi war and of the government's counterinsurgency and counterterrorism measures. The Congress began to make the White House and the Pentagon accountable for detainees, for prisoner abuse, for interrogation of prisoners, for bringing detainees to trial, and for other dimensions of the global war on terror such as mass electronic surveillance in violation of the 1978 FISA law. Federal judges issued rulings on detainees' right to legal counsel, lawyers' access to information on their clients' condition (e.g. whether they were force-fed during a hunger strike), their right to a hearing in federal court on whether or not they were lawfully detained, and other rulings limiting the powers of the executive branch. The professional military and the Congress insisted on their right over the contents of the Army Field Manual on interrogations. Human rights groups and news organizations took the administration to court about releasing reams of information under the Freedom of Information Act and complemented the actions of congressional committees and investigative commissions demanding and getting information. Officials in security agencies and executive departments leaked closely held secrets to the news media (e.g. the CIA's outsourcing of coercive interrogation and torture of terrorist suspects called "rendition"), which reported them. Retired generals spoke out on the conduct of the war.

The system of democratic checks operates slowly. The news media exercise self-censorship in wartime. The Congress is divided: many rest their chances of reelection on war's success and are unwilling to tie the hands of the executive branch. The federal judiciary has to wait until cases are brought before it. Critics within the military can be reassigned, demoted, or retired. The intellectual establishment is as split as the Congress and the public. For every public intellectual, human rights advocate, and international law professor counseling restraint in the global war on terror, an equally credentialed security analyst, public intellectual, and law professor insists on the extraordinary powers of the executive branch in a national security crisis.

Conclusion

1 In unconventional warfare, the insurgents attack the security forces, officials of the state, and civilians. The insurgents need the assistance of the population for manpower, resources, information and cover. If persuasion fails, they will get them by intimidation, fear and violence. The government in a security crisis is under great pressure to defend national security and to protect the public. The conjunction of unconventional warfare and security crisis sets off the dynamic of "dirty warfare."

2 The criminal law, the body of humanitarian law and crimes against humanity, and the codified laws of war do not regulate unconventional warfare and counterinsurgency appropriately. Total conformity to them by the state risks failure in confronting insurgents and terrorists.

3 Without restraints on the dynamic, both sides become brutal, arbitrary and barbaric in violence. Civilians suffer the most. Without restraints, a democratic state is at risk of adopting institutions and practices found in police states and military dictatorships.

4 British counterinsurgency has shown that crisis security measures for detention, interrogation, and incarceration of suspects, which violate the laws of war and peacetime justice and human rights, do contain

insurgency. They also show that extraordinary security measures do not result in victory. Only a political settlement ends violence and brings peace.

5 The lesson from the Bush administration's war on terror and the war in Iraq is that, without judicial and legislative checks, crisis security measures violate human rights, and the security apparatus generates human rights abuses on a vast scale. Crisis measures and abuses that have no demonstrable value for fighting insurgency and terrorism nevertheless keep expanding unchecked. In these crises, legal and moral restraints in a democracy are fragile and uncertain.

6 In a democratic state facing such crises, emergency laws and measures should be enacted by a lawful process, by the legislature, with accountability to an independent judiciary. The British government modified the rule of law, enacted emergency legislation that was periodically reviewed and renewed, and put the operation of the emergency security and justice apparatus under judicial and parliamentary oversight. The Bush administration mode of counterinsurgency and counter terror is for the executive branch to claim and assume extraordinary powers with minimal legislative consent. The experiences analyzed in this chapter indicate that the British institutions of restraint are preferable. To let the executive branch decide who is an "enemy combatant," what is "imminent danger," how to define "torture," what a "fair trial" is, and many other distinctions that make a difference between freeing a suspect who is not guilty of crime and keeping him in prison under indefinite detention without trial is to invite abuse on a large scale.

7 The temporary emergency rules for dealing with insurgency and terrorism should deal with and be based on realistic confrontations and behaviors of insurgents, soldiers, security personnel, interrogators, suspects, and civilians, and not on hypothetical, idealized, and highly unlikely scenarios, e.g. the "ticking bomb." What actually happens at a checkpoint where guards monitor hundreds of pedestrians and vehicles? What actually happens during a patrol of soldiers in a hostile urban neighborhood? How does one interrogate an uncooperative suspect in whose basement an arms cache was found? How does one interrogate an insurgent who was wounded and captured in a fire fight and who is likely to know where land mines have been planted? In combat and counterinsurgency, the right balance between obtaining information, saving lives, coercive treatment, and human rights has to be struck under realistic assumptions about human behavior and the "fog of counter-insurgency."

8 When the fighting eventually stops and a peace accord is negotiated and implemented, the legacy of "dirty war" is a huge liability to peace building. The adversaries have become polarized and post-war cooperation is problematic. "Dirty war" should be restrained and minimized for the sake of future peace.

9 The chances of peace building are improved when a political vision and resolution of the conflict is on the table throughout the hostilities, and when the adversaries exercise restraint. Imperfect as they are for regulating unconventional warfare, without the laws of war and international humanitarian law serving as an ideal and as a benchmark against which emergency measures are evaluated and justified, violence and human suffering in conflict would have no defined limits.

10 Responsibility for the security forces' non-compliance with emergency rules and measures should be located high in the chain of command and not simply blamed on a few "bad apples" among the rank and file. The higher officers are responsible for preventing a culture of "dirty warfare" and abuses from becoming pervasive in counterinsurgency and counter terror.

3 Peace intervention

Varieties of external intervention in ethnic conflicts

In the mid-1990s, the International Committee of the Red Cross counted 56 wars and insurgencies being fought, and some 25 million refugees and displaced persons around the world. They represented a formidable task for the United Nations and states assuming responsibility for international conflict management. How did they go about it?

Few civil wars and insurgencies deescalate into a peace process without intervention by external states and international organizations. From 1992 to 2000, the United Nations has deployed 34 peacekeeping missions, almost all of them in internal wars. Another count yields 38 peace missions mandated by the UN since 1989, of which 24 terminated without further conflict among the parties (Wallensteen 2002: chapter 9). The UN has played an important but by no means exclusive role in crisis management. It has not intervened or has played only a marginal peace-making role in several recent civil wars and major insurgencies, e.g. Northern Ireland, Chechnya, Sri Lanka, the Algerian civil war of the 1990s, the 20-year Southern Sudan civil war, and the South African peace process. In other instances, neighbor states have taken the responsibility of attacking rogue regimes, as Tanzania did against Idi Amin's Uganda, Vietnam against Pol Pot's Cambodia, and India against the Tamil Tigers in the north of Sri Lanka. The systematic study of what makes for success or failure in peacekeeping by international crisis managers and institutions has barely started. Critics tend to fault the conflicting interests and goals of the external stakeholders, the decision process in the UN and other bodies, the limited mandates and resources provided to peacekeepers, the obstructions to implementation by the host state, and the lack of commitment to peace by the adversaries.

Peacekeeping has been successful when the adversaries actually want peace. In many instances, they do not want it. More accurately stated, they verbally comply with demands by the external stakeholders for peacekeepers and humanitarian relief, which actually relieves them of responsibility for civilian victims, but in fact they obstruct the peace process. The international peacekeepers may themselves become victims of the intervention.

A peacekeeping operation is like the emperor who has no clothes, and the bluff is soon enough called by the combatants.

Because there is no scholarly consensus on how to classify different types of intervention and how to measure success and failure of external interventions, there are disagreements on what interventions achieve, let alone what would have happened had they not taken place. George Downs and Stephen Steadman (2002) found that, in 16 external interventions by the UN, a regional organization, or a single state, there were six failures, six successes, and four partial successes. On the other hand, Wallensteen writes that the UN "peacekeeping record since 1989 is impressive" (2002: 255). Roland Paris (2004: part 2) finds only two successful instances, Namibia and Mozambique, in the eight he studied, all of them also evaluated by others.

UN peacekeeping has varied on the use of force and the depth and range of external involvement (Bellamy *et al.* 2004). *Traditional peacekeeping* is based on the consent of the parties, impartiality, and minimum force. The typical case occurs when a ceasefire has been agreed to by two states, but before a peace treaty or settlement is negotiated. The adversaries want an impartial third party for separating their armed forces, monitoring the ceasefire, reporting on violations, and facilitating a permanent peace. After civil war broke out in Cyprus in late 1963 and the fighting escalated, a UN peacekeeping force of 6,200 soldiers, UNFICYP, was deployed to prevent recurrence of the fighting. Traditional peacekeeping has been stretched in decolonization wars and some other internal wars to managing the transition from ceasefire and peace accord to implementing the peace settlement itself, with the consent of the parties. In practice it means organizing the demilitarization of the conflict, organizing and monitoring a post-war election for choosing a new government in a democratic way, and launching the war-ravaged country on the road to stable peace. UN peacekeeping interventions in Namibia (1989–90) and El Salvador (1991–4) are instances. *Wider peacekeeping* occurs in an ongoing conflict when ceasefires by the adversaries are not complied with. In some instances, as in Bosnia and East Timor, the Security Council may try to impose peace by military means and organize a transitional administration and military force to enforce the peace and support peace implementation.

Intervention by the UN or by external states such as NATO in Kosovo is inhibited by the right of states to sovereignty and territorial integrity under article 2 of the UN Charter. Nevertheless, under chapter 7, if a conflict presents a "threat to international peace and security," the UN Security Council has the right to intervene in a domestic conflict. The UN can broker a ceasefire, deliver humanitarian aid and protect non-combatants, deploy peacekeepers and monitors, authorize military force to protect its peacekeepers and humanitarian workers, authorize economic sanctions by member states on the belligerents who violate UN Security Council resolutions on conflict management, authorize an international criminal tribunal for prosecuting perpetrators of war crimes and crimes against humanity, and other steps. Over time, a body of international humanitarian law has come to legitimize humanitarian intervention by external states against states that massively oppress and persecute their own people violently. The moral underpinning for such intervention is the just war principle (Walzer 1997). External intervention, according to the just war principle, has to conform to a number of conditions. There has to be a just cause; a legitimate authority has to conduct the war, usually sanctioned by the UN; force has to be the last resort and has to be proportional to the injuries and crimes perpetrated; intervention should be expected to make matters better rather than worse for the peoples on whose behalf it takes place; the interveners have to assume responsibility for the welfare of the people and for establishing peace, and have to end the intervention after completing their humanitarian mission, i.e. there has to be an exit strategy. Michael Walzer (2002) has argued that a just war is an effort to change the regime responsible for the atrocities, lest it repeat the massacres and other mass acts of inhumanity that the humanitarian intervention is meant to stop. Humanitarian intervention could well mean warfare against the regime and far-reaching responsibilities for post-war reconstruction.

The most savage offenses a government can perpetuate on its own people (and sometimes neighboring people as well) are genocide and ethnic cleansing. Ethnic cleansing is the use of force or intimidation for removing people of a certain ethnic or religious group from an area or territory that is their homeland. It used to be called "mass deportations." A host of criminal offenses take place during ethnic cleansing: murder, torture, arbitrary arrest and detention, executions, rape and sexual assault, military and paramilitary attacks on civilians, robbery and extortion, destruction of cultural and religious buildings and monuments, destruction of homes, confinement of civilians in camps, purposeful starvation, and some others. Some of these crimes are war crimes; others are crimes against humanity; still others are criminal acts by individuals. The purpose of these crimes is to get the target population to flee (kill and assault some, and the others will flee), to rob its property and make it destitute, to administer extra-legal punishment and revenge for alleged disloyalty or helping enemies, and to prevent return by having nothing to return for. In many cases, return is not possible. In others, only a fraction of the refugees and internally displaced persons return. Ethnic cleansing "works" as intended by the perpetrators.

Genocide is killing a part or all of an ethnic group. The 1948 genocide convention (Convention on the Prevention and Punishment of Genocide) defines it in article 2 as:

> any of the following acts committed with intention to destroy, in whole or in part, a national, racial, or religious group, as such: (a) killing members of the group; (b) causing serious bodily or mental harm to members of the group; (c) deliberately inflicting on the group conditions of life calculated to bring about its physical destruction in whole or in

part; (d) imposing measures intended to prevent births within the group; (e) forcibly transferring children of the group to another group.

Raphael Lemkin, the Polish scholar who first proposed the label and crime of genocide, explained that genocide does not only mean the immediate total destruction of a people, as in mass extermination, but is also a coordinated plan of many different actions aimed at destroying the basic foundations of life of a people and thus annihilating the people itself. Genocide against a politically defined group was not included in the convention, nor forced assimilation of a people by another one, because the Soviet Union would not have agreed to the convention. The crime of genocide, as well as mass political persecution and forced assimilation, consists of violent actions that are themselves war crimes and crimes against humanity, as is true for ethnic cleansing. All of these crimes are aimed at an entire group or people. Killing of civilians in a single incident, e.g. when a group extracts revenge for the death of its members by killing members of the alleged perpetrators, is termed a massacre, or ethnic riot. On the scale of horrors and tragedies that a human group inflicts on another, genocide and ethnic cleansing occupy the top.

Both genocide and ethnic cleansing are planned and organized murderous violence against a people by the authorities and their agents, take time to prepare, and require the complicity of large numbers of militants and passive acceptance by ordinary citizens who "look the other way," are intimidated or are confused. Collective violence tends to be perpetuated by authoritarian regimes that have a long record of oppression and human rights violations against minorities, between adversaries who have a history of hostile relations and of conflict, and during a major crisis such as insurgency, civil war, and secession. Research (Fein 1979; Mann 2005) has shown that in the preparatory period the target group is labeled and sharply distinguished from the perpetrator people by a name and hate symbols (yellow stars for Jews in Nazi Germany and Nazi-occupied Europe). It is dehumanized in official hate and threat propaganda, e.g. in cartoons, false atrocity stories and films, and the falsification of history, the target group is depicted as amoral, dangerous, and a threat to the perpetrators and their way of life. An elaborate justification is created for preparing the public for the collective violence and mass killings. Justification encompasses innocent civilians such as children, mothers, and old people because children will grow up to adulthood, women will give birth for the enemy group, and old folks may become troublesome witnesses, i.e. the entire group or people are tainted with the brush of guilt and should be struck preemptively before they strike the perpetrators. Armed fighters, including often special branches of the regular army and police, are trained, armed, and organized for the campaign of genocide or ethnic cleansing. A wall of concealment, falsehood, and denial is built to cover up criminal actions, such as the burial of bodies at remote execution sites in mass graves that are covered with dirt and leveled for escaping discovery.

Genocide and ethnic cleansing in the contemporary world are not rare events. Norman Naimark (2001) has described many, and others can be added from the non-European world: Armenian genocide in 1915; Greek and Turkish mutual ethnic cleansing in the 1920s; Nazi genocide of the Jews and some other groups in World War II; internal mass deportations in the Soviet Union against Chechens, Crimean Tatars, the Inguish, and the Volga Germans; mass atrocities between the various political and nationality groups in Yugoslavia in World War II; in the aftermath of that war the mass expulsion of German ethnics from Poland, Czechoslovakia, Yugoslavia, and other places; ethnic cleansing in Cyprus during civil war and partition; and repeated ethnic cleansing and atrocities during the Yugoslav wars and civil wars of the 1990s. In the rest of the world, just focusing on the period after World War II, there is the expulsion of the French settlers from Algeria after the war of independence, forced expulsion and mass killings during the partition of India, ethnic cleansing and mass flight of Palestinians during the Israeli war of independence and a lesser wave during the 1967 war, mass killings of communists and their supporters in 1965 in Indonesia, repeated ethnic cleansing in Kurdistan, genocide in Cambodia and Rwanda, mass killings in Algeria during the war between the Islamists and the army, mass killings and deportations from East Timor by the Indonesian army, and mass killings and ethnic cleansing in the South Sudan and again currently in Darfur by the Sudanese government and its allies. This is not a complete listing by any means. Nor do I put much stake on what precise word is attached to a particular episode of collective violence because they all are instances of mass suffering intentionally perpetuated by the authorities and their agents, and which external states singly and jointly have failed to stop.

What typically happens when an internal crisis unfolds? Diplomatic observers, NGOs, and news reporters will be the first to call attention to some violent events that become a continuing international crisis story. The NGOs, the United Nations, some stakeholder states, e.g. neighbors who are impacted by refugees, call for and sponsor fact-finding commissions, and publicly call on the adversaries to resolve their differences peacefully. Some external organizations and political leaders may offer their services for mediation and for talks. Debates take place in the United Nations Security Council about what is happening, who is responsible, and what should be done. The Security Council then passes resolutions calling for a ceasefire, for states and external bodies to stop assistance to the adversaries, for named aggressors to stop aggression, for talks between the adversaries, and the like, which, if not complied with, will result in sanctions (e.g. economic sanctions against an aggressor). The UN's various humanitarian agencies and other such organizations – UNHCR, World Food, International Red Cross – are called on for humanitarian relief to non-combatants and relief operations, and refugee camps are then organized. The UN may deploy lightly armed peacekeepers with a mandate for protecting the relief operations and for reporting ceasefire violations, and for protecting itself against attack. Since the UN has no permanent armed force, the Secretary General calls on member states to contribute soldiers, logistics, emergency assistance, and funds for the intervention, and may delegate some of these functions to other bodies, such as a regional organization (e.g. the African Union, the European Union, or NATO). Intervention is contingent on the consent of the state in which the conflict occurs. If the target government obstructs the peace operations or is incapable of ensuring the safety of UN and humanitarian personnel, the Security Council may strengthen the mandate, size, and armament of the peacekeeper, threaten sanctions and the use of force against those who defy its resolutions, and as a last resort authorize peace enforcement to stop assaults on protected civilians, refugees under its care, and international staff. The UN may also authorize a criminal tribunal for prosecuting those responsible for war crimes and crimes against humanity.

Traditional peacekeeping

When the UN and its functions were created after World War II, it was assumed that peacekeeping would be called upon when two states at war were moving to end hostilities and needed a neutral buffer force to interpose between two armies, to monitor the ceasefire, and to report violations. Peacekeeping was based on consent of the belligerents, impartiality of the peacekeepers, and minimum force ("Peacekeeping" 2002). An example is UNEF in Egypt in 1956–7 to bring the Suez crisis to a successful end. Its deployment facilitated the withdrawal of UK, French, and Israeli military from Egypt, and its presence reduced the risk of hostile incidents on the Israeli–Egyptian ceasefire line. Because the ceasefire did not progress to peace between Israel and Egypt, UNEF by itself did not deter the subsequent 1967 war between them, and UNEF was withdrawn. In Cyprus, after independence from the UK, violence erupted in 1963 when President Makarios proposed amending the independence constitution which protected Turkish minority status. UNFICYP was created as an interposition force between Greek and Turkish Cypriots with the mandate of "preventing recurrence of the fighting and contributing to maintenance and restoration of law and order," which it did from 1964 to 1973. When the Greek military government sought to incorporate Cyprus into Greece and the Turkish army invaded for protection of the Turkish Cypriots, UNFICYP's presence did not deter renewed armed conflict and huge refugee flows resulting from ethnic cleansing. Its mandate was modified to monitor a buffer zone along the 180-mile Green Line which for the next two decades became a barbed wire-filled no man's land between the Greek Cypriot South and the Turkish Cypriot North, cutting off the movement of people. However, UNFICYP may have reduced the risk of a wider war between Greece and Turkey. Similarly, UNMOGIP, a small military observer group deployed since 1949 in Kashmir to monitor the ceasefire between India and Pakistan, has not deterred later wars, cross-border insurgency, and terrorism. These traditional peacekeeping activities were a short-term fix for separation of the belligerents, but, without further successful diplomacy to bring a lasting peace, they did not deter renewal of armed fighting (Ramsbotham and Woodhouse 1999).

The UN has also conducted 32 peace operations in transitions from colony to independence, as UNTAG did in Namibia in 1989–90 and UNSF did in the Western part of New Guinea when it changed from Dutch to Indonesian possession, and in managing peace settlements after civil war, as in Mozambique, Angola, and Central American conflicts (Bellamy *et al.* 2004: 112). In El Salvador in 1991–4, ONUSAL was mandated to monitor the ceasefire between the army and the guerilla FMLN after a 14-year-long civil war and, following a UN brokered peace accord, the demilitarization of the adversaries. In the peace accord, the FMLN was to disarm and the government was to reduce and reform its army (Spear 2002: 164–5). Elections were held for a new government, which ONUSAL monitored with the help of 900 observers in March 1994. Disarmament was slow and punctured by violations. It took political pressure by Colombia, Mexico, Spain, and Venezuela to make the army reduce to half its size. These crisis managers and ONUSAL were instrumental in securing the transition of El Salvador from a war-ravaged to a peaceful state (Bellamy *et al.* 2004: 118–22).

Similar transitional peacekeeping operations after long, destructive civil wars in Southern Africa also achieved success after the Cold War ended and the adversaries could no longer expect diplomatic and military backing from external states, as was also true in Central America. In Mozambique an anti-colonial war by FRELIMO against the Portuguese (1964–74) was shortly followed by an even bloodier civil war between FRELIMO and RENAMO (1976–92) in which an estimated 1 million were killed and a third of the population uprooted. Both sides had armed civilians in their areas of control for self-defense purposes with hundreds of thousands of weapons only a fraction of which were handed in during demobilization of the fighting forces. ONUMOZ in Mozambique from 1993 to 1995 successfully managed the disarmament of the RENAMO insurgents, integration of combatants from both sides into a restructured army, and elections in conformity to the 1992 peace accords. An estimated 100,000 combatants were demobilized, 200,000 weapons were handed in at collection points, and a further 35,000 weapons were seized from 600 arms caches by joint South African police and Mozambique government operations after 1995, supplemented by a small-scale tools-for-arms buy-back program run by religious groups (Bonn International Center 2004). Because weapons could be used for crime, not just self-defense and protection in case the civil war restarted, and because there was a lucrative market for them across the border in South Africa, both governments had an interest in getting hold of them in their efforts to spread a culture of peace. The peace has held. ONUSAL and ONUMOZ are widely viewed as UN successes in transitional peacekeeping.

Humanitarian intervention: Rwanda and Kosovo

The machinery for international conflict management is slow and cumbersome, whereas ethnic crises and collective violence against civilians are fast paced. The intervention environment is more complex than for a natural disaster because an insurgency, civil war, and other armed conflicts are raging, and because external states, sometimes the members of the Security Council itself with veto powers, have a partisan interest in the conflict and are the allies or protectors of one of the adversaries. Economic sanctions hurt many innocent persons, as was the case with sanctions against the Iraqi regime after the first Gulf War. To remedy this flaw, the food-for-oil program was created, but its operation allowed huge sums to be diverted to the Saddam Hussein regime owing to collusion by member states and corruption within the implementation organizations. More generally, the delivery of humanitarian assistance is vulnerable to partial appropriation by the belligerents who in effect hold the victims of collective violence hostage. The same can happen to lightly armed UN peacekeepers. UN monitors deployed between the belligerents after a ceasefire are simply no match for the adversaries if they decide to resume armed fighting, as happened in Cyprus, in the Ethiopia/Eritrea war, in Kashmir, and elsewhere.

The effectiveness of international conflict management in humanitarian crises depends on the commitment of the external states, in particular the most powerful states in the Security Council, to stop the conflict and on compliance by the adversaries. If diplomatic efforts and peacekeeping result in the cessation of armed conflict and in a peace agreement, the UN and other interveners take on huge responsibilities for disarming the combatants and demilitarizing the conflict, for post-insurgency or post-war relief operations, and for the reconstruction of the society and its institutions.

Some external interventions from the past 20 years illustrate how international conflict management actually works. Rwanda had previous ethnic massacres and cleansing in 1962 at the time of independence. It was a divided society. It had a non-democratic military regime and France was its powerful international protector. All these are indicators of high risk for collective violence. In 1990, the Rwanda Patriotic Front, composed of Tutsi refugees and exiles, invaded with an armed force from Uganda, and was gaining ground against the Rwanda army. The goal of the invasion was the return of 500,000 Tutsi exiles and the restoration of their land and properties. Such an armed attack or insurgency is an additional indicator of high risk for collective violence against civilian populations. With the Hutu regime thus threatened, international diplomacy pressured it and the rebel movement into peace negotiations which resulted in a ceasefire and the Arusha peace accord signed on August 4, 1993 that included a provision on power sharing and the return of Tutsi refugees. The United Nations deployed a lightly armed military force of 2,500 peacekeepers with a limited mandate under General Romeo Dallaire to monitor the ceasefire. The Rwanda regime however stalled on implementing the Arusha accord. In the meantime, the Coalition for the Defense of the Republic, an extreme anti-Tutsi party that included many regime leaders, mounted a hate-Tutsi campaign on the radio and with leaflets, organized countrywide officials, militias, and ordinary people into a regime militia that was indoctrinated in weapons, and armed for leading the planned mass killings of Tutsi and anti-regime Hutu. Such preparations are a proximate indicator for ethnic cleansing and genocide.

These activities and instances of ethnic violence were noted by the diplomatic corps, UN agencies, the missions of the Catholic Church and other religious organizations, and NGOs. Alison Des Forges, a frequent visitor in Rwanda on behalf of human rights organizations, stated that:

> Exactly thirteen months before the genocide happened, we [Human Rights Watch] published a report which detailed massacres carried out by the government against the Tutsi minority. Then the August before, the RTLM [a radio station] started to broadcast clear incitements to hatred . . . and eventually to killing . . . This was over the public air waves. People knew about it. And the people who heard it informed everyone [the foreigners in Rwanda] . . . militia was being organized and recruited . . . we reported on that . . . the other part was the distribution of guns. That also drew public comment.
>
> (quoted in Fein 1994: 21–2)

Nevertheless, international aid donors were unwilling to suspend aid to the regime for non-compliance with the Arusha peace accord. When mass killings actually started in April 1994, General Dallaire asked for more peacekeepers and an expanded mandate for protecting and keeping safe innocent civilians, which was denied. Dallaire estimated that 5,000 well-armed UN soldiers might have stopped the mass killings in the capital and its spread to the provinces. The United States opposed this option and no African state actually volunteered troops. President Clinton explained that "The United Nations simply cannot become engaged in every one of the world's conflicts" (*Washington Post*, September 28, 1993). The UN Security Council extended UNAMIR for six weeks, but reduced it to 270 soldiers, and threatened to withdraw even those few unless all parties implemented the Arusha accords, knowing that they would not. Belgium and France flew in military forces for evacuating all foreigners, which they did, but not to stop the genocide. It is evident that international conflict management had failed in preventing, and if not that then limiting, the Rwanda genocide. It was a systemic failure of all components and all agents of the crisis intervention mechanism. This was later admitted and much agonized about, and some lessons were learned and applied in later crises. There wasn't a long wait before the crisis in Kosovo.

Kosovo had and has an Albanian majority population. It had been the scene of ethnic cleansing and massacres during the Balkan wars, after World War I and during World War II. In 1913, Leon Trotsky was a correspondent for a Ukrainian newspaper covering the fighting in Kosovo and was shocked by the destruction, killing, and looting: "The Serbs . . . are engaged quite simply in the systematic extermination of the Muslim population" (quoted in Malcolm 1999: 253). Land confiscations and Serb colonization boosted the Serbs to 24 percent of the population in the 1940s and 1950s. The Albanians were the only large ethnic group in Yugoslavia without a republic because of fears that Kosovo might secede and join neighboring Albania. Nevertheless, political and constitutional changes within Yugoslavia in 1974 and after Tito's death established regional autonomy which enabled Albanian nationalists to gain influence and power within the local communist party and its institutions, and in state enterprises, the courts, and local government. As a consequence of the higher Albanian fertility rate, emigration by Serbs in search of economic opportunities elsewhere in Serbia, and fear of Albanian nationalism, the Serb population dropped to about 10 percent in the 1991 census. Kosovo Serbs felt threatened and appealed to other Serbs for assistance. Between 1988 and 1992 Albanian and Serb nationalism clashed head on. The conflict precipitated the Yugoslav constitutional crisis that was the start of the country's breakup and occasioned Milosevic's rise to power in Serbia. Milosevic establish a post-communist nationalist regime based on his successful record of suppressing the Albanian nationalists and "retaking Kosovo" for the Serbs by coercion and military force (Judah 2000: chapters 1–2). In response, led by Ibrahim Rugova, the Kosovars (Albanians in Kosovo) organized non-violent resistance and non-cooperation with the Serb occupation forces and established parallel Albanian institutions from schools to courts.

The Dayton peace settlement was traumatic for the Kosovars. They expected to be included in an overall peace process for ex-Yugoslavia, but felt instead abandoned by the international community. The militant wing of the Albanian resistance formed the Kosovo Liberation Army (KLA), and obtained weapons after looting of arsenals in the anti-communist Albanian revolution created a huge black market for small arms across the Albania–Kosovo border. The KLA started an insurgency in the mountains against the Serb authorities and security forces; the Serb armed forces responded with a scorched earth policy; both sides claimed atrocities and massacres. An estimated 100,000 Albanians had fled the fighting from Kosovo and, by the fall of 1998, about 200,000 villagers had fled to the mountains and lived in makeshift camps. A major humanitarian crisis was in the making with the approach of winter and freezing temperatures. US and European leaders were in a quandary about UN-authorized intervention under chapter seven because the Russian government threatened a veto in the Security Council.

Frantic diplomatic moves resulted in a last-minute October ceasefire, 2,000 verifiers deployed under the Organization for Security and Cooperation in Europe (OSCE), the start of Serb–Albanian negotiations, and the return of the displaced thousands from the mountains. Ceasefire violations by the adversaries continued, including the massacre of 45 Albanian villagers in Racak in retaliation for the killing of a Serb police officer. Both sides used the ceasefire to rearm and reposition their fighting forces despite the OSCE monitors.

For the international community, Kosovo was at high risk for major ethnic cleansing. It was a divided society. Collective violence had occurred in the past. There was a history of animosity and conflict; armed groups had already started fighting, and civilians were being targeted. Vojislav Seselj, the leading Serb nationalist, called for the mass deportation of 360,000 Albanians in the Serb media and in the National Assembly. The Western Powers did not want to be responsible for inaction in a humanitarian crisis, as in Rwanda. Diplomatic talks between the international stakeholders, the Milosevic government, and the Albanians resulted in the Rambouillet peace plan. There would be another ceasefire, both forces would withdraw, but this time a 30,000-strong NATO force would become the peace enforcers. Kosovo would remain part of Serbia, the KLA would be demobilized, and safeguards for Serbs in Kosovo were to be assured by the peacekeepers. The plan was backed by the threat of NATO military intervention should Milosevic reject the deal. NATO's credibility as a peace maker in the post-Cold War era was at stake. The Kosovars were unhappy because the compromise fell short of independence, but signed under pressure on March 18, 1998. Milosevic decided to call "the NATO bluff" and refused to sign. He and other Serb leaders had already been indicted by the ICTY for war crimes and crimes against humanity in Croatia and Bosnia, but it did not deter them in Kosovo. Milosevic was counting on Russian assistance, and especially on obtaining their most advanced anti-aircraft missile system against a NATO air campaign. NATO justified its intervention on humanitarian grounds. The Kosovo war that followed revealed the uncertainties, moral ambiguities, and unanticipated consequences of a "just war."

Both sides expected the bombing campaign to last only a few days; it lasted instead for 78. The Serb military was keen on restoring lost prestige from the Croatian and Bosnian wars by holding out against NATO. As the OSCE verifiers pulled out, the Serb security forces and tanks moved in and the civil war resumed. The air campaign only slightly damaged the Serb military. Scattered in small units and camouflaged, and with NATO planes flying at 15,000 feet without forward air controllers locating targets, the Serb army evaded the bombing campaign. Nor did the campaign prevent the ethnic cleansing of 800,000 Albanians during "Operation Horseshoe" when villages and towns were surrounded by Serb armed forces, houses looted and arsoned, some killed and others expelled and put to flight in huge waves, most Kosovars ending in Macedonian refugee camps. The Milosevic regime claimed the people were fleeing NATO bombing. A major study by the American Association for the Advancement of Science (1999) demonstrated that the mass exodus of refugees from Kosovo occurred in patterns so regular that they must have been coordinated, indicating a deliberate campaign of mass expulsion. When the regime did not cave in, NATO extended the bombing campaign to Serbia proper and hit "dual use targets" such as Danube bridges, oil refineries, railroad depots, the television building in Belgrade, and some industrial plants that could be linked to war production. Altogether 23,000 bombs, 30 percent of them so-called "smart bombs," were dropped. Post-war studies based on death certificates and other records estimated about 500 civilian casualties, though Serbs claimed at least ten times that figure (UNC-CH 1999).

Milosevic signaled an end to his defiance of NATO just about when NATO was running out of military targets. It is thought that he did so because the Russians in the end denied him assistance against NATO and because the bombing campaign was slowly destroying the Serbian infrastructure and economy, without an end in sight for the stalemate. The peace agreement in June 1999 required all Serb forces to withdraw. Kosovo remained under Serb sovereignty, but only on paper; the provision was a face-saver for Milosevic. A huge NATO and Russian military force (KFOR) was deployed and assumed responsibility for peacekeeping. UNMIK, a UN civil administration, was installed in Kosovo, and beefed up with EU agencies and hundreds of NGOs. All these and the international community they represent have assumed responsibility for law and order, democratic institutions, and social and economic reconstruction. The cost of the intervention is in the billions of dollars and increasing. Some successes were achieved, e.g. the repatriation of thousands of refugees. The failures came swiftly. KFOR did not stop the reverse Albanian ethnic cleansing of some 150,000 Serbs who fled to the Mitrovica area on the Serbia border or to Serbia itself. Small pockets of Serbs remain in a few places and have to be heavily guarded. The probability of a multiethnic society in Kosovo is zero. In 2006, six years after the peace accord, the final stateness of Kosovo is still unresolved; democratic institutions are fragile; the UN "protectorate" is only slowly transferring control to local self-government; economic reconstruction is proceeding at a snail's pace. The good intentions and aspirations behind humanitarian intervention and international conflict management have run up against the tragedies of ethnic warfare and the realities of democratic institution building.

The Kosovo war unleashed a contentious debate over humanitarian intervention and just war. The debaters were knowledgeable about the Balkans, familiar with the conduct and facts about the war, steeped in the Geneva Conventions and international humanitarian law, and familiar with just war theory, and yet deeply divided on the Kosovo war. Some stated unequivocally that NATO had violated the UN Charter and international law and committed war crimes by bombing the Serb electricity grid (Hayden

1999). Most thought the intervention was justified, but poorly and irresponsibly executed, a reference to the high-altitude bombing for avoiding casualties while knowing it increased the risk of civilian casualties. Bozidar Jaksic (1999) believed that NATO's actions caused a humanitarian catastrophe on a wider scale than it was meant to prevent. Michael Walzer wrote that:

> Soldiers with guns, going from house to house in a mountain village [during ethnic cleansing] can't be stopped by smart bombs. They can only be stopped by soldiers with guns . . . Are countries with armies whose soldiers cannot be put at risk morally or politically qualified to intervene?
>
> (1998: 5)

Several questioned why the Kosovar non-violent resistance movement under Rugova had gotten no support for years, i.e. why international conflict management had waited until a violent crisis. And they pointed to the KLA provoking the Serb regime with acts of terrorism, knowing it would overreact by targeting civilians during counterinsurgency, and thus get the crisis managers to intervene on humanitarian grounds (Denitch 1999; Judah 2000: chapter 10). Just about everyone faulted NATO for not anticipating and stopping the reverse ethnic cleansing of Serbs by the KLA. Several critics faulted NATO for intervening without a longer-range vision and plan for Kosovo. Timothy Garton Ash observed that "Kosovo today is liberated and an almighty mess. Western leaders failed to prepare for peace, as they had failed to prepare for war" (2000b: 60).

The Independent International Commission on Kosovo headed by Judge Richard Goldstone (www.kosovocommission.org) concluded that the NATO military intervention was illegal but justified: illegal because the UN Security Council did not authorize it, and justified because diplomacy had exhausted other avenues and intervention had the effect of liberating the majority population of Kosovo from a long period of oppression under a Serb regime. But the Commission also faulted NATO on execution, and suggested three criteria for intervention based on just war theory: relief for suffering of civilians from severe human rights violations or the breakdown of government, overriding commitment to the protection of the civilian population, and a reasonable chance for ending the humanitarian catastrophe. The debate however underscored that applying these principles is fraught with controversy. The most troubling question was asked by David Rieff (2004) on the human rights approach to international crises. As it expands into a "crusading venture" for the betterment of the world, humanitarian language provides a convenient justification for the use of force that masks the true intent of political leaders and governments, as occurred with the manipulation of humanitarian arguments during the Iraq war by the Bush administration after no weapons of mass destruction were found.

In the aftermath of the Balkan wars, an international commission sponsored by the Canadian government on behalf of the United Nations researched and examined the 1990s experience with humanitarian intervention in armed conflicts and civil wars. On Bosnia, it concluded the following: "The Bosnian case . . . had a major impact on contemporary policy debate about intervention for humanitarian purposes. It raises the principle that intervention amounts to a promise to people in need: a promise cruelly betrayed" (International Commission on Intervention 2001: 1). During the Croatian war, the JNA (Yugoslav People's Army) had shelled the historic city of Dubrovnik and had destroyed Vukovar, which offended international opinion, intensified diplomatic efforts to stop the fighting, and led to a ceasefire and the deployment of a UN peacekeeping force, UNPROFOR, to monitor the ceasefire, "with tough sounding resolutions followed up with inadequate human and material resources" (Bellamy *et al.* 2004: 133). After fighting started in Bosnia, the UN extended UNPROFOR's mandate to include the safe delivery of humanitarian supplies in Bosnia to the burgeoning refugee and internally displaced population (IDP) seeking shelter in enclaves such as Bihac. Critics of the UN operation write that:

> UNPROFOR was not authorized to forcibly ensure humanitarian supplies be delivered . . . Both UNPROFOR and aid agencies . . . depended on the consent of the war lords to carry out their tasks . . . [and were] confronted with a traumatic dilemma: bargain with the war lords and deliver some aid or refuse to bargain and deliver much less aid. Most commanders chose the first option.
>
> (Bellamy *et al.* 2004: 136)

In one instance, "a UNHCR convoy had to negotiate its way through ninety roadblocks from Zagreb to Sarajevo, many manned by undisciplined, drunken soldiers of indeterminate political affiliation." Usually, "lorries were searched. Aid was diverted as tribute to areas controlled by those manning the roadblocks . . . sometimes it took days, even weeks to get a single convoy through" (Ramsbotham and Woodhouse 1996: 177, 182).

Nor was this peculiar to the Bosnian war. After assessing a number of UN peacekeeping operations, Dennis Jeff wrote that:

> Humanitarian assistance is usually considered to be unquestionably beneficial . . . [but] no armed group is going to go hungry while unarmed relief workers distribute food to non-combatants in areas under its control. The theft and sale of food also provides funds to sustain armies by providing the cash to buy arms, ammunition and the essentials of war or simply to enrich the combatants . . . there will always be a ready excuse for the combatants to seize the relief organization vehicles, radios, and satellite telephones . . . the temptation to appropriate them from well equipped aid workers is rarely resisted for long.
>
> (2000: 133–5)

Two officials of the International Committee of the Red Cross concluded in a comprehensive review that:

> in numerous armed conflicts the conditions required for conducting humanitarian operations are not fulfilled . . . during the last five years . . . there has been no conflict in which humanitarian workers have not been massively harassed, menaced, prevented from working, robbed, injured and even killed.
>
> (Rumbach and Fink 1994: 1, 11)

Crisis intervention: early warning and the rapid deployment force

Because of the shortcomings of crisis intervention in an ongoing ethnic violence and humanitarian crisis, in recent years some ideas and plans for earlier and more effective international conflict management have been proposed. All consist of an early warning system for imminent large-scale violent ethnic conflict and a rapid deployment force that would be placed at the center of the crisis until a more numerous, powerful, and permanent force can be deployed and diplomacy achieves a lasting cessation of the hostilities (Heidenrich 2001: chapter 12).

Quantitative research on indicators for large-scale ethnic collective violence and genocide has found that genocidal states have autocratic governments and a pattern of political exclusion and discrimination against some ethnic groups (Harff and Gurr 1998). They have a history of massacres and other violent modes of ethnic conflict against these groups, i.e. they are repeat offenders. They have an external protector (or protectors) that makes them resistant to international pressure. They engage in hate and threat propaganda against the future victims. They create an elaborate justification for brutalizing and killing the entire target group, not just insurgents. They organize armed groups for mass aggression against the future victims. And an insurgency or resistance movement against the autocratic regime by some of the future victims has started. All these factors increase the risk of genocide and ethnic cleansing. As shown above for Rwanda, Kosovo, East Timor, and Sudan, these indicators were present prior to the outbreak of collective violence. As is true for other diagnostic tests in social science, the methodology does produce some false positives and negatives, i.e. instances when the risk is high but no collective violence takes place or when the risk is assessed low but collective violence nevertheless takes place. Because some autocratic regimes keep the international community as much as possible in the dark about their internal problems and because some ethnic conflicts take place in remote regions, access to more and better information in high-risk states is needed. At the present, a huge network of international human rights and humanitarian NGOs that are linked to domestic counterparts is the source for much pertinent information, though in the absence of hard evidence there is a temptation by the news media and intervention advocates to report inflated estimates on victims. NGOs are vulnerable to expulsion by regimes that want to cover up their human rights record, or to limits on their activities and ability to get the pertinent information. Still, the methodology promises to be useful for conflict management decisions.

There are several proposals for a permanent UN rapid deployment force (RDF, also referred to as a rapid reaction force) (Brugnola *et al.* 1998). One idea was formulated by Brian Urquhart based on his long experience as UN crisis manager. The RDF would be a permanent military force under UN command ready for deployment at any time to trouble spots after early warning and before the outbreak of genocide. That would make it different from the current creation of a UN military force assembled from member states who have pledged standby military assistance for peacekeeping after a humanitarian disaster has already taken place. Standby arrangements have not prevented genocides. There were 19 standby arrangements at the time of the Rwanda genocide, and not a single one was activated.

A somewhat different idea was voiced by Saul Mendlovitz (1999), for a UN constabulary to enforce prohibitions against genocide and crimes against humanity. The constabulary would be a mixed military and police force whose mission is to stop the killing, establish safe havens for the victims and targets, and secure the delivery of humanitarian relief aid. It would be activated by the UN Secretary General, whose decision could be overridden by the Security Council after 45 or 60 days. The RDF is contemplated to be a stopgap and a deterrent, and not a substitute for a political settlement of the conflict and the stationing of a larger international military force for separating the military forces of the adversaries and for demilitarization of the conflict within an overall peace settlement. Both plans are feasible only if states, and in particular the great powers with a veto in the UN Security Council, are willing to surrender some of their sovereignty to the UN. It has not happened thus far.

The size of the RDF is estimated between 5,000 and 10,000, with additional logistic support from the states that have air transport capabilities for large military forces. The annual cost is estimated at $2 to 5 billion, and various ideas about financing, recruitment, training, arming, stationing in troubled areas, and mandate have been put forward. A core issue is how the deployment would be triggered in a timely manner and how the frequent gridlock in the UN Security Council on crisis intervention would be overcome. If the Secretary General has the authority to act without the UN Security Council blocking deployment in the two-month grace period, the RDF could be swiftly deployed before the violence becomes large-scale. Meanwhile international diplomacy would get two months to pressure the adversaries to stop the fighting with the UN force already in place. Attacking a UN peace enforcement force that can defend itself and that will get assistance would act as a formidable deterrent for the adversaries, on top of condemnation by the international community and the risk of sanctions.

In practical terms, for Kosovo after the Rambouillet accord, instead of unarmed international monitors of the ceasefire, the UN Secretary General would have deployed the RDF, and, instead of the unarmed UNAMET for organizing the referendum in East Timor, similarly the RDF would have been deployed. Such deployments could not have occurred without the consent of the Indonesian army and the Serbian regime. Armies on the ground can block airports and other access routes for peacekeepers. Nevertheless, the UN and the external stakeholders would have more leverage against the adversaries for cessation of the fighting or aggression against civilians with an RDF than without. In the case of Rwanda, the French and Belgian armies flew into the capital Kigali a sizable rescue mission, and the UN could have done the same with the RDF. In Darfur, at the 2004 ceasefire, a much more powerful force than the African Union peacekeepers would have been deployed, contingent on consent of the Sudan government. Whether the RDF might have been deployed prior to or in the early stages of ethnic cleansing in 2003 and whether it would have stopped ethnic violence against villagers in such a vast area is difficult to determine. It certainly could not have aggravated the Darfur tragedy that unfolded, and in all likelihood would have lessened it.

Both NATO and the European Union have created plans and started implementing a response force or a rapid reaction force meant for international crisis management and humanitarian emergencies, and for assisting regional crisis forces with logistic support. The EU deployed a small force of 1,500 troops in the eastern Congo where atrocities against civilians are being regularly committed by anti-government rebels, government troops, warlords, bandits, and even UN peacekeepers. As part of the UN reorganization plan, Secretary General Kofi Annan wants to devote more resources to peacekeeping (*NYT*, March 8, 2006). Mass violence against civilians is alive and well, and international crisis managers have little in their "humanitarian crisis tool box," nor are they any closer to coming to grips with the fundamental issues and dilemmas of humanitarian intervention than they were for Rwanda and for Kosovo.

The limits of intervention: Darfur

The international community is currently facing yet another humanitarian crisis due to ethnic conflict in the Darfur region of the Sudan. Paul Williams writes that "the UN Security Council decided that respecting Sudanese sovereignty was more important than conducting a military response capable of protecting the civilian population" (2006: 168). It chose instead to impose some sanctions, an arms embargo, and a no-fly zone, none of which were enforced.

Darfur is a society divided between nomadic arabized cattle herders and settled crop-growing African tribes. Competition and conflict over land use has been aggravated by years of drought and desertification which drives the cattle herders onto land claimed by the agriculturalists. Violent conflicts have broken out. The Sudan government sides with the nomads who are culturally and religiously closer to the Sudanese ruling groups and who have supplied many soldiers to its army. Insurgency started in February 2003 with attacks on military posts and government compounds by the Sudan Liberation Army. The goal is to achieve regional autonomy, not secession. In the words of an SLA leader: "if the Fur people get their fair share of wealth and power from Khartoum . . . we have no objection to continuing in the Sudan, provided we have supremacy in our land" (quoted in Judah 2005: 13).

Unable to contain the insurgents with its armed forces alone, the Sudanese government has recruited janjaweed militias from the nomad tribes, armed them with automatic weapons, provided them with helicopter gunship support, and unleashed them against the African villagers in a vast ethnic cleansing for ridding the rebel districts of people and resources. Villagers were attacked and killed, women raped, huts arsoned, crops destroyed, food stores looted, livestock stolen, and wells poisoned, amid other violence and destruction in a huge state-sponsored scorched earth and ethnic cleansing to deny insurgents local support and to punish the people. The janjaweed get to keep the loot and livestock as war booty, and eventually the land. An estimated 70,000 to 100,000 villagers have died and between 1.5 million and 2 million have fled to refugee camps where they live in miserable shelters and are kept alive by humanitarian food aid (Apsel 2005).

Despite Sudanese government denials of these crimes, world public opinion and the states that manage international conflicts have known about them since the summer of 2003. A UN fact-finding mission conclusively established intent and planning for the ethnic cleansing by the government and its collusion with the janjaweed (International Commission of Inquiry on Darfur 2005). Under pressure, the Sudanese government in April 2004 agreed to a ceasefire and to peace talks with the insurgents. A peacekeeping force of 7,000 soldiers under the African Union, lightly armed, with poor logistic support, with an observer mandate, has been deployed in an area the size of France. Darfur in the meanwhile has descended into chaos. The cease-fire keeps being broken by both sides. The peacekeepers are overwhelmed and sometimes themselves attacked by armed groups. In addition to the government forces, insurgents, and the janjaweeds, criminal groups and bandits prey on civilians. There is no protection for ordinary people who are attacked even in refugee camps across the border in Chad. As in other humanitarian relief operations, some of the relief aid is looted and aid workers attacked. Humanitarian assistance has been withdrawn in parts of the impacted area because relief workers were at risk of being killed or taken hostage. Malnutrition and disease have become the cause of most of the deaths. The Sudanese government refuses to disarm the janjaweed and other militias until the insurgents disclose the position of their forces, but the insurgents insist they only agreed to parallel disarmament. The seventh round of peace talks have opened but the peace process is at a standstill. In January 2006 a senior UN official in the Sudan admitted that the international strategy in Darfur had failed and that an intervention force of 12,000 to 20,000 troops was necessary to protect civilians and disarm militias (ICG 2006: 20).

Despite modest successes in Kosovo and East Timor, international conflict managers are once more stymied by an uncooperative state with valuable resources (e.g. petroleum), internal disagreements, unconventional warfare, and protecting and assisting civilian victims in a remote and forbidding environment. The international community capacity for providing humanitarian assistance in Darfur is quite limited and would be even with an RDF capability. Kosovo-style military intervention is not feasible for political, resource, and logistic reasons. Some "just war" criteria for humanitarian military intervention are lacking, in particular the expectation that intervention will reduce violence, improve the security and welfare of the victims, and lead to permanent peace in the region. For the foreseeable future, humanitarian peace intervention will remain a secondary mode of international crisis management, effective in limited situations, but not displacing traditional diplomacy.

4 War and peace in Bosnia

Mobilization for armed conflict in Serbia: crisis, threat, fear

The real problems and issues facing Yugoslavia, and Serbia in particular, were the end of communism and the transition to democracy and a market economy, as in Eastern Europe and the Soviet Union, and negotiating a constitutional design for a multinational state that provided security and human rights to ethnic minorities. Most Yugoslav leaders declined to consider seriously widely known models for territorially mixed, multinational, federal, democratic states such as India, Malaysia, and Tanzania. Instead they promoted a nationalist discourse and actions with high risk of armed conflicts.

Aleksa Djilas accounts for the emergence of a crisis frame in Yugoslavia as follows:

> The nationalist ambitions, fears and frustrations of Yugoslavia's constituent groups . . . were not the invention of nationalist intellectuals or political elites. However, the Yugoslav civil war would not have happened if elites . . . had not irresponsibly and deliberately manipulated nationalist sentiments with their propaganda and policies. The force of nationalist passions whipped up by these opportunistic leaders not only made conflict inevitable, but it also made the war extremely brutal.
>
> (1995: 85)

But why was much of the public susceptible to manipulation?

Yugoslavs experienced ethnic relations through two frames: a peacetime frame and a crisis frame. People possessed both frames in their minds. In peacetime the crisis frame was dormant, and in crisis and war the peacetime frame was suppressed (Oberschall 2000). Both frames were anchored in personal and family experiences, in culture, and in public life. In the peacetime frame, ethnic relations were cooperative and neighborly. Colleagues and neighbors, workers and class mates transacted routinely across ethnicity. They went to one another's weddings and religious holiday celebrations. Intermarriage was accepted. The crisis frame was grounded in the family and

Map 1 Bosnia and Hercegovina

Source: Courtesy of the University of Texas Libraries, The University of Texas at Austin

community memories of the Balkan wars and the two world wars, and repeated in collective myths and in history books and literature. In these crises, civilians were not distinguished from combatants. Old people, women, children, and priests were not spared. Atrocities, massacres, torture, ethnic cleansing, and other horrors were perpetrated by all adversaries. Ordinary people were held collectively responsible for their nationality and religion, and became the target of revenge and reprisals. Tito suppressed the crisis frame from public discourse but it simmered in the collective memory of each ethnic group, the families of victims, and the minds of intellectuals and of religious leaders. Milosevic, Tudjman, and other ethno-nationalists did not invent the crisis frame. They activated and amplified it with "our nation is threatened" discourse, based on a mixture of real events and fabricated falsehoods, relentlessly repeated in regime-controlled mass media.

A year before the outbreak of war, the Bosnian Serb leader Radovan Karadzic declared "The Serbs are endangered again . . . this nation well remembers genocide [in World War II]. Those events are still a terrible living memory. The terror has survived fifty years" (quoted in Sudetic 1998: 84). The ethno-nationalists activated and amplified the crisis frame through fear: fear of group extinction, fear of victimization, fear of assimilation. As David Lake and Donald Rothchild state, "ethnic conflict is most commonly caused by collective fears of the future" (1998: 4).

By highlighting the crisis frame, nationalists like Milosevic mobilized a huge constituency for getting elected on a "Save the Serb Nation" platform aimed as much against rival Serb moderates as against ethnic adversaries. Serb populist nationalism conferred new legitimacy for leadership when communism was becoming discredited as elsewhere in Eastern Europe. In the summer of 1988, high on the agenda was the "retaking of Kosovo" where the Serbs were threatened by the Albanians. In a dozen cities in Serbia, crowds of 10,000 to 200,000 organized by Milosevic and his supporters, still within the Serb communist party, demanded the resignation of moderate incumbents and their replacement with Serb nationalists. At the core of these assemblies were professional demonstrators dressed in folk costumes, carrying placards and banners rich with Serb national and Orthodox religious symbols. The coverage in the mass media became a vast learning experience for populist nationalism suppressed under Tito. The nationalist spectacle conveyed in the media coverage, the size of the crowds, and the theme of defending the Serb people legitimated Serb nationalism. Pressured by this "voice of the people," incumbents resigned from party posts and were replaced by Milosevic loyalists (Monnesland 1997: 319).

Political leaders, media professionals, and foreign observers all agreed on the importance of mass media propaganda for spreading nationalism and fear, and conditioning ordinary Yugoslavs for war and mass killings. In the Serb media, frequent stories of sexual assault and rape by Albanians against Serbs in Kosovo were highlighted and amplified the threat mindset, and were woven into a narrative of Muslim numerical domination over ethnic rivals, even though an analysis of violent crime statistics in Kosovo in the 1980s by Serb social scientists found that the incidence of rape in Kosovo was less than in Serbia and that offender and victim in rapes tended to be from the same, and not different, ethnic groups (Popovic *et al.* 1990). Biljana Plavsic, a professor of biology at Sarajevo University before she became a Bosnian Serb leader, wrote in the newspaper *Borba*: "rape is the war strategy of Muslims and Croats against Serbs. Islam considers this something normal" (quoted in Cohen 1998: 222). The media and intellectual rape discourse was widely believed by ordinary Serbs. A young Serb soldier told a reporter that "the Muslims expelled us from Kosovo with their sexual organs . . . they want to do the same here [in Bosnia] . . . the way they reproduce they need room. You will soon feel that elsewhere in Europe" (quoted in Cohen 1998: 222). The journalist Peter Maas (1995: 113) asked a Serb refugee couple why they had fled their village. They had heard on the radio that the Serb military had uncovered a Muslim plot: Muslims planned to take over the district, a list of names had been drawn up, the Serb men were to be killed, and the women were to be assigned to Muslim harems for the purpose of breeding Muslim janissaries (Ottoman soldiers from Christian families). And they believed this propaganda even though their Muslim neighbors "were decent people" who had never harmed them.

Fear of ethnic extinction was spread by both Croats and Serbs with highly inflated figures of the ethnic killings in World War II. The war of numbers sought to prove victimhood and a justification for preemptive aggression against the adversary. These fears polarized ethnic relations. The political scientist Bogdan Denitch recalls that:

> Everyone was traumatized by all the talk of world war two atrocities . . . even those who had seemed immune to nationalism. Old personal ties and friendships crumbled as many intellectuals I knew, as well as friends and family members, rallied to the defense of their own nation. The pressure to do so was immense.
>
> (1996: 81)

Political leaders, professionals, and foreign observers knew full well the importance of mass media propaganda for conditioning ordinary people to accept war and aggression against their fellow citizens from other ethnic groups. The sociologist and important politician Mira Markovic, the wife of Slobodan Milosevic, stated in an interview on March 15, 1991, when she was asked "Will there be a civil war in Yugoslavia?" that "Civil war is already happening in Yugoslavia. For the time being, [civil war] is one of information . . . its purpose is to cause national animosity to the point where armed conflict is unavoidable" (1996: 58).

After winning the 1990 Serbia election, the Milosevic regime gained control of the principal Serb mass media, in particular state television. Television journalists who lacked "patriotism" and obedience to the political masters were put on "compulsory leave" or marginalized (Thompson 1994: 56–95). Research on the Serb media and audience by the Belgrade Institute of Political Studies in 1994 concluded that the Milosevic regime controlled 90 percent of mass media penetration, i.e. 90 percent of information on public affairs and news reaching the public was through regime media (Kurspahic 2003: 41–2).

Questions about peace making in the Yugoslav wars

In 1990–1, the breakup of Yugoslavia set off armed conflicts over state-ness, i.e. over successor states, their boundaries, and their ethno-national demographics. From the start, the principal ethno-national adversaries and their ethnic allies in scattered territories were not the only parties to the conflict. External states and international organizations became stakeholders and attempted to limit the armed conflict, help the civilians trapped by war, and negotiate a peace settlement, which did not succeed until the Dayton Peace Accords (DPA). One question on peace making concerns the failure of several peace plans from 1991 to 1995, and why DPA succeeded. Another concerns to what extent the DPA not only brought an end to the fighting but settled the core issues of stateness, governance, and minority rights with finality. What are the prospects for a multiethnic democratic Bosnia? A third set of questions concerns the impact of the external stakeholders on duration of the war and on the protection of civilians from belligerents. A fourth question is whether and how external intervention changed the war and the peace settlement beyond what the belligerents might have achieved on their own.

Adversaries and stakeholders

I start with the principal adversaries and the external stakeholders, their goals, their strategies, and the major coercive and conciliatory actions they took. Next, I explain the linkage between military positions and strategies, the changing peace settlement plans advanced by the external stakeholders, and why the adversaries chose to accept or to reject them. At the end, I return to the four questions on peace making.

The principal adversaries were the Milosevic regime in Serbia, together with its Serb allies in Croatia and Bosnia-Hercegovina (BiH); the Bosnian Muslims and allied groups committed to a multiethnic Bosnia referred to as the Bosniaks; the Bosnian Serbs, who became a principal in the Bosnian war and were allied with the Milosevic regime; the Tudjman regime in Croatia, and its ally, the Bosnian Croats; the Slovenes, who quickly dropped out of the conflict and whom I omit from the analysis. The external stakeholders were all the major European states, separately and jointly in the European Community; the United States; the USSR and later Russia; the United Nations and its agents, the UN peacekeeping forces in UNPROFOR and other units; various groups of the above such as the Contact Group and NATO; and a large cast of NGOs and the international news media molding international public opinion.

The actions taken by these players were both conciliatory and coercive, and were extremely diverse. The principals and their allies formed assemblies and voted on seceding from states and political entities and forming alternative polities; they formed shifting alliances; their leaders engaged in negotiations on ceasefires and peace plans, but mostly engaged in coercive actions. They organized armed forces and fought other armed forces; they besieged cities and shelled civilian targets; they engaged in ethnic cleansing and massacres and looted the victims' property; they imprisoned civilians in detention camps; they blocked and robbed humanitarian aid to civilians; they took peacekeepers hostage; they agreed to and then violated many ceasefires; they traded resources, including war-making materials, across enemy lines for profit. The external stakeholders pursued a succession of ceasefires and peace settlements with the principals, disagreed with one another over conflict management, verbally condemned and threatened the principals for obstructing the peace process, created an international war crimes tribunal (the ICTY), passed many UN Security Council resolutions for peace making, protection of the civilian population, and delivery of humanitarian aid, but were reluctant to sanction the principals for war crimes, crimes against humanity, and defying Security Council resolutions, until the terminal stages of the wars.

Opening moves

The *Milosevic regime* first tried to change the constitutional design of Yugoslavia by negotiating with other ethno-national republic leaders for a more centralized state in which Serbia had more power. When that failed, it embarked on coercive actions for joining together all Serb groups and lands into a single state (referred to as "Greater Serbia" with the slogan "All Serbs in a single state") by conquering territories in between that had a minority of Serbs, and forcefully expelling most Croats and Muslims from these Serb lands. To achieve these goals, Milosevic made a deal with Croatia's President Tudjman in March 1991 at their meeting in Karadjordevo on partitioning BiH into Serb and Croat entities that would be annexed by their two states, with a small rump remaining for the Muslims as a buffer between them (Woodward 1995: 172). This common interest did not prevent war between the Milosevic and Tudjman regimes over the Serb minorities and lands in Croatia. The *Tudjman regime* wanted to join the Croats in BiH into a single Croat state, and to reestablish Croat authority in all the Serb-controlled areas of Croatia it lost in 1991 at the start of the Croatian war, as well as expel the Serbs from there. Subsequently Milosevic and Tudjman tended to agree with external stakeholders' peace plans that left open the possibility of annexation of the Serb and Croat populations and lands in BiH.

After Croatia and Slovenia seceded from Yugoslavia and gained international recognition as independent states, the *Bosniaks* wanted to maintain a multiethnic, sovereign state in BiH, and their war aims were to hold on to a large enough territory for a viable Bosniak entity within a single BiH state with Sarajevo as its capital. The *Bosnian Serbs* seceded from BiH at the start of the Bosnian war, when they already had seized power in many municipalities, and wanted to achieve an independent state that linked up all districts where most of the Bosnian Serbs lived, also with Sarajevo as its capital, expel Muslims and Croats from their territory and from non-Serb enclaves, and eventually join their state to Serbia. They rapidly conquered more than that territory, minus some Bosniak enclaves, in the initial months of the war. The *Bosnian Croats* also seized power early on before the Bosnian war started in several districts where they were a majority, but were divided on whether their stateness and security interest were better served by a BiH in which they would be an equal partner with the Serbs and Bosniaks, or by supporting Tudjman's goal of emasculating and dividing BiH and joining Croatia. The Bosnian Croats formed shifting alliances, pressed conflicting territorial claims against the Bosniaks, and eventually came under Tudjman's control.

The *external stakeholders* were at the time of the Yugoslav breakup preoccupied with the consequences of the fall of communism in East Europe, with the reunification of Germany, the development of the European Community, and even more so the successor political and economic system in the Soviet Union. They were a diverse group with some common but many diverging interests. Initially, they all wanted to preserve a Yugoslav state, albeit in altered form, and, when that became impossible, to limit state making to existing republics and their boundaries, with protection for minority rights. Once the wars became a reality, they sought to end them by negotiating seven major peace plans from 1991 to 1995, hoping to end the destruction and suffering, stem the flow of refugees, and prevent armed fighting from diffusing in the Balkans and beyond. When a refugee and a humanitarian crisis developed and the international news media publicized war crimes and atrocities unknown in Europe since World War II, public opinion and humanitarian and human rights organizations shamed them to intervene more forcefully, which they gradually did despite great reluctance to put their soldiers at risk. The external stakeholders engaged the wars with diplomatic conflict management, and were slowly sucked into peacekeeping, though there was no peace to keep and the peacekeepers often did no more than record ceasefire violations and attacks on civilians.

War

After the wars started, Serbia supplied ammunition, intelligence, heavy weapons, logistics, training, air defense, medical support, and other help, including officers' salaries to Serb forces in the war zone, especially to the Bosnian Serbs. Up to 25 percent of Serbia's budget was spent on support for the Bosnian Serbs (Norman Cigar, in Magas and Zanic 2001: 210). According to General Jovan Divjak (of the Bosniak army) (Magas and Zanic 2001: 153–4), by March 19, 1991, a year before the Bosnian war, the JNA had distributed 51,900 firearms to Serb volunteer units and members of the Serb SDS party in BiH. Those weapons enabled the SDS and the Serb militants to seize 50 of 109 municipalities by force in the summer and autumn of 1992. After the Croatian ceasefire of January 2, 1992, the JNA redeployed about 90,000 to 100,000 well-armed men, officers, 750 to 800 tanks, 1,000 armed personnel carriers, 4,000 mortars and artillery pieces, and 50 helicopters in BiH, some of which totally encircled Sarajevo by the end of 1991. In the general's words, "the JNA had occupied BiH by stealth, without resistance."

Before the start of the Croatian war, according to Croat General Martin Spegelj, "there was no question of waiting with arms folded . . . so in 1990 I began to arm Croatia. By the end of February 1991, we succeeded in mobilizing and training 65,000 lightly armed soldiers" (in Magas and Zanic 2001: 25). More than 3,000 officers and generals, most of them Croats, left the JNA and joined the Croatian army by the time the JNA attacked Croatia starting on September 19. By trapping JNA garrisons deep inside Croatia and occupying JNA depots, the Croats stopped the JNA withdrawal of heavy weapons and military hardware, and acquired 250 tanks, 400 to 500 heavy artillery pieces, 180,000 firearms, and 2 million tons of ammunition, which enabled the Croat army to stop the JNA from its first military objective of reaching the Virovitica–Karlovac–Karlobag line that would have "amputated" Croatia, leaving no more than a third of Croatia. Meanwhile the siege and shelling of Dubrovnik had begun, the Serb secessionists in Croatia were consolidating and expanding their territories, the JNA invaded Eastern Slavonia on Serbia's border, and the siege and leveling of Vukovar by artillery had started. Eastern Slavonia had only a 20 percent Serb population but was the land bridge between the Bosnian Serbs and the Krajina Serbs for the Greater Serbia.

In the fall of 1991, the external stakeholders proposed the first of several plans for stopping the fighting in Croatia and for a political solution of the stateness and minority rights issues at the core of the Yugoslav conflict. The *European Community* (EC) plan was to divide Yugoslavia into six sovereign republics recognized in international law and forming a loose economic association. The plan rejected republic boundary changes that would sanction territory seized by force. The Serb minority in Croatia would have a large degree of autonomy, and the Albanians in Kosovo would have a special status of autonomy which the Milosevic regime had abolished in 1990. None of the adversaries agreed to the plan. The Slovenes had by this time fought a successful three-week war that had expelled the JNA from its territory and were determined on independence. Because almost all Slovenes lived in Slovenia, and hardly any non-Slovenes, and because it had a compact territory bordering only on Croatia, Slovene independence was not contested. The special status of autonomy for the Krajina Serbs was not acceptable to them – they controlled almost 25 percent of Croatia's territory and wanted to secede from Croatia – nor to the Tudjman government. Greatest opposition to the EC plan was by the Milosevic regime because the plan defeated its two preferred outcomes, either a unitary Yugoslavia with a strong central government, or Greater Serbia with all Serbs in a single state (Woodward 1995: 182; Monnesland 1997: 368–9).

The war in Croatia continued and resulted in costly military and civilian casualties. The Serb political commentator Aleksa Djilas writes that "The Croatian–Serbian war was brutal. The civilian population suffered greatly.

Prisoners of war were tortured and murdered. Both sides engaged in 'ethnic cleansing' and there were over half a million refugees" (1995: 95–6, 99–100). According to Croat General Tus (in Magas and Zanic 2001: 60), in the battle of Vukovar alone both sides sustained huge losses: some 4,000 Croat and 5,000 Serb soldiers died, and 600 armored vehicles were destroyed. In his opinion, because of the losses and the Serb manpower shortage due to opposition to the call-up of reservists and draftees in Serbia, the JNA no longer had the forces to penetrate westward into Croatia. On the Croat side, one-quarter of Croatia was under rebel Serb control, and Croatia's army not yet ready to take them on. Both sides therefore accepted the Vance plan in January 1992 for a ceasefire and for deployment of 14,000 UN peacekeepers to separate the Croat and Serb forces, and for an international conference for settling the stateness and boundary issues. But the ceasefire in Croatia did not stop Bosnia-Hercegovina's rapid descent into civil war. Most of the JNA withdrawn from Croatia was put at the disposal of the Bosnian Serbs. For Tudjman, the ceasefire provided time for building a more powerful army that could retake the rebel Serb areas later and for pursuing his BiH partition ambitions.

A failed peace plan

Having failed to maintain the integrity of the Yugoslav state, the external stakeholders turned to an orderly and peaceful dissolution of Yugoslavia into successor states, their borders, the division of federal assets and economic obligations, and criteria for international recognition, most importantly republic borders. Their plan refused to accept the Serb referenda for autonomy and secession in the Serb-held Krajina of Croatia and meant to stop the Bosnian war. The plan for BiH was drawn up by an EC commission under the leadership of Jose Cutileiro and called for a single sovereign state of BiH made up of three constituent entities with much autonomy and the right to self-determination. Municipalities were allocated on the basis of absolute or relative ethnic majorities, which legitimated the nationalists' claim to territory based on ethnicity: 52 municipalities and 44 percent of the territory to Muslims, 35 municipalities and 44 percent of the territory to Serbs, and 20 municipalities and 12 percent of the territory to Croats, based on the 1991 census. BiH was so ethnically mixed however that 50 percent of Serbs, 58 percent of Croats, and 18 percent of Muslims would live outside their respective entities (Monnesland 1997: 382), and none of the entities would form contiguous areas. The Muslim leader Izetbegovic rejected the plan because it did not sufficiently protect BiH as a single state, and the Bosnian Croat leader Boban wanted more territory for the Croat entity and the option to join it to Croatia. The Badinter Commission called for EC states to recognize BiH only if all three ethnic groups voted in favor of BiH independence. EC members however could not agree on withholding recognition of the successor states and, with Germany in the lead, on

January 15, 1992 they recognized Croatia, Slovenia, and Macedonia as independent states.

Before the recognition of Croatian and Slovene independence, the three adversaries in Bosnia sought somehow to maintain a multiethnic Yugoslavia. With Croatia and Slovenia gone, the Bosnian political crisis heated up in as much as the Muslims and Croats there would be a small minority in a truncated Yugoslavia dominated by Serbia. The referendum on Bosnian independence was boycotted by the Bosnian Serbs and thus carried with 93 percent in favor (and a 63 percent turnout). Within days, the government of Bosnia declared its independence, the Bosnian war started, and the Bosnian Serbs seceded and organized the Republika Srpska (RS), and a truncated Federal Republic of Yugoslavia consisting of Serbia and Montenegro was proclaimed in Belgrade (called here Serbia for short). Thus the last-ditch attempts by the international community for an orderly dissolution of Yugoslavia and to prevent war in Bosnia failed.

War crimes and ethnic cleansing

The Bosniaks had no army. The historian Mark Hoare wrote (Magas and Zanic 2001: 183) that "the Bosnian government stumbled reluctantly into a state of war as the reality of aggression could no longer be denied." General Divjak described the formation of armed forces in Bosnia as the "self-mobilization" of people in defense of their cities, as reservists and volunteers rallied into patriotic leagues, local militias, and police units that were short on weapons (especially heavy weapons and armor), ammunition, trained officers, even uniforms (Magas and Zanic 2001: 158). Meanwhile, the JNA, by now a Serb army augmented by Serb paramilitaries and special forces, invaded across the Serbia–BiH border, and with the help of Bosnian Serb forces seized most of the Drina valley while elsewhere Serb forces seized power in municipalities and set siege to others, notably Sarajevo. Later on the Bosniaks obtained weapons and volunteer fighters, e.g. the mujaheddin from Iran and Muslim countries, which the Croats allowed through their military lines after a heavy "weapons tax" siphoned arms off to their army (Holbrooke 1998: 50–1). With the collusion of some of the external stakeholders, all sides in the Bosnian war managed to get some weapons and other military assistance despite UN Security Council Resolution 713 (September 15, 1991) calling for a "general and complete embargo on all deliveries of weapons and military equipment to Yugoslavia."

From the start, ethnic cleansing of non-Serb civilians and war crimes and atrocities were committed by Serb combatants. In Zvornik on April 8, 1992, after an ultimatum to surrender the city was rejected, the JNA, with artillery, tanks, and infantry units supported by Serb paramilitaries, stormed and took the lightly defended city. According to Jose Maria Meniluce, a UNHCR official who happened to be driving through Zvornik just when the White Eagle paramilitaries were overrunning the town and terrorizing the civilians:

> The fighters were moving through the town, systematically killing all the
> Muslims they could get their hands on . . . I saw kids put under the tread
> of tanks, placed there by grown men, and run over by other grown men
> . . . the Serbs doing the killing did not come from Zvornik.

Ethnic cleansing was followed by the organized looting of Muslim houses
and businesses (Neier 1998: 196–8; Rieff 1995: 201–2). These atrocities
were repeated elsewhere. The Serbs expected to seize Sarajevo in one week
and most of BiH in three to four months (Magas and Zanic 2001: 147).
Within a short time the Serb forces seized 66 percent of the territory of BiH,
but failed taking Sarajevo.

The Bosniaks had plenty of manpower but were short on weapons.
In 1992, the emerging Bosniak armed forces had 18 percent Croats and 12
percent Serbs, including some top officers like General Divjak. Ethnic cleansing forced the Muslims into a life-and-death struggle, but lacking heavy
weapons they were capable of waging only a defensive war. The military
analyst Norman Cigar believes that, throughout the war, the human factor
– morale, commitment, and leadership – made up for the Bosniak weapons
disparity (Magas and Zanic 2001: 203). As the Serb offensive was halted,
according to General Divjak, "the war took the form of classic trench
warfare as in WWI. In Sarajevo, two-thirds of the defensive lines remained
unaltered from June 1992 to December 1995" (in Magas and Zanic 2001:
161). Historian Marko Hoare observed that, despite the growth of their
army in 1993–5, the Bosniaks did not achieve any significant territorial
gains against the Serbs until the summer–fall offensive in 1995, with the
exception of the 5th Army Corps defending the Bihac enclave (Magas and
Zanic 2001: 198).

The Serbs had won a military victory and achieved most of their war
goals by 1994 less Sarajevo and some other Muslim enclaves, but faced the
problem of convincing their adversaries to accept defeat and make peace.
Bosnian Serb leader Karadzic stated "we have what we want. We control
70 percent of the territory, but we lay claim only on 64 percent" (quoted in
Monnesland 1997: 393). Serbia was hurting from the UN-imposed economic
sanctions. Milosevic would have liked to end the war in 1994 when
the Bosnian Serbs were at the peak of territorial control. In a speech to the
Serbian parliament in 1991 he stated:

> I believe . . . that the great powers will not intervene in Yugoslavia. The
> great powers will find it difficult to intervene in any European country,
> especially not in a country in which their [soldiers] could die. We are not
> Panama and Grenada.
>
> (quoted in Magas and Zanic 2001: 207)

The Bosnian Serb leaders did not feel any urgency for making concessions to
achieve peace. This disagreement made for an increasing rift between the
Milosevic regime and the Bosnian Serbs.

Faced with the reality of full-scale war in Bosnia, newsmedia reports of atrocities and massacres and detention camps in which civilians were tortured to death, and the mounting flow of displaced persons from the war and from ethnic cleansing, the external stakeholders acted through the UN for a cessation of the armed fighting and the protection of civilians, and restarted diplomatic initiatives for a peace plan.

From the spring of 1992 a series of UN Security Council resolutions were passed on the withdrawal of JNA (Serb) and Croat armed forces from BiH, economic sanctions on Serbia because of continued military assistance to the Bosnian Serbs, the deployment of UN peacekeepers (UNPROFOR) in mounting numbers for enabling the delivery of humanitarian aid to civilians, the effecting of ceasefires and the cessation of shelling of civilian populations, and the establishing of UN-protected areas, and similar measures, including establishing a commission to gather evidence on war crimes and crimes against humanity, and later establishing the International War Crimes Tribunal on the Former Yugoslavia (ICTY). Because the UN forces were lightly armed and with limited mandates – General Michael Rose commanding UNPROFOR stated in March 1994 that "We are here not to protect or defend anything except ourselves and our [relief] convoys" (quoted in Magas and Zanic 2001: 167) – and the belligerents kept violating the resolutions without penalties, the war continued and intensified. Croatian President Tudjman covertly deployed a huge Croatian armed force in BiH to assist the Bosnian Croats, and the Milosevic regime kept providing military assistance to the Bosnian Serbs.

More peace plans and more war

After the external stakeholders chose UN peacekeeping intervention that relied on the combatants for compliance with UN resolutions, they tried to negotiate the Vance–Owen plan with the adversaries in late 1992 to early 1993. BiH would be a single state consisting of ten provinces defined by ethnic, geographic, and historical criteria grouped into three non-contiguous entities with three provinces each for the three adversaries, and Sarajevo shared by all three. The power sharing central government would be weak. Compared to the earlier rejected Cutileiro ethnic cantonization plan, the Bosniaks would get less territory and the Serbs and Croats more. The division did not correspond to the "facts on the ground." The Serbs would have to give up conquered territory in eastern Bosnia, and would not get the Posavina corridor (assigned to the Croats) that linked their eastern and western held areas. Without the corridor, the Serbs were denied direct access from Serbia to the Krajina Serbs in Croatia, and thus were obstructed from the "Greater Serbia" goal. In a referendum the Bosnian Serbs rejected Vance–Owen. The stakeholders then came back with the Owen–Stoltenberg plan in the summer and fall of 1993 in which Bosnia would be a confederation of three ethnic states, with a 53 percent Serb, 30 percent Bosniak and 18 percent

Croat territorial division, allowing for the possibility of an eventual breakup of BiH with the Serb and Croat entities joining Serbia and Croatia. The plan would make possible the Milosevic–Tudjman goal of BiH partition leaving a small and weak Muslim buffer state. Because it did not meet the Bosniak minimum non-negotiable goal of a viable state, the Bosniaks voted it down (Monnesland 1997: 397–406; Woodward 1995: 302–12).

Meanwhile the war continued with some Serb gains against the Bosniaks. A new phase of the war opened with the Croats and Bosniaks fighting one another, a disastrous war for both that helped the Serbs to consolidate their gains and further threaten non-Serb enclaves. Although the Bosniaks and Croats had formed an uneasy alliance during the Serb assault in the spring of 1992, they were at the same time competing for control of territory with mixed Croat–Muslim populations. After the failure of Owen–Stoltenberg and with the Serbs in control of the part of BiH they wanted to merge into a Greater Serbia, Tudjman and his Bosnian Croat allies decided to go for Croatian annexation of Bosnian Croat territory, but determined Bosniak resistance defeated their aim. According to General Spegelj, "Almost half the tank arsenal left Croatia for BiH (70 tanks, and 200 heavy artillery and missile weapons)," with the Croat army disguised as the HVO, the army of the Bosnian Croats. In this war, the Croats suffered huge losses with 13,000 dead. General Divjak believed that "more Croatian soldiers were killed in battles against the ARBiH (the Bosniak army) than fighting in Croatia . . . against the JNA and the Serb Krajina forces." General Spegelj believes that, had the Bosniak and Croat forces joined against the Serbs, they could have defeated them, as they did later in 1995. What stood in the way were Tudjman's designs for annexing part of BiH to Croatia (Magas and Zanic 2001: 66ff. esp. 106–7). Because of huge losses, Tudjman accepted to end the "war within the war," and he and the Bosnian Croats signed the Washington Framework Agreement with the Bosniaks that established a federation of Muslim and Croat entities, more on paper than on the ground, and a military alliance.

After the failures of EC and UN diplomacy, the external stakeholders reconstituted themselves into the *Contact Group* (US, European Union, UK, France, Germany, Italy, and Russia) which took the leading responsibility for peace making. It proposed a single BiH state composed of two entities, the Federation of Bosniaks and Croats with 51 percent of territory, and the Serb entity, with 49 percent – which was less than the 53 percent in Owen–Stoltenberg, and much less than the 70 percent the Serbs held (Monnesland 1997: 412). The constitution was to be negotiated later. The Bosniaks and Croats accepted it. Serbia was hurting from the economic sanctions, and Milosevic favored acceptance for ending the war, and thus sanctions against Serbia. The plan left open the eventual joining of the Republika Srpska with Serbia, but the Bosnian Serbs rejected it because of huge territorial concessions uncalled for by their favorable military situation and because it would leave their territory in three separated parts.

Instead of peace, the Bosnian Serbs stepped up their goal of conquering the non-Serb enclaves of Tuzla, Zepa, Gorazde, Srebrenica, Sarajevo, and Bihac, which had been UN-protected areas since 1993 under UN Security Council Resolutions 819 and 824, and became more confrontational against the external stakeholders and the UN peace forces. In these confrontations, NATO war planes bombed Bosnian Serb military targets – so-called pinprick strikes because they inflicted little damage – in retaliation for Bosnian Serb shelling and attacking of the UN-protected areas. When the Serbs nevertheless took Srebrenica and Zepa and repeatedly took UN soldiers hostages, UNPROFOR became discredited and the external stakeholders were publicly humiliated. Despite UN resolutions, verbal threats, and NATO airstrikes, the mere possibility of the death of a few of their soldiers was sufficient to deter the stakeholders from taking effective military action on behalf of the promised "protection" of civilians. The Bosnian Serb leader Karadzic boasted in April 1995 "we will push for a final military victory" (quoted in Magas and Zanic 2001: 219). The greatest humiliation came with the surrender of Srebrenica by the outnumbered and outgunned Dutch peace-keepers to the Bosnian Serb forces under General Mladic, and no UN and NATO intervention. That surrender led to the largest massacre in Europe since World War II. At this time, some of the external stakeholders were considering abandoning the peacekeeping operation in BiH and made plans for withdrawing their soldiers (Holbrooke 1998: 66). For Timothy Garton Ash:

> During the last four years we [Europeans] have failed to prevent the destruction and partition of a once peaceful and still beautiful part of Europe, with some 250,000 killed and more than 3 million made homeless. To many a professional soldier's frustration and anger, British and French soldiers have had to sit on the ghetto walls while the people inside were humiliated and shot.
>
> (1995: 27)

Despite the appearance of strength, the Bosnian Serb military was stretched out on a 1,500-kilometer front line. Because of manpower short-age, its soldiers served long tours of duty, there was a shortage of officers, and as casualties mounted the Bosnian Serbs became war weary and morale suffered. Their army was successful against civilians protected by lightly armed soldiers and peacekeepers, but did not make any headway, despite a huge weapons advantage, against the Bihac enclave defended by a deter-mined 5th Army Corps. Completely cut off from the other Bosniak armies and left to fend on their own, they successfully resisted the Bosnian and Krajina Serbs and dissident Muslim forces for the better part of three years.

Military breakthroughs

What unexpectedly changed the Bosnian Serb threat of total military victory was developments in Croatia and on the western front in Bosnia, which once more underscores the linkage between the Croatian and Bosnian wars. Frustrated on his BiH aims and having to settle for the Federation of Bosniaks and Croats, Tudjman had withdrawn his armed forces from Bosnia and focused on regaining the regions of Croatia held by the Krajina Serbs. The first Croat offensive retook areas in western Slavonia in "Operation Flash," and shortly, in the three days of "Operation Storm," the Krajina Serb army together with most of the Serb civilian population was sent packing – an estimated 100,000 to 200,000, some fleeing, some expelled – into the Republika Srpska, in a huge offensive with 70,000 Croat soldiers and heavy shelling of Serb villages and towns to drive the people out. There were 900 Serb dead, half of them civilians, and many Serb villages were systematically arsoned to prevent the Serbs from ever coming back, with an estimated 20,000 houses destroyed (Magas and Zanic 2001: 114). The Bihac pocket was relieved from the three-year Serb encirclement. "Storm" was followed by the combined Bosniak–Croat offensive in western and central Bosnia, which retook some 20 percent of BiH territory from the Serbs whose army became disorganized to the point that Banja Luka, the largest Bosnian Serb city, was in danger of falling.

These military events coincided with decisive diplomatic and military moves by the external stakeholders. The Clinton administration decided not to allow the first major post-Cold War peace operation undertaken by the West to fail and assumed responsibility within the Contact Group for a renewed peace plan which affirmed the 51 percent/49 percent territorial division between the Federation and the Republika Srpska within a single sovereign BiH state. The Bosnian Serbs would lift their siege of Sarajevo by withdrawing their heavy weapons from the surrounding mountains and opening an access corridor, and stop the military pressure on the Gorazde enclave. Milosevic backed the US initiative because it would end the economic sanctions that were hurting Serbia. The Bosnian Serbs opposed the plan at first, but NATO backed it up with 3,000 airstrikes on military targets that destroyed communications, arms depots, and artillery emplacements – a decisive change from the earlier pinprick airstrikes (Monnesland 1997: 421–4). Under pressure from NATO, Milosevic, and the collapsing Western front, the Bosnian Serbs accepted a ceasefire, lifted the siege on Sarajevo, and agreed to peace negotiations on the basis of the US plan, which included a settlement for the Croatian war as well. The Serbs still held a part of Eastern Slavonia in Croatia they had taken in 1991. An intensive US-led shuttle diplomacy under assistant secretary of state Richard Holbrooke brought the adversaries and external stakeholders to the Dayton negotiations in November 1995.

Why did the external stakeholders not allow the combined Croat and Bosniak forces to achieve a total military victory against the Bosnian Serbs?

From the start of the war, the international community had committed to a unitary BiH in which the Serbs had a share of territory and power. Their goal was to contain the conflict and to achieve a peace settlement negotiated by the adversaries, and not to impose peace and stateness by force alone. Since every military advance had precipitated huge displacement of population and atrocities against civilians, they did not want further refugee and humanitarian crises. They were uncertain that Milosevic, with Russian backing, would not come to the rescue of the Bosnian Serbs to stave off a complete collapse, and they did not want to risk a major military rescue of the UN peacekeeping forces that might be trapped in renewed warfare. Moreover the Bosniak army's offensive had stopped as it had reached the limits of its resources and strength, and Tudjman halted the Croat offensive because he saw no point in pushing for territorial gains beyond the 51/49 Contact Group deal which the Croats would have to give up under the peace plan (Magas and Zanic 2001: 251–3, 273–4).

The peace negotiations start

The negotiations at Dayton were multistranded and the internal divisions of the players were as important for peace making as the divisions between them, as CCD maintains for peace processes. In addition to the three main Bosnian adversaries' negotiations, there were differences that had to be dealt with between Serbia and Croatia over Eastern Slavonia, between the Bosnian Croats and Bosniaks in the Federation, between the external stakeholders themselves (especially the US and the Europeans and Russia in the Contact Group), within the US government (between the Pentagon, the State Department, and Congress), between Milosevic and the Bosnian Serbs, and factions within the Bosnian Serb delegation itself. The war might have been ended with a partition, with the Bosniaks left in control of a smaller country, but the Bosniaks had rejected that outcome repeatedly, e.g. when they rejected Owen–Stoltenberg (Holbrooke 1998: 96). The US wanted to avoid another Cyprus where a temporary ceasefire had hardened into a permanent partition line or, as Holbrooke put it, "Two hostile ethnic groups divided for twenty one years by an ugly wall that cut the island in half" (1998: 133).

The informal negotiations prior to Dayton locked in on a single sovereign BiH state with two entities, with governance, power sharing, and territorial allocations to be negotiated. The Serbs and Croats wanted a weak central government and autonomy for the Republika Srpska. In the Federation the Croats wanted strong control in Croat majority areas. The Bosniaks wanted a strong central government for all BiH. An autonomous Republika Srpska opened the risk of a stronger link between it and Serbia than between it and the rest of Bosnia. The external stakeholders wanted the ceasefire to become a permanent peace and BiH to become a multiethnic democracy, and the US did not want to legitimize "Serb aggression and Croat annexation . . . that might unleash another round of ethnic and border conflicts in Central and Eastern Europe" (Holbrooke 1998: 232–3).

To achieve these goals, the stakeholders realized that, in addition to enforcing a cessation of the fighting by military means with deployment of a large NATO force, they would have to create a civilian implementation organization for compliance with the non-military dimensions of the peace settlement (Holbrooke 1998: 174). The Serbs and Croats wanted a limited mandate and limited authority for external enforcement, whereas the Bosniaks wanted a strong mandate with much international authority. The Serbs and Croats looked forward to achieving their war goals by non-coercive means following the end of the war, and for that they wanted a weak Bosnian central government and limited implementation powers for the stakeholders. The external stakeholders had some leverage against the Serbs. Milosevic was desperate to have the economic sanctions lifted, and was told he would have to compel the Bosnian Serbs to sign a peace agreement before that happened. Without that leverage, as Holbrooke knew, "we would have begun with almost no bargaining chips" (1998: 87). The resumption of NATO airstrikes was another bargaining chip, though there was opposition within the Contact Group for further involvement in peace or war should Dayton fail.

The external stakeholders imposed constraints on themselves that weakened their power in the Dayton negotiations. They wanted a rapid peace deal "looking good" – no secession, BiH state unity, human rights, refugee return, and multiethnic democracy – even if fundamental issues were not fully resolved or left to implementation. Germany wanted a quick repatriation of its 300,000 Bosnian refugees. All wanted to minimize the risk of casualties to peace enforcers: the Pentagon and the US Congress successfully opposed a strong mandate for IFOR, the 60,000-strong NATO Implementation Force in which 20,000 US troops would be deployed, and a quick one-year exit strategy (Magas and Zanic 2001: 216–17). The Europeans wanted only a weak commitment of resources and authority to the civilian implementation organization for which they would be responsible, which included the International Police Task Force (IPTF). With a weak IFOR and IPTF for implementing the non-military aspects of the peace agreement, the external stakeholders were closer to the Serb and Croat positions than the Bosniak. According to Norman Cigar (in Magas and Zanic 2001: 234), "Belgrade and the Bosnian Serbs . . . were able to obtain a better deal . . . than their deteriorating military position warranted . . . helped by an international desire for a rapid and cheap solution."

The Dayton Peace Accords

In the Dayton negotiations, Tudjman and Milosevic agreed to the transfer of Eastern Slavonia to Croatia under UN supervision with US and Russian troops, and guarantees for the Serbs to live there and thus avoid yet another round of ethnic cleansing. Yielding to US pressure, the Bosniaks and Croats strengthened the Federation structure on paper and agreed on the status of Mostar, the Federation capital, which was on the verge of renewed fighting. In the main negotiations on Bosnia, the peace makers broke up into several task forces. The core issues were constitutional design, governance, human rights, elections, and the territorial division. Derivative issues dealt with demobilization, demilitarization, security, and IFOR's role; refugees and displaced persons (RIDPs); civilian implementation and the IPTF's role; and a number of lesser matters such as the preservation of public monuments and the future of public corporations.

On *constitutional design and power sharing*, the authority of the central government was limited to foreign policy, trade, customs, monetary policy, immigration, and some other functions such as air traffic control. Governance was devolved to the two entities, the Serb RS and the Federation, and within the Federation to ten cantons, eight of which were dominated by either the Bosniaks or the Croats, and in the two mixed cantons further devolved to municipalities some of which, like Mostar, established parallel Croat and Muslim governance in their respective city territory. The central state presidency, council of ministers, state parliament, high court, and public authorities were organized on consociational principles modeled on the small, multinational European democracies of Switzerland and Belgium. Consociation assumes permanent distinct ethnic identities and boundaries, a minimum of shared public goods (each group would provide most of them separately), proportional representation by ethnicity on collective decision-making bodies and proportionate resources allocation, and ethnic veto on vital issues (Sisk 1996: chapters 3–4). It requires ethnic elite commitment to a single state and elite cooperation, which Bosnia lacked, and a territorially distinct ethnic population, which the RIDP return in annex 7 was meant to undo. Consociation in the DPA constitutional design and power sharing favored Serb and Croat goals. On *human rights*, the commission on human rights, the human rights chamber, and the ombudsman would investigate, hear, monitor, and decide human rights claims and issue binding decisions, but received no enforcement powers.

The Organization for Security and Cooperation in Europe (OSCE) would supervise the preparation and conduct of *elections*, but the stronger mandate of "running" the elections wanted by the US was shelved (Holbrooke 1998: 290). Although the Bosniaks wanted IFOR security for elections to prevent intimidation and fraud, they got only OSCE authority to do so but no obligation for doing it (Chollet 1997: chapter 8). The most disagreement was on the RIDP right to vote where they had resided in 1991 before ethnic cleansing instead of where they were actually residing; a compromise gave them the choice (Chollet 1997: chapter 9). The system of representation in elections does not appear to have been debated at all, yet it would determine whether multiethnic centrist parties would form and how they would fare against the ethno-nationalist parties, the very parties that had plunged

Bosnia into war. The US blocked any kind of an amnesty deal which would have undermined the ICTY, and insisted that indicted war criminals like Karadzic and Mladic would not be allowed to hold political positions or run for elected office. Because the US military did not want "mission creep," IFOR's mandate did not commit it to arrest war criminals, not even Karadzic and Mladic, although it did not preclude IFOR from doing so (Bass 2000: 243–5).

IFOR (later to become SFOR) got strong powers to enforce the military dimensions of the agreement and to protect its soldiers and managed to avoid any mandate on enforcing the non-military parts of the agreement and backing up the authority of the civilian implementation organization headed by the High Representative (OHR). This was done against the strong objections of the Bosniaks and at the insistence of the US military and NATO (Holbrooke 1998: 276–8; Chollet 1997: chapter 8, day 8). NATO and the US military also refused IFOR responsibility for merging the three Bosnian armies into a single force under the authority of the central government, which Holbrooke described as a "fundamental flaw in our post war structure" (1998: 276–7). Instead, the US government offered to equip and train the Federation forces "in order to level the field" so that it could defend itself in the event of renewed war and, not openly mentioned, also provide an exit justification for the US and NATO.

On *civilian implementation*, various external stakeholders and agencies wanted a piece of the action and got it: UNHCR would provide assistance and funding for RIDP returns; a Commission for Real Property Claims (CRPC) would handle occupancy, property rights, and compensation claims; OSCE would organize and supervise elections and monitor human rights through a variety of commissions and agencies; the United Nations Mission to Bosnia-Hercegovina (UNMIBH) was put in charge of supervising law enforcement, i.e. training and advising of police forces and monitoring and reporting on violations by police. The International Police Task Force under UNMIBH was however not given the authority to arrest people, including police who violated the Dayton agreements, because the European stakeholders did not want that responsibility, and because IFOR did not want the responsibility of having to back up the IPTF in case of trouble. General Wesley Clark prophetically observed that "We are leaving a huge gap in the Bosnia food chain" (Holbrooke 1998: 250–1). The Office of High Representative was made the final but weak authority over implementation of the accords and coordinating all these international organizations. Nor did OHR get authority over the military aspects of Dayton because of NATO objection. Annex 10 explicitly stated that "the High Representative has no authority over the IFOR." Holbrooke described annex 10 as "not a good agreement" (1998: 276).

The hardest-fought issue, and one that almost led to a breakdown of the Dayton negotiations, was *territories and borders*, in particular the status of Sarajevo which the Serbs wanted divided and the Bosniaks a single city under their control, a corridor linking the Federation to the Gorazde enclave wanted by the Bosniaks, the Posavina corridor linking up the eastern and western parts of RS wanted by the Serbs, the status of Brcko situated in the lynchpin of the Posavina corridor, and a 51 percent/49 percent territorial division which corresponded to the military situation at the start of the Dayton ceasefire. The Bosniaks had rejected 30 percent in Owen–Stoltenberg because of size and because their territory was in four disconnected, indefensible chunks (i.e. Sarajevo and Srebrenica totally surrounded by Serbs). The Serbs had rejected Vance–Owen because they would have to give up about 20 percent territory held and they would be left with four chunks and without the Posavina corridor. The Contact Group plan met the viability criteria for the Bosniaks and Croats, but left the Serbs with three chunks and without the Posavina corridor, which they rejected. The August–September 1995 Croat–Muslim offensive had linked up the Bihac pocket with the rest of the Federation and brought military territorial control close to 51 percent/49 percent, but left the Bosniak Gorazde pocket in Serb territory while the Serbs had failed to take the Posavina corridor. Sarajevo was still surrounded by Serb forces except for a dangerous access via Mt. Igman, and parts of the city were within the Serb front line. A trade on access to Gorazde via a corridor for a Posavina corridor was attractive for both Serbs and Bosniaks. As for Sarajevo, a compromise based on joint authority in a city divided into autonomous ethnic neighborhoods – the District of Columbia model wanted by the Serbs and staunchly rejected by the Bosniaks – turned out to be more contentious and unfeasible the longer the negotiators dwelled on the specifics. In the end, to avert a breakdown of the talks, Milosevic exercised his power over the Bosnian Serbs in conceding Sarajevo to the Bosniaks in return for some recently lost Serb areas in western Bosnia (Holbrooke 1998: 291–3; Chollet 1997: chapter 9, day 18). The Bosnian Serbs rightly felt that Milosevic had double-crossed them. When both sides agreed to arbitration on the future of Brcko, the last hurdle before the signing of the Dayton Peace Accords was overcome.

Compared to the adversaries' initial negotiation positions, the final deal favored the Serbs, except for Sarajevo, and that is because the external stakeholders by and large got what they wanted with an end to the war and a single state recognized by the international community without assuming the burden for "nation building," i.e. achieving a multiethnic democracy in Bosnia, or so they thought at Dayton. The Bosniaks were in a weak bargaining position because their recent military gains had needed the Croat military offensive and massive NATO airstrikes. Tudjman had gotten Eastern Slavonia and signed on to the accord. The US negotiators gave the Bosniaks an ultimatum to sign or else they would shut down the peace talks: "we must have your answer in one hour. If you say no, we will announce in the morning that the Dayton peace talks have been closed down. Not suspended, closed down. In one hour" (Holbrooke 1998: 305). Terminating the peace talks would mean that the UN peacekeepers and NATO would withdraw from Bosnia, the ceasefire would end and the fighting resume, this time with the Bosniaks on their own. Moreover, with Milosevic signing the accords, and the Bosniaks blamed as the "bad guys" undermining the agreement (Chollet 1997: chapter 9, day 30), sanctions on Serbia would be lifted and unlikely reimposed even if Milosevic were to continue military support to the Bosnian Serbs.

Reluctantly the Bosniaks signed. Izetbegovic stated: "It is not a just peace . . . but my people need peace" (quoted in Holbrooke 1998: 309). Norman Cigar observed that "the Bosnian Serbs . . . were able to obtain a better deal . . . than their deteriorating military position warranted . . . helped by an international desire for a rapid and cheap solution" (quoted in Magas and Zanic 2001: 234). The vice president of RS, Biljana Plavsic, agreed: "in 1995 we were defeated. However, that said, we did not look all that bad around the negotiating table . . . the people said 'it's good; we could have come out worse'" (quoted in Magas and Zanic 2001: 232). General Divjak also agreed:

> Dayton, alas, accepted the military outcome on the ground. We may say that there were no winners in war, but the greatest losers in human and territorial terms are the Bosniaks, who had no intention of making war on anyone, unlike some of their neighbors.
>
> (quoted in Magas and Zanic 2001: 102)

Assessments of the DPA

The DPA did not impose peace and democratic institutions by victorious powers on a defeated people and discredited political leaders as had been the case with Germany and Japan at the end of World War II. The peace was made by agreement with and among the belligerents whose leaders had chosen to wage war rather than create a multiethnic democracy in the first place. The citizenry of Bosnia was not consulted, nor was it asked to approve the DPA in a referendum. It was not an auspicious beginning for democracy and put the DPA's legitimacy in doubt. Even though the ethnic groups had lived cooperatively and peacefully with one another for 30 years before the Yugoslav stateness crisis erupted into war, after three years of massacres, ethnic cleansing, war crimes, and insecurity and deprivation in refugee camps and cities under siege, not to mention ethnic hate and fear propaganda, the people in Bosnia had lots of ethnic grievances, mistrust, animosity, and even hatred. Whether the consequences of ethnic war and ethnic cleansing could be reversed was uncharted territory. Commenting on the outcome of the first post-war elections in Bosnia in which the nationalists won, Ozren Zunec, professor of sociology in Zagreb, said that:

> the idea of multicultural Bosnia is an ideal to which we shall simply be unable to convert people, [and unable] to mobilize them to establish [a]

unified Bosnia . . . what worries and discourages me is the massive support of the population in the 1996 elections for the forces of destruction. My Bosnian friends . . . who in the terrible war chaos of 1993 and early 1994 tried to put the pieces of shattered Bosnia together again lost catastrophically in those elections.

(quoted in Magas and Zanic 2001: 250)

The country was devastated by war and the economy in shambles. The most glaring omission from the DPA was an economic reconstruction plan to put people to work and provide them with an income. To build institutions, especially democratic institutions, is difficult enough, and to do so amid widespread economic misery doubly so. The DPA was an ambitious attempt at building a democratic multiethnic state and society, a difficult and untried political engineering feat known as "nation building," without a "nation," without a democratic political culture and civil society, and without an economic base to prop it up.

Ten years later, Laura Silber wrote that:

the agreement that emerged [at Dayton] was probably the best one that could have been obtained at the time but it had serious flaws. Bosnia was to be a unified country . . . [with] a weak central government that ultimately lacked authority over the ethnically based entities. The accord created 13 overlapping constitutions [for the ten cantons of the Muslim–Croat Federation, the two entities, and the central government] as well as reams of laws and regulations that made the country a bureaucratic nightmare. Left to its own devices, this union of three distrustful groups, overseen by a weak central authority, would be deadlocked. And so an international administrator, the high representative, was given wide powers necessary to cajole and threaten Bosnia's leaders into action.

(*NYT*, November 21, 2005)

For Roger Cohen:

the agreement signed in Dayton . . . acquiesced the de facto division of the country along ethnic lines, masked by the fig leaf of weak national institutions. But the Dayton agreement had one conspicuous merit: it stopped the killing that had taken about two hundred thousand lives.

(*NYT*, November 20, 2005)

Two major flaws of the DPA were quickly exposed. When it came time to unify Sarajevo under Bosniak control in March 1997, there were about 70,000 Serbs there, most of whom wanted to remain, but the Serb leadership forced them to leave by deploying political thugs who arsoned their homes. Holbrooke (1998: 336) described the tragedy:

a steady stream of Serbs clogged the roads out of Sarajevo, most carrying furniture, plumbing fixtures, and even doors. Behind them rose the smoking remains of Grbavica and Ilidza [two Serb districts]. "We must not allow a single Serb to remain in the territories which fall under Muslim–Croat control," said [the Serb leader] Klickovic.

Klickovic, together with other Serb leaders, refused to allow multiethnicity a chance to succeed. IFOR and the IPTF did nothing to stop this outrage. IFOR, said a spokesman, "is not a police force and will not undertake police duties," while another remarked that the Serbs "have a right to burn their own houses" (Holbrooke 1998: 337). International public opinion was shocked.

The second flaw was exposed when:

> the rush to hold elections in Bosnia in September 1996, barely ten months after Dayton was concluded, made it all but impossible for moderate leaders to emerge. The very nationalist parties that had prosecuted the war entrenched themselves in power
> (Silber, NYT, November 21, 2005)

or as Holbrooke put it, "[the elections] were relatively trouble free, but none of the winners was in favor of a truly multiethnic government," and "the same leaders who had started the war were still trying to silence those who called for multiethnic cooperation" (1998: 344). The International Crisis Group (ICG) (1998) was more blunt: "the current electoral system is fundamentally inappropriate for a multi ethnic state such as Bosnia."

Faced with persistent obstruction on implementation of the DPA and even the possibility of a collapse of the agreement, the external stakeholders who had created the Peace Implementation Council in December 1995 for implementation of the non-military dimensions of the DPA kept increasing the powers of the High Representative. The Bonn Peace Implementation Council (PIC) summit at the end of 1997 authorized the OHR to dismiss elected representatives of both entities for non-cooperation and dismiss obstructive officials in local government (Chandler 1999: 78). The successive incumbents of the OHR increasingly exercised their powers at the cost of becoming external, authoritarian, "benevolent" nation builders. Critics described the OHR institutions as an "international protectorate" or a "transitional international trusteeship" (Chandler 1999: 35) imposing multiethnic and democratic institutions on unenlightened and resisting Balkan "natives." In a scathing critique of the external stakeholders' handling of Bosnia, Robert Hayden wrote that "Bosnia is . . . not a government of or by its own peoples . . . The method selected by the [O]HR to promote 'democracy' in Bosnia is to create a dictatorship of virtue" (1998: 47). Though the analogy is overdrawn – Robespierre's instrument was the terror and the guillotine, whereas the OHR withheld funding and fired officials

– it does highlight a fundamental flaw of the Dayton institutions and implementation.

What might have been different?

We can now revisit the questions at the start of the chapter. First, why did the Dayton peace plan succeed whereas the earlier ones were rejected? I don't believe there existed a mutually hurting stalemate for the two principal adversaries. As diplomatic activity for peace intensified before Dayton in October 1995, the Bosniaks were reluctant to sign the ceasefire and General Mladic was rallying his forces for a Serb counteroffensive (Holbrooke 1998: 187, 193). The Bosnian Serbs refused to sign the agreement at Dayton, and had to be pressured by Milosevic to do so two weeks later. It was Milosevic and the external stakeholders that were fed up with the war, and Tudjman needed international support for getting back Eastern Slavonia.

It is also an oversimplification to state, as Holbrooke did (1998: 172), that "map negotiations are taking place on the battlefield" and that "the diplomatic landscape usually reflects the balance of forces on the ground." None of the territorial division plans by the external stakeholders reflected the military situation on the ground, and that is one reason the plans were rejected: by the Serbs because they would have to give up too much territory, and by the Bosniaks when they would get less than a viable state. The location and shape of territorial control – the contiguity of territory, the corridors, which it would take bloody battles to achieve – was at least as important as the amount of territory. A major reason that the pre-Dayton plans were undesirable for the adversaries was that their control of territory would be scattered in several disconnected chunks. The conflict was about stateness, territory control and population control and defendable boundaries enabling sovereignty and control to be exercised effectively. Territory and boundaries were the most contentious issue at Dayton because they defined very sharply who would get control of what: a city at a transportation hub, a power station, a strategic road, and a bridge. Compared to consociational governance institutions that had no track record of success, and were shrouded in uncertainty, territory and boundary were concrete, had finality, and were not contingent on external stakeholder implementation.

Did the DPA settle the core issues of stateness, multiethnic governance, democracy, and human and minority rights with finality? There is close to unanimity that it did so only on paper and that everything hinged on implementation. As Holbrooke commented two years after Dayton, "The good news in Sarajevo was that joint institutions actually existed; the bad news was that they barely functioned" (1998: 352).

The third set of questions deals with the impact of the external stakeholders on the character and duration of the war and the final territorial settlement and borders. What would have happened if the external stakeholders had not intervened at all? Since the Bosniaks did not have an army at the start, the JNA would have easily defeated the scattered armed formations of the Bosniaks. That would have meant the Milosevic–Tudjman partition with a rump Muslim buffer state and huge forced expulsions and ethnic cleansing of the Muslims. Would a large NATO military deployment at the very start of the Bosnian war, e.g. preventive deployment along the Serbia–Bosnia border, have deterred war? It is hard to imagine Western governments deploying soldiers *before* atrocities, war crimes, and ethnic cleansing when they were so reluctant to do so in Kosovo *after* atrocities, war crimes, and ethnic cleansing had occurred in Croatia and BiH, and in Kosovo itself.

The low level of military intervention chosen by the external stakeholders, lightly armed peacekeeping forces in both Croatia and Bosnia with limited mandates, was inadequate to ensure the flow of humanitarian aid to civilians and to protect them from attack by the belligerents. Still, without it, many more would have been ethnically cleansed and starved to death. UNPROFOR did not stop military actions the armies undertook against one another or against civilians. Nor was the ICTY a deterrent for war crimes and crimes against humanity. UN Security Council resolutions and verbal threats had little effect on the war. What did matter for changing the military situation and bringing the adversaries to the negotiating table was the Croat–Bosniak military offensive, the massive NATO airstrikes, and the economic sanctions on Serbia, all three major coercive events.

Until the very end, the course of the Bosnian war was determined more by the shifting military and political alliances of the adversaries than by external intervention. According to General Spegelj, "However much the United States, Britain, France and Germany may have been involved in everything, they still had far less impact on events in Yugoslavia than the forces working from within" (quoted in Magas and Zanic 2001: 247).

Strategic analysis

The remaining question is on strategic analysis and CCD. Peace making takes place during "fight and talk" which needs to be steered toward "talk-talk," the cessation of open hostilities, and end in an uncontested peace agreement that is implemented. The process can be described in strategic terms as a set of games between players who make strategic moves by choosing conciliatory or cooperative and coercive or hostile moves. The number of players changes, e.g. an alliance makes one out of several players, and the players themselves may not be unitary, i.e. they might have factions or groups with different interests such as the State and the Defense departments in the US government, which complicates decision making. The game itself can change from zero sum when the players are foes to a Prisoner's Dilemma when the players have both common but also divergent interests, and back again. The issues at stake in the game – stateness, territory and borders, security, refugee return, etc. – possess various properties (divisibility, reversibility, finality) that are likely to make them more or less contentious, and the total peace package itself to be acceptable and made feasible. For a successful peace, the players' strategies and moves will have to shift from coercion to cooperation.

The more players are engaged in a peace process, the larger the number of games they are likely to play with one another, and the less likely they are all going to converge on cooperation at the same time. Much diplomacy consists of reducing the number of players, making internally divided players and alliances more cohesive if not unitary, changing the type of game and strategies the players are engaged in from coercive to more cooperative, redefining the issues to make them less contentious, and making outcomes feasible and acceptable.

In the diplomacy leading up to the DPA, the US eliminated one external stakeholder, the UN, and tried as much as possible to reduce the divergent interests and multiple voices within the Contact Group by assuming leadership. To sideline the UN and to get the CG states to agree to US leadership, concessions were made on including the UN in the peace implementation structure, on Russian peacekeeping forces in IFOR, and on symbolic prestige benefits to the French government by holding the actual peace accord signing ceremony in Paris, and calling it the Treaty of Paris, although everyone refers to it as the DPA. It was difficult to get the US government to develop a single negotiation position for the US delegation to pursue because the Defense Department, State Department, Congress, and President Clinton had somewhat different interests and responded to different constraints. For instance, after lots of internal debate in Washington, it was decided that IFOR should get a limited mandate because the Defense Department (DOD) wanted it that way and because it would after all be responsible for the 20,000 US soldiers in IFOR. Thus the DOD's position became the US delegation's position on IFOR at Dayton.

The US also tried to simplify the adversaries. The Washington agreement created a military alliance between Croats and Bosniaks who had been at war with one another and got them to agree on a Federation entity in a future undivided Bosnian state. It did not remove divergent Croat and Bosniak interests on some matters, but on others they had a unified voice against the Bosnian Serbs. Just as important, on the Serbian side, with the "Patriarch Paper" that created a joint Yugoslav–Republika Srpska delegation for all future peace talks headed by Milosevic, Holbrooke (1998: 105–7) managed to get Milosevic to assume responsibility for representing the Bosnian Serbs in addition to Serbia and to be the final decision maker for all Serbs. Thus the differences among Serbs were so to speak outsourced to Milosevic to deal with, which simplified the Dayton negotiations. Milosevic was more determined than the Bosnian Serbs to end the war and was more prepared to make concessions, as he did on Sarajevo. As for Tudjman, his main concern at Dayton was in the parallel negotiation with Milosevic over Eastern Slavonia.

That left three principal players: the external stakeholders under US leadership, all Serbs under Milosevic, and the Bosniaks. The Serbs and the Bosniaks had opposite interests on every issue. In the war, their military offensives aimed to conquer territory held by the other – our gain is your loss – and at Dayton the Bosniaks wanted a strong central state and strong implementation mandate whereas the Serbs wanted the opposite – again, our gain is your loss.

The externals and the Serbs had a zero sum conflict during the armed fighting. UNPROFOR was trying to protect Bosniak enclaves, territory, and humanitarian resources to largely Muslim populations, whereas the Serbs wanted to annex the enclaves and drive out the non-Serbs. The Serbs used a bully strategy against the externals. Probe the adversary with repeated coercive moves, and keep doing so regardless of whether the adversary responds with conciliation until the adversary responds with coercion that really hurts. Thus to threats, UN Security Council resolutions, and pinprick airstrikes as well as conciliatory moves the Serbs responded with hostage taking, holding up aid convoys, shelling civilians, attacking and taking enclaves, and ethnic cleansing. In these exchanges the externals were the losers and considered withdrawing from the conflict altogether rather than be further humiliated and discredited as international conflict managers. But on August 28, 1995, a mortar shell from Serb positions killed 41 civilians at a Sarajevo marketplace which outraged international public opinion, and justified more effective coercion against the Serbs. In Holbrooke's words, "It took an outrageous Bosnian Serb action to trigger Operation Deliberate Force [massive NATO airstrikes] – but once launched, it made a huge difference" (1998: 104). Coming at the time of the losses from the Croat–Bosniak offensive, the Serbs were willing to negotiate a peace.

Between the externals and the Bosniaks, there was a unilateral dependency relationship in so far as the Bosniaks wanted more protection against the Serbs and wanted peace making instead of peacekeeping, and had nothing to offer in return. When the military prospects dramatically improved for the Bosniaks during the pre-Dayton diplomatic initiatives, stopping the war is what the externals wanted, but not the Bosniaks. They knew, however, that they would not be able to defeat the Bosnian Serbs without NATO air cover and assistance from the Croat armed forces. They therefore accepted the ceasefire and negotiations for ending the war. Although the externals and the Bosniaks had a common interest in a single-state solution, they also had divergent interests in as much as the Bosniaks wanted vigorous implementation beyond a "cheap peace."

By the time of Dayton, the war itself and the earlier rejected peace plans had placed some constraints for core issue outcomes. The external stakeholders ruled out partition. The successful Bosniak defense against the Croats had blocked the Milosevic–Tudjman partition plan. The Bosniaks had demonstrated with their determination to continue fighting when they were close to military defeat that they would not compromise on a single

Bosnian state. The range of outcomes on the core issues, especially stateness, was thus narrowed.

Peace pacting at Dayton called for bargaining on the issues. Bargaining provides gains for both parties, but the gains are not necessarily equivalent, the outcome depending on the bargaining strength of the parties, on norms insisted upon by the external stakeholders (e.g. fairness, as in the 51 percent/ 49 percent territorial division, and insisting on refugee right of return), and on feasibility, acceptance, cost, and other criteria. The ultimate weapon of the parties in bargaining is to refuse the terms and choose to achieve outcomes by other means, which after failure in Dayton would mean resumption of war. Milosevic blocked that option for the Bosnian Serbs, and the threat of external stakeholders' and Tudjman's disengagement from the conflict blocked it for the Bosniaks. Without Serbia's assistance for the Bosnian Serbs and without external and Croat assistance for the Bosniaks, neither adversary was going to get more through war than in negotiations at Dayton.

International conflict management in the Croat and Bosnian wars consisted of much diplomacy and some peacekeeping military intervention, but the diplomacy remained fruitless until coercive measures were visited upon the aggressors. To get to the bargaining table at Dayton and to achieve a peace settlement, the adversaries and the external stakeholders managed to reduce the number of players, reduce players' and player alliances' internal divisions, limit the range of outcomes on key issues, and choose less coercive and more cooperative strategies. The DPA was no mean feat. But just as there is a "fog of war," there is also a fog that shrouds international conflict management. Though successful in ending the fighting and the war, some of the best diplomatic and scholarly minds in Western Europe and the US and some of the most senior and experienced political leaders, advisors, and military officers responsible for the agreements came up short on political and social engineering for a divided society. Consociational governance is premised on cooperating ethnic leaders, but Bosnia lacked them. Democracy is more than free and fair elections. It is also the rule of law and an independent judiciary, an executive accountable to the legislature, and human rights institutions, to mention but the most salient. Elections by themselves, under post-war Bosnian conditions, placed into power undemocratic ethno-nationalist political leaders who obstructed multiethnic democracy. Implementation without teeth is defeated by determined opposition. Without a major economic reconstruction effort in an economy of scarcity and misery, corrupt ethno-national political machines with patron–client links will control economic resources and perpetuate ethnic politics. To be sure, it may well be that after the horrors of war and ethnic cleansing the restoration of a multiethnic society is not feasible, at least not in the short run. The external architects of Dayton did not address a fundamental stateness question that comes prior to institutional design: "Is preservation of a multinational state desirable when a majority of citizens in two of three constituent groups do not acknowledge the state's legitimacy?" (Bose 2002: 4). Displaced persons and refugees return to their original towns and villages, which are no longer "home," and lead parallel but separate lives among those who expelled them, without shared institutions. By the time the external stakeholders became more intrusive on implementation with the "international protectorate" after 1997, the flawed institutional design had settled into a robust and successful structure of resistance to multiethnic democracy.

5 The Israeli–Palestinian peace process

What the conflict is about

The conflict is about how to divide the territory of Palestine between two peoples and the dual-state structure of the partition. The state of Israel was in 1948 and is internationally recognized by all but some Arab states; the other is the Palestinian state in the making which does not yet exist. Its constitutional design, borders, and relationship to Israel have been bitterly and violently contested for decades. Since the Arab revolt for independence against the British mandate in 1936–9 and the creation of a Jewish national homeland in Palestine, the conflict has engendered a three-cornered civil war (Arabs against the British, Jews against the British, and Arabs against the Jews), the war for Israeli independence in 1948–9 between the Jews and the Arab states and the Palestinians, the 1956 war, the 1967 Six Day War, the 1973 Yom Kippur war, and the 1982 invasion of Lebanon. In 1937, the British Peel Commission had concluded that partition and population exchange were the only means of establishing peace in Palestine. After World War II in 1947 when the Arab states rejected the UN partition plan and Israel declared independence on May 14, 1948, war broke out and was concluded with an armistice in 1949 that left the victorious Israelis with 77 percent of the territory of Mandatory Palestine, including most of Jerusalem. Jordan was in control of the West Bank and Egypt in the Gaza Strip. In the Six Day War of 1967, Israel gained control of 1 million Palestinians in the West Bank and Gaza, known as the Occupied Territories (OTs).

The dominant Israeli and Palestinian cognitive frames on Palestine are incompatible. Arthur Herzberg wrote that:

> Palestinians believe the Jews should not be in Palestine at all, and they are willing at best to acknowledge the unfortunate fact of their being there. The Likud believes it has already conceded the land east of the Jordan to the Arabs and that western Palestine is the least amount of territory to which the Jewish state is entitled.
>
> (Herzberg 1990: 46)

Map 2 Occupied Territories

Source: Reproduced by kind permission of Jan de Jong and the Foundation for Middle East Peace

The Israeli frame was embedded in a set of hard rock beliefs which denied that the Palestinians are a people – Golda Meir once stated, "Who are the Palestinians? I am a Palestinian!" – and maintained that Palestine was an empty land available for Jewish settlement. The few Arabs there had a dozen Arab states they could move to for making room for the stateless Jews.

From the beginning of these wars and armed uprisings, civilians were massively targeted in guerilla actions, ethnic cleansing, forced population movements, communal riots, massacres, armed resistance, and terrorism. Leaders on both sides – later Israeli prime ministers Menachem Begin in Irgun, Itzak Shamir in the Stern Gang, and Ariel Sharon, head of Israeli Defense Forces (IDF) commando units and architect of the Lebanese invasion, and Yassir Arafat, head of the PLO – had been responsible for terrorist acts against civilians.

The 1967 Arab–Israeli war ended with Israeli control of the West Bank, Gaza, East Jerusalem, the Golan Heights, and the Sinai, but with no peace treaty. International relations between Israel and the Arab states and the Palestinians were governed by UN Security Council Resolution 242 which called for Israeli withdrawal from the Occupied Territories and acknowledgment of the sovereignty, territorial integrity, and political independence of every state, including Israel. It also called for the "just" settlement of the (Palestinian) refugee problem. Israeli political leaders had to decide the stateness of the OTs and the status of its Palestinian inhabitants, and make those decisions acceptable to the Palestinians themselves and the Arab stakeholders, who in turn would make a lasting peace with Israel.

The Israelis

Israel has a complex political party structure which reflects a very heterogeneous population, and which necessitates coalition government composed of many small parties included into either a Labor- or a Likud-led government, or a Likud–Labor national unity government. *Likud* wanted annexation of the West Bank into the state of Israel. According to the historian Avi Shlaim:

> The Likud ideology could be summed up in two words – Greater Israel. According to this ideology, Judea and Samaria, the biblical terms for the West Bank, were an integral part of Eretz Israel, the Land of Israel. The Likud categorically denied that Jordan had any claim to sovereignty over this area. Equally vehement was its denial that the Palestinians had a right of self determination there . . . [Its] party manifesto for the 1977 election [read]: "The right of the Jewish people to the Land of Israel is eternal and is an integral part of its right to security and peace. Judea and Samaria shall therefore not be relinquished to foreign rule; between the sea and the Jordan, there will be Jewish sovereignty alone."
>
> (2001: 352–3)

Likud established settlements in the West Bank and around Jerusalem, hoping eventually to achieve a Jewish numerical majority there, and through land annexation and economic pressures get the Palestinians to emigrate. As for the remaining Palestinians, Likud was willing to grant them some rights as residents of Israel, but not citizenship. Benjamin Netanyahu, Israeli prime minister in the mid-1990s, rejected the principle of a Palestinian state in the OTs, and proposed instead that "the Palestinians be granted autonomy in urban zones, with the understanding that the Israeli army would not only retain freedom of action throughout the whole territory but would also control all strategic positions" (Enderlin 2003: 44).

His Likud successor Ariel Sharon, the architect of the settlement policies and of the invasion of Lebanon, hoped that the Palestinians would over-throw the Jordanian monarchy and establish their Palestinian state there. In 1991, he wanted to cut the West Bank into three cantons encircled by settlements (Enderlin 2003: 147). When he became prime minister, he implemented that policy. Amos Elon writes that "Sharon is ready to allow a Palestinian state to be established only in Gaza and a very few small disjointed enclaves in the West Bank surrounded by Israeli settlements and military installations" (2004: 26). Sharon undertook the forced evacuation of the Gaza settlers for security reasons, against tremendous opposition from the settler movement and religious parties. Defending 6,000 settlers from daily attacks by Palestinian insurgents with 20,000 soldiers and with no end in sight was too costly for overall Israeli security.

The *Labor* party is progressive on social and economic issues but hawkish on security and Arab policy. After the 1967 war, Labor denied the right of self-determination to Palestinians and a Palestinian state on the OTs, but was more flexible on accommodation with the Palestinians than Likud. Simon Peres, its most permanent leader, believed that annexation of the West Bank would be disastrous because it would undermine the democratic and Jewish character of Israel. He favored Jordanian sovereignty over the heavily populated areas of the OTs with Israel retaining control of strategically important areas for security reasons. Yitzak Rabin, the other prominent Labor leader, also opposed a Palestine state next to Israel. He realized that an Arab–Israeli peace settlement would have to involve Israeli withdrawal from most of the OTs, which would become part of Jordan or be admin-istered under a joint authority. He was determined to keep Jerusalem, Jordan valley settlements, and other places of strategic value for Israel. In accord-ance with these views, he was reluctant to establish Jewish settlements in the OTs but ended up doing so (Shlaim 2001: 328–30, 429–30).

The *settlers* were another important player in Israeli policy on the OTs and an important ally of Likud. The first settlements were established as security outposts on the Jordan border to stop Palestinian guerilla infiltra-tion and attacks after 1967. By 2004, there were about 235,000 settlers in the OTs and another 180,000 on the eastern side of Jerusalem. A quarter of settlers lived in the West Bank for religious reasons. When an interviewer asked Rabbi Moshe Levinger, Hebron's first Jewish settler, about the scriptural claim to the biblical land of Israel, he read verses from Genesis and added, "All my ideas are formed from the Torah. It's not complex. This land is ours. God gave it to us. We're the owners of the land" (quoted in Goldberg 2004: 50). In downtown Hebron, an entire Israeli armored infantry regiment is needed to protect 300 settlers. The religious settlers are part of the Gush Emunim movement and are directly represented by small parties in the Knesset whose power derives from their ability to defeat the government they are part of in a no-confidence vote. Their view of the Palestinians was expressed by Benny Elon, the head of the Moledet party, in 2001:

> if the Arabs want a Palestinian state, it already exists, in the form of Jordan. Our solution, the voluntary exodus of Arabs out of Judea and Samaria, will lead to peace . . . we are willing to negotiate with them over some form of autonomy, with its capital in Amman . . . if they are not willing to [live with us in peace], then the painful price they will have to pay will be [population] transfer.
>
> (2001: 7)

Amos Elon comments that "the settlers now make up Israel's most vociferous political lobby. Military deployments . . . are nowadays largely determined by their interests and personal wishes. For years they have vehemently opposed every peace initiative and blocked every possible compromise" (2002: 16).

The reasons that three-quarters of the settlers have chosen to live in settlements are tax breaks and housing subsidies, a lifestyle they could not achieve in crowded Israeli cities, and convenient commuting distance to their jobs within Israel. Most settlements are commuter suburbs and lack an economic base. Polls showed that the majority of Israelis favor accepting a Palestine state and evacuating the settlements in return for real peace and security, though they had many doubts about the feasibility of peace. The settlement movement had a powerful triple hold on the polity. Religious motivations and ideals intersect with economic interests and the armed forces' security concerns. The idea of the Land of Israel and Jewish settlers in the West Bank resonated with fundamental religious and cultural beliefs that are attractive to even some secular Zionists. Consequently, though the hard-core religious settlers and their supporters are a tiny minority of the Israeli population – about 2 percent – "they have driven Israeli policy in the occupied territories for much of the thirty past years" (Goldberg 2004: 51).

Only *Peace Now*, the movement and party, sought unequivocally a two-state solution, withdrawal of the settlers, and reaching out to moderates among the Palestinians for joint peace building and reconciliation. Started in 1977 with 350 reserve officers in an open letter calling on Prime Minister Begin to accept the Israeli–Egyptian peace plan, the movement held huge rallies in Tel Aviv one of which was "the largest political demonstration in

Israeli history" (Shlaim 2001: 371). Peace Now opposed the Lebanon war and the occupation of southern Lebanon. It was ignored for the most part and became weakened and demoralized by the failure of the peace process at Camp David in 2000. It revived with the joint Israeli–Palestinian citizens' peace initiative that produced the Geneva Accord in 2005 whose goal was to restart the stalled peace process.

The Palestinians

Founded in 1964, the Palestine Liberation Organization (PLO) joined Palestinian political, paramilitary, and refugee groups under one loose umbrella, and relocated in Lebanon after being expelled from Jordan when it tried to overthrow the government there. The PLO sponsored armed resistance to Israeli occupation, including terrorism, airplane hijacking, border raids and shelling of Israeli civilians, civil strife, and other violent activities (Wieviorka 1993). Its most spectacular terrorist action was the Munich massacre on September 5, 1972 when Palestinian terrorists killed 11 Israeli athletes in a dormitory at the Munich Olympic Games. The PLO established itself as the governing body in the Palestinian refugee camps in Lebanon and gained increasing international recognition and observer status at the United Nations as the voice and advocate of the Palestinian people. From its founding to the mid-1980s, its stated goal was the destruction of the state of Israel by armed struggle. It defined itself as a national liberation struggle against European and Israeli colonialism, and claimed to be the sole representative of the Palestine people. The Palestine National Council in exile declared an independent state of Palestine on November 15, 1988 although it had no formal presence anywhere in that territory. A month later, the PLO announced its renunciation of terrorism and acceptance of Israel's right to exist, steps insisted upon by the US government as the ticket of admission for talks on the future of Palestine. Israel refused to recognize and negotiate with the PLO so long as it pursued violent and terrorist means. The Palestinian National Charter (PLO Covenant) declared that "Palestine is the homeland of the Arab Palestine people," "its boundaries are those of the British Mandate," and "it is an indivisible unit." Only Jews who resided in Palestine before the beginning of the Zionist invasion are considered inhabitants of Palestine. The Charter thus did not recognize Israel and the right of almost all Jews to live there (Lea 2002). It maintained the right of Palestinian refugees and their descendants to physical return to Israel which is graphically expressed in Palestinian homes and schools by maps of Palestine that do not indicate Israel and cities like Tel Aviv, showing in their stead Arab villages that have long gone out of existence. It denied any historical claim of the Jews to Palestine and to Jerusalem. It rested its claim on the West Bank and Gaza on UN Council Resolution 242 which stated that "territorial acquisition by war is inadmissible" and called for the "withdrawal of Israel's armed forces from territories occupied in the recent [1967] conflict."

Hamas, the PLO's main rival, is an offshoot of the Muslim Brotherhood and was first established as a social welfare and education organization in the Gaza Strip in 1970. It became politicized during the first intifada and has been totally committed to the full destruction of Israel. It developed a military wing, the al-Qassam brigades, and champions an "Islamic state." Hamas gets about $20 million to $30 million a year from Iran, and an undisclosed amount from various Saudi Arabian sources and Muslim charities from all over the world, including the US and Western Europe (Stern 2003: 48–9). Because money is fungible, the donors have little control over how the contributed funds are internally allocated between humanitarian and military–terrorist purposes. Hamas's covenant holds that Palestine from the (Jordan) river to the sea is an Islamic endowment and that no Muslim has a right to cede any part of it, calls for the obliteration of Israel by force, and asserts that the Jews are the source of evil in the world.

As the first intifada declined in the early 1990s, Hamas and other Palestinian armed groups increased assaults on Israeli soldiers and civilians in Gaza, which Israel countered with the arrest and deportation of 418 Hamas and Islamic jihad leaders and activists. Starting in 1994 Hamas undertook a campaign of car bombs and suicide bombing in Israel against civilian targets, the aim of which was to undermine the Oslo peace process. On April 9, 1994, a Hamas operative drove a car bomb into a bus killing eight inside Israel, and, on October 19, 22 people were killed and more than 50 wounded when a Hamas suicide bomber blew himself up in a Tel Aviv city bus. And that was just the beginning. Hamas reframed the concept of suicide – opposed in traditional interpretations of Islam – into martyrdom as a religious duty based on an Islamist interpretation of Koranic texts and teachings centered on the notion of jihad. It challenged the authority of the newly installed Palestine National Authority (PA) in Gaza, which led to lethal clashes between Hamas demonstrators and the PA police and the arrests of many Islamist militants (Kepel 2002: chapter 14).

Suicide bombings since 1993 have played a big role in undermining the peace process from the Palestinian side. According to data assembled by Avishai Margalit (2003) from a number of sources, from the start of the Oslo peace process in 1993 to August 2002 there have been 198 suicide missions, of which 136 succeeded in killing both victims and the attacker. Research indicates that suicide bombers come from a wide range of educational and socio-economic backgrounds, recently also including women. Many live in refugee camps and have spent time in Israeli prisons. They are angry and vengeful but not psychologically impaired. They are motivated by national humiliation of the Palestinian people, personal and family experiences of humiliation due to life under the occupation, and the attraction of martyrdom as a religious duty that will be celebrated in the Islamic world. The pollster Khalil Shikaki found that the most support for suicide bombing and violence among Palestinians is among those who have experienced humiliation at checkpoints or in other encounters with the occupation authorities (talk, March 1, 2005, Duke University).

Recruitment, training, indoctrination, and logistics are provided through charitable and paramilitary groups within Hamas that harness anger and organize the martyrdom operations down to the last step of public statement by a "living martyr" on videotape shown after the suicide bombing. The video statement legitimizes and spreads the culture of violence and makes last-minute backing out personally costly. The infrastructure for suicide bombing includes generous support for the families of martyrs. Jessica Stern found that:

> The organizations that recruit suicide bombers encourage youth to donate their lives, and their parents' quiescence, in a variety of ways. The parents are showered with gifts and attention, including substantial financial rewards offered by a variety of charities. They hold celebrations for the "shaheed" (martyr) to celebrate his purported marriage in paradise. Death notices in Palestinian papers often take the form of wedding announcements.
>
> (2003: 54)

The glorification of suicide bombing by Hamas has resonated with the Palestinian public after the collapse of the Camp David peace process. A poll conducted by Bir Zeit university with over 1,200 Palestinian respondents indicated that 80 percent supported violent attacks on Israel, including suicide bombing, compared to 44 percent in mid-1998 when hopes for peace were high (*NYT*, November 15, 2000). A Hamas leader told Jessica Stern that suicide bombing is a cost-effective weapon: an attack on an Israeli shopping mall requires a bomb, a detonator, and a moment of "courage": "'Courage' is the scarce resource. Hamas' job . . . is to find youth with the capacity to feel this courage and then to find ways to nurture it" (2003: 40).

The external stakeholders

First and foremost external stakeholders were the Arab states that had signed an armistice but were still in a state of war with Israel. The most important of them was Egypt, which had large parts of its territory under Israeli military occupation after the 1967 and 1973 wars. Syria had lost the Golan Heights. Jordan had been the sovereign on the West Bank until 1967 and remained the internationally recognized agent on behalf of the population there. Second was the United States which had been the principal external architect in the 1947 United Nations creation of Israel and subsequently became its principal international ally. That remains deeply resented in the Arab world, and in some Muslim countries like Iran.

As in other peace processes, the external stakeholders derive benefits from the conflict that conflict with their interest in a peaceful resolution. For some Arab states, the Israeli–Palestinian conflict is a convenient scapegoat for domestic problems. The US has ended up footing the bill worth several billions of dollars annually to Egypt and Israel for making peace with one another. US pressure on Israeli governments for more responsiveness in the peace process is constrained by domestic politics. Thus the US kept selling weapons to the Israelis, including sophisticated weapons systems, makes loan guarantees and provides other resources to the Israelis, and vetoes UN Security Council resolutions against Israel, while making empty threats against the Israeli government on settlement expansion and on stalling the peace process. For instance, in September 2003, according to a *New York Times* story (September 17), the US reduced loan guarantees to Israel because of settlement expansion, but:

> the action was almost totally symbolic. It came on the same day that Israel sold $1.6 billion of bonds on Wall Street backed by a loan guarantee of repayment by the U.S. government under legislation passed last spring that provides Israel with up to $3 billion in loan guarantees annually for three years.

On Middle East conflict management the US is perceived in the Arab world as a partisan intervener rather than an impartial mediator and honest broker, as was noted by President Clinton (2004: 747).

Israel has not had to pay the full cost of the conflict, but neither have the Palestinians. The Palestinian economy is heavily supported from external sources. The Palestinians in the OTs are a huge dependent population in a permanent disaster area kept from starving by external donors. According to Peter Hansen, the United Nations Relief and Works Agency commissioner, the UN has the largest humanitarian operation on the ground in the Middle East, with 10,500 staff members in the West Bank and Gaza alone, and its food aid reaches almost 220,000 families: "as the Palestinian economy has stagnated, the demands on agency resources have soared" (*NYT*, July 30, 2002). Should the conflict wind down, the total external support to them would diminish. The Palestinians are the world's largest per capita recipients of international aid, nearly $300 per person in 2004 (*NYT*, December 17, 2004). In 2005 the Palestine Authority's yearly revenue of about $1 billion derived from donor states – Arab, European Union, US and UN agencies for refugees – and from $50 million per month customs duties and taxes collected by Israel on the PA's behalf. According to the Saudi ambassador to the US, the Saudi government transfers $200 million a year to the PA, and another $200 million to UN agencies that maintain the Palestinians (CNN, February 5, 2006, Wolf Blitzer). Most of these revenues are spent on 140,000 PA employee salaries, about one-third of total employment and an enormous jobs program lacking an investment dimension for economic development (*NYT*, January 8, 2006). In the 1990s, 40,000 to 50,000 Palestinians worked in Israel except during temporary border closures when that number dropped to 10,000 to 25,000 (Brynam 2000: 47–9). Two-thirds of funding for charitable societies comes from external sources. All these resources pouring into the OTs still leave them with an unemployment rate of about 25 percent, as high as 75 percent for the young men ages 16 to 25 in refugee camps who are the most fertile recruiting pool for armed fighters and terrorists. In retaliation for violent attacks on Israel, the Israelis withhold the customs duties and limit the migrant labor force, which causes economic pain, resentment and anger, and more armed fighters and terrorists.

Conflict dynamics

Faced with over 1 million Palestinians in the OTs after the 1967 war, Israel gradually imposed a civil and military administration that replaced the Jordanian government. The Palestinian economy became a dependent, labor-exporting segment of the Israeli economy with resources and infrastructure such as water, electricity, telephone grid, and roads under Israeli control (Lustick 1993; Ron 2003). Though the Palestinian economy benefited from the Israeli link, it was at the expense of civil and political rights. Former Israeli foreign minister Abba Eban characterized the condition of the Palestinians as follows in 1987:

> The Arabs cannot vote or be elected at any level, have no degree of juridical control over the government that determines the condition of their existence, have no right of appeal against the judgments of military courts, are not free to leave their land with assurance of a right to return, are not immune from judgments of expulsion from their birthplace and homeland, have no flag to revere, do not possess the same economic and social conditions as their Jewish neighbors, nor the same status for their newspapers and universities . . . There is a society in the West Bank and Gaza in which a man's rights are defined not by his conduct . . . but by his ethnic identity.
>
> (quoted in Rosenberg 2003: 22)

Wendy Pearlman, a US researcher living in Bir Zeit on the West Bank, witnessed routine daily encounters between Palestinian civilians and Israeli soldiers:

> Last March the Israeli army used bulldozers to tear up the road, halting movement between 35 villages and the town of Ramallah. Although the Palestinians came together to repair damage and to reopen the road, Israeli tanks and armed soldiers have remained stationed here . . . For the past two weeks the soldiers have been forcing almost everyone traveling from one point to another to get out of their taxis, abandon their cars and cross the checkpoint on foot. At best this requires the people to gather their belongings and walk a long distance in the sun

before catching another ride. Yet it is not unusual for soldiers to stop people and turn them back, inspect their identity cards, confiscate car keys or fire tear gas bombs and rubber bullets.

(*International Herald Tribune*, June 15, 2001)

Within both adversaries, the least conciliatory, extreme groups held the peace process hostage. Settlement expansion was at the core of the Israeli mobilization paradox in the peace process (Margalit 2001; Foundation for Middle East Peace 2002). The Labor–Likud rivalry made the balance of power in the Knesset, and therefore the fate of the government, depend on pro-settler religious and nationalist parties. Peace moves by Labor were balanced by concessions to the Likud and its allies on settlement expansion for the sake of preserving the government in power. The alternative Labor–Likud national unity government created gridlock over an issue the partners profoundly disagreed on, and settlement expansion continued. Settlement expansion provoked violent incidents with Palestinians and magnified the security dilemma: every settlement meant more land seized, and more roads, checkpoints, outposts, and military installations to protect them, which in turn increased Palestinian attacks and insurgency, which in turn fostered Labor–Likud outbidding on more security, yet more security was not achieved. The occupation generated a predictable coercion paradox. Although the insurgency kept being contained in the short run, it also fueled more insurgents and more extreme modes of violence. Coercive control and collective punishment from Israeli counterinsurgency tactics, border closings, and other economic restrictions on the Palestinian economy expanded the pool of unemployed, humiliated, and angry Palestinians recruited into militant groups dedicated to violent attacks on the settlers, on the IDF, and on civilians within Israel. Palestinian attacks in turn strengthened the hand of the Likud and its allies for opposing the peace process.

On the Palestinian side, there was a parallel mobilization paradox. When the Oslo peace process was delivering some tangible gains, the PLO strengthened its position within the Palestine population and support for Hamas and other militant groups declined. Hamas countered with suicide bombings, which predictably provoked a coercive Israeli response and a slowdown of the peace process. The PLO then responded to the Hamas challenge by outbidding it with unconciliatory posturing against Israeli demands for curbing violence.

Peace initiatives before Oslo

Following the 1973 war, under strong pressure from the US and other stakeholders, the Israeli government decided to explore a peace deal with the Arab states, starting with Egypt which wanted to regain Egyptian territory lost in the Sinai Peninsula. Egypt insisted that some plan to end the occupation of the OTs had to be part of a comprehensive peace settlement with Egypt and the other Arab states. The Labor government led by Prime Minister Rabin was unable to negotiate an acceptable plan without risking its Knesset majority because that depended on the ten votes of the National Religious Party (NRP). The NRP sponsored Gush Emunim (Block of the Faithful), the militant neo-messianic settlement movement, which opposed the return of any part of the "biblical homeland" to Arab rule. Rabin himself at this time refused to negotiate with the PLO and opposed a two-state solution, although he was willing to consider local autonomy under Jordanian authority for the densely settled urban Palestinian areas. Labor lost the May 17, 1977 election to Likud, and the new Prime Minister Begin formed a government in alliance with the NRP, which thus continued to hold the balance of power in the Knesset. Begin and Likud were just as opposed to negotiating directly with the Palestinians as Rabin and Labor had been, and were totally opposed to surrendering sovereignty to them or to Jordan on any part of the OTs.

Under continued pressure from the US, which wanted peace between Israel and Egypt, the Begin government signed the Camp David Accords in September 1977. These included "A Framework for Peace in the Middle East" that dealt with the Palestinian issues. Egypt, Israel, Jordan, and representatives of the Palestinian people were to participate in three stage negotiations. First, ground rules for a self-governing authority and its powers in the OTs would be defined. Second, a transition period would occur during which the Palestinian Authority would establish an administration, the Israeli civil administration would be gradually withdrawn, and the Israeli military would be redeployed in security locations. Third, final status negotiations would begin within three years of the transition period start (Shlaim 2001: 374–5). Israeli public opinion was 82 percent in favor of the Framework, but it barely passed in the Knesset because most Likud and NRP members voted against it. The Framework was a roadmap to a peace settlement, and was a model for subsequent roadmaps, including the Oslo Accords of 1993, yet 16 years elapsed between the Framework and Oslo. The problem with every roadmap was the same: the adversaries had totally different destinations in mind.

Implementation of the first stage was something else again: "Begin managed the autonomy talks in such a way that nothing could be achieved" (Shlaim 2001: 381). Meanwhile, settlement expansion was the order of the day. Private Arab land was expropriated not just for security purposes but for civilian settlements, and cuts were made in the defense budget to free funds for settlements. By stalling the peace process, Begin was creating "facts on the ground" that he knew would be very hard to undo. In the 1981 election, Likud stayed in power with the help of the right-wing parties after the bombing of the Osiris nuclear reactor in Iraq proved popular with the voters. Settlement expansion continued and extended to densely populated Palestinian areas. The Golan Heights was opened for settlement. The government's official policy became permanent jurisdiction over the

1.3 million Arabs in the OTs and was in complete contradiction to the 1977 Camp David Framework.

During the Lebanese war, 1981–4, the peace process was at a complete stall. Because of lack of success in the war and high inflation, both Likud and Labor lost Knesset seats to other parties in the July 1984 election, but decided to form a national unity government headed by Simon Peres and Yitzak Shamir. Their disagreements ended in paralysis on Palestinian and OT issues for the next four years. Contributing to the paralysis was stepped-up rivalry between Jordan and the PLO on who would represent the Palestinians in peace negotiations. Israel refused to negotiate with the PLO so long as it didn't recognize Israel and renounce violence and terrorism. PLO attacks and terrorism against Israeli targets continued and also against non-PLO Palestinian moderates like the pro-Jordan mayor of Nablus. Israel retaliated tit for tat against the PLO – the airstrike against the Tunis headquarters of the PLO was in answer to the killing of three Israelis on a yacht in the port of Larnaca in Cyprus. Peres nevertheless managed to reach an agreement with King Hussein in September 1987, called the London Agreement, for keeping the Foundation for Middle East Peace process alive with plans for an international peace conference. Because the plan was opposed by his Likud coalition partner Shamir, the conference was not convened until October 1991 in Madrid.

In the meanwhile unforeseen events changed the parameters for the restart of the peace process in the 1990s. In December 1987 the Palestinian street started the first intifada against Israeli occupation. The Palestine National Council in November 1988 voted to recognize the state of Israel, accept all UN resolutions concerning Palestine, and in effect accept the principle of a two-state solution. The Cold War ended with the collapse of the Soviet Union. Jordan renounced any territorial claim to the West Bank and cut the financial and administrative ties it had maintained there. Joint authority with Jordan over Palestinian areas was finished as an option; the Israelis would have to deal directly with the Palestinians about the future of the OTs. Jordan however agreed to include Palestinian representatives in a joint delegation at future peace talks. Meanwhile, after the Israeli general election of November 1988, the Likud–Labor national unity government continued in power under Prime Minister Shamir and required the consent of both partners on settlement policy. Settlement expansion continued.

Would a peace agreement be attainable?

In the 1990s, the peace deal that emerged as doable was a "land for peace" exchange based on UN Resolution 242: Israel would return all occupied territory from the 1967 war and all Arab states would recognize and sign a peace treaty with Israel, and normalize relations. The deal implied the creation of a Palestinian state. And there the problems started since the PLO was ambivalent about recognizing Israel and renouncing violence, and Israel refused to recognize and negotiate with a terrorist organization. Though the recognition issue was formally overcome by both parties at the start of the Oslo process in 1993 (see page 143), there remained uncertainty on both sides' willingness and capacity for delivering a two-state solution with secure borders and peaceful relations after a peace treaty. Whoever negotiated and signed for the Palestinians might not be able and willing to curb the rejectionist organizations (Hamas, Jihad, Hezbollah, al-Aqsa brigades, etc.) that were intent on continuing the armed struggle against the very existence of Israel. Whichever Israeli government negotiated and signed for Israel might not be able to deliver on an independent, viable Palestinian state since thousands of Israeli settlers would have to be forcefully evicted and since Greater Jerusalem was incorporated into Israel, including East Jerusalem, which was claimed by the Palestinians for their future capital.

The settlements had become a contentious core issue in Israeli–Palestinian relations. In January 2001, there were approximately 180,000 inhabitants in the East Jerusalem Jewish neighborhoods beyond the Green Line, about 200,000 Israeli settlers in 146 settlements in the West Bank, and about 6,500 Jewish settlers in 16 settlements in Gaza (www.peacenow.org/settlements). Every settlement expansion increased the trust deficit needed for peace making. In the words of a Palestinian negotiator, "For the Palestinians, the settlements are the equivalent of blowing up a bus in Tel Aviv" (quoted in Enderlin 2003: 68). The Palestinian side would have to reframe the right of refugee return for the 3.2 million UN-registered Palestinian refugees from physical return to token return and only financial compensation for the vast majority (Hollis 2000). Other major issues in a peace settlement were borders and viability of a Palestinian state, demilitarization, the status of the holy places in Jerusalem, and equitable allocation of shared resources such as water.

The peace process was engaged by both sides with fundamental disagreement on all core issues that would have to be dealt with in final status negotiations. Because of disagreements avoided for the sake of getting a peace process going, the energies of the adversaries and of the external stakeholders were focused on "roadmaps" that neglected the underlying conflicts. Neither leadership had prepared their publics for the painful compromises and sacrifices required for a doable peace agreement. Both Palestinians and Israelis have incorporated Jerusalem into their collective national myths (Benvenisti 1995). The national myths of Israelis and Palestinians deny Jerusalem to the other. Ninety-two percent of Palestinians say that Jerusalem is very important to them personally, but 86 percent do not believe Jerusalem is important to Israelis as a national capital. Palestinians, including Arafat, deny that there was ever a Jewish Temple (of Solomon) on the Temple Mount, which they call Haram al Sharif (Noble Sanctuary). Conversely, 80 percent of Israelis believe that the Palestinian claim to East Jerusalem as a capital is not justified, and 70 percent will not accept the Temple Mount under Muslim religious control in a peace settlement (Segal *et al.* 2000: 19). Many Jews believe that, when the Jews started immigrating to Palestine at the turn of the century, there were hardly any Arabs living there. The Zionists had created the myth of Jewish settlers returning to the Palestine homeland, taming the wilderness with manual labor, and establishing an egalitarian society in an empty space that had plenty of land for two peoples without any harm to the Arab inhabitants.

On top of tough core issues, uncertainty remained about good faith in negotiations and trust on implementation. Arafat spun one tale in English to the Israelis and the international community on refugee return, on accepting the state of Israel, and on curbing Palestinian violence, and he spun a different story in Arabic to the Palestinians and Arab audiences. On the Israeli side, even the most conciliatory Labor prime minister, Peres, approved settlement expansion, and so did Rabin and Barak, and of course the Likud prime ministers Shamir, Netanyahu, and Sharon, with all of them knowing how the settlement issue complicates the peace process and poisons Israeli–Arab relations. Prime Minister Barak admitted that:

> if you think you can evacuate 10,000 to 15,000 settlers from the Golan Heights – which will take you to the brink of civil war – and then evacuate tens of thousands of others from Judea and Samaria, then you don't understand anything about the reality of Israel.
>
> (Enderlin 2003: 137)

In the peace process, Palestinian rejectionist violence targeting civilians inside Israel and Israeli settlement expansion are the most disruptive moves by each side, feeding on each another. Though they were totally and predictably disruptive of the peace process, they kept being made. None of this made for inevitable failure in the peace process, but it highlights the necessity for fundamental shifts in the mentality of political leaders and citizenry before any peace agreement is signed and implemented. The worst-case scenario for both adversaries is for an Israeli–Palestinian peace agreement to be followed by civil disorders, possibly even civil wars, within each camp: Palestinian moderates and rejectionists taking up arms against one another over stopping terrorism for political ends and over recognizing Israel and, in Israel, government coercively removing settlers from the OTs, some of them, with allies, violently resisting the IDF. Fratricidal violence lurks just below the surface of peace making: Sadat and Rabin were assassinated by their own extremists for making peace between Israel and Egypt.

The Oslo peace process 1991–2001

The Israeli–Palestinian peace process started at Madrid on October 30, 1991 during the first intifada, and ended in the aftermath of Camp David in 2001. Starting in December 1987, the first intifada in the OTs was a spontaneous, grassroots movement against Israeli occupation consisting of mass demonstrations, strikes by merchants and by workers, refusal to pay taxes, blocking roads and confronting the military authorities, and the ubiquitous stone-throwing youth. According to Lustick:

> Five years after its initial outburst, though the intifada may have faded away . . . the depth of anger it expressed and generated [was] understood by the vast majority of Israelis to mean that ruling the Arabs of the territories required repeated use of harsh, sustained and politically costly repressive measures.
>
> (1993: 398)

The impetus for Madrid was pressure on Israel and the Arabs by both the US and the external stakeholders during several years of diplomatic efforts and a variety of proposals for a peace conference and a new window of opportunity for change after the first Gulf War. Palestinians were part of the Jordanian delegation because Israel did not recognize the PLO. Over several meetings in many locations until June 1992, Israel and the Arab states met for peace making, but the "land for peace" exchange was rejected by both sides. Meetings bogged down over procedure, e.g. whether Palestinians from East Jerusalem could be included in the Palestinian team. The Shamir government dragged the negotiations out, announced increases in the Jewish settlements in the West Bank and Gaza and around East Jerusalem, and intended to create "facts on the ground" (i.e. settlements in the OTs). The Palestinian rejectionists (Hamas, Islamic Jihad, Hezbollah) engaged in violent actions, the IDF retaliated tit for tat, and other forms of Palestinian protest such as hunger strikes by prisoners continued during the Madrid talks.

The June 1992 Israeli general election became a referendum on peace (Shlaim 2001: 497–9). Likud's Shamir wanted a "big Israel" – a codeword for annexation of the OTs – for settling the Russian immigrants and for preserving the Land of Israel. Labor was flexible on Palestinian autonomy and on freezing settlement expansion during the peace talks. The voters put Labor and left-of-center parties into power under Prime Minister Rabin with a decisive mandate to run the government and pursue territorial compromise for peace.

Under Rabin, the Madrid–Washington bilateral peace negotiations also deadlocked. The Israeli historian Shlaim writes that "It proved impossible for the two sides to agree on a first step . . . The Palestinians wanted to end the occupation; the Israelis wanted to retain as much control as possible for as long as possible [during the interim period]" (2001: 509). Spoiler violence was another major cause and was to set back the peace process over and over again during the coming years. To be sure Israel had to take measures against Palestinian violence, but its government frequently reacted out of proportion to the offense. Moreover, even the powerful state of Israel was unable to stop Israeli spoiler violence by settlers against Palestinian civilians and even against Israelis themselves, as Rabin's assassination clearly demonstrated. To expect the divided Palestinians to control every militant group in their midst was unrealistic and became for the Israeli opponents of the peace process a pretext to put it on ice. When militants kidnapped and murdered an Israeli border policeman in December 1992, Rabin arrested and deported more than 400 Hamas activists to a Lebanese border detention camp, a level of collective punishment that outdid the coercive measures of the Likud government. The deportations occasioned a chain reaction of protests, violence, civil strife and coercive social control, much unfavorable international condemnation, and a phased return of the deportees. The Rabin government came to realize that the Madrid framework was leading nowhere, and that it would have to negotiate directly with Yassir Arafat and the PLO.

Started as a non-governmental initiative under Norwegian auspices, secret face-to-face talks between Israelis and the PLO had been going on and got the Oslo peace process started. Yassir Arafat and the PLO were internationally isolated after backing the loser in the Gulf War and were hoping to restore acceptance of the PLO as the sole representative of the Palestine people. On his part, Prime Minister Rabin was alarmed at Hamas and Islamic Jihad's growing support in the OTs, and expected the PLO to rein them in (Rosenberg 2003: 155; Kepel 2002: chapter 14). The Declaration of Principles on Interim Self-Government Arrangements (DOT) at Oslo unlocked the stalemate over mutual recognition and drafted a credible game plan of gradual exchange of land for peace and security in step with the formation of an interim Palestinian administration that would end with the so-called "final status" negotiations on the core issues at a later time – sovereignty, borders, security, settlements, Jerusalem, holy places, and refugees. It set down an agenda and timetable for negotiations. In the Oslo A agreement (September 1993), Israel recognized the PLO and the Palestinians' right to self-determination implying a right to statehood; the PLO recognized Israel, pledged to change the PLO covenant, and renounced terrorism and violence. Palestine control of Jericho and the Gaza Strip started the roadmap to Palestinian self-rule. The agreement was signed on the White House lawn and sealed with the historic handshake of Rabin and Arafat. Israeli public opinion was 65 percent in favor and 13 percent "very much against." The Knesset approved it 61 votes to 50. Benjamin Netanyahu, the Likud leader who had succeeded Shamir, rejected it and stated that, when the Likud returned to power, it would cancel it. The Palestinian leadership was split, with the radicals accusing Arafat of a sell-out because the DOT did not guarantee an independent Palestinian state (Shlaim 2001: 522). The internal divisions within both adversaries were an omen for trouble to come.

Oslo A was followed by a series of specific agreements and protocols on territorial control and on transfers of economic, fiscal, health, education, and other functions from the Israeli government to the Palestinian administration that was coming into being. Joint committees supervising cooperation on water, electricity, transportation, communications, tax transfers, labor relations, and investment were formed. Israel committed itself to Palestinian state building in the OTs, even supplying weapons to a Palestine Authority police force, with which it would negotiate a final status for ending the 40-year-long conflict.

Oslo B (on September 25, 1995), officially the Palestinian Interim Agreement on the West Bank and Gaza Strip, was a complex document of some 300 pages. It mapped the path to autonomy and statehood with the election of a Palestinian Council (legislature), transfer of authority to it, withdrawal of Israeli forces from cities, and the division of the West Bank into three areas where Israeli civil and military authority would be gradually and conditionally transferred to PA control. In area A, Palestine urban areas, 4 percent of the total area, the Palestinians would have full control. In area B, villages, 25 percent of the West Bank, Palestinians would exercise civil authority and Israel retain military authority. In area C, Israeli settlements and roads, 71 percent of the West Bank, Israel would have full control. The condition was the Palestine Authority (PA) curbing violence by the militant groups. The last parts of the Occupied Territories to be transferred would be some Jewish settlements, access roads, and military bases of the IDF. How much of area C was to be eventually transferred to the Palestinians was left for the final status negotiations.

The Oslo agreements were a bold and comprehensive joint undertaking that was meant to build confidence, overcome suspicion and hostility, increase trust between the adversaries, and end with a normalization of their relationship as two neighbor states. Oslo required conciliation unique in Israeli–Palestinian relations and enjoyed near unanimous approval in world public opinion. It was a gradualist scheme of more control and responsibility by a Palestinian administration in the making with Israeli assistance and cooperation. There were two flaws in the scheme. It assumed full commitment and good intentions, yet a substantial part of the leadership and public of both adversaries was opposed to it. The second flaw was apparent by viewing a color-coded map of the West Bank indicating a jumble of 2 million Palestinians living in some 650 towns mixed with 200,000 Israeli settlers living in 130 settlements (not including the Greater Jerusalem area), main roads, bypass roads, Israeli military bases, special areas, and other landmarks. How to separate these enemies when every change entailed risk of confrontation would be a monumental undertaking.

Oslo A set the stage for a showdown between the PLO and Hamas who vowed to pursue their goal of a Palestine state from the Jordan River to the sea, i.e. driving the Israelis out of Israel, by violent means. In elections for chambers of commerce, university councils, and the Palestine legislative council, Hamas and Islamists took on the PLO, and often prevailed. On several occasions, during 1994 and 1995, the PA police opened fire on Hamas-backed demonstrators and jailed Islamist leaders and militants. The PA and the PLO were incapable of controlling the violent rejectionists in their midst and were unwilling to risk all-out civil war (Kepel 2002: chapter 14).

The first act of spoiler violence was the suicidal killing by a lone Israeli settler (Baruch Goldstein, a member of the extremist Koch party) of 30 Muslim worshippers in the Tomb of the Patriarchs, a mosque in Hebron. Rabin refused the Palestinian demand for the removal of the 400 militant Israeli settlers from the heart of Hebron. After an interruption, the peace process continued with agreement on transfers of control in Jericho and Gaza, but Hamas and its militant allies vowed revenge for the Hebron massacre with the October 20 Hamas suicide bomb attack killing 22 in Tel Aviv and another Islamic Jihad suicide bomb attack killing 21 in Netanya. Because of the Hamas/Islamic Jihad suicide bomb campaign inside Israel, the Israeli public failed to get a security benefit from the peace process: to the contrary, the intifada had spilled over from the Occupied Territories into Israel itself. From 10 to 20 yearly deaths from political violence in Israel in 1990–4, the figures had risen to 51 in 1995 (B'tselem 2002). Each Palestinian attack generated its own Israeli tit-for-tat retaliations, such as border closings, detentions, arrests, and other modes of collective punishment which made Oslo a turbulent peace process. In a few short months, the earlier pattern of coercive moves by the adversaries was restored and threatened to undo the conciliatory pattern of the Oslo process. Violence continued and, to placate the Israeli nationalist and religious right, settlement expansion continued. Predictably it weakened the good will Prime Minister Rabin had earned among Palestinians.

Still, the Oslo process had acquired a certain momentum. Oslo B, the next interim peace agreement, was signed on September 28, 1995 and started the transfer of Israeli control in the Occupied Territories to the Palestinians, prisoner release, and other cooperative exchanges. The aftermath of Oslo B was the high point of support for and optimism about the Oslo peace process among both Palestinians and Israelis. Eighty percent of Palestinians approved the peace process, and only 20 percent approved violence against Israel. For Israelis, the Oslo Peace Index (measuring approval of Oslo and belief that it would result in peace) rose from the 40s and 50s into the 60s (Shikaki 1998; "Peace Index" 2003). Thereafter there was an erosion in support for the peace process in both populations punctured by some temporary increases in response to further agreements and the opening of the Camp David peace talks in the summer of 2000.

The hope and good will generated from Oslo B received several shocks. The first was the assassination of Rabin by a Jewish religious rejectionist. The second was the Hamas and Islamic Jihad suicide bomb campaign within Israel (February/March 1996), which led to border closings and other social control measures and the suspension of transfers of Palestinian territory and population to Palestinian control by Prime Minister Simon Peres, who had succeeded Rabin. The third was the Likud victory in the Israeli election (May 29, 1996), a predictable reaction to the suicide bombings. Benjamin Netanyahu became prime minister in no small part because security in Israel itself had worsened.

As Netanyahu had vowed to do, his government slowed and obstructed the peace process. He relaxed restrictions on settlement expansion, which precipitated Palestinian protest strikes, followed by civil strife over a tunnel opened next to the Temple Mount that led to rioting and the death of 15 Israeli soldiers and 80 Palestinians, and a deadly three-day battle in Nablus over control of Joseph's Tomb, a disputed religious site. In that confrontation, six IDF soldiers and 55 Palestinians were killed, and Palestinian police joined Palestinians against the Israeli army, which had to use tanks to prevail. At this point the peace process would have been ready for burial had it not been for a crisis summit called by President Clinton (29 September 1996) which barely salvaged it with an agreement on the Hebron redeployment. A zone for 160,000 Palestinian inhabitants received 80 percent of Hebron, and an Israeli zone under IDF protection got the other 20 percent for 450 Jewish settlers. When a Jewish settler opened fire in a Hebron market on Palestinians, spoiler violence actually backfired in as much as negative Israeli public reaction and international condemnation of the shootings swayed Knesset and cabinet approval for the Hebron agreement.

Shortly thereafter, the Netanyahu government became embroiled in a domestic crisis that could have led to Prime Minister Netanyahu's impeachment. To mollify the nationalist and religious hardliners in his coalition, and at the expense of the peace process, he announced settlement expansion at Har Homa for 6,500 housing units and 32,000 future settlers. The Palestinians responded with predictable protest strikes (three Palestinians were killed and 500 injured in the anti-Har Homa construction protests), the international community responded with a predictable UN Security Council resolution that condemned the construction, the US responded with a predictable veto of the resolution, Hamas predictably resumed suicide bombing in Israel, and the Israelis responded with the equally predictable border closings, stopping of revenue transfers, hunts for terrorists, and suspension or slowdown of the Oslo peace process. All these moves had become the ritualized repertoire of Israeli–Palestinian relations. Under US pressure, the Wye One and Wye Two agreements resumed the peace process following a one-and-a-half-year suspension. They provided for Israeli withdrawal from 13 percent more of the West Bank (giving the Palestinians full or partial control of 40 percent of the West Bank), and set a timetable for final status negotiations. After an initial pull-out, the Netanyahu government suspended implementation of Wye because of disagreements on interpretations of what had actually been agreed to. Land confiscation for settlements and roads continued.

The Camp David final status negotiations

The internal political dynamics of the two adversaries were damaging to the peace process, as Senator George Mitchell later remarked (2002). Process was blocking outcome. Neither adversary was a unitary actor; each was deeply divided. Good faith implementation of interim agreements was doubted, and uncertainty shrouded all agreements. Internal domestic difficulties of the PA over corruption and the falling standard of living led Arafat and Fatah to accommodation with the rejectionist wing of the Palestinian movement, and signaled to the Israelis Palestinian duplicity and non-compliance on the foremost security issue of suicide bombings. Rejectionist violence cost the Palestinians enormously because of Israeli countermoves: lost income from border closings; lost revenue from tax transfer freezes; suspensions of the Oslo process and thus transfers of population and territory to the Palestine Authority; arrests, detentions, deportations, house demolitions, injuries, and deaths. The fact that violence continued during the Oslo process, in fact against the Oslo process, and escalated to suicide bombing attacks in Israel itself demonstrated to the Israelis how difficult it was for the Palestinian movement to break with its history of violence and terrorism and how ambivalent the PA and chairman Arafat were on suppressing the rejectionists. How was a peace agreement under these circumstances going to result in actual peace? In a major Israeli opinion survey on the peace process in 1996, only 33 percent of the respondents believed that a peace agreement would bring a true, lasting peace (Segal *et al.* 2000: 19).

Internal domestic difficulties of the Israeli governments over holding a Knesset majority coalition and dealing with the nationalist and religious right were the motor behind settlement expansion, access road building, and lenient social control of settler violence and land occupations. To the Palestinians these policies and actions signaled Israeli uncertainty and bad faith on the final status borders, viability, and independence of the future Palestinian state. Stopping and especially rolling back settlement expansion would have earned the Israeli government international support, diminished protests and incidents that led to cycles of violence, and demonstrated good faith on final status talks. The fact that despite these benefits the settlement policy was unchanged indicated to the Palestinians the extent to which Israeli governments were hostage to the Likud, nationalist, and religious hardliners opposed to any Palestinian state.

Despite non-conciliatory moves in the peace process and turmoil in the Occupied Territories, conflict-related Palestinian deaths reached an all-time yearly low of eight in 1999. The security situation in Israel also improved with only one conflict-related death in 1998 and one in 1999. Low death figures did not translate into public opinion support for the peace process and an expectation of peace, because protests and violent resistance against the occupation in the OTs continued on a daily basis. When Barak became prime minister after the May 17, 1999 elections, the situation he faced was visually depicted in newspapers and on websites with a multicolored map of the West Bank whose complexity defied comprehension: settlements, out-posts, military bases, access roads, bypass roads, checkpoints, areas under Palestinian control, under Israeli control, under joint control, areas to be transferred in future negotiations, etc. reveal a Byzantine mosaic suited for

an abstract painting but questionable for an atlas (Enderlin 2003: 238ff.).
A multitude of Israeli–Palestinian interfaces had high risk of daily clashes
between Palestinians, settlers, and the IDF.

Prime Minister Barak had campaigned on making final status peace with
the Palestinians, Lebanon, and Syria, in one huge peace effort. In the head-
to-head election for prime minister, Barak got 56 percent to Netanyahu's
44 percent, an impressive victory. The Knesset results showed a more
polarized electorate. Both Labor and Likud lost seats; the main gainers were
the extreme right and the extreme left, the Shas and Meretz. Barak formed
a Labor-led coalition government with them and with Sharansky's Russian
language party, which amounted to an internally divided team on core peace
issues and on settlements. The head of the NRP party became minister of
construction, and settlement expansion planning and construction continued
and actually exceeded the Netanyahu record. Barak's campaign promises
– the four "Nos" – to the Israeli public, later reiterated to the Knesset, were
not helpful in the prelude to Camp David (Enderlin 2003: 112):

1   no to any change for unified Jerusalem under Israeli sovereignty, as the
    eternal capital of Israel;
2   no withdrawal to the 1967 borders (the Green Line);
3   most settlement dwellers in Judea and Samaria to remain under Israeli
    sovereignty;
4   no foreign army west of the Jordan River.

For his part, Arafat told President Clinton "Jerusalem must be the capital
of the two states, and there can be no peace if Jerusalem is not the capital of
the two states" (Enderlin 2003: 163).

In preparatory talks, there were huge differences on procedure and on
substance. Arafat wanted continuation of redeployments under Oslo B
and the Wye accords, whereas Barak wanted final status negotiations first.
On territory and borders the Israelis offered 66 percent, later 78 percent, as
a start, and the Palestinians wanted 96 percent with 4 percent offset by
territory swaps. On refugees, according to Abed Rabbo, "The Israelis didn't
want to hear about a 'right of return.' But only about 'family reunification'
. . . today there are almost no families in need of reunification" (Enderlin
2003: 124–46). In the end a "Framework Agreement on Permanent Status"
was drafted, leaving core issues unresolved. Abu Ala stated "on the core
topics there are no points of agreement." Arafat said to President Clinton,
to Secretary of State Madeleine Albright, and to Israeli cabinet minister
Shlomo Ben Ami that "it was much too soon to organize the Camp David
summit," "we need a lot of preparation," and "we're not ready, we haven't
talked about Jerusalem or the refugee issue." Sandy Berger, Clinton's
National Security Advisor, reports that "Arafat has lost all trust in Ehud
Barak . . . we aren't against a summit, but it is ten to one it will end in
failure" and suggested further steps that had failed earlier (Enderlin 2003:

162–9). Arafat threatened to unilaterally proclaim an independent Palestine state on September 13, 2000. Barak's coalition government fell apart when the NRP, the Shas, and Sharansky's party quit the government. On July 10, a day before the Camp David summit opened, the Knesset passed a motion of censure against Barak: he ceased to have a majority in the Israeli legislature. The summit started with mostly strikes against it.

Barak believed that further delay worked against peace making because the occupation in the OTs and increasing Palestinian resistance risked another insurgency. As he told *Newsweek* on November 8, 1999: "I was elected telling people I am going to physically separate us and the Palestinians in order to encourage cooperation, mutual respect and trust." The final status talks had been repeatedly postponed owing to suspensions in the Oslo process and more such delays were likely. External pressure from President Clinton, who wanted a foreign policy success before leaving office (or being forced out by impeachment), was also a factor. As for Arafat who was reluctant to engage in final status talks without preliminary understandings on substantive issues in informal contacts with the Israelis, he feared that, if an agreement was first reached between Israel and Syria over the Golan Heights, it would weaken the Palestinians' bargaining position. With a deteriorating standard of living and mass protests in the OTs against the occupation such as the May 15–18 Palestinian Days of Rage, he knew that Hamas and Islamists were gaining at the expense of the PLO and the PA, and he needed an initiative that put him back in the driver's seat.

The agenda of the Camp David talks on July 11–25 was clear cut: two states, Israel and Palestine, were to recognize each other's existence and live in peace, and were both to be recognized by all states, including all Arab states. Borders had to be agreed on. The status and partial evacuation of Israeli settlers in the OTs had to be negotiated. The Israeli claim on all Jerusalem as its capital and the Palestinian claim on East Jerusalem as its capital had to be compromised. The status of the holy places, in particular the Temple Mount and the Western Wall, had to be decided. Palestine refugee return rights and claims had to be dealt with. A number of lesser yet important issues premised on resolution of the already listed ones, such as water resource allocation, airport location and overflight rights, security issues and limitations on the Palestinian military and its weaponry, a connecting corridor between the West Bank and Gaza, and the like, also had to be settled (ICG 2002).

President Clinton thought a peace accord was doable. After it failed he still believed that any future peace settlement would be very much like the proposals at Camp David/Taba that were not agreed to (Clinton 2004: 945). Senator George Mitchell, head of the commission to investigate the causes of the al-Aqsa intifada, agreed in a television interview (2002):

> One of the tragedies of the deaths that are occurring now [during the al-Aqsa intifada] is that if you talk to Palestinians and Israelis, and I talk

to them all the time, to government officials and private citizens, there is a consensus on both sides about the way it's going to end.

Interviewer: How do you think it is going to end?

Mitchell: It's going to end just about the way President Clinton outlined before he left office in January of 2001 . . . and that is about where it is going to end. It is the only way to end, and people recognize that. Despite all the turmoil, violence, conflict, a steady majority of two thirds of Israelis and Palestinians believe that the only way out of this is through a negotiated two-state solution. It is the only way.

Failure of the Oslo process

What actually happened at Camp David, and why no agreement was reached, has been fiercely contested by the participants and by commentators. Blame for the breakdown of the peace process, which extended beyond Camp David to subsequent talks at Taba where the offers and counteroffers narrowed some of the Camp David differences, has generated an enormous literature based on interviews, insider accounts, scholarly analysis, and self-serving statements (Pressman 2003). Since not only Israeli, Palestinian, and US participants disagree, but participants within each camp, such as Dennis Ross and Robert Malley who had played key roles in Middle East conflict management for years, I will focus on the deeper causes of the failure which stemmed from the dynamics of the entire Oslo process rather than on the personalities of the Camp David negotiators.

They were not even a firm offer put into writing, but a set of American proposals subject to a variety of interpretations. Israel was to annex 9 percent of the West Bank, presumably in addition to the already annexed East Jerusalem, where most of the Israeli settlers lived, in exchange for a fraction of that area in unspecified locations in Israel. Nothing specific was discussed on the refugee issue. As for East Jerusalem, there would be Palestinian sovereignty over many Arab neighborhoods and over the Muslim and Christian quarter of the Old City, custody but no sovereignty of the Haram al Sharif (Temple Mount), which was the status quo, and Israel would retain sovereignty over some East Jerusalem Arab neighborhoods. It was not made clear whether the Palestinian Jerusalem segments would be contiguous and have access to the rest of the West Bank, free of Israeli controls. On this score, Khalil Shikaki said in an interview that:

> The Palestinian public will not tolerate less than full sovereignty over all East Jerusalem, including the Haram al Sharif. Palestinians will not tolerate Israeli border police and Israeli checkpoints. That is not sovereignty, that is control. Palestinians no longer want to ask Israel for permission to build their houses, to educate their children, to live their lives.
>
> (Sontag 2000)

In the Clinton compromise formulae for East Jerusalem and the holy places, there are many euphemisms falling short of sovereignty: "degrees of sovereignty," "a sense of sovereignty," "virtually full sovereignty," and probably others that did not guarantee "immunity from external interference in domestic authority," the benchmark of Westphalian sovereignty defining stateness.

Had there been more trust on both sides, between negotiators as well as the people they represented, there might have been an agreement. But during the entire Oslo process, Palestinian rejectionist violence and Israeli settlement expansion poisoned the fragile good will from episodic conciliation. Further talks at Taba where the Israelis sweetened their offer were overshadowed by the Sharon Temple Mount incursion and the start of the second (al-Aqsa) intifada. It amounted to a massive uprising against Israeli occupation, and was answered by massive IDF repression. By the time Camp David started, the negotiators, Israelis and Palestinians, profoundly mistrusted one another and doubted each other's good faith. Their vocabularies and cognitive maps were opposites. For Israelis, surrendering land in the West Bank to the Palestinians was a "concession"; to the Palestinians, "getting back" what had all along belonged to them was no concession at all. Was the West Bank a "liberated" or an "occupied" territory? What are the boundaries of Jerusalem? Are the Israeli inhabitants of East Jerusalem housing estates "settlers"? Are suicide bombers "terrorists" or "martyrs"? The negotiating teams as well as the US mediators came away with differing interpretations of Camp David: Israelis believed they had conceded 95 percent of what the Palestinians had wanted, and the Palestinians believed they had been offered a dependent and unviable ("Swiss cheese") truncated state. Such mistrust and cognitive disconnects had increased despite hopes of a peace settlement among many Israelis and Palestinians.

The Oslo process was slow, piecemeal, step by step, taking years. Prime Minister Rabin thought there would be peace within six to nine months following Oslo A, a colossal underestimate. As the process slowed, Palestinians were getting disillusioned with lack of results and worsening living conditions, while Israel increased the number of West Bank settlers from 116,000 in 1993 to about 200,000 in 2000. Lengthening the peace process made for accumulation and aggravation of issues. Suicide bombers and other terrorist acts worsened security for Israelis within Israel itself. Confidence in the peace process and a peaceful outcome was undermined for most Israelis and Palestinians when the political leaders on both sides were hostage to their extremists. The public opinion data indicate that a six-month window of opportunity existed after Oslo B in 1995 for a concentrated peace thrust such as Prime Minister Barak mounted four years later under far less favorable circumstances. The opportunity was missed ("Peace Index" 2003; Shikaki 2002).

The Oslo process lacked transparency. Contentious core issues (Jerusalem, refugees) were left to the final status negotiations and purposely left vague.

Arafat's "right of refugee return" was not spelled out, and left the existence of Israel clouded in uncertainty. Vagueness on East Jerusalem, its boundaries, its sovereignty, its access roads to the West Bank, and south-to-north territorial linkage on the West Bank raised questions of just how viable any Palestinian state would be.

There was an asymmetry of power. According to Timothy Sisk, "asymmetry in power relationship is a high risk to productive conflict management" (1996: 81). Israel was under less pressure to make concessions since the status quo was quite acceptable to many Israelis. The outcome of such bargaining is not likely to satisfy the weaker party. One way for the weaker side to reduce the asymmetry of power and try for a better outcome is to create a high cost to the other player through civil unrest and violence, which is what the Palestinians kept doing. It got them a destructive stalemate instead of a stronger bargaining position (1996: 82). Derivative and security issues from continued violence derailed progress on core issues. There was also lack of symmetry in the "land for peace" exchange. Control of land from Israeli redeployments was tangible; peace is a promise. Israel wanted a visible indication of that promise with a crackdown on Palestinian violence by the PA.

There was insufficient pressure by external states with real clout to penalize the parties for failure to agree. The United States was not an impartial mediator but a partisan ally of Israel that kept up a steady stream of financial, military, and diplomatic support for Israel regardless of verbal condemnation and threats on various occasions. The Arab states, on their part, and the European Union and the United Nations kept financing the Palestinians regardless of violent Palestinian actions against the peace process. Had the United States withheld all support from Israel, and had the Arab states withheld all support from the Palestinians, external pressure for peace in the Middle East might have been effective. Because of the domestic politics of the US and the Arab states and their foreign policy goals, they did not apply decisive pressure.

Both adversaries had "agency" problems. Neither was (or is) a unitary actor, and that fueled the mobilization paradox. Both sides were hostage to their rejectionists who did not want a peace agreement founded on two independent states. Given internal divisions, the "negotiating process is vulnerable to outbidders who oppose accommodation" (Sisk 1996: 82). The security response of the Israeli government against violence weakened the Palestinian moderates vis-à-vis the rejectionists. And the violence of the Palestinian rejectionists weakened conciliatory Israeli groups and augmented support for the nationalist and religious hardliners and the Likud right wing. The principals in such negotiations kept appeasing their extremists lest they be ousted from leadership by rejectionist rivals. And they hesitated repressing their extremists for fear of igniting internal civil strife.

Acceptance and feasibility of a peace accord were problematic. Had the two sides agreed on a deal somewhere between the most generous offer and the concessions that were made, the Likud, the religious and nationalist parties in the Knesset, and a large segment of the Israeli public (in a referendum) were not likely to have voted for it. In Israel, acceptance of the Oslo process fell from the upper 50s on the Peace Index in 1996 to the mid-30s in 2000 ("Peace Index" 2003). In 1996, the peace process had the most public support, yet two-thirds of the Israeli public did not believe that a peace agreement would bring a true, lasting peace. Of these, two out of three rejected a compromise on Jerusalem, i.e. Palestinian sovereignty in Arab East Jerusalem (Segal *et al.* 2000: 19). Palestinian acceptance was also uncertain. Expectations of a peace settlement had sunk to 24 percent from a high of 80 percent in early 1996, and approval of violence against the occupation had risen from a low of 20 percent in 1996 to 86 percent in 2001 (Shikaki 2002).

As for feasibility, armed Palestinian militias hostile to a peace treaty would have to be disarmed and their fighters integrated into an economy already high on unemployment and rife with corruption. Several thousand settlers would have to be relocated to Israel, many against their will. With Gush Emunim supporters obstructing coercive removal of settlers, there was a great risk of civil disorder in Israel. The settlers would require financial compensation and other expenses amounting to a huge sum of money; the compensation scheme for the Palestinian refugees would total several billion dollars, probably to come from external sources. On top of these funds, the Palestinian state would start as a bankrupt and economically devastated entity requiring billions in investment to jump-start it. A RAND Corporation study (2005) estimated a capital investment of $33 billion for the first ten years of a Palestinian state. A Camp David peace treaty would have severe implementation problems.

The aftermath of the failed Oslo peace process

After the failure of Camp David, the conflict became far more violent than during the Oslo process. To what extent the al-Aqsa intifada was a spontaneous uprising or was provoked by Ariel Sharon's controversial walk accompanied by hundreds of Israeli police on September 28, 2000 on the Temple Mount will remain debated but does not alter the fact that the peace process had broken down in the minds of many Palestinians and Israelis. Whatever else it meant to accomplish, Sharon's walk symbolized Israel's claim to sovereignty over the Temple Mount in the context of incompatible sovereignty claims which were one of the causes of failure of the summit.

What began as youth throwing stones and some shootings the next day turned into a major insurgency with armed ambushes, car bombs, and suicide bombers, and was answered with border closings, mass arrests, sieges of Arab cities, targeted killings, and other counterinsurgency operations. Israeli deaths in Israel had been 1.5 per month during Oslo and rose to 7.1 per month during the al-Aqsa intifada (September 29, 2000 to February

15, 2006, the latest figures available), with a high of 26.8 per month in early 2002. There were 138 suicide bombs exploded from September 2000 to September 2004. Two-thirds of the 916 Israelis killed were civilians. Palestinians killed by Israeli security forces in the OTs were 3,318, or 52.8 per month, of which 213 were targeted killings (calculated from data in B'tselem (2006). The impact of deaths and injuries on the Israeli and Palestinian publics goes far beyond the actual numbers: one has to grasp the apprehension besetting routine everyday activities, and visualize the daily violent television fare, the unending funerals, and fears about boarding buses and shopping in markets, or just being in the wrong place at the wrong time.

Prime Minister Ariel Sharon convinced many Israelis that there was no credible Palestinian partner for peace, and that a unilateral, Israeli-imposed, and enforced separation of Israelis and Palestinians was the only realistic solution to their predicament. In a wide-ranging set of interviews with Ari Shavit, Sharon stated and explained his views:

> The conflict isn't between us and the Palestinians. The conflict is between us and the Arab world . . . It may be that we will never have peace, and it may be that it will take a great many years . . . The greatest danger is in signing some document and believing that as a result we will have peace. This is not going to happen

and "deterrence is what enables us to live here. This is how it was in the past, this is the way it is in the present, and this is also the way it will be in the future" (Shavit 2006). Sharon's separation plan consisted of a physical barrier on the West Bank that would be the de facto border with Israel, annexation of about 10 percent of its territory into Israel, including the five largest settlement blocs (actually cities) and the eastern portions of Jerusalem, sovereignty over the Temple Mount, continued Jewish presence in Hebron, strategic Israeli withdrawal from the Gaza Strip (completed), ceded to the Palestinians together with some vulnerable West Bank settlements, and east of the barrier a demilitarized Palestinian state, "security zones" in the Jordan valley, and Israeli control of water resources (Shavit 2006; *NYT*, April 13, 2004). Ehud Olmert, the acting prime minister following Sharon's heart attacks and coma, has affirmed the Sharon plan in its essentials as the platform for their new Kadima party, and contested the March 28 elections on that basis (*NYT*, March 10, 2006.) On the Palestinian side, Hamas, the winner of the legislative elections on January 26, 2006, holds that the entire land of Palestine, which includes Israel, belongs to Allah and is a Muslim holy land, considers the Oslo process agreements null and void, and is dedicated to the destruction of Israel (*NYT*, January 29 and February 1, 2006). The state of Israel–Palestinian relations is back to what it was before the Oslo process in 1993; actually it is worse now than at that time because of the additional bloodshed and shattered hopes from Oslo's failure.

6 The peace process in Northern Ireland

What the conflict is about

Starting in 1968, the Catholic civil rights movement for equality in Northern Ireland, its coercive reception by the Unionist government and Protestants, and armed Republican insurgency against the British Army and government set the stage for almost 30 years of violence, insurgency, terrorism, and counterinsurgency known as "the Troubles." The Troubles were a complex mixture of conventional electoral politics, peaceful marches and demonstrations, huge public gatherings and protests such as the Orange Order parades and the Ulster Workers' Council strike, communal rioting and ethnic cleansing at sectarian interfaces of Protestant and Catholic residential areas, prison hunger strikes, terrorist shootings and bombings by paramilitaries, house searches, the internment of terrorist suspects, and other collective reprisals typical in counterinsurgency. In conflict and conciliation processes, parallel to and interspersed with violence and coercion there are varied peace-making initiatives for opening channels of communication between the adversaries, for a ceasefire, for an agreement on procedures for peace talks, and for peace negotiations themselves, and that was also true for the Troubles. Some were overt, others "backdoor"; some were conducted by advisors and lower-echelon officials, others by the prime ministers of the UK and Republic of Ireland (Eire); and some were negotiations among political leaders chaired by mediators.

Given the history of Anglo-Irish relations, it was inevitable that a challenge to Protestant domination in Northern Ireland and the demand for equality of citizenship by Catholics would make stateness the core issue in short order: shall Northern Ireland remain part of the UK as unionists were determined it should, or shall it become the northern part of a united Ireland, as nationalists wanted. Over the stateness issue in Ireland two bloody civil wars had already been fought in the twentieth century: the Irish nationalist insurgency against the UK started with the Easter Rising in Dublin in 1916, then the Irish Republican Army (IRA) insurgency against the Irish Free State over the Anglo-Irish Treaty to partition the island when the six northern counties with a Protestant majority – Ulster – remained in the UK.

At the start of the Troubles, preferences on stateness were clear. In 1968, 76 percent of Catholics considered themselves Irish, and 71 percent of Protestants identified themselves as British and 84 percent were opposed to a united Ireland (Boyle and Hadden 1994: 59–62; Rose 1971). Moreover, 82 percent of Protestants approved "the right for people in the North to take up arms . . . and to fight to keep Northern Ireland British." Although the adversaries are frequently referred to as Protestants and Catholics, and the conflict as "sectarian," it is more accurate to designate them as unionists and nationalists, which highlights the stateness issue. Nevertheless, in conformity with usage, I will retain "sectarian" in addition to ethnic, and use religious as well as political designations for the adversaries.

Religious dogma, freedom of worship, and other religious issues are not disputed in Northern Ireland. Unlike Bosnia where churches and mosques and religious monuments were blown up, they were not targeted in the Troubles. The religious terminology stems from the pre-modern origins and history of the Irish–English conflict when ethnic and proto-national adversaries in Europe were designated by the dominant religion of their ethnic group and of their state. There is a religious and cultural dimension to the antagonism between the two groups, which reverts to the historic conflicts between European states – France and Spain associated with Roman Catholicism and England with Protestantism. When the Protestant leader and firebrand Reverend Ian Paisley orates on "Home rule" being equal to "Rome rule," he draws on the history of anti-Popery discourse in England and in Ulster. But his rhetoric is not about religious freedom and toleration, the core of the seventeenth-century religious conflicts which is commemorated in his Belfast church, the Church of the Martyrs, with busts of Protestant leaders and clergymen persecuted by the Church and Catholic states in the Reformation. It is rather an emotional threat and fear discourse aimed at contemporary unionists on the danger to the Protestant-English heritage and way of life posed by a united Ireland and the historical association of Irish nationalism with Irish Catholicism (Alcock 2002).

A better analogy to the Northern Ireland conflict is privileged European settler societies in colonies dominating indigenous peoples: Europeans in Southern Africa and French people in Quebec and later in Algeria, and Jewish settlers in Palestine. The Protestants colonized Ireland from the seventeenth to the nineteenth centuries, or were "planted" there in the vocabulary of the time, starting about the same time that other English Protestants planted themselves in New England and Virginia, when the French colonized Quebec, and when Dutch Protestants started colonizing the Cape region in South Africa. To justify their "planting," the European migrants constructed collective myths. The Protestant settlers invoked the biblical imagery of migration to the Promised Land for fulfilling God's design for a New Jerusalem that will be a model to mankind, whereas the French articulated their civilizing mission ("mission civilizatrice") for non-European peoples. Each of these settler societies developed some unique features. In Northern

Ireland in the 1960s both adversaries possessed a threatened minority mentality – the Catholics because they were a minority in Northern Ireland, and the Protestants because they would become a minority in a united Ireland. Both groups had developed a siege mentality – a response to these perceived threats – and considered themselves the principal victims in their relationship, the Catholics because of discrimination and second-class citizenship and the Protestants because of violence targeting them and fear of abandonment by the UK (Mitchell 1999: 13). Commenting on these states of mind, Seamus Mallon, the former Deputy First Minister of the Assembly, said "the UK does not want us; Eire does not either" (author interview, Belfast, July 10, 2003). For Patrick Mayhew, the Secretary of State for Northern Ireland in 1992–7, "Protestants fear the UK will abandon them; Catholics fear that the UK will surrender to the Protestants' demands" (author interview, London, June 24, 2003). Threat, fear, and victimhood are a triple obstacle for conciliation in a divided society.

The Troubles

The Troubles had three major clusters of collective violence and three principal peace initiatives. The first cluster started with the civil rights campaign of 1968 to 1972, a huge mobilizing venture for the Nationalist population and for Unionist countermobilization. It ended with the first major British peace and reform plan at Sunningdale in 1973 whose implementation was blocked by the 1974 election outcome and a massive Unionist Ulster Workers' Council strike in 1974. The second cluster was fueled by opposition to British counterinsurgency measures such as internment and support for the hunger strike of Republican detainees in prisons, which rallied Catholics behind the insurgency against the authorities. The British and Irish governments undertook the second major peace initiative that resulted in the Anglo-Irish Agreement (AIA) in 1985 which was torpedoed by a massive Unionist non-cooperation campaign and Republican and Loyalist violence. The third cluster of violence was the intensification of the IRA bombing campaign in 1990–3 in Northern Ireland and Britain, including a mortar shell that nearly missed Prime Minister Major and his cabinet during a meeting at 10 Downing Street. Nevertheless, a third and persistent, albeit slow "on again, off again," peace initiative started with the secret John Hume–Gerry Adams talks and the Downing Street Declaration (DSD) in December 1993 and ended with the Northern Ireland Peace Agreement (NIPA) in Belfast on Good Friday, April 10, 1998, signed by both the UK and Eire and all but one of the major political parties, followed by ratification in two referenda separately by the voters of Northern Ireland and of the Irish Republic, and the installation of a power sharing government in December.

As measured by annual political deaths, political violence waxed and waned with the major episodes of collective action, yet also took on a dynamic of its own with tit-for-tat Republican–Loyalist paramilitary shootings, tit-for-tat shootings of Catholic and Protestant civilian bystanders, murders of suspected informants, bombings, and shootings between British security forces and the Provisional IRA (the Provos, here referred to as the IRA) and its various offshoots. The coincidence of internment and unionist opposition to the Sunningdale Agreement marks the highest level of annual deaths from 1972 to 1976, with more than 200 a year and peaking with 467 in 1972 ("annualdeaths," www.cain.ulst.ac.uk/events/index.html). Thereafter in most years deaths declined below 100, and below 20 in 2000 and 2001 after NIPA.

As I described in Chapter 2, the British authorities deployed a formidable security apparatus against the insurgents. The shootings and casualty figures did diminish during the 1980s, but the security response did not end the insurgency. Indeed one would not have expected that in view of the coercion paradox. According to Fintan O'Toole, "the IRA has been the most effective terrorist organization in the world. A huge apparatus of repression (British troops, electronic surveillance, internment without trial, covert special forces, networks of informants) contained it, but did not defeat it" (2002: 14). To the end, the IRA maintained a terrorist bombing capability throughout the UK.

Throughout the Troubles, sectarian mobilization and polarization continued in response to coercive events and in frequent elections. From 1969 to 1999, there were four elections to the Northern Ireland Assembly, eight Westminster (UK) elections, five elections to the European Parliament, seven district council elections, ten by-elections and two special elections (Constitutional Convention, Forum), and a referendum on NIPA. As was true for Yugoslavia and other divided societies caught in stateness crises, elections tend to become an ethnic census that favors the hardliners and rejectionists over the moderates who try to forge a cross-ethnic compromise and political party (Snyder 2000: chapter 7). Public manifestations of sectarian solidarity such as the annual Orange Order parades and the display of sectarian flags, sectarian curb coloring, graffiti, and paramilitary murals, signaled and reaffirmed the dichotomous division in Northern Ireland. Dominic Bryan's research (2001: 43–4) on Orange parades found that the "blood and thunder" marching bands of Protestant working-class youth, some with links to Loyalist paramilitaries, enact an intentionally provocative symbolic sectarian repertoire with flags, banners, songs, and music closely tied to the political culture of antagonism, territorial control, and Protestant domination. These parades occasion clashes between these youths and Catholic residents along contested routes, and between the youth and the police when the parades are banned or rerouted, and attract violent partisans from both sides who join the rioting. In addition, talks, debates, and declarations on policy proposals and peace initiatives gave political leaders lots of opportunities for hostile rhetoric and for staking out intransigent positions in public. In keeping with the mobilization paradox in peace processes, on the verbal front as on the action front, the public was flooded with non-conciliatory messages. In both the Catholic and the Protestant communities, the political rivalries and mobilization between moderates and rejectionists, the hostility and mistrust between the two principal adversaries, and the antagonism of both adversaries towards the British government kept feeding on the stream of elections and violence.

The adversaries and their strategies

There were six major players in the peace process: the *UK* and *Eire*; the *Nationalists* and the *Republicans* on the Catholic side; and the *Unionists* divided also into a more *conciliatory* group and a diehard, no-change *rejectionist* group. The two principal adversaries were divided on the core issue of stateness. In a nutshell, Nationalists wanted a united Ireland. The constitutional nationalists, led by John Hume in the Social Democratic Labour Party (SDLP), sought that goal by non-violent democratic means. The Republicans, led by Gerry Adams in Sinn Fein and their allied military arm, the IRA, sought it through coercive means, with the IRA employing a "Brits out" bombing and shooting strategy. On the Unionist side, the more moderate Ulster Unionist Party (UUP) under the leadership of David Trimble was willing to compromise on reforms and on power sharing but opposed change on stateness. The rejectionist cluster of Unionist political parties led by the Democratic Unionist Party (DUP) and its most extreme advocate the Reverend Ian Paisley were firmly opposed to any change at all. They wanted to maintain total UK sovereignty unconditionally and rejected power sharing with nationalists.

Other core issues stemmed from the non-violent civil rights movement for equality and for an end to discrimination in housing, employment, policing, and justice. Although some reforms were enacted under British direct rule, e.g. the Fair Employment Act of 1976 and the Standing Advisory Commission on Human Rights in 1973, power sharing in governance, police reform, and minority protection and access remained core issues. Kevin Boyle and Tom Hadden report that "statistical evidence on voting patterns in Northern Ireland [shows that] in terms of political solidarity the two communities were more clearly defined and stable in their allegiances than in other comparably divided societies in Europe" (1994: 54). Given the reality of sectarian voting in Northern Ireland and the difficulty of forming a cross-ethnic centrist party and voting, demonstrated by the Alliance Party's limited success, the major electoral competitor, and thus also the major competitor for political office and power, resided within each community: Sinn Fein against SDLP among nationalists, and DUP and other diehard unionist parties against UUP and allies among unionists. The more extremist parties and blocs engaged in a sectarian "outbidding" strategy against the more moderate ones within their own community.

The goal of the UK government was first and foremost to end the insurgency and the violence, and to do that it chose a security strategy that in time became full-fledged counterinsurgency. It had been in favor of internal reform on equality and economic issues for some time before the Troubles started, and had backed the moderate Unionists' reform attempts in the early 1960s under the Northern Irish Prime Minister Terrence O'Neill, but his reforms failed. The lack of change became the impetus behind the Catholic civil rights movement. On stateness, initially, the UK stuck with the status quo because it did not want to awaken unionist apprehensions about abandonment by the UK. Nevertheless, when the security strategy failed to suppress the Republican insurgency, the British government started exploring changes on stateness that might be acceptable to Unionists and to the Irish government.

The most antagonistic relationship in the conflict was between Sinn Fein and the IRA against the UK, with both using violent means until the mid-1990s. They expected the British government to quit Northern Ireland rather than keep sustaining losses from terrorism. The UK also had an adversary relationship to unionists because without the consent of a substantial majority of them there could be no peace. The unionists' weapons against the British government were massive protests and strikes that brought the province to a standstill, and electing rejectionist legislators who gridlocked government and blocked change. The message was the same: without unionist consent, the province is ungovernable and peace unattainable.

The UK government's positions and policies were constrained in other ways as well. Northern Ireland, minus the Troubles, was of little consequence to the government and to British public opinion. Peter Brooke, the Northern Ireland Secretary, admitted in an important 1990 speech that "the British government has no selfish strategic or economic interest in Northern Ireland" (Mallie and McKittrick 2001: 83). With the Troubles, it was a liability for Britain's standing in international opinion, a £4-billion-a-year financial drain for economic subsidies and security, and terrorist danger within Britain itself. The overrepresentation of Northern Ireland voters in Westminster gave Unionists undue influence on British politics and public affairs when the Tories were in power with Unionists' support. Moreover, how the British government handled the stateness issue might have repercussions for constitutional changes in Wales and Scotland.

Nor could a British government, whether Labour or Conservative, simply withdraw unilaterally from the Troubles without provoking a huge Protestant insurgency and Loyalist terrorism which would plunge the province into more civil war, with a risk of international war should the Irish government intervene to rescue Catholics from massacres and ethnic cleansing. Patrick Mayhew was explicit: "if we [the UK] gave up Northern Ireland to Eire, civil war would break out" (author interview, London, June 24, 2003). There was also a "kith and kin" factor that was important for British national pride as a people of substance with moral values, strong sentiments that supported Prime Minister Thatcher's decision to defend the Falkland inhabitants against the Argentine invasion. Britain did not abandon people who were British and wanted to remain British and who had sacrificed for Britain. Anyone visiting the churches and cathedrals of Ireland can view evidence of the sacrifices the Protestants in Ireland had made in the many wars of the British Empire and in the two world wars by reading the names of fallen men in battle from various regiments carved into marble memorials. Last but not least, it was an unwritten principle of stateness change that it had to be orderly and consensual, not chaotic and coerced. Except in rare instances, the UK had done that for the transition of its colonies to independent states. Northern Ireland was no exception.

The Irish government wanted a united Ireland, eventually. It was a historic aspiration of its citizenry and was enshrined in its constitution. Yet that goal had to be pursued peacefully and cautiously. There was a violent nationalist tradition in Ireland, and the outlawed IRA was operating with help from Republicans within Ireland, which might put Eire on a collision course with the UK. As a result of the Troubles, Sinn Fein and the Republicans were gaining in elections in Ireland. The policy of modernization and economic development, with much aid from the European Community, was paying off and was at risk should Sinn Fein gain power and the violence spill over from North to South. Irish public opinion was hesitant about acquiring a North inhabited by close to 1 million Protestants opposed to becoming Irish citizens and inheriting sectarian conflicts. Sean Duignan, an advisor to Irish prime ministers in the 1970s and 1980s, said that:

> Northern Ireland is a huge headache for the Irish government . . . the people in the street [in Dublin] believe both sides in Northern Ireland are lunatics, one is as bad as the other . . . yet history and sentiment for a united Ireland transcends such matters, as in West Germany and East Germany.
>
> (author interview, Dublin, June 13, 2003)

Then there was the £4 billion UK subsidy to Northern Ireland: how would a small country be able to afford anything like it? The Irish strategy was thus cautious incremental change on stateness. Eire had two bargaining chips with the UK: it could intensify the crackdown on insurgents' use of the South, a vital security matter for the British government, and it could exercise its influence with the nationalists in the North on non-violent transition to stateness.

UK–Eire cooperation: the key to the peace process

The success of the peace process hinged on the gradual strengthening of a cooperative relationship between the UK and Eire despite a history of adversarial relations. According to Martin Mansergh, a key advisor to Irish prime ministers, "a psychology of mutual resentment lingered in Anglo-Irish relations" until "both countries became members of the European Community and had to treat with each other in a multilateral setting as partners" (2000: 3). Anglo-Irish cooperation became the engine of the peace process (Mac Ginty and Darby 2002: 58).

A successful accord on contentious issues must have the three properties of *feasibility, acceptability*, and conformity to *shared principles*. Feasibility refers to models and precedents for institutions that have worked or can be made to work. Political leaders and advisors ruled out some stateness options on feasibility grounds. Acceptability refers to consent and co-operation by the political leaders, parties, and citizenry for institutional change. It was early on defined by Eire and the UK as democratic consent by the citizens of the two parts of Ireland and negotiated by the parties, thus not imposed on them. Acceptability was the Achilles heel of the peace process. Shared principles refer to norms of international law and democratic values that states like the UK and Eire abide by. One hopes that feasible and acceptable institutions that conform to shared principles will also possess *finality*, i.e. a stable, uncontested outcome. This was not to be in the Northern Ireland peace process, for what was acceptable on stateness did not have finality, and what would have had finality was not acceptable.

Options on stateness were considered and discussed by each government separately and jointly, in formal and informal meetings. Prime Minister Heath and his cabinet, on September 3, 1970, considered repartition, con-dominium, joint authority, phased sovereignty, and some others (Heath 1998: 430). Although Prime Minister Margaret Thatcher pursued a security response to the insurgency, she and her Irish counterparts discussed several constitutional designs in the years leading to the Anglo-Irish Agreement of 1985, including joint authority, joint sovereignty, confederation of two states, and repartition, which she rejected (Thatcher 1993: 415). The Irish government in the 1970s and 1980s considered federation and confederation between Eire and Northern Ireland, condominium, joint authority, and full independence for the North, and argued these options with UK officials in formal and informal talks (author correspondence with Dermot Nally, a key advisor in the Irish government, July 10, 2003). These options did not meet the three criteria for stateness. For instance, united Ireland and varia-tions thereof (confederation) were not acceptable to the Unionists and would start a second armed conflict. Repartition risked ethnic cleansing and more violence. Shared sovereignty lacked feasibility because there were no prece-dents for it (author interview with Robert Hazel at the London University Constitution Unit, London, May 29, 2003).

The two states agreed on the principle of power sharing governance. In one form or another power sharing governance remained a part of all peace plans. It is difficult to conceive of democratic political reform in a divided majority–minority society without power sharing. For the UK and Eire, the specific power sharing mode was for the Northern Ireland political leaders and parties to decide since imposition was ruled out by shared principles, and that is what happened during the NIPA negotiations (Horowitz 2002: 200).

My analysis of the peace process focuses on three key peace initiatives in the 35-year conflict, two that failed to bring peace – Sunningdale in 1973 and the Anglo-Irish Agreement in 1985 – and NIPA, which was successful in 1998 and which is being implemented. On core issues, the agreements are remarkably similar: constitutional change on stateness to be approved by a majority of the people; a power sharing executive and assembly; UK–Eire–Northern Ireland institutions for cooperation on matters of mutual concern; and cross-border cooperation against insurgency and terrorism. To be sure the 1985 and 1998 agreements spelled out in greater detail the substance on these topics, in particular the Irish government role in Northern Irish affairs, and NIPA details the steps for long-term peace building. Still, the similarities are striking. Why were the earlier peace plans defeated, and why and how was NIPA agreed to?

Sunningdale

The context for the 1972 Sunningdale Agreement was the most violent year of the Troubles till then, with 500 political deaths, 2,000 explosions, 5,000 injured, and 10,000 shooting incidents. To put down communal violence the British government had brought in the army, a move at first welcomed by the nationalists who needed protection from unionist attacks. A pattern familiar from other armed forces' attempts to control communal violence in divided societies followed. As in Yugoslavia when the JNA was deployed to stop clashes between Serbs and Croats in contested areas and became a partisan on the Serb side, so the British Army turned partisan on the Protestant side. Prime Minister Ted Heath realized that the British security response would not end communal violence and insurgency without political reforms. He suspended the Northern Ireland Assembly and introduced direct rule from Westminster.

Meetings were held with the more conciliatory political leaders among the Unionists led by Brian Faulkner, with the SDLP, and with the Alliance Party, trying to forge a cross-community political alliance for political reform. At Sunningdale, on December 6–9, 1973, the British and Irish governments and the three Northern Ireland political parties agreed that constitution change on stateness would be based on the consent of the people of Northern Ireland, that a power sharing executive would be formed and that the UK would devolve power to the Assembly and its executive, and that the UK and Eire would cooperate against terrorists and a Council of Ireland would be established with seven ministers from the UK and seven from Eire, together with a consultative assembly from members of the Northern Ireland Assembly and the Dail, the Irish parliament. The Council would enable the Irish government to consult with the British government on the development of resources, trade and industry, tourism, sports, electricity, public health, transportation, and environmental protection.

The inducement to the moderate Unionist parties was the restoration of the Northern Ireland Assembly – "devolution" – albeit with power sharing with the SDLP and the Alliance Party. The majority of unionists massively rejected Sunningdale. In the February British general election the Unionist rejection bloc, the UUUC, put up a single candidate in each constituency and campaigned with the slogan "Dublin is just a Sunningdale away," playing on Protestant fears that the Council would become the opening wedge on the path to a united Ireland. It worked. The UUUC won 11 of 12 seats and received a huge 51.1 percent vote, compared to 13.1 percent for the moderate Unionists. Martin Mansergh (2000: 6) called it the "clearest exercise of the unionist veto" on political reform. This outcome represented an almost 20 percent gain for the rejectionists compared to the outcome of the 1973 Assembly election a year earlier when power sharing, termed "partnership government" in a British White Paper, but not the Council of Ireland, was the issue. In 1973, the Unionists had split almost evenly between the official Unionists under Faulkner (29.3 percent) and the anti-power sharing Unionist bloc (32.1 percent). Far from supporting compromise and peace, democratic elections polarized the electorate and defeated the attempt to build a centrist cross-community political coalition. The second-largest loser in 1974 was the Alliance Party, which dropped from 9.2 percent in 1973 to 3.2 percent, which suggests that moderate Protestant voters were likely to desert the center over the stateness issue and back the rejectionists. The constitutional Nationalists in the SDLP remained steadfast with 22.4 percent compared to 22.1 percent (Elliott and Flackes 1999: 533–80).

In spite of the 1974 election outcome, the Assembly voted for a power sharing executive, and the rejectionists answered with the Ulster Workers' Council Strike. There were blocked roads manned by masked armed men, factory lockouts, power outages, loyalist bombs exploded in the Irish Republic, and two weeks of chaos by rejectionists whom the British Army and the Royal Ulster Constabulary (RUC) were hesitant to subdue. These civil disorders ended devolution, the power sharing executive, and the Sunningdale Agreement. Two years of hard negotiations went down the drain. The British government resumed direct rule. The mistrust between the Unionists and the British government over a sell-out on stateness intensified, and the Catholics' belief that Protestants would not compromise on political domination was strengthened. Nevertheless, as Martin Mansergh commented, "Although the Sunningdale Agreement, with its twin principles of power sharing and an Irish dimension, collapsed after a few months, it nevertheless defined the basic ingredients of a political settlement" (2000: 8).

The Anglo-Irish Agreement

Several British peace probes failed between Sunningdale in 1973–4 and the Anglo-Irish Agreement of 1985. Republicans gained over Nationalists among Catholics during the campaign for supporting the hunger strikes at the Maze prison – an example of the coercion paradox at work – and Sinn Fein emerged as a major political force in several 1982–5 elections. The UK's security strategy continued in force and managed to contain but not suppress terrorist violence. The most spectacular instance came when the IRA exploded a bomb intended to blow up Prime Minister Thatcher and the Tory leadership at the annual Conservative Party conference at Brighton, killing five but no leaders. Prime Minister Thatcher needed Irish help for intensifying the security strategy. Her Irish counterpart Garret FitzGerald was worried about the growth of republicanism, North and South, and was convinced that a political solution was the only way to bring the Troubles to an end. When interparty talks in the North led to dead ends, the UK turned to an inter-state approach and found a willing Irish partner. After two years of consultations, the two governments' heads of state signed the Anglo-Irish Agreement in November 1985. Thatcher wanted more defense of borders, hot-pursuit zones by British security forces, and a security zone on both sides of the border, and toyed with the possibility of repartition for security reasons, which meant ceding to Eire some areas adjoining the Irish Republic with a predominantly Catholic population. FitzGerald advocated creative solutions to stateness which were unacceptable to Thatcher, who stated: "I have made it clear that a unified Ireland, that is out. A confederation of two states, that is out. Joint authority, that is out" (quoted in Mallie and McKittrick 2001: 59).

The AIA was a deal between two state elites from which the Northern Ireland political parties had been excluded. It reaffirmed the consent principle for stateness change and power sharing governance. Cross-border cooperation on security and for combating terrorism was intensified. The biggest addition to Sunningdale was on Irish–British institutions. An Anglo-Irish Intergovernmental Conference (AIIC) and a Council with a permanent secretariat would allow the Irish government to advocate on behalf of the Catholics, but there would be no "derogation of sovereignty" from the UK to the AIIC (Elliott and Flackes 1999: 164–6). According to Martin Mansergh, the AIA "institutionalized the Irish government's right to be heard in relation to the nationalist community" (2000: 8).

Elliott and Flackes believe that the AIA was "the most far-reaching political development since 1920 and the creation of Northern Ireland" (1999: 164). As in 1974, the unionist rejection was massive opposition to any role of the Irish government in Northern Irish affairs, which was framed as an "opening wedge" to a united Ireland. Unionists rallied more than 100,000 protesters in Belfast and started a mass campaign of non-cooperation with the authorities. Fifteen Unionist Members of Parliament resigned in protest against the role of Eire in the internal affairs of the UK. In the 1986 by-elections two months later the Unionists in the rejectionist bloc got 71.5 percent of the Unionist votes, compared to 62.3 percent in the 1983 election. Rejection had a huge electoral payoff. The consequence of the protests was the dissolution, yet again, of the Assembly in May 1986, and direct rule, yet again, by the British government. Despite such opposition, the AIA and UK–Eire cooperation for peace remained the key to the peace process and NIPA in 1998.

The road to NIPA

Seven years elapsed between the AIA in early 1986 and the next major peace initiative by the UK and Eire with the Downing Street Declaration in December 1993. Urgency was lacking on the British side. The armed conflict had been contained at a low level of about five British Army casualties per year in 1990–3; deaths to Northern Ireland civilians were about 60 per year; the financial cost could be absorbed by the UK without economic harm. John Chilcott, Permanent Undersecretary of the Northern Ireland Office in those years, explained that, "despite Canary Wharf [IRA bombs in London], there was no pressure to settle the Troubles at any price" (author interview, London, June 25, 2003). Northern Ireland was not Bosnia with huge Muslim populations trapped in enclaves and food convoys to starving families blocked by the besieging Serb army.

The impetus for advancing the peace process came from the Irish government of Albert Reynolds which was apprehensive about the growth of republicanism in Eire and the risk of the violence in the North spilling over to the South. After a lot of negotiations the two governments issued the Downing Street Declaration in December 1993. In it they reaffirmed the peace process of the past 20 years, the democratic consent principle for stateness, i.e. the right of self-determination was "for the people of the island of Ireland alone, by agreement between the two parts respectively, on the basis of consent, freely and concurrently given, North and South" (Elliott and Flackes 1999: 235). All parities to the peace process had to commit to exclusively peaceful and democratic means. Eire in effect recognized the Unionists' right to reject the unification of Ireland, but the declaration also affirmed the right of the Irish government to participate, with the British government and the Northern Ireland political parties, in the creation of new structures and institutions for the North. The DSD was well received except by the rejectionist Unionists. The Reverend Ian Paisley condemned it by charging that the prime minister had "sold Ulster to buy off fiendish Republican scum" (quoted in Elliott and Flackes 1999: 238).

From the DSD in December 1993 to the start of substantive peace negotiations on the core issues on November 10, 1997, there were four years of contention over procedural issues and preconditions for the Republicans to enter the peace negotiations. After some preliminary bargaining, the IRA announced a ceasefire on August 31, 1994 and the Loyalist paramilitaries halted their campaign of violence six weeks later. At that point the peace process stalled over the decommissioning of IRA weapons and Sinn Fein joining the talks, "an issue which for years to come would remain central to the peace process" (Mallie and McKittrick 2001: 211) and would time and again derail it. The UK and some Unionist parties wanted the paramilitaries to decommission their arms as a commitment to the peace process before the political parties associated with them could enter the peace negotiations. Eire and the SDLP wanted no preconditions to negotiations. Sinn Fein and the Unionist parties linked to paramilitaries wanted no disarmament before a peace agreement. Gerry Adams argued that "decommissioning has to be part of finding a political settlement" (quoted in Mallie and McKittrick 2001: 213). Former Senate majority leader George Mitchell, who headed the International Body on Arms – referred to as the Mitchell Commission – and was called upon to mediate in the peace process, writes that, "in the real world of Northern Ireland, prior decommissioning simply was not a practical solution" (1999: 29).

Mitchell offered a compromise: parallel decommissioning under an independent commission headed by a Canadian general, and adherence to the Mitchell principles. In brief, "to be eligible to participate in negotiations a party would have to promise to adhere to specific principles of democracy and nonviolence" (1999: 35). Eventually the Mitchell proposals were accepted. In the meanwhile, frustrated by a year-and-a-half-long ceasefire without negotiations, the IRA resumed its bombing campaign at Canary Wharf in London on February 9, 1996, which killed two and injured hundreds. Despite this setback, ground rules were agreed to and elections were held in June to the interparty talks under the Mitchell rules. Delays were caused by mistrust among the participants who scrutinized and debated the nuances of every term: "for several weeks," Mitchell recalled, "the participants debated the rules. In the end, the precise words had little effect on negotiations" (1999: 58). Sinn Fein was excluded so long as the IRA did not resume the ceasefire. In June the interparty talks started but stalled over the voting rules, followed by more disputes over the agenda, and following that came a deadlock over decommissioning. By March 1997 there had been no progress on substantive issues. A frustrated Mitchell wrote that:

> We had been meeting for a year and a half. For hundreds and hundreds of hours I had listened to the same arguments, over and over again. Very little had been accomplished. It had taken two months to get an understanding on the rules to be followed . . . Then it took another two months to get agreement on a preliminary agenda. Then we tried for fourteen months to get an accord on a detailed final agenda. We couldn't even get that.
>
> (1999: 127)

Substantive talks would not start until November 10, 1997, four years after the Downing Street Declaration. In a television interview, commenting on his experiences as mediator in both Northern Ireland and in Palestine, Senator Mitchell reflected that:

> what you find in all these situations is a complete absence of trust . . . they don't believe anything the other says. They assume the worst of the other side. And as a result it infects their own actions. And so you have to try to bring them to a point where they are at least willing to listen . . . not what I would call a really trusting close relationship . . . but the minimal level necessary to permit political compromise.
>
> (2002)

NIPA: agreement at last

A speed-up of the interparty negotiations came after the Labour landslide election victory in May 1997 when Tony Blair became prime minister. He and Mitchell set a May 1998 deadline for the peace talks. The IRA announced a new ceasefire in July, Sinn Fein joined the talks, two rejectionist Unionist parties exited in protest, and negotiations got underway on November 10. The substantive issues had been sorted into three strands: on governance in Northern Ireland, on North–South institutions, and on UK–Eire institutions (East–West). Teams of civil servants, advisors, and lawyers from both governments had worked up drafts on every issue based on proposals, declarations, statements, and minutes of meetings that had accumulated over the past 30 years. Norms of acceptance had been decided earlier: there was to be a referendum in the North and in the South on any peace agreement followed by elections to the Assembly and changes in the constitution of Eire and in British law allowing for a new constitutional design in Northern Ireland.

On the core issues, Senator Mitchell characterized the adversaries' position as follows:

> The unionists wanted a continuation of the union – Northern Ireland as part of the United Kingdom – and a strong, majority run Northern Ireland Assembly; they desired only minimal North–South institutions, with power derived from the Assembly, not independent of it. The nationalists wanted just the opposite: a united Ireland, north and south joined together in a single sovereign state; short of that, they looked for an Assembly in Northern Ireland in which power would be shared between the Protestant majority and the Catholic minority; and they wanted strong North–South institutions created directly by the British and Irish parliaments and therefore independent of the Northern Ireland Assembly.
>
> (1999: 148)

And, Mitchell added, "Each side was deeply suspicious of the other with a presumption of bad faith."

On stateness, UK union or united Ireland, the two governments had at the AIA and all subsequent declarations insisted on democratic consent as the means of change, and the political parties had pledged in the Mitchell principles to "democratic and exclusively peaceful means of resolving political issues." Continuation of the union for the time being was conceded by the Nationalists. What remained contentious was the North–South institutions. During the negotiations, the Unionists' leaders managed to reduce the authority of the North–South Ministerial Council by making it contingent on the Assembly: "It is understood that the North/South Ministerial Council and the Northern Ireland Assembly are mutually interdependent, and that one cannot successfully function without the other" (in Strand Two, paragraph 13 of NIPA, formally the Agreement between the Government of the United Kingdom of Great Britain and Northern Ireland and the Government of Ireland), and limiting its functions to 12 innocuous ones (including agriculture, fisheries, environment, inland waterways, tourism, and education, but only teacher qualifications and exchanges) (NIPA, Annex to Strand Two).

By the time of the negotiations, it was understood by the majority of unionists and nationalists that there would be *power sharing* governance, but the mode of power sharing and many details on elections to the Assembly, the organization of the executive, Assembly voting rules, and other matters had to be decided, and were left by the two governments for the Northern Ireland political parties to decide. Donald Horowitz writes that:

> There are two main approaches to interethnic conciliation in severely divided societies that operate along democratic lines. One approach is for those ethnically based parties most willing to compromise to join together and, by joining, to . . . marginalize the extremes. The second aims to coopt the extremes and include them as participants in and beneficiaries of compromise.
>
> (2002: 193)

The first approach had been tried at Sunningdale and had failed. The second approach, consociational power sharing, prevailed. Consociational power sharing assures the minority in a divided society participation in a grand coalition executive and legislative veto on important decisions. It is most suited for societies that are territorially divided by ethnicity and have cooperating ethnic elites. Neither condition existed in Northern Ireland. Why did the negotiators choose it?

According to Horowitz, "As an official of the Northern Ireland Office remarked, the British government cared only that the parties agreed [on the mode of power sharing]; for the most part, it did not care what they agreed to" (2002: 200). The SDLP wanted consociationalism and David Trimble, who represented the majority of Unionists, agreed. John Hume, SDLP party head, declared "We are totally committed to a completely inclusive system of government in Northern Ireland where all parties would be included, including Sinn Fein, so that all sections of our people would be represented in government" (quoted in Mallie and McKittrick 2001: 267). Hume believed that without some representation of the extreme groups governance in Northern Ireland would not work. Jeffrey Donaldson, a Unionist negotiator, objected: "I just found it difficult, if not impossible, to envisage a situation where you would have a coalition government, a compulsory coalition government, containing political elements that were diametrically opposed to each other" (quoted in Mallie and McKittrick 2001: 267). As for why Trimble accepted consociational power sharing for the Unionists, Horowitz believes that "Leaders of the Ulster Unionist Party were willing to accept arrangements crafted to benefit nationalists, in part because they were thought to be beneficial in the future, in the event that unionists, rather than the nationalists, should find themselves in the minority" (2002: 203).

Under the Northern Ireland electoral system agreed to, a candidate for the Assembly could be elected by as few as 14 percent of the constituency voters and thus could appeal successfully to a narrow ethnic segment without bothering to build cross-ethnic support. The members of the Assembly had to register as Nationalist, Unionist or other. Assembly decision rules required parallel consent or weighted majority on important decisions to ensure joint Nationalist and Unionist majority consent, which gave the minority a powerful veto. The arrangement was a blow against cross-community centrist parties such as the Alliance Party and the Women's Coalition. Stephen Ferry, the head of the Alliance Party, said that many in the middle class, the most likely supporters of a cross-ethnic party such as his, consider politics a "tribal mess" and have retreated into private life, despairing of any change (author interview, Belfast, June 18, 2003). Committee chairs, ministers, and committee memberships were to be allocated in proportion to party strength and not by agreement to adhere to a common program and policies. That ruled out cabinet government: a minister might pursue policies and programs in disregard of the first minister and other ministers, remain in office until the next election, and escape accountability. There is no real political opposition in such a form of government. If the voters are dissatisfied with its performance, unless they totally desert their parties and vote for an entirely new party – quite unlikely – the same parties get reelected with perhaps small shifts in strength and form the same executive. Consociational governance is premised on a "cartel of elites" (Horowitz 2002: 195).

NIPA was flawed political engineering for achieving ethnic cooperation in government. The strand one political institutions turned out to accomplish the opposite, i.e. government gridlock and the growth of the more extreme parties, Sinn Fein and DUP at the expense of the SDLP and UUP. As for why the SDLP and the UUP did not forge a centrist cross-ethnic coalition after

NIPA, in view of the fact that the two parties with the help of the Alliance and the Women's Coalition had enough members in the Assembly to meet the "parallel consent" criterion, the Deputy First Minister Mark Durkan of the SDLP said "we can't lock ourselves in with just one party . . . we are social democrats, the UUP are conservatives . . . we differ on much beyond sectarian issues" (author interview, Belfast, July 16, 2003).

Other issues were settled by compromise, as on prisoner release to take place two years after the signing of an agreement, or by postponing decisions and sidetracking them to independent commissions on weapons decommissioning, police reform, criminal justice, contentious parades, human rights, and equality and social justice. Postponed decisions were going to hinder implementation of NIPA. The broad principles of cross-ethnic integration favored by the British and Irish governments were expressed in the terms of reference of these commissions and public bodies, but clashed with the sectarian political institutions in Northern Ireland. The least satisfactory postponed decision which was to plague implementation of the agreement for years was on decommissioning. For the signers of NIPA, the decommissioning provisions included only a vague verbal "commitment to the total disarmament of all paramilitary organizations . . . intention to work in good faith with the Independent Commission, and use influence . . . to achieve the decommissioning of all paramilitary arms within two years following endorsement [of the agreement] in referendums" (NIPA, 1998, "Decommissioning," paragraph 3). There was no timetable and no definition of what decommissioning meant concretely. David Trimble wanted the actual destruction of some weapons to start when the new Assembly met and, failing that, the power to exclude Sinn Fein from the executive. Sinn Fein's position was that, "if decommissioning were a precondition to joining the executive, that was something they could not accept" (Mallie and McKittrick 2001: 278). Prime Minister Blair provided Trimble with a face-saving "side letter" affirming British help on both concerns, which was just enough to get most UUP negotiators to sign on to the agreement. Decommissioning remained an extremely contentious issue.

Acceptance, finality, feasibility

Despite last-minute brinkmanship by the Unionists on North–South institutions and by Sinn Fein over decommissioning and the refusal of the DUP to sign the agreement, Senator Mitchell announced at 5 p.m. on Good Friday (April 10) that the two governments and the political parties had reached an agreement. *Acceptance* was positive. In the simultaneous referendums in May, the voters approved with 71 percent yes, an estimated 90 percent of Catholics in favor and Protestants split half and half, and an overwhelming yes vote in the Irish Republic. The June Assembly elections produced a pro-Agreement majority, but among Unionists the rejectionist parties polled only 2 percent behind David Trimble and the UUP, showing deep divisions and polarization within the Protestant community. As is true for other peace pacts, spoiler violence by extremists followed. The Real IRA, one of several small republican paramilitary offshoots from the IRA, planted the Omagh bomb that killed 29 and injured many more, and in July the ban of the annual Drumcree Orange Order march resulted in loyalist protests, roadblocks, and rioting. Still, the public wanted peace and wanted NIPA to work.

Finality was problematic. The agreement was sold to unionists as an assurance for lasting UK stateness, and to the nationalists as an opportunity for future union with Eire. The agreement left "self determination on the basis of consent" to the people of Ireland, North and South, "to bring about a united Ireland." Owing to a combination of migration and fertility, demographics favored a slow population trend in favor of Catholics, with a majority estimated two decades away. Poll data supplied by the *Northern Ireland Life and Times* showed that Catholics want equality within Northern Ireland more than a united Ireland, and they believe that they are on the way to achieving it (*NILT* 2002). What constitutional design "united Ireland" might have is uncertain and was not part of the NIPA public discourse (Reynolds 1999–2000).

Rejectionists have kept mobilizing against the agreement with a fear and threat strategy on stateness. The fear was of a Catholic, theocratic Ireland, a collective myth sustained by the oratory of the likes of Paisley, whereas in reality Eire had become prosperous, secular, tolerant, and European. The threat was from North–South institutions enabling Irish government penetration in Northern Ireland, aided and abetted by connivance and deception from the UK and nationalists. The reality was articulated by Dennis McCarthy, a civil servant attached to the North–South Inter-Ministerial Council (IMC):

> What this office and the IMC are doing is slight, the perception much larger . . . While the government is suspended, civil servants here meet with their counterparts from Eire. We are just continuing existing policy. When the Assembly resumes, we have to be accountable to it.
>
> (author interview, Stormont, July 7, 2003)

The future of stateness remains contingent and uncertain.

Feasibility has been the Achilles heel of NIPA. Consociational power sharing has not brought ethnic cooperation. The political parties of the extremes have steadily gained at the expense of the centrist nationalists and unionists, and have become the largest party in their respective camps. In its first five years, the agreement produced four suspensions of the Northern Ireland power sharing government and three polarized elections. In the 2005 Westminster election for the UK Parliament, compared to the 1998 Northern Ireland Assembly election, the DUP got 33.7 percent compared to 18.1 percent seven years earlier, and Sinn Fein increased from 17.6 percent to

24.3 percent. The UUP dropped from 21.3 percent to 17.3 percent and SDLP from 22 percent to 17.5 percent. As for the Alliance Party which runs on a cross-ethnic appeal, it declined from 6.5 percent to 3.9 percent. During most of this period, power sharing government was suspended and the province was ruled directly from Westminster. According to Mallie and McKittrick:

> The Ulster Unionists refused to go into government with Sinn Fein because the IRA had not given up any weapons. Trimble encapsulated the policy when he declared: "the position of the Ulster Unionist party is and will remain . . . no guns, no government." The Sinn Fein position was that Republicans were prepared to talk about decommissioning, but would not contemplate delivering up guns . . . in advance of the formation of an administration.
>
> (2001: 298)

Many different formulae were offered up in compromise but none amounted to transparent public weapons destruction and none was accepted by unionists.

Decommissioning was and is a very important concern for both the Unionist leadership and the Protestant citizenry. For Protestants NIPA was asymmetric and a violation of reciprocity and balance norms in negotiated agreements. Nationalists got most of what they wanted: the possibility of a future united Ireland, power sharing, police reform, a commitment to justice reform, prisoner release, North/South institutions. The one assurance unionists wanted in return was security and non-violent politics and in particular weapons decommissioning, which was the public commitment to total non-violence. The agreement was based on trust and reciprocity with each side delivering its side of the bargain, but the unionists were not getting decommissioning. They only got selective implementation and felt betrayed by the nationalists and by the UK.

A 2003 study of public opinion on NIPA and its implementation found that support for NIPA had fallen among Protestants from 50 percent in 1998 to 36 percent in 2003 (Irwin 2003). Of 22 issues, decommissioning was the source of the most dissatisfaction. Nevertheless 60 percent of Protestants wanted the Belfast agreement to work, but it hadn't. Robin Wilson, director of Democratic Dialogue in Belfast, reflected that "the . . . mistake was to adopt a model of power-sharing based on the principle that high fences make good neighbors . . . The agreement institutionalized sectarian divisions," and recommended "re-engineering the Belfast agreement to foster integration" ("The Hard Liners Tighten their Grip," *International Herald Tribune*, May 10, 2005).

The critique of consociationalism has to be qualified. Some of its basic principles, like proportional representation of Catholics and Protestants on commissions and in agencies, express widely accepted justice and fairness norms, and have been successfully applied in Northern Ireland, as in police reform (see page 178). Some dimensions of governance actually worked well. In several interviews, my informants kept insisting that during devolution in 2000–1 the Northern Ireland executive had performed well. Ministers appointed from all the major parties ran the branches of government in a satisfactory manner. Government services in health, social services, education, trade and industry, tax collection, etc. were smoothly provided to the citizenry. District councils were functioning. Urban development agencies were working. Independent boards, such as the election commission that ran the frequent elections in Northern Ireland, were not controversial. In most divided societies elections are the occasion for fraud and violence, even in the presence of international monitors. Such was not the case in Northern Ireland where a commission consisting of three technocrats and three impartial citizens (a high court judge, a retired civil servant, and a lady prominent in civic affairs) oversaw a huge operation at polling places and a central Belfast transparent manual counting and checking process which, but for occasional minor fraud allegations, is considered fair, valid, and above sectarian politics (author interview with Dennis Stanley, chief election officer, Belfast, July 7, 2003).

Implementation: decommissioning and police reform

Since the AIA in 1985 when the British and Irish governments forged an alliance on resolving their joint Northern Ireland problem, the contours of a settlement on core issues, on stateness, power sharing, human rights, and non-discrimination, were set, the details only to be negotiated. One is struck, as indeed Senator Mitchell was in his reflections on peace making in both Northern Ireland and Palestine, by how contentious the derivative issues are in the peace process: the procedural issues of recognition of the adversaries during ongoing armed conflict, rules about inclusion and exclusion and pre-conditions for talks, rules about talks themselves, lining up political support, and preparing public opinion. All that consumed enormous energies and lots of time because of animosity, lack of trust, and political gains to be made from obstruction, with every delay increasing the risk of violence and outrages setting back cooperation. The mobilization paradox captures this dimension of peace making, which in the Northern Ireland conflict was fueled by frequent elections and disputes over NIPA implementation.

A fundamental flaw in the Northern Ireland peace process was that obstruction and non-cooperation held more benefits than cooperation. One is struck by the number of times the parties and leaders to talks and negotiations boycotted, refused to participate, threatened to withdraw, withdrew, did not take their seat, made it impossible, resigned, walked out, refused to meet face to face, refused to sit down at the same table, and got away with these non-cooperative moves (Elliott and Flackes 1999: 612–13). Sinn Fein and the IRA held the negotiations hostage over arms decommissioning while the UK gave up its strongest bargaining chip, prisoner release, so important to the IRA. Patrick Mayhew noted that "it was a great mistake to let prisoners go before guns were turned in," and Mark Durkan agreed that "100 percent of prisoners were released, but no arms were turned in" (author interviews, London and Belfast, June 24, July 7, 2003). John Darby argues that "there is a need to orchestrate reciprocated concessions on demilitarization and decommissioning during peace negotiations, and do this very early on in the proceedings" (2006a: 158). The NIPA negotiators failed on that score.

Weapons *decommissioning and demilitarization* of insurgency and civil war are a major stumbling block in peace processes. Decommissioning prior to a peace agreement is a problem of asymmetric security. If the insurgents hand in their weapons and give up violence, they become totally vulnerable to their adversary who remains armed. Charles King writes that "credible guarantees of physical survival to belligerent leaders must be provided" (1997: 64), and one might add not only to the leaders but to the rank-and-file insurgents as well. The threat of violence is the main bargaining power of the insurgents in negotiations because the only inducement they can offer to their adversary is giving up their weapons and the restoration of peace. For the government and for public opinion, decommissioning is a symbolic issue on top of a security issue. They want the insurgents to cease using violence as blackmail in peace bargaining and to commit to non-violence and peace beyond just cheap words. Giving up some weapons is a clear signal of that intent. For unionists, decommissioning remained a trust issue, not just a matter of military hardware destruction.

Barbara Walter argues in a study of 41 civil wars that, even when disarmament of the insurgents is not prior to but part of a peace pact, "civil war adversaries do . . . require the added reassurance of outside security guarantees before they willfully implement peace treaties . . . resolving underlying issues over which wars are fought is not enough to bring peace" (1997: 36). The guarantors in Northern Ireland would be the Irish and British governments, who were expected to honor and enforce any peace agreement they signed. In the Bosnian war peace negotiations, prior disarmament was not an issue because all sides clearly understood that, if the negotiations failed, the adversaries would resume war and had the means of doing so. After the DPA, the outside guarantor of security to both sides was the powerful 60,000-strong NATO implementation force IFOR that was responsible for the collection and cantonment of heavy weapons and for providing security.

After seven and a half years of crisis management, decommissioning was achieved. On July 28, 2005, the IRA announced "the ending of the armed campaign," that "all IRA units have been ordered to dump arms," and cooperation "with the IICD [Independent International Commission on Decommissioning] to complete the process to verifiably put its arms beyond use." In October the commission and two religious witnesses, one Protestant and one Catholic, verified that this had been done. In February 2006, the

International Monitoring Commission reported that the IRA had ceased recruitment and training for paramilitary purposes and that except for some handguns kept for personal protection disarmament was complete. The commission also noted with concern that some other, both republican and loyalist, paramilitaries were still active in terrorist, violent, and especially criminal activity, as was true of former members of the IRA "heavily involved in serious organized crime." The commission reported that the IRA was well on its way in the difficult transition from a terrorist and outlaw body to a lawful organization. These events opened the door to a power sharing government and devolution.

The second most contentious, unresolved issue at the NIPA negotiations was police reform. The parties agreed to an independent commission headed by Chris Patten, the last British governor of Hong Kong who successfully led the transition of the colony to the People's Republic of China. After consulting widely with political parties, the public, and human rights and police organizations, the commission's reform plan included a 50:50 Catholic/Protestant recruitment plan at entry for the next ten years and appointments of senior-level Catholic police officers from Eire and abroad, accountability to community boards, a police board and 26 district police partnerships (DPPs), professional norms of policing assuring fairness to all citizens, neutral replacing sectarian symbols, i.e. name change from Royal Ulster Constabulary to Northern Ireland Police Service (NIPS) and other symbol changes, and an independent oversight commissioner to monitor and report on implementation. For the next three years, between the issuing of the Patten Report in July 1998 and the passage of the police law in the Assembly in November 2001, the political parties insisted on numerous changes and engaged in brinkmanship that put the cross-community support necessary for passage at risk. In the end, the police law closely matched the Patten Commission recommendations. Sinn Fein and the DUP continued their opposition during implementation.

Two years later in 2003, the police reforms were taking hold. The NIPS was recruiting from a large pool of applicants including 2,000 Catholics and had chosen 50 percent Catholics of 300 police recruits in the first year. Some 400 citizens had been appointed to the DPPs. In each DPP ten members were allocated to political parties according to election outcome and nine "civil society" appointments representing age, gender, and religion demographics in the district (author interview with Desmond Rae, chair of the Police Board, Belfast, July 10, 2003). The NIPS is considered a highly professional force; in fact it has become a model for police reform in Bosnia. The DUP and Sinn Fein remained critical.

Peace building

Police reform, security issues, arms decommissioning, prisoner release, and other derivative issues remained contentious after NIPA. The dilemma for republicans was that if NIPA was successfully implemented many Catholics would make their peace with UK stateness rather than want a united Ireland. For Protestant rejectionists effective government under NIPA institutions was a steady slide towards a united Ireland. Thus the rejectionists on each side had reasons to obstruct power sharing. The conflict within each adversary came to dominate the implementation of the peace process as much as the conflict between the principal adversaries, what I have termed the paradox of peace making.

The UK–Eire alliance reduced the conflict from six to four major adversarial relationships which improved the chances of an overall agreement. Even so, one is struck by the 13 years between the AIA in 1985 and NIPA in 1998 compared to the two and a half years between the start of the Bosnian war and the DPA which ended it. I believe that, because of the far higher casualties and human misery in the Bosnian war, the urgency of peace for the Bosnian parties and the external stakeholders was greater there than in Northern Ireland. Even with 17 years to work with, NIPA has serious flaws. The stateness issue was not settled with finality, acceptance by the majority of unionists has not happened, and political reforms have had consequences opposite to what the UK and Eire had intended. Stephen Ferry, of the Alliance Party, comments on NIPA that:

> the paradox of the Agreement is that while the intensity of the conflict in Northern Ireland has been reduced, divisions have become even more clearly defined and entrenched . . . To be successful in the long run, the Agreement will have to . . . reduce sectarian and communal segregation. However much of the Agreement is based on the institutionalized assumption of two communities, separate but equal, and living in peaceful coexistence . . . at the worst extreme, this separation could amount to territorial partition.
>
> (2003: 1, 13)

Ferry is joined by other academics and political leaders who are critical of the top-down crisis management and are calling for parallel bottom-up grassroots institution building for achieving lasting peace. Mark Durkan says simply: "The peace process has to be broadened to business, to the churches, to the communities, not just the political sector" (author interview, Belfast, July 7, 2003). Can civil society resolve stateness and moderate ethnic identity, and foster cross-community cooperation?

Stateness in the narrow sense is defined by sovereignty – UK or Eire. Absent shared sovereignty, a possibility ruled out for the time being, the authority of the sovereign over a minority can be diluted through federation, confederation, and local autonomy, as it has been in some multiethnic states. Whether Northern Ireland remains in the UK or becomes united to Eire, it will be in a multiethnic state and remain a multiethnic province, and will have a distinct constitutional status and power sharing governance in either state. Whichever group, Catholic or Protestant, remains or becomes a minority, they will be included in governance and state institutions. Most people have made their peace with this state of affairs. According to *NILT* surveys (2002, 2005), though 84 percent of Protestants would like Northern Ireland to remain in the UK, 68 percent would accept unity with Ireland if a majority ever voted for it. Among Catholics, although 50 percent would like to become part of a united Ireland, 93 percent accept continued UK stateness. These preferences and attitudes are in line with the 1998 referendum on NIPA. Whether the province remains UK or becomes Eire, the people there, by and large, will live in the same homes, attend the same schools, work in the same organizations, worship in the same churches, speak the same language, watch the same television programs, take the same holidays, pay the same taxes, shop in the same malls, become ill in the same way and be treated in the same hospitals, be subject to the same laws, as they now do. Why should stateness matter? Or, to put it somewhat differently, what is it about stateness that matters?

According to ethnic conflict theory, national identity and symbolic politics matter. Identity – the sense of "Who am I?" – is an internalized social construction composed of many elements: gender, age, family status, physical and intellectual qualities and accomplishments, profession, lifestyle, and so on. These are recognized and validated by others and by public symbols in various contexts, and provide self-esteem, dignity, security and other psychic benefits. National and/or ethnic identity – what people do I belong with, and what are our qualities? – is an important dimension of overall identity in a multiethnic society. To reduce the salience of ethnicity, *identities shared across groups* have to assert themselves. In public affairs, it might be municipal pride: inhabitants of Derry, Catholic and Protestant, both take pride in its urban redevelopment. It might be attachment to a political philosophy: social democrats from both groups share the values of social justice. It might be what both groups have in common as Europeans. It might be attachment to Northern Ireland.

The elimination of sectarian *public symbols* is a second way of reducing the salience of ethnicity. Changed symbols for the reformed police signaled that it belongs to all citizens, not just the Protestants. Symbol changes in the short run offend diehard ethnics, and that was true for the Police Service of Northern Ireland, yet acceptance was widespread. In the longer run, ethnic rivalries and their symbolic dimensions might be diverted into non-political channels, as with sports. *Cooperative problem solving* also reduces the saliency of ethnicity. Whether Northern Ireland remains in the UK or becomes Eire, whether one is Catholic or Protestant, unemployed youth, gang violence, drug addiction, and other social problems in a shared city and neighborhood diminish quality of life, a collective good. Both groups have an interest in economic and social programs for dealing with them.

A fourth mode for reducing the salience of ethnic identity is *shared institutions* for those who want to break out of ethnic encapsulation, e.g.

mixed schools. For people in a divided society, an institutional and political underpinning for shared institutions and community relations work have to be provided. People want to live in a normal society, free of threat, intimidation, violence, and fear. They view separation, both in the physical sense of peace walls and separate territory, and in the psycho-social sense of avoidance and ethnic encapsulation, as a guarantor of normalcy in everyday life. Shared institutions are burdened with uncertainty. Parents want not only quality education. They want their children treated equally and fairly by professional teachers and administrators. They want their children protected from peer harassment. They want the curriculum, both statutory and "informal," to be free of bias against their ethnic group. The school house and classroom are not just a production line for knowledge but an ethnic microenvironment in which children spend thousands of hours growing up. As long as these parental concerns are not addressed, they will prefer separate schooling even though they are favorably disposed to shared education. Individual preferences and dispositions favorable to inter-group relations do not translate automatically into integrated neighborhoods and schools. Public policy has to facilitate that transition.

Cooperation in problem solving and participation in shared institutions do not occur in a political and social vacuum. As explained in Chapter 1, on the causes of ethnic conflict, ethnic violence everywhere results in ethnic separation because of coercion and security concerns (Horowitz 2001: 424; Varshney 2002: 9–11). After a peace agreement, security is never 100 percent: militants keep control in impacted populations on both sides of ethnic boundaries. John Darby (2006b) and his collaborators have shown that a rise in violent crime after peace accords is common. Much of it is intra-communal and is perpetuated by criminal gangs that became entrenched during the conflict when regular policing was surrendered to paramilitaries and other vigilantes with links to lawful political organizations. Territorial and ethnic population control by gangs and paramilitaries heightens the territorial and numerical dimensions of ethnic threat and fear. When outside agents, be they NGOs, international agencies, or commissions, organize cross-ethnic reconstruction programs and inject resources into communities devastated by war and insurgency, ethnic political machines appropriate the resources and programs to strengthen ethnic patronage and clientelism to the detriment of cross-ethnic ties.

In these settings, cooperation and shared institutions have to be established with bold top-down and bottom-up steps that Ashutosh Varshney refers to as an "institutionalized peace system" (2002: 9–11). Based on his study of cities in India at risk of communal Hindu–Muslim violence, at a minimum it entails cross-ethnic political alliances, peace committees from both groups, and routine cooperation of civic groups and business associations, but, "if politicians insist on polarizing Hindus and Muslims for the sake of electoral advantage, they can take the fabric of everyday engagement apart." In recognition of the need for a civil society initiative on cooperation and shared institutions, the Community Relations Unit of the Office of the First Minister and the Deputy First Minister published in January 2003 *A Shared Future: A Consultation Paper on Improving Relations in Northern Ireland*. Public debate has been engaged. NIPA intended to promote a non-sectarian civil society with top-down structures and initiatives that would transplant them to the grassroots. There is no lack of laws, commissions, agencies, and programs for improving community relations, advancing social justice, and achieving lasting peace. There is the Community Relations Council and the District Council Community Relations Programme, an Equality Commission, the EMU and Cultural Heritage mandates, the Human Rights Commission, a Targeting Social Needs initiative, and the statutory duty placed on public bodies to promote good relations between persons of different religious persuasion, political opinion or racial group. These organizations and programs finance many local activities, including the work of non-governmental organizations. What has been accomplished?

Avoidance

Data from the 2001 census indicate that residential segregation in Belfast has increased since the IRA ceasefire in 1994: two-thirds of the population of Northern Ireland live in areas that are 90 percent or more Catholic or 90 percent or more Protestant (Ingram 2002). Sectarian encapsulation and polarization during the most violent years 1969–74, especially in working-class neighborhoods of Belfast, were partly a legacy from the history of past ethnic violence and partly a response to the security dilemma for ordinary people. Data from the 1901 census indicates that 60 percent of Belfast residents lived in streets that were highly segregated (90 percent or more Catholic or 90 percent or more Protestant). The figure increased to 67 percent by the late 1960s and 77 percent in the early 1980s (Boal 2002: 689). The increments were due to communal violence. Over time Belfast became more segregated and residents of the central city moved out to safer neighborhoods. The first "peace walls" were built by residents at sectarian interfaces using arsoned buses and autos because barriers reduced communal rioting. The authorities, the army, and the police eventually recognized the reality on the ground and authorized and built additional ones. Of the 27 walls in Belfast, including two built since NIPA, none has been taken down. Surveys indicate the closer one lives to a wall, the more opposed one is to dismantling it. The Housing Authority tried to attract both groups to mixed public housing with rent reduction, but families avoided them because they attracted vandalism, bombing, and arson. In the end, public policy on residential integration failed because security was inadequate and because of in-group preferences. The authorities accepted community self-segregation. They couldn't well build housing that just stood empty or was destroyed (Bollens 1998). Peter Shirlow (2003) found that, in the troubled Ardoyne district of Belfast, fear, mistrust, and neighborhood social pressures result in robust sectarian separation and boundaries despite the fact that quite a few residents privately approve cross-community interaction. The majority of residents refuse to shop, get medical services, and use recreation facilities in places dominated by the other religion, and only 5 percent work in such places. This contrasts to the middle-class neighborhoods near Queen's University which are mixed, tolerant of ethnic interaction, and peaceful. Housing moves there are chosen for life stage and household composition change, and not because of sectarian animosity and rejection (author interview with the geographer Fred Boal, Belfast, June 17, 2003).

Avoidance isn't happening just in working-class Belfast. In Derry, only one Protestant neighborhood remained on the Catholic side of the river Foyle, and only one Catholic neighborhood on the Protestant side of the river. During the Troubles, people came to view physical and social separation as guarantors of security in daily life. They view cross-community relations as burdened with uncertainty and potential trouble

Since the ceasefire and NIPA, sectarian political violence has much diminished. There are indicators that violence has turned inward and has become linked to gang violence, criminal rackets, the illegal drug trade, and interpersonal aggression. Working-class Belfast abounds in street gangs. Similar problems exist in underclass areas of cities all over the world. As in other cities, a strong economic and education program targeting the youth and disrupted families has helped, yet the culture of violence and sectarian avoidance remains resilient.

The paramilitary presence complicates a civil society strategy for social reconstruction. Paramilitaries had assumed the role of "community defense" against the police and outsiders, and continue enforcing community norms in the name of "community justice" with kneecapping and beating offenders without accountability to lawful authority, even as some of them participate in criminal activities. According to informants, Republican neighborhoods are better organized and controlled than the Loyalist areas. The IRA raises funds from US donors, extorts from local businesses (e.g. taxis) and controls a share of NGO and local government funds which are distributed to those in need (unemployed, older people, families that have lost a breadwinner, etc.) in addition to rewarding their adherents. They have become a "little state" within localities, what I refer to as an ethno-political patronage organization. The Protestant working class is more disorganized and bitter. Employment in manufacturing and in policing has diminished; nondiscrimination in employment now means competition with Catholics; the police which they considered "theirs" now arrest them in sectarian clashes; public funding has been funneled to Catholic districts because of their "minority" status. In their view, NIPA, the political process, and civil society programs have worsened their well-being.

Research has found that the public is ahead of the political leaders on peace building. From the results of a major survey in 1996, the authors conclude that "most people in Northern Ireland want to live together rather

than apart, and . . . even on those matters on which there is most disagreement there are some possible compromises" (Hadden *et al.* 1996: 48). These
findings indicate a lot of change since 1968 when a majority in both groups
agreed that "people with the same religion ought to stick together" (Rose
1971: 495). Three surveys tracking community relations from 1989 to 1999,
analyzed by Jane Hughes and Caitlin Donnelly (2003), found that a substantial majority of Catholics and Protestants in 1999 preferred living in
mixed neighborhoods, working in a mixed environment, and schooling their
children in a mixed school. Ninety-one percent agreed that government
should give top priority to equal treatment, and 64 percent believed that
this was actually the case. This contrasts with 69 percent of Protestants in
1968 who opposed anti-discrimination legislation in employment and housing (Rose 1971: 481). The *NILT* survey (2002) found that large majorities
among Catholics, and a majority among Protestants prefer mixed neighborhoods, mixed schooling for their children, and an integrated workplace.
Three out of four respondents would not mind if a close relative were
to marry out of their religion. Almost none report having been abused
verbally on account of their religion or having been unfairly treated in a shop
or business.

No political party, movement, group, or policy initiative has so far
managed to mobilize the pool of citizens willing to cooperate and share
institutions across the sectarian divide. There is no institutionalized peace
system. To the contrary. Sectarian party politics polarize ethnic relations.
Disappointed expectations and public disillusionment over the decommissioning gridlock, devolution, and the implementation of NIPA have eroded
support for the Agreement though not for achieving peace. Commenting
on the findings from a survey by the Centre for the Study of Ethnic Conflict,
Colin Irwin puts it thus: "the people of Northern Ireland appear to be
moving away from the voices of moderation and accommodation and back
to their separate political camps" (2003: 49). In February 2003, a majority
of supporters of all three Unionist parties would have voted to reject the
Agreement "if the referendum were held today." In the 2005 Westminster
elections, the two top political parties chosen by the voters were the DUP
with 33.7 percent and Sinn Fein with 24.3 percent, the two parties that in
the past seven years did the most for obstructing implementation of NIPA.

7 Peace building

The peace process

Conflict and conciliation dynamics puts the accent on obstacles to peace making in civil wars and insurgencies. The end of hostilities finds the adversaries and the society more divided than before violent conflict:

1   Internal armed conflict has devastating effects on the polity, society, and the economy. Peace institutions and capabilities weaken, and violence institutions and capabilities strengthen.
2   According to the paradox of mobilization, leadership groups and the population change during the conflict in ways that make peace making problematic. Hardliners displace moderates, and splits between conciliators and rejectionists factionalize each adversary; bystanders are mobilized, polarized, and encapsulated in partisan subcultures; external interveners have been added to the internal adversaries.
3   The insurgents and the security forces perpetuate massacres and atrocities against one another and against civilians in violation of the laws of war, human rights, and humanitarian law. An emergency system of surveillance, fighting, detention, and prosecution of insurgents and terrorists suspends the justice system and leads to abuses.
4   Issues have accumulated. On top of the core issues, the armed conflict and the emergency institutions for counterinsurgency keep generating contentious conflicts over responsibility for killings, violence and security, refugees, relief operations, failed peace efforts, and the safety and welfare of civilians.
5   Some external intervention tends to increase the conflict because it is partisan rather than conciliatory. Well-intentioned humanitarian relief and peacekeeping operations are diverted by the combatants for increasing their war-making resources and enable combatants to relinquish responsibility for non-combatants. International intervention with military force is improvised as the crisis deepens and is often too little, too late.
6   The stakes in a peace settlement are very high since adversaries will continue living in the same state and will need to cooperate for peace implementation, yet they continue pursuing war goals by other means.

> According to the paradox of peace making, the adversaries' relationship has become more hostile and less trusting; rigid and extreme views about one another have embedded in collective myths that have the force of truth; each considers itself the victim of the other's aggression.

Accessible information about conflict and peace processes around the world is tracked and analyzed by research and policy organizations. The International Crisis Group (www.crisisweb.org) tracks conflicts on a monthly basis and publishes analyses with policy recommendations on ongoing crises. The Center for International Development and Conflict Management (CIDCM) at the University of Maryland (www.cidcm.umd.edu) updates the Minorities at Risk data set and publishes analyses and trends every other year titled *Peace and Conflict: Global Survey of Armed Conflicts, Self-Determination Movements and Democracy*. The Human Security Centre (www.humansecuritycentre.org) publishes the annual *Human Security Report* which analyzes trends on the causes and course of international and internal conflicts. Their websites link to the other conflict and peace research institutes around the world and to government and international organization websites such as the UN Department of Peacekeeping Operations (www.un.org/Depts/dpko).

Peace negotiations are preceded by informal probes and exploratory communications between the adversaries through intermediaries who may be external stakeholders, neutral states without a direct interest in the conflict, prominent public figures such as retired statesmen and Nobel prize winners, or mediators appointed by international organizations such as the European Union and the United Nations. Peace negotiations are not institutionalized to the same extent as other modes of conflict management, e.g. collective bargaining between management and trade unions under labor law. In collective bargaining for a labor contract, who the adversaries are is recognized by law, the date of contract expiration is known, there are rules for negotiation according to law and precedent, the mode of acceptance for a new contract is lawful – ratification by vote of the union members – and coercive actions undertaken during negotiations, such as striking and picketing and countermoves by the employer, are also protected by labor law and violations (e.g. strike breaking) negatively sanctioned by the state. Thus labor negotiators can focus on the substantive issues because the procedures for negotiation are set down in the law. By contrast in peace negotiations, the who, when, how, and what (the agenda) are subject to disagreement; the mode of ratification of the settlement has to be determined; coercive moves by the adversaries continue and are not subject to sanction mechanisms; and the enforcement of the peace settlement is also to be negotiated (Oberschall 1973: 244–5). The preparatory talks and intermediaries attempt to create an orderly and normative framework for peace talks and get the adversaries to commit to that framework ahead of the negotiations. Thus talk/fight eventually shifts to cessation of open hostilities and to peace negotiations.

Darby and Mac Ginty (2000: 7–8) have identified five criteria defining a genuine peace process:

1   The adversaries negotiate in good faith and do not stall with pre-conditions and non-negotiable demands.
2   The key players are included in the process, which necessitates mutual "recognition" by the adversaries.
3   The central issues in the conflict are addressed – both the core and the derivative issues.
4   The players do not use force to achieve their goals, or use a ceasefire merely for rearming and repositioning their forces.
5   The players are committed to a sustained process, not just exploratory talks.

Add a sixth criterion: the external stakeholders and interveners assume some responsibility for implementing the settlement with resources, monitoring, enforcement guarantees, and reconstruction aid.

These are the ideal circumstances: the Oslo, Dayton, and Northern Ireland peace processes were short on several criteria yet went ahead. In the Oslo process through Camp David, the good faith of both adversaries was questionable because of their use of or reluctance to stop coercive moves that each knew obstructed the negotiations. In Northern Ireland, some major players were excluded or took themselves out of the negotiations: Sinn Fein until the final phase; the DUP refused to sign the peace accord. Some of the most divisive issues such as decommissioning and police reform were outsourced from the negotiations to post-accord commissions. Before and at Dayton, the Bosnian Serbs had to be bombed by NATO into participation in peace talks and coerced by Milosevic for compromising on borders and for signing the DPA, which they did their utmost to undermine during implementation. In the Kosovo peace negotiations, the central issue of stateness was not decided. Because of these shortcomings of peace pacting, implementation of peace accords is beset by uncertainties.

Peace agreements

Research on peace agreements since the end of the Cold War (Darby and Rae 1999; Wallensteen 2002: 149–56) shows that they encompass security, demilitarization and demobilization, humanitarian assistance, refugee return, power sharing governance and elections, human rights and minority protection, and reconstruction aid. When stateness is a core issue, the agreements also deal with a constitutional design for the new state or states, even when it is an interim rather than a final status. When the fighting has devastated the state and society and instability is a threat to the international order, peace-building responsibility is assumed by external stakeholders, as in Bosnia and Kosovo. In the aftermath of civil war, it is one thing to grant refugees and internally displaced persons the right of return and compensation for property and quite another to implement such rights. Legal rights have to be established on the basis of documents and records which may have been purposely destroyed; the predicament of current residents who may themselves be displaced persons and whose occupancy rights had been recognized and legalized by the authorities has to be dealt with; security of the returnees who may be harassed and intimidated has to be provided. These steps assume a functioning political authority and a legal and administrative process of functioning courts and municipal administration which have to be rebuilt.

Some agreements also deal with truth and justice, long-term economic reconstruction, political reforms, and ethnic reconciliation. A civic culture of tolerance and respect for minorities is not conceivable without truth and justice in human affairs. Justice after ethnic warfare and crimes is demanded by the victims and restores the rule of law in place of private revenge and cycles of retribution. It uncovers truth, removes offenders from public office, holds individuals rather than groups responsible for crimes against humanity, and gives offenders an opportunity to reintegrate into society after they have served their sentences. Truth and justice however run up against the culture of denial of the adversaries. Both sides claim to be the victims and both have justified aggression and violence with collective myths of legitimate defense under threat. These myths and sentiments have been promoted by the political leaders and mass media and continue to be spread by them even after the peace settlement. "We bury our dead and live with our killers" is the context for return of displaced persons and refugees. A former political prisoner who returned to Prizren in Kosovo told Mark Baskin: "On my way to work I greet the judge who sentenced me to nine years in prison" (2002: 13). Long-term peace gets a chance only when security becomes normal, when justice and truth have punctured the culture of lies and denial, and when political reforms and economic reconstruction have established cooperation between adversaries.

State failure and peace building

After insurgency and war, peace building is contingent on unfavorable conditions that exist at that time and in all likelihood for some time to come: physical destruction, an economy in shambles, flourishing black markets and smuggling, refugees and internally displaced persons living in camps and temporary residences, unemployed young men with access to cheap weapons, high levels of both property and violent crime, dependence by many on humanitarian relief, and spoiler groups who continue violent attacks. Within these typical parameters there is a great deal of variation on *state failure* and on *effective authority*. At one extreme there is total state failure, as in Somalia; at the other extreme there exists a functioning state and administration, as in Northern Ireland. Between the extremes there can be state failure at the center but an effective administration in particular provinces and municipalities. A typical instance is when the central state administration is weaker than ethno-political patron–client machines that effectively run the government administration in their domains, as in Bosnia after Dayton. Another instance is when the state administration is eclipsed by ethnic and religious groups with militias that become rivals and substitutes of the state. They provide some security and justice in areas they control, run their own schools and other social services, and collect compulsory "taxes" from the population to finance their activities, which approximates post-war Afghanistan.

Effective local authority can be exercised by a multitude of small groups, leaders, parties, warlords, clan leaders and/or insurgents rooted each in a district, province, or town, but who fight one another and block effective authority beyond localities. At times one group ends up controlling the capital and many control the periphery, as in Afghanistan, or else the civil war ends with a few territorial authorities without an effective overarching central government, which was the case at the end of the Bosnian war. Another possibility is that a strong man and party end up controlling the central government and most of the state's territory and population, which was the situation in Cambodia after the ouster of the Khmer Rouge. Disarmament, demilitarization, refugee return, power sharing, economic reconstruction, and other provisions of a peace settlement will have to be implemented in such messy worlds (Baskin 2004).

In the past decade, the UN and external stakeholders in peace building have improvised a variety of post-conflict administration and reconstruction modes that differ on intrusiveness, responsibility assumed, and resources invested by external stakeholders. Mark Baskin describes them as:

> a new type of loosely bounded political system in which the policy-makers are both international and national, and the exercise of policy depends on the cooperation and coordination of a range of military, political administrative and non-governmental organizations. They borrow elements from the UN trusteeship system, from colonial administration and governance, and from post-Second World War reconstruction in Europe and Asia.
>
> (2003: 162)

The most intrusive and comprehensive mode of intervention has been termed an *international protectorate*, as in Kosovo and East Timor, where UN operations had much formal authority to establish security, administer public affairs, and build state institutions. *Supervisory operations*, as in Bosnia, are less intrusive, yet, in the face of refusal by ethnic leaders to implement the Dayton accords, the external stakeholders provided the High Representative with increased authority to make binding decisions and to dismiss obstructing officials. At a low level of intrusiveness are *advisory operations*, as in Afghanistan, when the UN Security Council mandate assists a formally sovereign government in security operations and reconstruction. In some armed conflicts and crises the UN is only minimally involved, as was true in the Rwanda genocide and is the case thus far in Darfur.

When the authorities fail to secure life and property in an armed conflict, people seek security in a viable mode of social organization, usually their ethnic and/or religious group. In an extreme case of state failure and fragmentation close to anarchy, everyone is caught in a security dilemma and submits to the local strong man with the guns. Mancur Olson has analyzed how such anarchy evolves into a decentralized warlord state:

> [in anarchy] even when there is a balance of power that keeps any one leader or group from assuming total control of a large area or jurisdiction, the leader of each group may be able to establish himself as an autocrat of a small domain. A dispersion of power and resources over a large area can result in a set of small-scale autocracies, but no democracy.
>
> (1993: 573)

The group leaders or warlords will rule by organizing an ethnic group with a territorial concentration, although during protracted insurgency the group may change to a motley collection of adherents for whom fighting and loot have become a way of life.

The civil war and insurgency scenarios of new war theory (Jean and Ruffin 1996) and the "conflict trap" model of civil war developed by the World Bank group (Collier *et al.* 2003) agree with Olson's warlord control in a failed state. In these civil wars, according to Collier:

> once a rebellion has started it appears to develop a momentum of its own. Getting back to peace is hard, and even when peace is reestablished it is often fragile . . . Most entrepreneurs of violence have essentially political objectives . . . Loot is not usually the root motivation for conflict, but it may become critical to its perpetuation, giving rise to the conflict trap.
>
> (2003: 79)

Afghanistan as a failed state

An example will flesh out the analysis. Before the US war against the Taliban in Afghanistan, the country had already experienced 20 years of war, civil war, and insurgencies. Unlike the Yugoslav wars, these wars were not about secession, i.e. stateness. Afghans have a national identity based on a long history of statehood and resistance against foreign invaders. The wars were over control of the state, territory, and population, and were brutal. Millions of refugees fled to Pakistani refugee camps across the border, and the country was awash in weapons funded and supplied by Saudi Arabia and the US during the anti-Soviet war.

In the early 1990s, poppy for opium making earned 25 times more than the wheat, rice, and cotton that farmers traditionally grew, and a war-torn criminalized narco-economy had taken root. The journalist Pankaj Mishra writes that "Local Mujahideen 'commanders' – the word in Afghanistan refers to men with guns and bands of their loyal supporters . . . set up toll checkpoints on roads. Extortion, arbitrary arrests, killings and kidnapping, and rape had become commonplace" (2005: 46). This description corresponds to what Olson meant by anarchy in a failed state. Under the Taliban, autocratic Islamist rule by an alliance of ethnic and religious leaders and jihadis had been imposed in the Pashtun-dominated southern and eastern provinces. The Taliban continued the civil war against the ethnic leaders and militias forming the Northern Alliance. The Taliban correspond to Olson's "stationary bandit" – the autocrat – extending his domain against rival warlords in order to achieve a monopoly of control in a territory and who provides some public goods like security of life and property. To be sure, for secular Afghan women, barring them from employment outside the household was a public bad, not good. The point is that the Taliban had effective authority and exercised it for governing.

When al Qaeda based in Afghanistan conducted the 9/11 terrorist actions against the US and the Taliban refused to surrender Osama bin Laden and its other leaders, the US declared war and invaded. Rather than use American ground troops for that purpose, the Bush administration hired the regional commanders and militias in the Northern Alliance for $70 million and provided weapons, airstrikes, and cover, and a small cadre of Special Forces and CIA officers in what amounted to outsourcing the fighting to local mercenaries and private contractors (Mishra 2005: 46). The Taliban were routed but regrouped across the border in Pakistan where the Pakistani government had no effective control. With international help, the US instituted an ambitious program of nation building centered on the capital Kabul under Hamid Karzai. Eighteen thousand US soldiers were deployed, a constitution was ratified, two elections were held for a national government, yet a few miles beyond Kabul the warlords who had been ousted by the Taliban, beefed up with US weapons and funding, recreated the previous warlord state based on armed militias (many masquerading as police) and opium trading. According to Mishra, "twenty-eight out of the country's thirty-two provinces now grow poppy, often with the support and involvement of local officials" (2005: 47). Chris Mason, the Afghan policy officer in the State Department during 2001–5, writes that "half the seats [in the national legislature] . . . [are] held by the same old war lords, ex-communists, and hard line Islamists who helped complete the destruction of Afghanistan" and "as many as 90 percent of Afghanistan's police chiefs reportedly are involved in or protecting the drug trade" (2005). In 2006, the Taliban has resumed fighting in the southern provinces with sizable military forces.

The US and the coalition of states engaged in nation building have an ambitious program. The US is trying to create an Afghan army. The UK, Netherlands, and Germany are organizing provincial reconstruction teams. The US and Germany are training police officers. There are a number of poppy eradication programs. There is lots of road construction for linking major cities. There are schemes for agriculture development meant to wean farmers from poppy growing. Three million refugees have returned from Pakistan. NATO armed forces are poised to take over security from the US. But even the most basic security measures have so far failed. For instance, though some 30,000 of an estimated 150,000 private militiamen have turned in weapons under the disarmament program, they are old weapons no longer needed. The militias are keeping the new weapons acquired from the US when the warlords became allies in the war on the Taliban and the global war on terror. No doubt the constitutional design, democratic power sharing governance institutions, economic development programs, and state building devised by experts and external stakeholders are well intentioned and conceptually sound on paper, but peace building has to be applied in the Afghan political and military environment where security has not been provided and there has been state failure for almost 30 years.

Peace-building measures are context contingent and especially vulnerable to state failure and lack of effective authority. Disarming insurgents and a military bloated during civil war is quite a different operation in varying contexts. When a security dilemma persists during peace implementation as in Afghanistan, fighters are not likely to turn in their weapons and disband. When there is little likelihood of the resumption of war, as was the case in Mozambique, fighters hold on to arms because of their value in an arms black market, but peace builders can match the black market price in a buy-back program or supply tools, cash, and goods of equal value for farming. Where there is a robust state and effective authority some fighters can be integrated with the regular armed forces, as was done in South Africa (du Toit 2000: 41–2). In many instances, to get around the security dilemma, insurgents as well as members of the armed forces are granted some form of political amnesty and other ways of clearing their change of status from combatant to civilian. In other peace processes, the insurgents insist on parallel phased disarmament lest the authorities be tempted to play them for suckers by turning against them once they turn in their weapons. Such parallel disarmament is not going to work unless an external stakeholder is a guarantor, as NATO was in Bosnia after Dayton with a huge military force. The mode of disarmament and demobilization has to be adapted to context.

Other measures for stopping the fighting and establishing security are also context specific. The World Bank researchers (Collier *et al.* 2003: 141–4) describe a number of ways for "cutting the rebel financial jugular" and "curbing rebel access to commodity markets," diamonds in Angola and timber in Cambodia. These measures depend on the external stakeholders' influence with governments, multinational corporations, and international banks for shutting down the black market in these commodities. This is not going to work for the opium, heroin, and cocaine trade which is conducted through channels that are already criminal. Thousands of ordinary farmers grow poppy in Afghanistan with the collusion of the local authorities. The trade is taxed at hundreds of checkpoints and collection places. Eradication by spraying the fields destroys the livelihood of the farmers as well as some of the food they grow. Such programs have not been effective and have created support for insurgents and drug traders. An agricultural development program and rural non-agricultural employment on a vast scale will have to compete successfully with the narco-economy and official corruption, and these are contingent on a functioning state and effective authority in the poppy growing districts.

Security, law and order, stability

John Darby, Roger Mac Ginty and their associates (Darby and Mac Ginty 2000; Darby 2006b) have identified the most common and contentious implementation obstacle as the continuation and/or resumption of violence and other security issues. Virginia Gamba writes that:

> Ultimately conflict and peace are interrelated. Nowhere is this more evident than in the complex environment of demobilization, disarmament, and reintegration . . . In the manner in which these three issues are tackled early on – in the grey period between war and peace – lies the roots of a successful transition or the making of a failed state.
> (2006: 55–6)

Darby's research shows that continued violence and security problems result from state violence, from insurgent violence, from community violence, and from crime. State violence and insurgent violence are due to fractionalized adversaries. The government has to bring under control elements in the security forces that continue repression and illegal rackets that were part of counterinsurgency. Restoring the emergency security and judicial apparatus of the state to peacetime operations is a major undertaking especially when some violence continues. The government is also tempted to use fraud, intimidation, and violence in post-accord elections for staying in power, which will be responded by its political rivals in kind. External election monitors and the certification of the electoral process on a "free and fair" scale help restrain the adversaries.

The insurgents have rejectionist factions who did not sign on to the peace accords and who continue spoiler violence. Community violence and crime are facilitated by a culture of violence which becomes entrenched during armed conflict. The adversaries mobilize ethnic identities and solidarity with marches, rallies, funeral processions, and celebrations in which symbols,

songs, flags, insignia, taunts, and insults offensive to their enemies are promi-
nently displayed, and which precipitate communal rioting. These collective
actions do not cease just because a peace accord has been signed. Elections
called for in a peace accord legitimize and amplify these manifestations
of partisanship and mutual hostility. The violence capability inherited from
armed fighting continues. Insurgents establish transnational organizations
and networks for smuggling weapons and combatants, financing their operations through criminal activity, and laundering their cash flow to escape
detection. They are capable of doing the same for narcotics, contraband,
illegal aliens, prostitutes, and criminally obtained resources when armed
conflict subsides. Ethnic encapsulation in wartime leaves paramilitaries and
other groups not committed to peace accord implementation in control of
ethnic enclaves and territories. Absent lawful alternatives for making a
living, organized and individual crime is likely to continue (Darby 2006a).

Creating the Kosovo state

A case in point was Kosovo at the end of war in 1999. The Serb population
fled with the retreating Serb army or were expelled by ethnic cleansing and
regrouped in an enclave at Mitrovica along the Serb border. For the pre-
ceding decade all government and staff had been Serb or controlled by Serbs
– elected officials, bureaucrats, judges, prosecutors, jailers, police, schools,
hospitals, the law, administrative procedures, language, driver's licenses,
auto registration, etc. The Kosovars totally disengaged from the Serb state
they viewed as illegitimate and organized parallel underground Albanian
institutions through the non-violent Democratic League of Kosovo headed
by the unofficial president, Ibrahim Rugova. Following the Serb debacle,
the Kosovo Liberation Army came from mountain hideouts and other safe
enclaves to establish control just when the UN deployed the Kosovo Force
(KFOR) made up of NATO soldiers. Chaos ensued. A daily television news
story showed angry Serb and Albanian mobs assaulting one another on the
Mitrovica bridge, which had become an ethnic interface, with hapless French
KFOR peacekeepers trying to separate them and being themselves assaulted
by angry Kosovar and Serb mobs. The Albanians wanted to reclaim the
houses and apartments whence they had been expelled, and the Serbs who
now occupied them and who had been expelled from other places and had
taken refuge in Mitrovica refused to yield unless KFOR repossessed their
houses and apartments and provided security. Timothy Garton Ash
characterized Kosovo in the winter of 1999/2000 as a "worsening state of
anarchy":

> the Albanian mafia has entered with a vengeance . . . what began with
> Albanians murdering Serbs ends with Albanians murdering each other
> . . . there are still virtually no police, and there is no effective law . . .
> KFOR forces have set up detention camps, with hundreds of suspected

murderers and violent criminals . . . then the Albanian judge comes and releases all Albanians, and the Serb judge does the same for Serbs.

(2000a: 50)

Under UN Security Council Resolution 1244, a four-pillar structure for Kosovo peace building was established. Pillar one headed by UNHCR was responsible for humanitarian assistance, and became the UNMIK "justice and police" pillar after humanitarian assistance was terminated. Pillar two dealt with civil administration under UNMIK (United Nations Mission in Kosovo). Institution building headed by OSCE (Organization for Security and Cooperation in Europe) was pillar three, and economic reconstruction under the EU (European Union) was pillar four. UNMIK was:

> given an unprecedented mandate both in terms of its scope and struc-tural complexity. UNMIK was tasked with re-establishing and running a complete transitional civil administration responsible for everything from security, justice, law enforcement, health and education to matters as mundane as garbage collection . . . [it] amounted to re-establishing all the state institutions . . . and the development of provisional democratic self-governing institutions.
>
> (UN Security Council Report, 10 February 2006, no. 3, Kosovo)

At the start UNMIK had no judges and police to work with. Only 30 of 756 judges and prosecutors prior to the NATO war were Kosovar Albanians, and they faced threats because they were seen as Serb collaborators. An international police force was slow in getting started and too few for effec-tive law and order. In lieu of police, UNMIK enlisted KFOR to deal with violent crime and disorder. The KLA tried to seize and appropriate local administration, businesses, communications media, and other resources and functions of local government that were UNMIK's responsibility. Garton Ash writes that, "In small towns and villages, the self-appointed KLA bosses behave as if they are the masters now. Local people complain bitterly about the unjust way they distribute international aid" (Ash 2000a: 50). Kosovo had a socialist civil and property rights legal system and Serb criminal and emergency law from the 1990s Serb military administration. Habeas corpus for detainees had been suspended under the Serbs. The body of law was reestablished to what it had been in 1989 before Serb domination, but, since much organized violence continued and judges and witnesses were intimidated when KLA members were prosecuted, the detention of suspects and witness protection programs were continued. Interim international judges and prosecutors were recruited for restarting the court system. There were inevitable conflicts and misunderstandings between the inter-national staff and the locals, e.g. over the higher pay, perks, and protection the internationals got (which was similar to the two-tiered system of compensation and status between expatriates and natives in colonial services before independence). A crash program to train judges and other court personnel and for police was instituted (Baskin 2002). The physical infrastructure of courts, police, and corrections needed repair and new resources, e.g. even the electricity supply to the court buildings and offices was problematic. An inspectorate for oversight of the judiciary and for evaluation of judges' performance was started. A bar exam was introduced, and the appointments of judges were lengthened when their competence and fairness warranted it. As these institutions rooted and a new cohort of law faculty graduates came online, slowly a new justice system emerged in Kosovo. Municipal elections were held in October 2000 and a legitimate local government was installed, but remained under UNMIK supervision.

Peacetime institutions slowly replaced violence and chaos. The cost is high. In 2005, UNMIK still had 910 international and 2,900 local staff, and had spent $2.2 billion. KFOR had 17,000 troops from some 35 countries, and UNMIK civilian police totaled 3,300 officers from 49 countries (most from Germany, India, Jordan, and the US). Not counted in these staff and cost figures are the OSCE and EU missions with a total of 424 international and 1,234 local staff. Bearing in mind that 2005 is five years after war's end, that its final stateness had not been decided, that Kosovo is a small country with only 2 million people (in 1991), and that because of the ethnic cleansing at war's end there are few ethnic interfaces where violence typically flares during peace building, one can imagine the enormous task of repairing a failed state and creating democratic governance institutions in much more populous and ethnically diverse and mixed states like Afghanistan and Iraq.

Democratic governance

In Chapter 1 I highlighted "stateness" as the core issue in some civil wars and insurgencies. There is much debate and lack of scholarly consensus about whether state formation by partition, secession, and other means is effective for ethnic conflict reduction both within the new state and between the new and the original state(s). The pivotal variables are the number, size, homogeneity, mixing, and territorial concentration of ethnic groups in a multiethnic state. Some research suggests that, if a minority has a territorial concentration in a region – a homeland – where it is the majority group, it is more likely to engage in rebellion for secession (Toft 2002/3: 84). Chaim Kaufmann concludes from his comparative and quantitative research that "restoring civil politics in multiethnic states shattered by war is impossible because the war itself destroys the possibility for ethnic cooperation . . . there are strong reasons to believe that violent conflicts cannot be 'reconstructed' back to ethnic harmony" (1996: 137, 153). Both Lijphart (1990) and Horowitz (1985) argue that with suitable constitutional design and power sharing ethnic conflicts can be managed non-violently in multiethnic states, though they differ on the specific governance institutions for doing so.

Multivariate quantitative studies (Doyle and Sambanis 2000; Fearon and Laitin 2003; Collier *et al.* 2003) of the risk of ethnic warfare and the difficulties of peace making due to ethnic and religious divisions in multiethnic states operationalize and measure these variables in a flawed manner and with flawed data. Collier's religious factionalism is based on nine categories: Catholic, Protestant, Muslim, Jew, Hindu, Buddhist, and three Eastern religions. This omits the quintessential religious conflicts within Islam, Shia versus Sunni, and between the Islamic religious fundamentalists and ruling secularists in Algeria, Afghanistan, Pakistan, Turkey, Egypt, and elsewhere. The ethno-linguistic factionalism (ELF) index in these studies is based on data from a 1964 Russian ethnographic world atlas (*Atlas Narodov Mira* 1964) which confounds language, ethnic group, and national origin. For the US the *Atlas*'s ethno-linguistic figures are what in the US census for 1960 are listed as "foreign or mixed parents" added to "foreign born." Using these figures for categorizing ethno-linguistic groups in the US assumes zero assimilation and zero English language acquisition by immigrants and for Americans who have one native-born parent. The US census does not ask what language is spoken in the household or whether the householders speak English. There are similar problems of categorizations for other countries of immigration like Canada and Australia. Using these methods, on a 0 to 100 ELF scale the US is 50, which is similar to Switzerland (50) and Zimbabwe (54) (Mauro 1995: 708–9). Such figures cast doubt on the validity of the ELF index. In African countries the *Atlas* omits lingua francas that have made for national unity. Tanzania gets a 93 index even though most Tanzanians speak Swahili. Until improved methods are used in country-based multivariate studies, conclusions on causes of ethnic conflict and the consequences for peace making due to ethnic and religious divisions should be viewed with caution.

If an ethnic group achieves constitutional and political change short of full sovereignty in an independent state, there is further disagreement on just what mix of federalism, autonomy, and group rights is appropriate for ethnic conflict reduction and for peaceful conflict management. No governance theory that simultaneously links size, relative size, number, heterogeneity, and territorial mix of ethnic groups has yet been formulated for understanding ethnic conflict management, although promising starts have been made (Horowitz 2000: chapter 15; Toft 2002/3). It is, however, widely agreed that democratic states should and do reach substantial accommodation with minorities on power sharing, within reasonable limits, as a matter of democratic principle as well as sound conflict management.

In a democracy, the powers of the executive branch are limited by the constitution and checked by the legislative and judicial branches. Political leaders are elected by the people in free and fair elections. The state functions within the rule of law. Individual human rights are protected. In multiethnic democracies, government is inclusive of minorities: there is no self-perpetuating and permanent ethnic majority ruling group that excludes minorities. In most cases, minorities have some group rights, e.g. on language. There is a large range of activities for citizens and groups which is not controlled by the state, e.g. religion. Democracy works best when individuals and groups pursue a variety of interests that cross-cut social categories and cleavages – age/life stage, social class, urban–rural, lifestyles, professions and occupations, gender, private sector versus state sector, in addition to ethnicity, nationality, language, and religion. Groups and individuals that are adversaries on some issues find that they are allies on other matters. A variety of shifting coalitions are formed, disbanded, and reassembled routinely in the political process. All citizens have an interest in good roads. Businessmen from all groups have an interest in low-transaction costs for economic activity and limits on bureaucratic state controls. All low-income people, regardless of ethnicity, have an interest in a decent minimum wage, safety in the workplace, state support for health care, and preschool. Democratic power sharing in multiethnic societies should provide incentives for the transition from identity politics based on ethnicity to democratic interest politics, the inclusion of the hitherto excluded, equal access to state services, fairness in justice, and tolerance between groups. To the extent that these conditions are in the making, one can refer to the process as "democratic consolidation" (Linz and Stepan 1996).

Political scientists have formulated two incompatible models for democratic power sharing in ethnically divided societies. Both models agree that the winner-take-all, single member constituency electoral system and a majoritarian organization of the national legislature as in the US and the UK are inappropriate for ethnic conflict management in multiethnic societies. Political institutions that frame inter-ethnic relations as a zero sum game should be avoided. The models disagree on: (1) the organization of the three branches of government with respect to inclusion–exclusion of ethnic minorities and checks and balances between majority and minorities; (2) the electoral system of voting rules and constituency size and boundaries that translates actual votes into elected political office holders; (3) the balance between human rights and group rights; and (4) fairness, non-discrimination, and access norms for inter-ethnic relations.

Consociational power sharing was formulated by Arend Lijphart (1990). The core idea inspiring it is that ethnic identities and groups are robust and permanent and that in a multiethnic democracy they will persist and continue to be the principal axis of governance and politics. The art of political engineering is to channel ethnicity and ethnic relations towards cooperation, accommodation, and peace. The state should be decentralized and federal, with an ethnic majority entrenched in each federal unit. At the center of the state a grand coalition executive that includes all ethnic groups governs. Each ethnic group has a veto on the most important constitutional and policy issues. Legislative, executive, and government positions and resources are allocated on a proportionality principle that is considered fair and equitable. The electoral system should be some variation on proportional representation which is the rule in continental Europe and which provides for inclusion of all groups in a coalition government. Ethnic groups have group rights and practice group autonomy, sometimes referred to as segmental autonomy. There is cooperation rather than conflict among the governing class because they have divided up power and resources among them – a "cartel of elites" – and there is peace among the rest of the population because inter-ethnic relations rest on separation and avoidance, both in territorial and in functional terms. Consociational governance perpetuates ethnic groups and divisions, but these provide stability because they are properly managed. It works best when there is a sharp territorial separation of the ethnic groups, as in Switzerland, but its advocates also claim its usefulness for territorially mixed ethnic societies as in Northern Ireland, Bosnia, and Lebanon.

"Incentives"-based democratic power sharing – also referred to as "integrative" – was formulated by Donald Horowitz (1990). Horowitz takes a far less benign view of ethnicity in democratic politics than Lijphart. Unless tempered and tamed, ethnicity will tear the body politic apart; consequently institutions should provide incentives for decoupling politics from identity and ethnicity and align them instead with interest politics based on other cleavages, e.g. social class, social democracy, economic policy and strategy, and the like. Horowitz advocates a unitary state with a non-ethnic federal structure (federal units not to coincide with the ethnic groups); majoritarian but ethnicity-neutral executive, legislative, and administrative bodies and jurisdictions; a "vote pooling" electoral system such as proportional representation with an alternative vote or single transfer vote which has incentives for pre-election political party pacts between moderates cutting across ethnicity and a post-election coalition of moderates; and "ethnically blind" policies rather than proportionality, e.g. policies that benefit all low-income groups regardless of ethnicity rather than a policy that specifically benefits an economically disadvantaged ethnic group. These institutions reward inter-ethnic cooperation and foster identities other than ethnicity. They provide incentives for a mixed ethnic governing coalition and for aligning policy and politics on non-ethnic interest articulation.

A huge literature on the merits and the shortcomings of the two models now exists (Sisk 1996; Reynolds 2002; O'Flynn and Russell 2005; Noel 2005). The advocates and critics on both sides are competent professional analysts and are knowledgeable on the same limited number of cases from the past 20 years or so when power sharing in divided societies has been introduced in peace settlements. They refer to earlier instances of political transitions from colony to independent state, from communist regime to post-communist political systems, and from earlier European history, and yet profoundly disagree on the lessons learned from the comparative history of power sharing institutions.

One problem with the controversy is that, in addition to the complex bundle of political variables in the models, the success and failure of power sharing democratic governance depends on many variables linked to state failure, continued violence, economic collapse, external intervention, and others. The models are formulated within the context of simplified domestic and international environments which are non-transferable to complex conflict-ridden situations. What could the Swiss and Canadian experience with federalism and democratic power sharing have in common with what governance in post-war Iraq, Afghanistan, and the Sudan has to cope with? Any model that assumes inter-ethnic elite cooperation is going to have severe application problems in Northern Ireland and Bosnia where it does not exist. A model that assumes free and fair elections is going to be flawed where political power is appropriated by means foul and illegitimate. How can one divide resources proportionately among ethnic groups when elites control resources and positions and award them to their adherents? Does it make sense to analyze the inner workings of a legislature when political power is in the hands of warlords and political bosses who control the legislators? In application to post-civil-war divided societies, the consociational and incentives-based models of democratic power sharing institutions are normative ideals that point the way to a future end state, but they are incomplete roadmaps on how to reach the promised land. What is needed is realistic implementation models or scenarios for governance in divided societies that are in the transition from violent armed conflict to more peaceful modes of conflict management (Wallensteen 2002: chapter 7).

Putting Humpty-Dumpty together again

Peace negotiations and peace building have a low success rate despite sound research and promising theorizing on democratic governance by credentialed academics, despite mediation by experienced and sophisticated diplomats and technical staff, and despite an outpouring of aid and good will by humanitarian agencies. Peace building has to be feasible and it has to be acceptable. There are five explanations for low success:

1   Sound knowledge is lacking. Despite impressive research, knowledge about peace building remains incomplete. The operation is so complex and contingent that unanticipated results keep coming up and derail the effort. Success and failure are not clear cut. Well-meaning observers will disagree about whether the cup is half full or half empty, and whether one should persist or change course. Some peace-building plans are not feasible, yet it is difficult to tell *ex ante* which are and which are not, and *ex post* it is not evident how to increase the chances of success.

2   What is feasible is not acceptable. A sound peace settlement is obstructed by the leaders and the publics of one or both adversaries.

3 Political agenda trumps informed knowledge. Informed knowledge is provided to political leaders about conflict management and state building by experts, but is rejected because it does not fit the leaders' political agenda and ideology.

4 Implementation is bungled. The organization and management of complex peace building involving many and different types of stakeholders are convoluted, ad hoc, and full of rivalries and contradictions. Though feasible and acceptable, implementation is deficient.

5 There is a lack of resources. Peace building takes longer and necessitates a wider scope of activities and institutions than anticipated. Insufficient resources are allocated to it. Peace building is feasible, but not on the cheap.

Examples from Bosnia, Northern Ireland, Iraq, and Cyprus will speak to these explanations. Iraq and Cyprus merit more detailed analysis.

Limits to knowledge

The attempted transition from communism to democracy in Yugoslavia was undermined by the outcomes of the 1990 elections which put into power parties and leaders that pursued a nationalist agenda. Goati writes that "The electoral system has strongly influenced the election results in both Serbia and Montenegro as well as the remaining Yugoslav republics" (2000: 36). The reform communists and non-party intellectuals in both Serbia and Croatia believed their chances of winning against ethno-national parties were better with a majority two-round system instead of proportional representation (PR), and they were sadly mistaken. The majority system gave the ethno-nationalists a majority of seats in the legislature even though they obtained less than a plurality of votes in the first round: Milosevic's SPS got 46 percent of votes in the first round and ended with 78 percent of the Serb Assembly seats, whereas Tudjman's HDZ got 41.5 percent of votes and ended with 67 percent of the seats in the Croat Assembly. This meant that in Croatia and Serbia the ethno-nationalists were able to pursue their agenda without effective legislative opposition.

The consensus from political science is that in multiethnic states the majoritarian (Westminster first-past-the-post) electoral system should be avoided because it benefits ethnic bloc voting that favors the majority at the expense of minorities and mixed ethnic parties, and that is what happened. Yugoslav communists were not experienced about democratic multi-party elections since the 1990 election was the first one ever, but they were not ignorant of developments elsewhere in Eastern Europe. But consider what happened in Bosnia where a PR system was in place for the 1990 elections: "the three nationalist parties gained votes and seats almost directly proportional to individuals' choices of national identity in the 1981 census" (Woodward 1995: 122). Together they accounted for 82 percent of all votes and badly defeated the reform communists and other centrist reform parties with an all-Yugoslav constitutional agenda. That outcome was no better than what the parties of moderation and Yugoslav unity achieved in Serbia and Croatia. One might conclude that it is the interaction of electoral system, ethnic demographic mixing, and crisis politics rather than electoral system alone that accounts for outcomes on the moderate to extremist dimension, and that both political leaders and academic experts need more knowledge about the dynamics of such interaction.

In Northern Ireland in 1973, the Heath government tried a new political initiative with a 78-member assembly elected by PR designed to give non-sectarian moderates and nationalists a better chance of representation in the legislature and in governance than with a majoritarian system. It worked. The three parties in the pro-reform power sharing coalition won 60 percent of the votes and 51 of 78 assembly seats. Nevertheless the majority of unionists defeated power sharing in a follow-up constitutional convention and with a massive loyalist strike and civil disorders in the streets. What was sound political knowledge for political design and proved feasible turned out to be unacceptable to a substantial part of the people whose consent was needed for power sharing to work.

Consider constitutional design for Bosnia. One of its cornerstones was meant to be the Croat–Bosniak Federation which is one of the two political entities of the Bosnian state; the other is the Republika Srpska. The Federation was devised by US, Russian, and EC experts and negotiated with the Croats and Bosniaks in March 1994 for signing as the Washington Framework Agreement. Its purpose was to stop the Croat–Bosniak fighting which was especially savage in Mostar, block Croat secession of Herceg-Bosna (the part of Bosnia claimed by Croats) and its annexation by Croatia, and become a military and political counterweight to the Republika Srpska. It was also thought that an overall constitutional settlement for Bosnia would be more feasible if it proceeded in two steps, first a ceasefire and governance agreement between Croats and Bosniaks, and then an overall settlement between all three adversaries (Monnesland 1997: 411–12). Further details of the Federation structure were negotiated at Dayton between Croats and Bosniaks and consumed a lot of time and energy. Other negotiations dealt with the governance structure of the two entities, Federation and Republika Srpska (Chollet 1997: chapters 8–9). At the time the Federation looked like an important element of the overall constitutional design for Bosnia. As it turned out, it created a layer of bureaucracy and authority that complicated the already complex structure of government in Bosnia without contributing anything of value. Redesigners of Dayton want to abolish it altogether. In 2004, the European Stabilization Initiative put forward a plan for "making federalism work" by abolishing the Federation:

> The Federation is largely a historical accident . . . it ended up as a . . . federation inside another federation . . . in practice it consumes an

important share of resources while providing few practical services . . .
many of the original responsibilities of the Federation have been moved
to the state.

(ESI 2004)

Experts thought the Federation feasible, indeed crucial, for peace building
and expended political capital on establishing it, and they were proven
wrong.

If the Federation level of government turned out to be void of authority,
and a weak central government was legitimized at Dayton to accommodate the Serbs despite the objections of the Bosniaks, where does authority
reside in Bosnia? The answer is cantons and municipalities in the Federation
and municipalities in the Serb entity. The cantons have powers over police,
appointing judges, education and cultural policy, land use, public housing,
social services, local businesses, and television and radio programs.
Sumantra Bose notes that:

> The Bosnian state is a consociational confederation . . . between its two
> political entities – a radically autonomous RS and a Federation of BiH
> in which most competencies are devolved to the ten cantons (eight of
> which have clear Bosniak or Croat majority populations).

(2005: 326)

The canton idea originated in the last European Community constitutional
plan for Bosnia in March 1992 before the start of the Bosnian war. Named
after the Portuguese foreign minister Cutilheiro, the plan called for a confederation of three regions themselves divided into many small cantons.
At this time Bosnia already had held a referendum on independence that
the Serbs boycotted and which was approved by 99 percent of the remaining Croat and Bosniak voters. The plan was signed by Izetbegovic for the
Muslims, by Karadzic for the Serbs, and by a Croat representative, and
was understood to be the basis for further negotiations. As armed fighting
broke out, Izetbegovic thought the plan amounted to an ethnic partition
of Bosnia and urged the Bosnian assembly to reject it. The Bosnian Serbs
rejected the cantonization plan when they voted for a constitution for a
"Serbian Republic of BiH" and seceded unilaterally. In April the Bosnian
war started full-scale.

Later peace plans by the European Community and the Contact Group
all included a confederal dimension with ethnically defined cantons or
provinces and, as I previously explained in Chapter 4, were rejected by one
or another of the adversaries. At the Dayton negotiations themselves,
territorial definition of the entity borders and the consociational dimensions
of the central government were assiduously debated without any reference
to the authority and powers of the cantons and municipalities. Despite
the presence of a blue ribbon collection of advisors, experts, diplomats, and

mediators from a number of countries and international organizations, for the better part of three weeks the adversaries and external stakeholders debated and negotiated over those aspects of Bosnian governance that would prove irrelevant, like the Federation, or would not work, like the consociational dimensions of the central government, and omitted plans for the effective post-Dayton authority and administrative structure of Bosnia, which are not even mentioned in the Dayton General Framework Agreement and the 11 annexes. The irony of the peace building at Dayton story is that democratic governance institutions the adversaries found unacceptable were coerced on them by the external stakeholders in a consociational mode that proved unfeasible. In the end, government was made to work by an "international protectorate" in a most undemocratic fashion.

In both Northern Ireland and Bosnia the implementation of the peace settlement proceeded under favorable conditions since the external stakeholders managed to shut down the fighting and most of the violence, assured security of life and property, and invested huge resources into peace building. What of the prospect of peace and nation building in a deeply divided country in the midst of insurgency, terrorism, and military occupation of a hostile population, as is happening in Iraq?

Political agenda trumps informed knowledge: Iraq

Two years before the Bush administration assumed office in Washington in January 2001, Republican neo-conservatives and influential former Reagan officials agreed on regime change in Iraq as the centerpiece of a new US military and foreign policy strategy in the Persian Gulf and Middle East. In a letter sent to President Clinton on January 26, 1998, they wrote that "the only acceptable strategy is one that eliminates the possibility that Iraq will be able to use or threaten to use weapons of mass destruction . . . the strategy should aim, above all, at the removal of Saddam Hussein's regime from power." Containment was no longer working, they claimed. "The safety of American troops in the region, of our friends and allies like Israel and the moderate Arab states, and a significant portion of the world's supply of oil will all be put to hazard." Among the 16 signers were Donald Rumsfeld, Paul Wolfowitz, James Woolsey, Elliott Abrams, Richard Armitage, John Bolton, Richard Perle, Robert Zoellick, William Kristol, Francis Fukuyama, and Zalmay Khalilzad, which reads like a blue ribbon team of Republicans who would shape foreign and military policies and public opinion during the Bush administration. This was three years before the al Qaeda terrorist attack on the US on September 11, 2001, before the Afghan war, and before President Bush declared a global war on terror.

During the 2000 presidential campaign, candidate Bush "mocked the idea of nation-building as a dangerous Democratic folly . . . and repeated that the function of the American military was to 'fight and win wars'" (Taub 2004: 34). Within the military and the State Department, however, much debate and planning about peacekeeping and peace stabilization were taking place in reaction to the Bosnia, Somalia, Kosovo, and Haiti experiences of the 1990s. General Gordon Sullivan, the then army chief of staff, created a Peacekeeping Institute at the Army War College, and the Pentagon established a new Office of Peacekeeping and Peace Enforcement Policy. The Clinton administration began work on a "generic political-military plan" for future missions drawn up in the National Security Council. A vast literature on peacekeeping "lessons learned" and "how to do it" proliferated (Taub 2004: 35).

A consensus developed in these circles and among academics that peacekeeping and peace stabilization is a long process consisting of an intervention phase during which security, establishing order, and humanitarian relief are the first and foremost concern, followed by an interim administration for reconstruction of a functioning state and democratic political system in lieu of a failed autocratic regime and economy, and ending with full return to sovereignty and exit of the external interveners. Several conclusions were drawn. The initial phase requires about "twenty soldiers per 1000 inhabitants to stabilize an unsettled population," according to James Dobbins who was a top Clinton peacekeeping official. For Iraq it comes out to a huge deployment of nearly 500,000 troops (Taub 2004: 36). The second conclusion was that, even though the military plays the dominant role in the security phase, peace building is at bottom a political process, i.e. in order to establish stable democratic institutions one has to confront and change the political structures that caused the conflict to begin with, or, as Marina Ottaway put it, "nation building is not a task for the 82nd Airborne" (2002: 18). A third insight was expressed by Paul Schroeder when he wrote that:

> Some people seem to think that states and governments are somehow fungible, replaceable – that if one is destroyed or overthrown, another can take its place – and that if the state or government overthrown was evil and dangerous, anything that replaces it will be better . . . There have to be powerful grounds for overthrowing any regime effectively governing a state, and a clear idea of how to replace it.
>
> (2001/2: 31)

A fourth conclusion disputes the facile equation of state and nation building with democracy. "Let us not indulge in fantasy," writes Ottaway. "It is politically correct to equate state reconstruction with democracy building . . . the international community has to set more modest goals . . . and then tailor those goals to each country's reality" (2002: 22). Moreover, scholarly research indicated that the early stages of transition from autocratic regimes to democracies have been rife with violence. "The danger is not just that the transition will be chaotic and violent, but also that anti-democratic groups and ideas will be mobilized and will become a long-lasting fixture on the political scene," write Edward Mansfield and Jack Snyder (2005/6). A fifth conclusion was that "democracy does not flow out of the barrel of a gun," as Chris Patten phrased it (2003: 40). Mansfield and Snyder labeled the same idea the "oxymoron of imposed democracy," and Ottaway applied it to Iraq by stating: "The United States cannot shock and awe Iraqis into accepting a new political system, nor can it impose one with force once the occupation ends" (2003). When President Bush and his advisors "argue that ousting Saddam Hussein will allow the United States to build democracy in Iraq and that doing so will stimulate a wave of democracy around the Middle East," Tom Carothers and Bethany Lacina of the Carnegie Endowment described it as a "fantasy" (2003). Further conclusions and guides to policy for the specific case of post-war Iraq were that democracy building was especially difficult in an Arab-Muslim state and that one might well end up with an Islamist state like Iran rather than a polity like Turkey, and that any attempt to create stability in the Gulf/Middle East region needed a truly international effort and the cooperation of Iraq's neighbors. The Carnegie Endowment for International Peace made these scholarly research and policy guides available in non-technical summaries titled "From Victory to Success: Afterwar Policy in Iraq" in a special issue (no. 117) of *Foreign Policy* magazine in 2003.

Nor was such knowledge and policy advice provided only from outside the military. Conrad Crane and Andrew Terrill, of the Army War College Faculty, researched American military occupations and their post-war reconstruction record and presented their findings at an inter-agency workshop in December 2002 whose purpose was to examine how "American and coalition forces can best address requirements that will . . . necessarily follow from operational victory in war with Iraq." Crane is a Stanford PhD and has served in the US military for almost 30 years; Terrill is a well-known Middle East expert. The research was published in February 2003 by the Army War College with the title *Reconstructing Iraq* and had a strong security and policy focus on the Arab/Muslim context. In it the authors discuss and predict just about every problem that has beset the Iraqi occupation. They doubted that the Iraqi population would welcome the US forces, and warned about chaos and looting at the fall of the regime and the consequences for security of disbanding the Iraqi army, Sunni Baathist resistance feeding urban guerilla warfare and terrorism, the danger of Iraq breaking up along the Sunni/Shi'ite/Kurdish divide, the problems of disarming the population, the hostile reaction of Iraqis to the detention and interrogation of suspects in counterinsurgency operations and the possibility of suicide bombers as an anti-occupation tactic, the huge size and funding necessary for an effective occupation and transition, and the likelihood of more and violent resistance as the US presence is maintained. They warn that "the possibility of the US winning the war and losing the peace is real and serious" (2003: 41). This analysis was provided *ex ante* before the war's start and is based on research and information that had been available for some years.

It wasn't just the thinking of "armchair" military analysts. When Jim Lehrer asked General Anthony Zinni (retired) in a PBS *NewsHour* interview on September 30, 2003, "Do you believe what is going on on the ground now postwar in Iraq could have been avoided?" Zinni answered:

> Well, I think we should have anticipated that if you take down the government of an authoritarian centrally controlled organization like Saddam Hussein had, and you pull it out, rip it out, if you dismantle the Army, if you tell all the businessmen that were ever "Baathist" they can't do business again because they were Baathists . . . If you are going to take out institutions and remove them, then you have to be prepared to restructure them from scratch . . . I think that should have been anticipated . . . I think the potential for civil war, the potential for outsiders, the Jihadis coming in . . . that should have been seen clearly . . . those responsible for planning in the Pentagon should have seen this.

Informed knowledge about the issues and problems of post-war Iraq occupation and reconstruction was available and made available in the scholarly community, in the policy community (RAND Corporation, United States Institute of Peace), within the military itself (Army War College, Institute for National Strategic Studies of the National Defense University), and within the State Department (the Future of Iraq Project), the CIA, and other branches of the US government. The Bush administration, i.e. the White House and the civilian leadership in the Pentagon, chose to ignore it because it did not sit well with their political agenda. Why the Bush–Cheney administration chose this course is the subject of at least a dozen books already and will be argued and criticized for years to come. Francis Bacon, the English philosopher-statesman, famously wrote that "knowledge is power," but one does well not to equate the pursuit of political power with the pursuit of knowledge and of truth.

What is feasible is not acceptable: Cyprus

Since Turkish troops invaded the north of Cyprus in 1974 and divided it into Greek and Turkish zones, there have been many initiatives for the reunification of the island. The latest was the UN Secretary General's "Annan Plan," a 192-page document titled *Basis for a Comprehensive Settlement of the Cyprus Problem*, which included a draft of a proposed constitution (www.cyprus-un-plan.org/MainArticles.pdf). The Annan Plan designed a new state of Cyprus in which Greek and Turkish Cypriots would live side by side as good neighbors in a bi-zonal, bi-cameral federal state with power sharing institutions. As for peace building in other divided societies, the external stakeholders and experts came up with a peace settlement incorporating key consociational principles of elite cooperation, minority veto, proportionality, and segmental autonomy. A distinguished panel of diplomats, political leaders, and academics from Cyprus and elsewhere assembled at the Harvard Kennedy School of Government in September 2003 "asserted that nearly all of the components of the Annan Plan were reasonable and appropriate" (Rotberg 2003: 13). On April 24, 2004, the plan was rejected by the Greek Cypriot voters in a referendum with a 74 percent no vote although the Turkish Cypriots approved it with 65 percent.

The Turkish army invasion in 1974 led to de facto partition of the island into North and South, with an estimated 180,000 Greek Cypriots fleeing North to South, and many fewer Turkish Cypriots in the opposite direction. In the ensuing 30 years, South Cyprus became a thriving country with a market economy and a GDP per capita of $17,000 viewed favorably by the European Union for admission, whereas the relatively less developed Turkish North had a GDP per capita of $5,000 in a state capitalist, protected economy. Settlers from Turkey had immigrated to make up some of the population loss after 1974. Many peace attempts were made, the most recent being the Kofi Annan plan of 2002–4 which went through several versions during negotiations. The core of the plan was a single federated state with limited powers made up of two entities that had most of the power to govern, border adjustments, demilitarization, a reconciliation commission, complex power sharing with many blocking powers and vetoes for the benefit of the Turkish Cypriots, right of refugee return, and property settlement. Despite the safeguards in the Annan Plan, it raised Turkish fears of being economically and demographically overwhelmed by the more prosperous and more numerous Greek Cypriots (700,000 Greeks in the South versus 150,000 Turks in the North).

Under the citizenship and political rights provisions of the Annan Plan, voting rights and the right to stand for political office were to be exercised at the place of residency. But the Turkish North entity could limit residency return (with the exception of returnees over 65 years old) during a six-year moratorium. After six years, a complex and graduated timetable based on ethnic mix thresholds in each locality was meant to slow down the acquisition of residency in the North by returnees from the South. Such gradual return assured continued political control for Turkish Cypriots in districts with many Greek returnees. Thus a Greek Cypriot family originating in a village in the North and managing to go through the hurdles of repossessing a farmstead or house they used to own and to relocate there would not have a right to vote and stand for office in their village or district for perhaps more than two decades, the number of years depending on how many other Greek Cypriots resettled in the same village or district. Exceptions were made for a few designated Turkish and Greek villages. The status of minority rights in the two entities was not spelled out beyond prohibition of discrimination. In a town or village a 20 percent minority might have to finance schooling for its children in its language from private funds rather than have the right to state support. These provisions meant to calm the fears of the Turkish Cypriots were unattractive for Greek Cypriots who hoped to repossess their ancestral northern properties. According to Trove Malloy of the European Centre for Minority Issues (ECMI), "While a major return of Greek Cypriot refugees to the north was rather unlikely, the property regime of the Plan could have resulted in a major landownership by non-residents in the Turkish Cypriot entity" (Malloy and Soyan 2004: 8).

In the property settlement provisions, a claimant could opt for compensation or for return of the property under a process run by an independent property board made up of an equal number of Turkish and Greek Cypriots and some international members. Compensation was based on the value of the original property, but calculations for appreciation of value after 30 years and economic changes and the value added from improvements were somewhat uncertain, with each side anticipating being short-changed. As for property return, it was contingent on several factors: the dispossessed residents were eligible to receive property elsewhere in exchange, or get compensation for having to move, or receive temporary alternative accommodations, all of which would slow property repossession. A complex timetable of reinstatement of properties by locality was devised that would slow it down in villages and districts where the returnees exceeded certain quotas. In districts where many returnees were granted property rights, there could be thus further delays. Refugee return reflected minority veto and proportionality ideas from consociation theory.

Last but not least, who was going to finance the property settlement? There were some references to "donor funds" by external stakeholders, but to some Greek Cypriots it looked like they themselves were going to have to pay for repossessing their properties. That violated basic fairness notions. Outsiders expected most claimants to opt for compensation, but for the Turkish Cypriots repossession was fraught with uncertainty. The consociational safeguards built into property settlement and political rights and citizenship provisions to relieve Turkish fears of Greek domination made the Annan Plan unattractive for the Greek Cypriots. Without freedom to settle and own property where one wanted, and to enjoy citizenship in place of residence, the peace settlement ratified a de facto partition that had existed all along. With trust and good will between ethnic elites assumed in consociational theory, the Annan Plan could be made to work reasonably, but such trust and cooperation were lacking. The plan was part of an externally managed peace process precisely because Greek and Turkish Cypriot leaders did not trust one another and did not cooperate. The failure of the Annan Plan highlights the zero sum cross-ethnic dimensions of consociational design: by sweetening the successive proposals for accommodating the objections from Turkish Cypriot leaders, the designers ended making it unacceptable to the Greek Cypriots.

Refugees and refugee return

Wars, civil wars, and insurgencies produce flows of refugees and internally displaced persons (RIDPs) owing to ethnic cleansing and fleeing the fighting and personal danger. Many peace agreements make some provision for refugee return. At the end of fighting, RIDPs want to leave their camps and temporary homes and resume their former life. Can ethnic cleansing and large-scale ethnic population transfers be reversed? This is probably more likely in countries like Angola and Mozambique where many refugees had lived in villages, where land for farming is available for cultivation, and where RIDPs hadn't possessed valuable property usurped by squatters. In more urban and developed countries, as in the Balkans and in Cyprus, and especially in the aftermath of ethnic cleansing designed to permanently expel an ethnic group, RIDP return is complicated by repossession of property, financing compensation, removal of occupants from the property, and community opposition to return of RIDPs. RIDP return is not simply humanitarian and physical resettlement because of its linkage to wider issues of state borders, ethnic cleansing, and population policy of the adversaries that are at the heart of their original conflict and of any peace settlement.

These issues get more contentious with time. A case in point is the Palestinian refugees from the 1947–8 and 1967 wars between Israel and the Arab states. Originally they numbered somewhere between 500,000 and 1 million from 1948 and then another 300,000 (of which about 100,000 were uprooted for the second time) from 1967. They and their descendants have grown in 2004 to 4 million registered refugees, living in Jordan, the West Bank, Gaza, Lebanon, and Syria for the most part. In Jordan they have become citizens; in Syria and Lebanon, they are non-citizens. In Lebanon and Gaza, they are poor, crowded, and angry.

Together with the other peace issues discussed in Chapter 5, the "right of return" of the Palestinian refugees, spelled out in UN resolutions and voiced by their leaders and organizations, remains a major impediment to a Middle East peace. A physical right of return exercised by more than a small proportion of the Palestinian refugees would be the end of the state of Israel as it now exists and would create utter chaos. What does right of return actually mean after half a century? The townhouses, villages, farms, olive groves, and pastures of 1948 do not exist anymore. They have become Israeli towns, apartment blocks, shopping centers, industrial parks, agro-businesses, and highways. Many agree that, when two peoples have had such a long and destructive history of conflict, a peace settlement has to provide for sharp separation into two states, and not for mixing them together under one roof. Only token refugee return is acceptable to the Israeli public. Other options have been proposed by the most conciliatory groups in both Israel and Palestine who drafted the Geneva Convention, such as symbolic recognition of refugee rights with some compensation and limited humanitarian return, plus voluntary resettlement of other Palestinians in a future

Palestinian state (*Geneva Accord* 2004: article 7, "Refugees"). Whether these proposals would be acceptable to Israelis and Palestinians, and how to finance such a refugee return and compensation scheme remain a big question mark.

Refugee return and compensation may be viewed along five dimensions:

1   The broader political and demographic conflict over political power and institutional control in peace making has to be resolved through constitutional design and power sharing before refugee return can become a humanitarian and human rights issue. Sadako Ogata (2005), the UN High Commissioner for Refugees in the 1990s, argued persuasively that there are seldom, if ever, humanitarian solutions to refugee problems.

2   There has to be a viable and acceptable plan of compensation and/or return of RIDPs. A morally defensible plan – aggression does not pay, innocent victims of armed fighting are compensated – should not make those who are not responsible for the original wrongs, and who often are RIDPs themselves, worse off.

3   The process of submitting claims and of processing and adjudicating conflicting claims has to be transparent, fair, non-discriminatory, and enforced. In practice it means that an external agency has to be authorized to manage the process because the local authorities typically were complicit in expelling the refugees, in robbing their properties, and in assigning abandoned dwellings to their own ethnic supporters and often to themselves.

4   Some way of financing the return and compensation process has to be devised, and that at a time of much destruction and reconstruction which strains resources. In practice, it is again external donors – governments, multilateral agencies, NGOs – that are expected to foot a large share of the costs.

5   The security of returnees has to be assured against local resistance, intimidation and violence, and concurrent reforms have to be made in local government, the justice system, and schooling so as to make the returnees' life tolerable and normal. In practice, that means effective enforcement of minority rights for RIDPs against the same local authorities that had been responsible for expulsions and other systematic human rights violations.

Refugee return in Bosnia after Dayton

As described in Chapter 4, in the Bosnian war of 1992–5 ethnic cleansing had been the principal means of the Serb and Croat ethno-nationalist leaders and parties for establishing ethnically homogeneous territories. About half the total population of 4.3 million had been uprooted from their homes by the end of the war (UNHCR 2004). The goal of the Dayton Peace Accord, of the Bosniaks, and of the external stakeholders referred to as "the international community" was to prevent the dismemberment of Bosnia on ethnic lines and to reestablish an independent multiethnic state. RIDP return to their pre-war homes, especially so-called "minority returns" to a district where they would be a minority and thus contribute to ethnic re-integration, was an important component of that goal. Annex 7 of the Dayton Agreement (www.incore.ulst.ac.uk/cds/agreements/dayton_ annex7 .html) dealt with refugees and displaced persons. Chapter 1, article 1 stated:

> All refugees and displaced persons have a right freely to return to their homes of origin. They shall have the right to have restored to them property of which they were deprived in the course of hostilities since 1991 and to be compensated for any property that cannot be restored to them. The early return of refugees and displaced persons is an important objective of the settlement of the conflict in Bosnia and Hercegovina.

In article 2, "refugees and displaced persons are permitted to return in safety, without risk of harassment, intimidation, persecution, or discrimination." That was the agreement. The reality on the ground was something else again.

The Dayton accords created a Commission for Real Property Claims (CRPC) of displaced persons and refugees to oversee the return of property rights but gave it no power to implement claims settlement decisions. This power rested with the local authorities, which found numerous ways to obstruct implementation. Without property restitution, one would expect little minority refugee return, and that is what happened: in the five years 1996–2000, minority returns to the Federation were only 139,400, and to the Republika Srpska only 50,300. At that time, only 52,000 of a total of 189,000 "minority" claims involving about 500,000 property units had been disposed of (UNHCR 2004). In frustration, the Peace Implementation Council created a Reconstruction and Return Task Force (RRTF), an inter-agency coordinating committee composed of all the international agencies and NGOs in reconstruction and return projects, to organize and assist return. The Office of High Representative acquired greater powers for removing obstructionist local officials, an authority the OHR increasingly exercised. According to research on Bosnia returnees:

> Obstructionist mayors, council members, assembly representatives and even housing office officials were removed from office and usually banned from political life. During his tenure [as OHR head, 1999–2002], Petrisch sacked 64 local hard liners and passed 246 laws including those designed to protect minority ethnic groups and advance democratic governance at the state and entity levels.
>
> (O Tuathail and Dahlman 2004: 149)

With such enforcement, the CRPC's work bore more rapid fruit. In the three years 2001–3, it settled 137,000 minority property claims (compared to 52,000 in the previous five years), and minority RIDP returns were 223,300 (compared to 50,300). By the time the CRPC terminated its work on property repossession, 300,000 claims involving 1.2 million property units had been successfully disposed of, benefiting an estimated 1 million RIDPs (about 3.4 people per claim, the average family size) (CRPC 2003). At an international conference (Malloy and Soyan 2004: 31–5), Hans van Houtte, head of the CRPC, explained its success as follows. The CRPC was a public international institution, subject to international law. The commission consisted of three internationals appointed by the European Court of Human Rights, and six national members, two from each of the major ethnic groups. It hired 250 local staff deployed in offices all over Bosnia, with commissioners and staff given international diplomatic protection important for withstanding pressures from the local community. It conducted a mass media information campaign on the entire property claims process, and assembled a huge computerized database for its work. A successful claimant was issued a CRPC certificate with three options: return of property (chosen by 54 percent), which could then be occupied, sold, or rented; compensation (chosen by 24 percent); and simple confirmation of property rights (chosen by 22 percent) which was sufficient to reclaim property. Only 1 percent of its decisions were contested and, despite some resistance, by 2004 80 percent of its decisions had been implemented. The total cost over seven years was $33 million. The process was deemed fair, transparent, and efficient by the Bosnian public and the international community. When enforcement became effective owing to the RRTF and OHR actions in 2000 and later years, minority returns were unblocked in Bosnia. According to UNHCR (2004), as of August 31, 2004, 1,001,000 RIDPs had returned and only 312,000 remained. Of the returnees, 446,000 were minority returnees, including 157,000 to the Republika Srpska (RS), the entity where the most ethnic cleansing had taken place. That meant that the RS, with 1.1 million population, would have a substantial non-Serb minority, though nowhere near the pre-war figures.

Neither the CRPC nor any other agency kept track of whether those who got their property back had actually physically returned, as opposed to renting and selling their property. According to Daniela Heimerl (2005: 386), a defensible estimate is that 75 percent of returned property is sold or exchanged. Impressionistic accounts are that older folks return when impediments to pension transfers across jurisdictions and health and other service delivery to returnees were removed by OHR action. Families with school age children were less likely to do so because of lack of employment and lagging school reforms on integrating minority pupils into the school systems. In a few places like Prijedor a concerted large-scale effort by Bosniak returnees managed to achieve some political power, a minority school, and tolerable ethnic relations with Serbs. In the municipality of Kiseljak where Muslim Bosniaks expelled by the Croats returned in large numbers, Tone Bringa made a case study of the return and reconciliation process and reports that "The Bosniaks are back, but they are made to feel that they do not belong" (2005: 197). In both Kiseljak and the Prijedor district, large-scale return was possible only after the local leaders who were responsible for killings and ethnic cleansing were indicted by the ICTY and arrested, and other officials obstructing the return were removed from office by the OHR. Elsewhere, returnees experienced problems and avoidance by the majority ethnics, and pre-war friendships and neighborly relations were not resumed, at least not in the short run (Stover and Weinstein 2004: chapter 7). A UNDP report (2003) states that the dominant attitude (in BiH) is that everyone should be educated in his/her own culture, language, and history, and not share a common schooling in these subjects and topics, and thus minority children, including children of minority returnees, were expected to learn according to the majority definition of language and social studies if they attended the local schools or, as was more typical, be bussed to their own, often inferior, schools. As of 2004, the OHR and international agencies were pushing to develop a common school curriculum, the same textbooks, uniform teacher training, and schooling under the same roof, with eventually schooling of all the children in the same classrooms, but little of that had been implemented (personal communication on BiH school reforms researched by Ken Palmer, October 2004).

The same UNDP report and a large World Bank study (2001) with 25 focus groups and 675 residents from a dozen sites in Bosnia, which included minority RIDPs, highlighted the problems of reconstruction and normalization of a society after civil war. At the end of 2001, the unemployment rate was estimated at 20 percent. GDP per capita was about 50 percent of pre-war figures, relegating Bosnia from middle-income Central and East European levels of living in 1990 to third world a decade later. Nearly half the workforce earned just above the poverty line or below. Twenty-nine percent lived in houses without adequate property or occupancy rights. The citizenry was skeptical about a better future, and 60 percent of citizens, including 50 percent of civil servants, believed corruption was widespread. The people were caught in a number of simultaneous changes: in addition to post-war reconstruction, there were the shift from socialism and state-centered enterprises to a market economy and private enterprises, rebuilding of a failed state with diminishing revenues, democratization of authoritarian regimes, urbanization speeded in the war by refugees and others seeking security in cities, and resettlement of refugees involving contentious property return and repossession. Social services, pensions, support for war veterans and their families, income relief, and other institutions that citizens expect from governments, especially when they are needy and poor, were all in decline. Many had grievances and a sense of victimhood from war service, and resented the war profiteers driving luxury autos. In this impoverished population, competition for jobs, housing, and services was keen, and many sought favors through political patrons. Families associated with kin and neighbors within limited ethnic circles and continued ethnic encapsulation and polarization set off by the war. All of this made for surface cooperation but little reconciliation between ethnic groups. There was little RIDP integration at their former neighborhoods. An exception was good cross-ethnic cooperation and understandings in workplaces, but mixed workplaces were few because of discrimination in hiring. Poverty and competition for scarce resources hindered cooperation. Few opportunities existed for common goal achievement across ethnic groups which would weaken the mistrust, negative stereotypes, discrimination, and antipathy inherited from the war years. These UN and World Bank findings underscore the importance of economic reconstruction, job creation, and non-discriminatory labor markets for improving post-war ethnic relations in divided societies.

Truth, justice, reconciliation

The peace process and settlement frequently include some institutions for justice and truth, and more broadly reconciliation. First and foremost, victims want justice, as was the case for "las abuelitas" in Buenos Aires, Argentina who marched once a week around the Plaza de Mayo in front of the presidential palace carrying the photographs of vanished family members. External stakeholders insist on it, as was true for the Allies in World War II for both Germany and Japan. Judge Richard Goldstone who played a leading role in both the South African Truth and Reconciliation Commission (TRC) and the United Nations International Criminal Tribunal for the former Yugoslavia (ICTY) stated that:

> It is my belief that when nations ignore the victims' call for justice, they are condemning their people to the terrible consequences of ongoing hatred and revenge . . . But for the TRC, there would have been widespread denials of most of the worst manifestations of apartheid and those denials could have been believed . . . by the majority of white South Africans. That is no longer possible. Nor would the same result have been achieved through the normal criminal process.
>
> (2000: 60, 71)

Truth and justice confront a culture of denial on the facts of war crimes and crimes against humanity and on responsibility for them. In ethnic conflicts and continuing in their aftermath, closing ranks in ethnic solidarity against truth and justice becomes a condition for good standing in one's ethnic group. Collective action is joined against acknowledgment of the adversary's claims. The most public manifestation of opposition is against public monuments that symbolize the legitimacy of the adversary's presence. When the international community raised a monument to the 7,000 Muslims massacred at Srebrenica in 1995, a large NATO and International Transitional Police Force contingent had to protect the Muslim attendees who wished to honor their dead. The local Serbs put up their own separate monument to honor their war dead. The official Serb story was that in July

1995 the Muslims decided to leave as a group, and denied that they were expelled and massacred. In Banja Luka, the capital of the Republika Srpska, in May 2001, Muslim returnees and international dignitaries in Bosnia gathered for laying the foundations for the reconstruction of the historic Ferhadija mosque that had been dynamited and razed by Serb militants in 1993. Local Serbs rioted in protest and the local police stood by. In another incident, Bosnet reported on October 18, 2000 that "A Bosnian Serb war crimes suspect who blew himself up when peacekeepers tried to arrest him was given a hero's funeral by hundreds of his compatriots" (www .bosnet.org).

There is no easy and sure way from truth and justice to reconciliation. Justice is often perceived as victor's justice, and it is sometimes biased since the victors are more likely to indict their adversaries than their own offenders. Justice is framed by the peace makers and the judges as individual accountability for crimes, yet the population experiences it as their collective guilt. The people are partly right in so far as they know that many had been complicit in the crimes, some by omission and others by cheering the perpetrators from the sidelines and profiting from ethnic cleansing. Collective myths justifying the culture of denial must be confronted with a truthful, plausible, and defensible world view that is less threatening to ethnic identity than collective guilt. A common cognitive frame holds that good people do good things and bad people do bad things. No group is willing to admit that they are collectively bad; hence they deny that they have done bad things. Social science argues a more truthful and empirically supported frame based on the ordinary man thesis: the worst crimes and wrongs are committed not by bad people for personal gain and moral depravity, but by ordinary people for a group cause in a crisis, with their peers' support. That is the tragedy of the human condition, and it applies equally to the adversaries. Such a "tragedy of the commons" frame is now widely accepted for explaining environmental degradation. It would do well for truth and justice.

What might one expect from truth, justice, and reconciliation between adversaries? Germany and France had fought several wars against one another since the wars of the French Revolution, resulting in millions of deaths, many war crimes and atrocities (e.g. mustard gas in World War I), occupation and insurgency in World War II France, massive state propaganda dehumanizing the enemy, a punitive and humiliating peace settlement at Versailles that occasioned extremist nationalism and sentiments of revenge by the Nazis, and much else that fueled hostility between the leaders and peoples of France and Germany. After World War II, the Nürnberg war crimes trials meted out justice to the Nazi leadership responsible for the holocaust and crimes against humanity. Together with the prosecution of lesser offenders, mountains of documentation on Nazi crimes were made public. Truth could no longer be denied. The top leaders in both countries, de Gaulle and Adenauer, did not stop there. They instituted policies for national reconciliation sponsored by their governments, professional associations, and civic bodies on a broad front for changing their historical adversarial relationship to a cooperative one that penetrated into popular culture. Universities established relations under the auspices of a conference of rectors; twin-city partnerships were established starting in 1949; a Franco-German commission of secondary school teachers instituted changes in the history and geography curricula; secondary school partnerships were created for pupil exchanges; Franco-German intellectual associations were established under the leadership of highly regarded public intellectuals like Alfred Gosser, Carlo Schmidt, and Theodore Heuss; and the entire enterprise was capped by the state visit of de Gaulle to West Germany in 1962 and the Franco-German treaty a year later (Dicht 1984). Reconciliation worked. Franco-German cooperation became the core of the European Community and the subsequent European Union.

None of this is simple after bloody ethnic conflict. Milan Kundera once wrote that "The struggle of man against power is the struggle of memory against forgetting" (quoted in Hutchins 1989: 160), and that proved to be the case in the Central American peace processes. At the end of civil war in Nicaragua the victorious government of Violeta Chamoro accepted the amnesty that the Sandinistas had passed and that forgave them and their Contra adversaries for politically motivated crimes. All parties realized that amnesty was the price of peace. In El Salvador, the UN mediated an end to 12 years of civil war between the government and the FMLN insurgents with UN monitoring for insurgents turning in their weapons with personal security assurances. The peace settlement established a UN truth commission that examined and publicized human rights abuses by both sides including the activities of death squads. Given the absence of an impartial justice system for trying offenders, the March 1993 UN Report named some of the war crimes perpetrators and recommended a ten-year ban on holding office for offenders, and the National Assembly passed an amnesty law. An ad hoc commission called for the dismissal or transfer of 103 army officers including some top generals. President Cristiani did not dare implement all the dismissals and transfers though UN and US pressure resulted in the removal of the top two generals from office. There were no penalties for crimes in an estimated 75,000 deaths, two-thirds civilian deaths. Some truth emerged, a little justice, but the peace held (Neier 1998: chapter 3).

After a 30-year insurgency against military governments in Guatemala during which 200,000 people were killed, a peace settlement was signed in December 1996 following five years of UN-mediated negotiations. Under the agreement, the insurgents turned in their weapons and their leaders entered peaceful politics with some getting elected to the Guatemalan Congress. Both sides agreed to a general amnesty for war crimes, but not for crimes against humanity, i.e. against civilians. A truth commission called the Commission for Historical Clarification (CEH) was created for establishing and publicizing the truth about the war years. In its 15-volume report submitted to the United nations in 1999, the commissioners wrote that:

> The main purpose of the Report is to place on record Guatemala's recent bloody past . . . the gravity of the abuses suffered repeatedly by its people has yet to become part of the national consciousness . . . knowing the truth will make it easier to achieve national reconciliation.
>
> (CEH 1998)

Both the armed forces and the insurgents cooperated with the commission to only a limited extent. It worked behind close doors and its recommendations were non-binding. Despite these handicaps, the Report documented a clear record of mass human rights violations, 90 percent of which were committed by the military and the state against mostly Mayan civilians. It attributed the violence not to lapses of individual morality and group discipline alone but to a centuries-long political culture of intolerance and exclusion of Mayans from political life.

Because of the limitations of the CEH, the Catholic Church created its own truth commission, called the Recovery of Historical Memory (REMHI), using its countrywide network of church volunteers who collected thousands of victim testimonies in open hearings using local languages. Its investigators reconstructed 70 massacres, all by the military. It named 55,000 killed civilians and named war crimes perpetrators. It too found that 90 percent of the crimes had been committed by the security forces and that 90 percent of the victims were Mayan civilians. When its four-volume report was published, the head of REMHI was murdered in his home (Beristain 1998). Despite this setback and the continued high level of criminal and political violence in the country, Stephen Kinzer reports that:

> Peace has created the space for political debate. It has brought a grudging acknowledgement on the part of some large landowners and powerful businessmen that the feudal structure of society must be changed so that social tensions never again explode into rebellion.
>
> (2001: 61)

The legacy of the two truth commissions is the spread of "historical memory" projects and a pan-Mayan cultural rights movement: monuments, community memorials, touring dramas by high school students on collective violence themes, video presentations, teaching human rights and tolerance in school curricula. With this truth-seeking process, Guatemala may have turned around a centuries-long political culture of authoritarian and military rule.

The South African Truth and Reconciliation Commission (TRC)

The TRC was part of a complex peace process between the South African government and the African National Congress (ANC). From 1985 to 1990 there had been secret informal talks on preconditions to formal negotiations and some confidence-building moves with Nelson Mandela's release from prison, lifting the ban on opposition organizations, and ANC rejection of violence and insurgency which committed both sides to compromise and created trust. Upon his release on February 2, 1990, Mandela promptly described whites as fellow South African citizens whose fears about African majority rule he recognized and was prepared to deal with. Formal talks led to the National Peace Accord of September 1991 which demilitarized the armed conflict and opened the way to substantive negotiations on constitutional design and transitional power sharing capped by national elections and Mandela's assumption of the presidency on May 10, 1994.

As is true in most peace processes, criminal and political violence increased during peace implementation (du Toit 2000). During the transition to majority rule a total of 23,609 political deaths occurred from September 1994 to December 1997 in what amounted to low-intensity armed warfare. According to Brandon Hamber:

> By the early 1990s, the situation had spiraled out of control, and a cycle of murder and retribution permeated most of the South African townships. Multifarious forms of orchestrated and seemingly random violence proliferated across the country. Violence flared between the ANC and the Inkatha Freedom Party, paramilitaries from all sides armed themselves in the name of defending their communities, targeted assassinations and massacres left hundreds of fatalities, drive by shootings became commonplace, violence against commuters on trains and at taxi ranks ensued, and the White extreme right vocally threatened armed insurrection if minority rule were ended.
>
> (2001: 238)

A commission of inquiry to investigate violence in black townships implicated both government and opposition organizations, and found evidence that military and police intelligence had armed and incited rival African groups to commit violence against one another.

In this security crisis a huge citizen movement for an end to violence mounted peace demonstrations and formed NGOs such as the Network of Independent Monitors (NIM) whose members participated in peacekeeping at potentially violent encounters between members of the unbanned African opposition, white extremist groups, and the police. One peace activist described the work of these NGOs as follows:

> Thousands of peace workers across South Africa placed their minds, hearts, and bodies between chaos and a fragile equilibrium. Through them and the peace committees they represented, the Peace Accord took shape in the streets. The regional and local peace committees absorbed the real impact of the transition to democracy, dealing daily

with the conflict and violence it generated and working to heal broken communities.

(Marks 2000: 65)

The citizens' peace movement became a key component of what Varshney (2002: 9) referred to as an "institutionalized peace system" for controlling communal rioting as well as post-settlement violence.

In view of the troubling pattern of violence and human rights abuses, the adversaries made an amnesty deal. Legislation to exempt an estimated 3,500 security forces officials from prosecution for most human rights abuses was passed, and the ANC disclosed intra-African human rights crimes and torture but declined to dismiss the offenders from the party organization. In May 1994 when Mandela became president, the temporary constitution superseded De Klerk's blanket amnesty legislation but granted amnesty to both sides for politically motivated crimes committed up to December 1993. The new ANC government responded to public demand for full disclosure and accountability for both state and insurgent violence by establishing a Commission on Truth and Reconciliation known as the TRC:

> to enable South Africa to come to terms with its past . . . If the wounds of the past are to be healed, if a multiplicity of legal actions are to be avoided . . . indeed if we are to successfully initiate the building of a human rights culture – disclosure of the truth and its acknowledgement are necessary.
>
> (quoted in Neier 1998: 41)

The TRC had a number of goals. Telling the truth and accountability for crimes following lawful procedures in a public forum would affirm the rule of law. Victims and their families would receive public recognition and support for their loss, apology from offenders, and compensation from the state. Offenders would get conditional amnesty – conditional on telling the truth and publicly apologizing to the victims – for politically motivated crimes and a chance to reintegrate into society. Truth would emerge from the testimony of hundreds of victims and offenders as well as documentary evidence of the policies and actions of the state and the insurgents' organizations. Reconciliation depended on whether the public and the victims perceived the TRC process as fair, i.e. there would be accountability and justice at all levels of responsibility in the chain of command.

Headed by Archbishop Tutu, the TRC was composed of three committees. The Human Rights Violation Committee investigated human rights abuses from 1960 to 1994. It established the identity of victims, the harm they suffered, the identity of the offenders, and the complicity of state and insurgent organizations. It determined whether abuses resulted from the deliberate actions of these organizations or were motivated by personal gain or revenge. The committee held open hearings all over the country, in

11 languages, many broadcast on radio and television, which offered the victims a public forum to tell their story and offenders to acknowledge their actions and publicly make an apology, and apply for amnesty to the Amnesty Committee. Both individuals and organization leaders appeared before it, including ex-Prime Minister De Klerk and ANC leaders Tembo and Mbeki. A total of 16,700 victims testified before it. The evidence could be used by the public defender to indict offenders who were not granted amnesty, and offenders who refused to participate in the TRC process could be prosecuted. The final report of five volumes (TRC 1998) massively documented human rights violations by every major political party, insurgent organization, and state agency and their leaders, and declared that apartheid was a crime against humanity.

The Amnesty Committee was empowered to determine whether the applicant's actions met the criteria for amnesty in exchange for full disclosure, or whether the case was to be referred to the justice system for prosecution. By 2000, of 7,112 applications, 849 were granted and 5,392 refused, and some had other dispositions. The Reparation and Rehabilitation Committee identified 16,700 victims, who got an average compensation of about $500 that observers labeled "symbolic." The legislature had limited the total reparations fund.

An actual case will illustrate how the TRC worked. Rayner Moringer was an applicant for amnesty. He was a foreign-born businessman in the aircraft industry and had lived in South Africa for 30 years before he became involved in the kidnapping of a business acquaintance, Mr. Mbotoli, by Transkei Military Intelligence. Mbotoli was implicated in a coup attempt in the Transkei. Moringer set up a business meeting with Mbotoli on April 12, 1991 during which Mbotoli was abducted to a Special Forces base in the Transkei. At his trial for treason, Mbotoli received a 20-year prison sentence. He was released in 1995 under the amnesty legislation.

Moringer admitted helping the abduction and agreed that his actions were unlawful, but denied getting paid for them. His motivation was to prevent the Transkei coup, and to save Mbotoli's life who would have been assassinated had he not been captured. He was reluctant to name Transkei agents in the abduction but was reminded by the commissioners that "he had to make full disclosure," which he did. When the South African police tried to arrest him, he fled to the Transkei and lived for two years in a house provided by the Transkei government. Under sharp questioning by commissioners, he convinced them that residence in the house was not a payoff for his help to the Military Intelligence. Called as a witness, Mbotoli stated that, "in the spirit of Mandela and reconciliation, he advises the TRC to grant amnesty to the applicant" and Moringer declared publicly "I am sorry and regret the harm to you." The commission attorney pointed out that full disclosure was made, that the applicant was totally honest in his answers, and that the motive was political, i.e. coup prevention. In 1999, amnesty was granted to Moringer (TRC 2000).

Truth and justice commissions help adversaries remake a damaged political culture. Victims heal when they tell their stories in public and their losses are acknowledged. Offenders who cooperate with full disclosure of their crimes and apologize to the victims for political crimes can get amnesty, and can be reintegrated into society. The public learns about the killings and torture that they found convenient to ignore. A "historical memory" is put on record by authoritative commissions that will make it more difficult for extremists to practice fabrication and misinformation in public debate. Just as important, the police, the security services, and the courts who perpetrated and condoned the culture of violence can be reformed. Judge Goldstone reflected on the TRC when he wrote that:

> It should be recognized that in a perfect society victims are entitled to full justice, namely trial of the perpetrator and, if found guilty, adequate punishment. That ideal is not possible in the aftermath of massive violence. There are simply too many perpetrators. Even the most sophisticated criminal justice system would be completely overwhelmed . . . Some societies simply forget about the past and attempt to induce national amnesia in its people. Of course that is bound to fail – the victims do not, indeed cannot, forget. And their unanswered call for retribution develops into hate and hate is directed collectively at the group from which perpetrators came.
>
> (1997)

There are formidable obstacles to justice making in some situations owing to the volume and violence of crimes in a country lacking the most elementary resources for justice. The Rwanda genocide involved a far larger percentage of the population than elsewhere. Penal Reform International estimated that 607,000 offenders could be accused of participation in genocide in some fashion. A 1996 law created special courts to try suspects in four categories of offenses: (1) leaders and those who planned, supervised, organized, and killed with cruelty; (2) those who killed under orders; (3) those who caused serious body injury; and (4) those who committed property crimes. The last three categories of offender would be tried in gacaca courts modeled on traditional justice in Rwanda, where judges elected from the local community would try the accused in public trials with mass participation. In 2004, ten years after the genocide and with more than 100,000 accused languishing in jails and camps for years, some 758 out of a planned 9,000 gacaca courts were operational. The physical impossibility of incarcerating all but the most brutal offenders led to sentencing them to community service in camps under the National Unity and Reconstruction Commission as a step before reintegration in their communities. Systematic monitoring of the gacaca process by NGOs uncovered many problems with the Rwanda justice process (PRI 2004). There is a lack of community participation though it is mandated by law. Both perpetrator Hutus and their village fellows and the Tutsi survivors are reluctant to confess and/or to testify. Omissions, half truths, lies, and false witnesses are common. Offenders who confess believe their families will experience difficulties. The survivors fear the return of the offenders. Many whose families were killed depended for survival in the community after the genocide on help from the perpetrators and were reluctant to testify against them. Another study of the gacaca courts also found that, when villagers were meant to name suspects and provide evidence of crimes, "participation is . . . reduced and in many cases silence prevails" (Reyntjens and Vandeginste 2005: 119). The typical strategy for cohabitation in the same locality between offenders and victims is avoidance, "not wanting to attract enemies," which is similar to the finding about the reception of minority returnees to their home places in Bosnia (Stover and Weinstein 2004: 78–9).

The ICTY

The United Nations International Criminal Tribunal for the former Yugoslavia was established in 1993 after the international media publicized mass killings, detention camps, and other crimes against humanity in the Bosnian and Croatian wars. The purpose of the ICTY is to "insure some measure of accountability during extraordinary periods of lawlessness. International criminal justice is justified by the failings of national justice to respond to ethnic persecution" (Teitel 1996: 84). The Tribunal is also an exercise in truth telling: it was meant to provide a public record of what happened to counter the lies, propaganda, and misinformation spread about them, and to hold specific individual persons and groups responsible rather than taint entire groups and nationalities with collective guilt. The historian Ivo Banac expressed it best in the context of the Yugoslav wars:

> The horrors of the twentieth century are directly connected to the living influence of false history . . . [the past] is a distorted and misconstructed past of nationalist ideology, with its stress on the continuity of victim-hood and redemption, loyalty, and treason . . . this coming to terms with the past means not only accepting responsibility but also overthrowing the caricature version of the past.
>
> (2001: 102)

The ICTY was also meant to deter further war crimes and atrocities, but the worst mass killings at Srebrenica occurred after it was established.

In its tenth annual report (ICTY 2003) the Tribunal disclosed that it employed 24 judges from 23 nations, 16 of them permanent judges. Its annual budget ran to about $100 million, and it had over 1,000 authorized positions. In its ten years it had indicted 80 or more defendants (some of them were secret), completed trials of about 30, completed appeals of ten, and 30 defendants were in various stages of trial, pretrial proceedings, or detention awaiting trial. Twenty indictees were still at large, among them the high-profile Bosnian Serb leaders Radovan Karadzic and General Ratko Mladic. The Tribunal had gotten limited cooperation from governments on arresting and surrendering indicted persons because they were viewed as national heroes rather than war criminals by public opinion. The leverage the Tribunal had on Balkan states was the threat by the European Union to delay or block admission unless their governments cooperated with the ICTY.

Patricia Wald (2002: 1120) estimated that there were 20,000 to 50,000 potential war crimes offenders in the Balkan wars responsible for an estimated 250,000 deaths – most civilians – and many more victims of ethnic cleansing. The Tribunal would handle only a small fraction of the offenders, at a high cost in resources and time, with most of the justice to be meted out in the courts of the Yugoslav successor states. The ICTY will wind down its operations from 2008 to 2010 and preparations have started for the transfer of cases (ICTJ 2004). In Bosnia, a reformed justice system is a cornerstone for the rebuilding of a failed state by the external stakeholders. Police, judges, and other officials, some of whom were complicit in ethnic cleansing and war crimes, were screened, retrained, and certified, and new legislation and courts for prosecution of war crimes were established. The hope is that the reformed justice system will establish the rule of law and replace the ethno-national political patronage system. Reforms have been slow. According to the International Center for Transitional Justice (ICTJ), "The state of BiH presents the classic dilemma in the area of transitional justice: it is a context marked by an unusually high demand for justice and an unusually low capacity or willingness to deliver it" (2004: 5).

According to the OSCE mission to Croatia (2004), the government and the public believe that these trials are not for justice but to satisfy external stakeholders. Most of the prosecutions thus far have been of Croatian Serbs (many in absentia) rather than of Croats who in any case get off with light sentences. As for Serbia, until well into 2005 it refused to cooperate with the ICTY despite international pressure, but since then a number of prosecutions for war crimes have taken place in Serbian courts (Wood 2006). Without the ICTY, even this low level of justice for war crimes and crimes against humanity would not be taking place. Vojin Dimitrijevic writes that in Serbia:

> the notion of individual responsibility for crimes committed in the Yugoslav wars has been persistently swamped by the "feeling of belonging" to a group of victims, to a people who have been horribly wronged . . . [In Croatia] trained jurists, including the president of the Supreme Court of Croatia, who should have known better, defended the indicted [Croatian] officers by adducing self-defense in response to an aggressive war.
>
> (1996: 86)

A great deal of information about what happened and who was responsible has been uncovered by high-profile ICTY trials at The Hague, among them those of General Radislav Krstic, the senior Bosnian Serb commander at the Srebrenica massacres and of other top military officers, several indictees for the Ahmici massacre in April 1993, the commanders of the Prijedor district detention camps where detainees were tortured and killed, Bosnian Serb General Stanislav Galic who commanded the siege of Sarajevo during which civilians were targeted and killed, Blagoje Simic, mayor of Bosanski Samac, who was responsible for the ethnic cleansing of Muslims and Croats from that city in April 1992, and former President Milosevic who died of a heart attack during his trial after the prosecution had already presented and argued its case but before he had finished his defense. All of it was cutting through the mass media propaganda and falsification spread by the adversaries. In the high-profile cases, the Tribunal would have to prove "command responsibility" in a complex and purposely covert military and state organization that had no "smoking gun" evidence on the top leaders. These were no easy prosecutions in view of the destruction of records, non-cooperation by governments, refusal of indictees to testify against their peers, the reluctance of witnesses to come forward despite witness protection programs, and other impediments. As the chief prosecutor Carla Del Ponte stated, "There is no classic paper trail . . . you need to establish what the real chain of command was. And it may not be the same chain of command that is written down" (2001).

Biljana Plavsic was indicted for ethnic cleansing and other crimes when she was deputy to wartime leader Radovan Karadzic in the Republika Srpska. She pleaded guilty to one count of persecution, and in return seven other charges were dropped. She refused to testify against her former associates. Her defense was that her wartime actions were driven by "blinding fear" of Serbs becoming victims, and that in their defensive zeal Serbs became "victimizers." She was sentenced to 11 years in prison. Milomir Stakic was charged with two counts of genocide, five counts of crimes against humanity, and one count of violating the laws and customs of war (i.e. murder, extermination, deportation, inhumane acts and torture, persecution, and murder). His trial lasted from April 16, 2002 to May 2003. The prosecution called 37 witnesses and submitted 19 written statements over 80 sitting days of the Tribunal. The defense called 38 witnesses and seven witness statements during 67 trial days. Thirty-four witnesses were granted protective measures because of threats – use of pseudonyms, facial and voice distortion on video, and closed sessions. There were 1,448 exhibits admitted as evidence. The sentence was pronounced in July 2003: Stakic was guilty of murder, deportation, and persecution but found not guilty on genocide. He was sentenced to life with a minimum term of 20 years. The Stakic case shows the fairness and thoroughness of the ICTY prosecution and explains the slow pace and high cost of justice in war crimes.

What is accomplished by transitional justice? How have nations and ethnic groups dealt with their less-than-sterling history? Austria simply denies its Nazi past, and Turkey keeps in denial of the Armenian genocide. The West Germans were forced by the Allies to confront it; Japan still avoids acknowledging the full extent of war crimes and massacres in Korea and in China during its twentieth-century wars. France has for decades shunned opening the wounds of its collaboration with the Nazis during the Vichy regime. Gary Bass writes that "even liberal states tend not to push for a war crimes tribunal if doing so would put their own soldiers at risk . . . this is perhaps the single biggest impediment to the creation of robust institutions of international justice" (2000: 28–9).

There are several arguments for a truth and justice process for achieving closure about human horrors on a large scale in civil war and ethnic conflict: beyond the matter of justice, punishing criminal leaders removes them from leadership and makes for a stable peace; deterrence of more and future war crimes; stopping the cycle of retribution; placing responsibility on individual perpetrators instead of condemning and labeling entire nations and ethnic groups. The risk of transitional justice is also clear. The rejectionists get a chance to condemn it as "victor's justice" and cultivate and exploit resentment and collective victimization (Bass 2000: 284–312). The uneasy compromises about amnesty made in the Central American peace processes indicate how peace and stability prevail over morality and justice owing to realism. The South African process managed to strike a better balance because the magnitude of the crimes was not on the same scale, because South Africa was not a failed state, and because it had a vigorous civil society. Serb public opinion opposes the ICTY because it perceives the Tribunal as biased against Serbs. Surveys in Bosnia also indicate that most respondents perceive the ICTY as incapable of conducting fair trials (Stover and Weinstein 2004: 33–4). Bosnian judges interviewed thought that economic development would contribute more to social reconstruction than legal accountability. The well-known Belgrade intellectual and journalist Aleksa Djilas (in Judah 2003: 23) stated that the Tribunal was concerned mainly with justifying NATO bombing of Kosovo and Serbia. Serb voters turned against Milosevic not because he was responsible for starting the wars but because he had lost them.

What has been the consequence of the ICTY for truth and justice in the short term? Tim Judah (2003: 23–4) toured the most ethnically cleansed regions in Bosnia in 2003 to get a sense of it at the grass roots. In Kosarac, a town that was ethnically cleansed of Muslims by the Serbs in 1992, he found that every house had been rebuilt and that half the original population of 20,000 had returned because the returnees felt safe. They felt safe only because 19 of the local organizers and killers in the ethnic cleansing had been arrested, indicted, or effectively removed from public life. Clearly where justice had been done the survivors had benefited. One wonders how different would have been the response to the constitutional crisis in

Yugoslavia in 1990–2 had there been a robust truth and justice process under Tito for dealing with the war crimes and crimes against humanity during World War II.

Can the cycle of revenge be broken without transitional justice? The assassins of Prime Minister Zoran Djinjic on March 23, 2003 told the special prosecutor that they had killed him because he was a "Hague traitor," i.e. had surrendered Milosevic to the ICTY. A year before the Bosnian war Radovan Karadzic stated: "The Serbs are endangered again . . . this nation well remembers genocide [in World War II]. Those events are still a terrible living memory. The terror has survived 50 years" (quoted in Sudetic 1998: 84). The deputy mayor of Prijedor justified the Omarska camp where Croats and Muslims were tortured and put to death in 1992 as a payback for the World War II Jasenovac camp where thousands of Serbs were killed. "There is a connection," he said. "During world war two the Croats killed us; this time it was the other way round, we killed them. Perhaps in fifty years, it will happen to us again" (Cohen 1998: 479). In my view, the collective myths and crisis frame on ethnic relations that justified a war of aggression against civilians can only be defeated with a truth and justice process or, in Jack Snyder's words: "intellectual combat against falsifiable myths . . . is a key instrument for containing ethnic conflict" (2000: 334).

Economic reconstruction

Economic reconstruction is the neglected stepchild of peace accords. Emergency economic and humanitarian aid are discussed during peace negotiations, but the external stakeholders usually commit themselves to reconstruction and state building in post-warfare donor conferences at which states pledge various amounts but only a fraction ends up being provided. The World Bank and regional banks are brought in to contribute loans, make studies of needs, draft programs, and set conditions for repayment. Conditions at the end of fighting are widespread poverty, much destruction of housing and infrastructure, industrial activity at a standstill, a criminalized economy, human trafficking, high unemployment, relief dependence, brain drain of the most capable professionals and educated youth, and a poorly paid civil service supplementing salaries with bribes for routine services. There is no "peace dividend" at the cessation of warfare (Gupta *et al.* 2002). In post-conflict socialist countries like Bosnia and Kosovo, state property in the form of enterprises and housing has been appropriated by ethno-political leaders who perpetuate their rule through patron–client relations: "you vote for us and we give you a job and a living, sometimes also a low-rent apartment." In a few cases the country has a viable economic sector for jump-starting the economy if some investments are made, like Croatia with tourism on the Dalmatian coast. Even countries with valuable resources like oil in Iraq are left with a run-down industrial plant that needs huge investments and modernization before it becomes profitable. Business is burdened with huge transaction costs from bureaucratic regulations, juris-dictional fragmentation, and corruption. Post-war economies run on cash transactions avoiding taxes. An Albanian economist working for the World Bank in Kosovo quipped at a conference I attended that:

> In the Balkans, the police is there to beat up the minorities, the judges and courts to protect the criminals in their ethnic group, the Ministry of Finance to divert foreign aid into their own pockets, and the army to make war on civilians.

He meant that economic reconstruction has to run parallel with institutional reforms of the police, courts, and government services, i.e. building a functioning state.

Surveys in post-conflict Bosnia find that the people are more concerned with jobs and making a living than with governance and human rights issues and underscore the "limits of social policy in a context of massive poverty and unemployment" (Poggi *et al.* 2002: 24; Stover and Weinstein 2004: 149–58). Despite these concerns, recovery policy seldom includes a massive labor-intensive job and infrastructure program similar to the Work Programs Administration and Civilian Conservation Corps during the 1930s Great Depression in the US. Utilizing macroeconomic modeling, the international agencies debate how to keep inflation down, clarify property rights, privatize the socialized sector, integrate with the global economy, curb corruption, eliminate the narco-economy and criminal rackets, reduce poverty, and raise incomes and growth rates. Collier *et al.* at the World Bank recognize that "The returns to early rehabilitation of key infrastructure destroyed during the conflict can be extremely high . . . The restoration of transport connections is also important for reintegrating the rural subsistence economy into the market" (2003: 152–9). Yet the most obvious way to putting the unemployed to work receives short shrift.

Practitioners of post-conflict recovery use a dual strategy of state building and economic revival for peace building. The High Representative in Bosnia stated in OHR's Twenty-fourth Report to the UN Secretary General on peace implementation that, "When I arrived in Sarajevo, I outlined my priorities as first justice, then job reform" (2003: 2). Concretely this meant a "complete restructuring of the court system," implementing the recom-mendations of the "Bulldozer Committee" for removing 50 roadblocks to economic growth, and equipping Bosnia-Hercegovina with a modern state-level system of indirect tax collection (for a value added tax) and a single efficient customs service. A sympathetic observer gives the OHR higher grades for political reform and state building than for economic recovery:

> Bosnia's situation and future are precarious. But that is not because – at least not primarily because – of the institutional structure of the Bosnian state . . . It is due [to] the dire condition of the economy and

mass unemployment: the emigration of highly educated and qualified citizens that began in 1992 and continued after the war; the extremely poor quality of post-secondary education that, coupled with poor job prospects, encourages emigration by bright young people.

(Bose 2005: 329–30)

The World Bank's LICUS (low-income countries under stress) approach for underdeveloped countries puts the accent on economic growth through macroeconomic policies and has been adapted to post-civil-war societies. Collier *et al.* (2003: 91) believe that their findings show that "economic development is the critical instrument in preventing rebellion and in building the conditions in which groups engage in their conflicts through normal political means." Others who have evaluated policy and programs by the World Bank, the IMF, the United States Agency for International Development, and UN agencies are unconvinced that these organizations deliver on what they promise and pressure weak governments to accept. Joseph Stiglitz (2002) is extremely critical of the IMF's growth and stabilization policies. Robert Muscat is skeptical about the macroeconomic modeling approach by the World Bank and others for guiding economic recovery in post-war situations: "large scale inductive models grind out enormous amounts of data . . . that do not establish a causal link between the variables and the outcome . . . one cannot come away from a reading of the burgeoning econometric examination of conflict without strong reservations" (2002: 150–1).

Data on the most elementary variables from many underdeveloped countries are guesstimates, and that is especially true for countries caught up in warfare and its aftermath. When I taught at the social science faculty of the National University of Zaire (now the Democratic Republic of the Congo) in Lumumbashi in 1977, the government's demographic advisor told me that his office was simply increasing the population figures by 3 percent every year from the 1960 base recorded in the last year of the Belgian colonial administration, which itself was a crude estimate since no census had ever been held in the Congo. In the course of our researches in Lumumbashi my students and I found other instances of phony economic statistics. The cost of living index compiled by a Belgian market research firm was based on prices at a single supermarket patronized largely by Europeans rather than on prices in markets where Africans purchased food and other goods. The official statistics underestimated African incomes by a huge factor because they omitted most economic transactions among Africans which were in self-employment in small businesses. For instance, about half the African housing was built by self-employed local craftsmen, carpenters, brick makers, roofers, and builders whose employment, wages, and materials were ignored in the official statistics and which amounted to about $1,200 per house on average according to information we obtained from the owners and builders. Demographic and economic data collection and reporting in countries similar to the Congo are just as unreliable as my research team determined about the revenues of Zambian small businesses and market traders in field studies and surveys (Beveridge and Oberschall 1979). Economic policy ought to be based on microeconomic realities in addition to macroeconomic modeling.

The conventional economic wisdom at the IMF, World Bank, US government, and other leading world development agencies, termed the "Washington Consensus," is that growth and poverty reduction won't happen without well-defined property rights, contract enforcement, privatization, and the rule of law. As Stiglitz points out (2002: chapter 7), China achieved the highest rates of growth and the largest reduction of poverty despite violating the Washington Consensus. Dale Perkins, a specialist on the Chinese economic transformation, points out that "Chinese owned businesses knew how to operate in a world in which legal contracts were often not enforced. They had established working relationships with local governments and could turn to them for help when needed" (2000: 234). Chinese business had a long history of circumventing a powerful predatory state bureaucracy, a practice that continued between work units and among individual Chinese under the communist party-state with the "guanxi" (personal influence) system. Public–private cooperation based on township enterprises and later on overseas to mainland Chinese ties were made possible by shared culture and ties that freed market forces and entrepreneurship without the benefit of the formal institutions in the Washington Consensus. The Chinese were drawing on social capital that was temporarily put on ice in the Mao decades and was revived when state controls for economic activity were loosened. Economic recovery and development feed on social organization, not just investment, human capital, and a functioning state.

Social reconstruction

The goal of social reconstruction in a multiethnic society is institutionalized cooperation and a culture of tolerance in ethnic relations. The majority should reasonably accommodate the minority (or minorities), but the minority has to reciprocate and accommodate the majority in turn. Public policy in shared institutions should firmly oppose ethnic colonization by militants who promote ethnic identity agendas and the ethnification of social relations. Ethnic colonization refers to importing the divisions and conflicts that caused ethnic conflict into shared institutions by militants with an ethnic identity and separatist agenda. Ethnification of social relations is the predominance of ethnic identity and group membership over other identities and statuses.

One design for social organization in multiethnic society is maximum separation and group autonomy with a weak center for cooperation and conflict management. It is based on the principle of "good fences make good ethnics and good citizens" that justifies consociational power sharing in the polity. It legitimizes the divided society, but, unlike colonial regimes of domination and subordination, the segments are equal. Such a design is feasible when there is sharp territorial separation, as in Switzerland. There is no controversy over language in the public schools when all the pupils speak a German dialect in a German-speaking town, and all pupils speak French in a French-speaking town. If there are few shared institutions at the grass roots, how to accommodate to one another is simply not an issue. Whether Czechs and Slovaks are part of the same state, form a loose confederation, or split into two states does not present major issues in ethnic relations and conflict management at the grass roots. Social organization is an issue when the ethnic groups are territorially mixed, as in Northern Ireland and South Africa, or had been territorially mixed before armed conflict and ethnic cleansing and some want to reconstitute a shared homeland, as in Bosnia.

Morality, trust, social ties, shared institutions, and social capital are in short supply after ethnic wars. Ethnic identity and encapsulation are prominent; attachment to collective myths and symbols offensive to other groups is strong; avoidance is practiced and is legitimate; minority returnees are not welcome; all groups harbor deep-seated grievances and feel victimized by the others; identity politics is thriving. How do institutionalized cooperation and a culture of tolerance get started in such a social milieu? The prescription for social reconstruction in a multiethnic society is identities shared by the adversaries, non-partisan public symbols, and shared institutions rather than segregation and avoidance.

Reversing ethnification

To understand the salience of ethnic identity and the persistence of identity politics, one must understand the mechanisms that sustain them. People have many identities which are shared with other ethnic groups: senior citizen, graduate of a secondary school, wage earner, inhabitant of a particular village or town. In a pre-crisis social milieu, people maintain a balance between several identities. In some activities and statuses, ethnicity is exclusive, but in others it is shared. A Croat in a mixed Croat–Muslim town is a member of the Catholic Church, which signals membership and good standing among Croats, and he can also belong to the town's soccer team that includes both Croats and Muslims, which stands for inter-ethnic cooperation. In a crisis, ethnicity becomes more salient owing to social pressures that are biased in favor of ethnicity, i.e. there are greater social pressures to be recognized as a good Croat who cuts ties to Muslims than to remain on the town soccer team, and similarly among Muslims. A formal model of identity formation based on the social construction of ethnic identity shows that in a crisis most Croats and Muslims sever their ties and will quit joint activities like soccer (Oberschall and Kim 1996). For an individual the experience is ethnification; at the aggregate level, the town experiences ethnic polarization. This tendency is enhanced by a competitive process within each ethnic group for increasing their ethnic reputation against rivals by stepping up their ethnic activities (Kuran 1998). Ethnification explains how behaviors that signal ethnic identity diffuse rapidly and assume ever more intense, exclusive, and visible forms, as in ethnic dress and life-style codes, ethnic voting, and other manifestations of ethnic solidarity and loyalty.

Ethnification is grounded on the same principles as a much larger category of behaviors that model the consequences of positional competition in rank-ing systems, like conspicuous consumption, fashion, teenage behavior fads, political correctness, and competitive sports (Hirsch 1976; Frank 1985). Formal models demonstrate that such processes have bandwagon properties. There is a stable equilibrium at low incidence, but, once unleashed, ethni-fication runs the course until high incidence is reached, and remains stable at that level.

Sanctions by the authorities against such behavior may in fact increase its attractiveness because personal sacrifice for a group cause increases one's reputation in the peer group and stimulates others to do likewise. Ethnification is difficult to reverse from within the group for the same reason that norms and customs tend to be stable. Max Weber explained it a century ago: "the stability of custom essentially rests on the fact that whoever does not conform to it . . . pays a cost for non-conforming . . . so long as the majority in the social milieu expects conformity with the custom and counts on it" ([1923] 1956, vol. 1: 30). James Coleman (1969) has shown that non-conformity to majority norms belongs to a class of processes he referred to as "innovator-loss," i.e. the first who try to change a norm pay a high price, which discourages others from trying. Because the social construction of ethnicity and ethnification are powerful shapers of the social world, better human relations and communication programs for ethnic relations and reconciliation by themselves have a limited impact. Conformity to opinion and norms entrenched in the social fabric, like race discrimina-tion in the South before the civil rights movement, can only be broken by vigorous public policy or a broad-based and determined opposition social movement.

Social reconstruction during peace building has to pursue policies that encourage identities other than ethnicity, provide inducements for inter-ethnic cooperation, distribute resources by need rather than ethnicity, and outlaw ethnic discrimination from public institutions and programs. A good example of such a program is economy recovery starting with massive infra-structure projects that generate jobs and incomes and are ethnically neutral, i.e. all are eligible to participate and none are excluded. We know from studies of inter-group relations that mixed teams of peers – such as sports teams and military combat units – collaborating on a joint enterprise foster positive inter-ethnic relations (Hewstone and Cairns 2001). We also know from refugee and displaced person returnee studies that a mixed workplace has a more positive impact on ethnic relations than residential mixing (Poggi *et al.* 2002). Finally we also know that poverty is an inhibitor of all manner of social and civic engagement, and thus is also an impediment to improved ethnic relations. Infrastructure construction would thus deliver results for inter-ethnic cooperation on all three dimensions of team activity, work context, and poverty relief.

Sharing institutions without ethnic colonization

In any society, activities take place in organizations and groups which deliver both an individual and a collective benefit or good: sports, professional associations, business and workmen organizations, religious groups, education organizations, book clubs and country clubs, exercise groups, and many, many others. Some of these organizations are in the public domain, like most education, health services, and pension plans in many societies, others are public–private partnerships, and still others are voluntary associations.

Many collective goods in mixed populations cannot be separated by ethnicity by redrawing boundaries, like sunshine, rain, air quality, traffic congestion, beach erosion, etc. For some other collective goods, joint production and consumption are not a contentious issue, e.g. shared use of highways, electricity grid, airports and harbors, and the like. Some other collective goods are sought by majorities and minorities alike, e.g. state pensions, health care, and non-discriminatory labor markets. Although it is possible through administrative means to deliver these collective goods separately by ethnicity rather than jointly, there is no benefit realized and no demand for it. The issue for minorities is non-discriminatory access to such collective goods and equality under the law, not separate institutions. Finally there are shared institutions where cultural and language differences require cooperation and accommodation.

Democratic states have made far-reaching accommodations on cultural autonomy and sharing with non-state groups, especially religious institutions, as with religious schools, and on language, as with minority language rights in state administration and in the courts. Equal rights and access to state majorities and minorities in principle do not depend on territorial jurisdiction though from a practical standpoint it makes little sense to give a minority language parity in places that have very few or none using that language. Thus the state might require its employees in a particular jurisdiction to speak a language when a certain proportion of the citizens in a particular area speak that as their first language, but not in other jurisdictions. Multinational organizations face the problem of language communications and deal with it in terms of efficiency, cost of training, and other practical criteria. A state, however, cannot deal with language differences as simply a problem of efficient communications because language is also a very important

234 *Peace building*

expression of ethnic identity. In multilingual states such as India, Canada, Belgium, and Switzerland it makes political, cultural, and practical sense to match linguistic with political jurisdictions. For some other identity-linked collective goods, e.g. television programming, the state can provide access to religious, cultural, and other groups, both majority and minority, in the state-controlled mass media on an equitable basis, and provide financial support for them. Even so it is inevitable that culture has a distinct majoritarian tone and is not a smorgasbord of unconnected symbols and practices. National holidays and symbols, school recesses, and cultural events of all types will to some extent reflect the historical and religious traditions of the majority or founding people in the country. A democratic state will try to accommodate to the prescriptions and sensibilities of minorities. For religious minorities with dietary prohibitions and a distinct worship, appropriate meals are served in the armed forces and in prisons, and appropriate chaplains and religious worship are provided. Some states will exempt minorities from civic obligations when they are contrary to deeply held religious beliefs, as with conscientious objectors and Quakers serving in the armed forces.

The state's accommodation to minorities on identity-linked collective goods does have limits. If a minority claims the right to exercise certain customs and practices because they are fundamental to its ethnic and religious identities, and these customs are just as fundamentally contrary to the state's constitution and laws and the values of the majority of the people, there is an inevitable conflict. A state and the majority should prevent the Balkanization of shared institutions by ethnic militants. Suppose a religious or ethnic group practices child marriage, private revenge for wrongs such as blasphemy, female genital mutilation, withholding health care to its critically ill, or other practices founded on custom and religious belief, the state must set limits to claims of differential treatment, as Lord Justice Devlin famously argued (1968). It is true that colonial empires had legal pluralism, with European law and courts for European settlers and administrators and customary law and courts for the indigenous peoples, but these societies were not democratic nor was there any pretense that the dominant and subordinate group had equal rights or indeed would become equals at some future time. Some measure of accommodation on family law duality between Hindus and Muslims exists in India and in other places where laws and practices of traditional societies with different ethnic and religious customs have been carried forward into a modern state. But in a contemporary democratic state, legal pluralism that criminalizes the same behavior for one ethnic or religious group while legalizing it for another is unlikely to be acceptable and unlikely to bring ethnic peace. It did not in the end work in the case of slavery for the United States, and it creates lots of ethnic and religious conflicts in states like Nigeria over Sharia law for Muslims and secular law for non-Muslims.

Conflict management in shared institutions

Peace settlements like those in Northern Ireland and in Bosnia leave many loose ends on key issues in the conflict to be dealt with during implementation by commissions, task forces, voluntary groups, and public–private and international partnerships, from police reform to job programs, community relations, and education. Contentious issues that were pursued violently in civil war and insurgency continue to be sought in shared institutions but have to be managed peacefully. In a multiethnic society, the state can remove incentives and benefits it has created for those who exclude others from groups and institutions, and provide incentives for those who include and participate in sharing groups. Any sharing institution will have to devise ways of including and accommodating minorities without becoming Balkanized by minority identity politics and self-encapsulation. If the choice is parallel separate institutions, the authorities should not permit them to become incubators of the divisions and ideologies that caused the ethnic conflict to begin with.

Consider the recurring and persistent conflicts between citizenship and multiculturalism in education. T. H. Marshall writes that:

> citizenship . . . postulates that there is a kind of basic human equality associated with the concept of full membership of a community . . . citizenship requires a sense of community membership based on loyalty to a civilization which is a common possession . . . If citizenship is invoked in the defense of rights, the corresponding duties of citizenship cannot be ignored . . . [the citizen's] acts should be inspired by a lively sense of responsibility towards the welfare of the community.
>
> (1965: 76, 89, 101, 123)

Education has been the battlefield between citizenship and ethnic and religious groups that claim control over culture reproduction, between majorities and minorities, secularists and cultural traditionalists, the state and ethno-national minorities. Ever since the state and the public made schooling compulsory in the nineteenth century because they viewed a literate population as an important national resource, an educated mind a basic human right, and moral character useful for nation building, they competed with already established, mostly religious organizations which claimed the right to the moral and cultural development of youth. Some sort of accommodation had to be reached on the continuation and financing of parallel religious education organizations and state supervision of their curricula and standards for licenses and certificates recognized by the state. Accommodation was reached but not without a great deal of conflict.

In France the time series of annual protests and demonstrations has a peak in the 1902–5 years over church–state separation and the status of separate Catholic education (Tilly *et al.* 1975: 57–9, figs. 6–8). More recently Muslim fundamentalists are confronting the French public schools on female head-scarves. They are an affirmation of fundamentalist Muslim identity that symbolize rejection of the citizenship ideal of the French state and the French people, i.e. "liberté, fraternité, égalité." In the United States when New York and other states prohibited the teaching of religion in public schools in the 1840s, the Catholic Church decided to set up its own school system amid a great deal of controversy (Glazer and Moynihan 1963: 234–8). The white South resisted desegregation of public schools after the 1954 Supreme Court decision. For the next decade, the start of the school year was greeted by widespread protests and some violent incidents at school sites in many Southern and border state localities. In our own time Protestant funda-mentalists are battling against "secular humanism" which they believe is taught in public schools and is subverting the faith and morality of children and youth. They have established Christian academies and religious schools that give them control over socialization and culture reproduction, and the authorities have given them a wide latitude for running their parallel institutions in the name of freedom of religion (Oberschall 1993: chapter 13). In other societies, the compulsory use of the dominant group's language in schooling and in other state institutions gave rise to demands for local autonomy and self-determination. Language and education have always been contentious issues in a multiethnic society. What is an appropriate education policy for a multiethnic society?

Education can be produced in various mixes of private and public, shared or separate for ethnic groups, state subsidized and compulsory to varying degree. Ethnic groups by and large have similar preferences on how much and what kinds of education their children should get, just as they have similar preferences for clean air and road safety. Parents want not only quality schooling for their children's career prospects, but they want the curriculum not to be biased against their ethnic group in civics, history, and literature. They also want the school administration and teachers to treat their children fairly and equally, and they want their children protected from harassment by other kids, i.e. they have fairness and security concerns. As long as discrimination is embedded in the process of schooling itself, minorities will prefer separate rather than shared schooling. When the state outlaws discrimination and enforces it, and when its agents, be they teachers, police, tax assessors, hospital workers, etc., conduct their activities as pro-fessionals and not as partisans, it will attract minorities and majorities to shared institutions. At the same time, the majority and the state have an interest in schools and universities that promote national unity and citi-zenship, as T. H. Marshall noted, and public policy should prevent ethnic insularity and separation in public institutions and sharing groups. No group should be compelled to attend these mixed schools rather than their own separate schools, but separate schools should not subvert citizenship. If the mixed schools offer a supportive social and cultural milieu for learning and are less expensive than separate schools, all groups will be attracted.

Sharing increases inter-ethnic transacting, and innovator-loss barriers are breached with interaction volume, i.e. the lone non-conformists who usually pay a price for first transacting across ethnicity will have plenty of company and will not be negatively sanctioned. In such shared institutions, ethnic groups discover that they have similar preferences for some collective goods – crime-free streets, after-school youth activities, public transportation from homes to schools, a good computer course – and that they possess personal qualities and talents for rewarding transactions with one another – good looks, good brains, a sense of humor, sports skills, or a helping disposition. Education policy can structure schooling opportunities for more integration. Instead of offering the same level of computer and science curriculum in every school, a special school with an advanced curriculum in computers and science that attracts pupils from all groups can be created. Pupils will study and participate in mixed teams on common problems, which research has shown to be a cooperative mode of cross-ethnic activity.

Reasonable accommodation to minorities within schools is desirable in mixed institutions: the school might offer special elective courses of interest mainly to one or another ethnic group, but forbid identity ethnification with no educational purpose. Micromanagement of identity and culture conflicts is unavoidable, and school administrators will have to deal with demands for special dishes in the cafeteria due to religious diet rules and what to do when some students display offensive symbols on their dress. Within shared institutions some self-segregation based on in-group preferences will persist, and that is to be expected. Increased contact between ethnic groups may also stimulate group competition and ethnic identities, and that too is expected. The school will become a learning experience for ethnic conflict management. In the long term, the logic of ethnic separation will lose force both within and outside the schools, and ethnicity will reduce to in-group preferences in private and intimate domains that it is not the business of the state to interfere with in a free society. The reason that sharing is preferable to separation and avoidance is that recent history has repeatedly shown how "live and let live" separatism rapidly descends into ethnic warfare in a crisis, as in the Balkans.

Some lessons for public policy during peace building follow. Separate ethnic institutions and transacting are fastened to four anchors. The first is in-group preference; the second is distinct collective goods preferences; the third is ethnification; the fourth is the legacy of unequal treatment, stereotyping, hostility, fear, and habits of avoidance. The first two stem from the logic of ethnic groups and are not meant to cause harm to other groups. The last two purposely create and maintain ethnic separation and inflict harm and losses in inter-ethnic relations. A democratic multiethnic state is committed to equal treatment of its citizens for philosophic, moral, and legal reasons. It should outlaw discrimination and enforce equal treatment in public policy. When ethnic groups have similar preferences for collective goods and when public policy opposes bias and unequal treatment, most citizens from all walks of life will choose shared institutions. Ethnification does not self-destruct after ethnic fighting, and public policy should oppose ethnic colonization in public institutions. When ethnic groups have different preferences, public policy ought not to subsidize conduct, practices, and institutions that make for separation, although it should not ban them so long as they are voluntary and benign. Ethnic politics in sharing groups and throughout the society will be contentious but can remain non-violent and amenable to non-coercive conflict management. Trust, inter-ethnic relations, social capital, cooperation, and ethnic conflict management are learned in shared institutions and are transferable to all domains of ethnic relations and from one generation to the succeeding ones.

Conclusion

It is customary to end a book such as this with an assessment of "what we have learned" about ethnic conflict management and peace building and what should be done differently. Peace building rests on security, political reform, truth and justice, and social and economic reconstruction. In the chapters on the Israeli–Palestinian conflict and the peace process in Bosnia and Northern Ireland I have presented a detailed methodology based on CCD and the "feasible" and "acceptable" dimensions of peace settlement implementation. More broadly, the literature is filled with excellent ideas on what we have learned and what lessons to apply in ethnic conflict management and peace building. The literature has a strong normative and policy orientation, e.g. power sharing governance as peaceful conflict management. We don't lack good ideas so much as knowledge of how to implement them in realistic, difficult conflict and conciliation environments. Most analysts recommend incentives for a bridge between adversaries that builds on the moderates in both camps, early intervention for peace by external stakeholders, and external monitoring and enforcement of demilitarization and demobilization. They warn that lack of post-war security is the greatest threat to peace, and that hurried post-war elections risk legitimizing intransigent ethnic leaders in what amounts to an ethnic census. Implementing these good ideas and policy prescriptions is the problem.

Take the notion that violent rejectionists have to be brought into the peace negotiations rather than excluded; as Prime Minister Rabin put it succinctly in 1993 at the start of the Oslo peace process, "peace is not made with friends, it is made with enemies" (Shlaim 2001: 512). The downside of implementing this good idea is that one loses important domestic support for peace from the rejectionists within one's camp, as Rabin and his successors found out soon enough. By negotiating with Sinn Fein and thus indirectly with the IRA, the UK government lost the support of half the unionists, and that was to plague implementation of NIPA. There is no simple way out of this dilemma. To get around the resistance of the Bosnian Serbs to the Dayton peace process, US diplomacy threatened President

Milosevic with continued economic sanctions on Serbia. Milosevic in turn bullied the Bosnian Serbs into signing the DPA, but they proceeded to undermine implementation. The contentious issues at Dayton were transferred unresolved from the negotiation table to post-settlement implementation.

Research shows and experience with peace accord implementation confirms again and again that early post-conflict elections advantage ethnic nationalists and disadvantage ethnic moderates and a moderate cross-ethnic coalition. What are the practical implications for peace building? Is it a realistic option to delay elections until a law-and-order state and civil society are well on their way, which might take years? Should and can an "international protectorate" or "trusteeship" mode of governance be imposed on the adversaries against their consent, and what sorts of issues and conflicts does that create for peace implementation? Is it possible to delay resentment and obstruction of the international protectorate with local elections and the transfer of governmental functions in a gradual, limited, bottom-up process?

We know that humanitarian aid is a moral hazard. The adversaries will appropriate some of the aid to their combatants and will use RIDPs, the international aid program, and aid workers as hostages for advancing their military plans. In fact, humanitarian aid may prolong a civil war because the combatants outsource responsibility for civilian survival and welfare to the international community that otherwise they would have to shoulder. Is there a clear-cut lesson for humanitarian aid?

We know that early intervention in ethnic conflicts by external stakeholders has a better chance of preventing a humanitarian crisis and anarchy, and we have drawn up plans for quick military intervention when diplomacy fails. But in actual crises, in a difficult ethnic and logistic environment, the international conflict managers are not intervening effectively, although there is endless talk about it. Knowledge, as I have argued, is one thing; implementation of what is known is far more problematic. One may know that a critical mass of uranium atoms can set off a chain reaction that will produce a huge explosion and still be far from producing a nuclear weapon, which in that instance is very fortunate for mankind. For peace building, limits of knowledge about implementation are a huge liability.

One may well ponder why ethnic cooperation in governance is so often contentious whereas multiethnic, multinational, multilingual organizations are managed reasonably well and without violent conflict. There are multinational corporations; international conventions on postal services and air and sea transportation; international governance organizations such as the UN and the European Union, and many of their agencies and programs, e.g. WHO and WFO and UN peacekeeping; transnational humanitarian bodies like the ICRC; religious organizations; military organizations like NATO, which, following in the footsteps of armies since the earliest empires, are multiethnic and multilingual; scientific, scholarly, educational, and professional activities and associations which are multinational and global, as are international sports federations, the Olympic Games, the World Cup, and chess and other games federations; international tribunals and courts and trading bodies and banks; and, for the sake of completeness, crime syndicates and terrorist organizations. All these multiethnic organizations are rule-abiding and recognize a common authority that makes and enforces the rules. Why should it be more difficult to make ethnic groups cooperate in governance and social organization?

Examine international sports like soccer and the World Cup. It is very competitive, and encounters are zero sum, i.e. one wins and the other loses. There is lots of national pride invested in the outcome, and the ritual of anthems, flags, colors, spectator facial paints, chants, and other symbols of national identity are prominent. The media build-up and coverage are ubiquitous and all-pervasive. The emotional involvement of hundreds of millions of fans is visibly displayed and legitimate. The financial stakes are measured in multibillion dollars and range from advertising to international tourism and the construction of facilities. Group identity and interest are central to international sports. Yet the activities are cooperative and peaceful.

International sport possesses a number of dimensions that favor coopera-tion. Over time, the outcome is reversible: a loser can become a winner. There are many sports and the outcome thus made divisible: some countries do well in winter sports, others in summer sports, some in long-distance running, others in cycling, and still others in Greco-Roman wrestling. In some sports size is important for winning, in others quickness and team work. There are no incentives for changing the rules because whatever they are they apply equally to all competitors. Everyone agrees that rules and referees are necessary for the game: the collective good of a sports contest cannot be produced through coercion or in anarchy. Participation is volun-tary. No matter what one's emotional engagement and national pride, one does not cease to be a father or mother, professional, citizen of a town, and member of a religious and political group because one is a sports fan, or maybe only for short periods of time.

In so far as ethnic governance and group relations assume the character of international sports they can be made more cooperative and more peaceful. Interest and identity need not be, indeed cannot be, suppressed, as they are not in sports, but have to be modified with incentives and institu-tions. The political rules have to benefit all groups, and power sharing and institutional reforms are meant to do that. Ethnification has to be downsized through multiple group memberships and sharing institutions that express other identities and a multiplicity of interests. Diversity and autonomy in some cultural pursuits, like diversity in sports, allow minorities to excel and benefit even when they are at some disadvantage in other cultural pursuits and competitive arenas. New ideas and designs for institutions that decouple sovereignty, territory, identity, and interest have to be studied, tried, and applied. Changing the rules of ethnic relations by violence rather than public policy has to be firmly opposed. It has been said that language is a dialect with an army, and that has been the conviction of ethno-national leaders. To the contrary, for peaceful ethnic management in a multiethnic society, every dialect, with or without an army, should be a language in some institutions, districts, and circumstances, even if not in all of them.

References

Abbreviations

Other items cited in the text by acronym are alphabetized accordingly among the references.

CNN Cable News Network
NPR National Public Radio
NYRB *New York Review of Books*
NYT *New York Times*
PBS Public Broadcasting System

References

9/11 Commission Report: Final Report of the National Commission on Terrorist Attacks upon the United States, authorized edn., New York: Norton, 2004.

Ajdukovic, Dean and Corkalo, Dinka (2004) "Trust and Betrayal in War," in Eric Stover and Harvey Weinstein (eds.), *My Neighbor, My Enemy*, New York: Cambridge University Press, chapter 14.

Alcock, Antony (2002) "Religion and the Conflict in Northern Ireland," *CIFEM News*, December, 14–18.

American Association for the Advancement of Science (1999) *Policy or Panic? The Flight of Ethnic Albanians from Kosovo, March–May 1999*, hrdata.aaas.org/Kosovo/policyorpanic.

Anderson, Kenneth (2003) "Who Owns the Rules of War," Crimes of War Project, http://www.crimesofwar.org/special/Iraq, April 24.

Apsel, Joyce (ed.) (2005) *Darfur: Genocide before Our Eyes*, New York: Institute for the Study of Genocide.

Ash, Timothy Garton (1995) "Bosnia in Our Future," *NYRB*, December 21.

—— (2000a) "Anarchy and Madness," *NYRB*, February 10, 48–52.

—— (2000b) "Kosovo: Was It Worth It?" *NYRB*, September 21, 50–60.

Atlas Narodov Mira (1964) Moscow: Glavnoe Upravlenie Geodezi I Kartografi.

Baldy, Tom (1987) *Battle for Ulster*, Washington, DC: National Defense University Press.

Banac, Ivo (2001) "The Weight of False History," *East European Constitutional Review*, Spring/Summer, 101–9.

Bandura, Albert (2004) "The Role of Selective Moral Disengagement in Terrorism and Counterterrorism," unpublished paper, Department of Psychology, Stanford University.

Bartlett, Robert (1993) *The Making of Europe*, Princeton, NJ: Princeton University Press.

Baskin, Mark (2002) *Lessons Learned on UNMIK Judiciary*, Pearson Papers, vol. 8, Clementsport, Nova Scotia: Canadian Peacekeeping Press.

—— (2003) "Post-conflict Administration and Reconstruction," *International Affairs*, 79(1): 161–70.

—— (2004) "Between Exit and Engagement: On the Division of Authority in Transitional Administrations," *Global Government*, 10: 119–37.

Bass, Gary (2000) *Staying the Hand of Vengeance: The Politics of War Crimes Tribunals*, Princeton, NJ: Princeton University Press.

Bellah, Robert (1967) "Civil Religion in America," *Daedalus*, 96(1): 1–21.

Bellamy, Alex, Williams, Paul and Griffin, Stuart (2004) *Understanding Peacekeeping*, Cambridge: Polity Press.

Benjamin, Daniel and Simon, Steven (2006) "Al Qaeda's Big Boast," *NYT*, January 25.

Benvenisti, Meron (1986) *Conflicts and Contradictions*, New York: Villard Books.

—— (1995) *Intimate Enemies*, Berkeley and Los Angeles: University of California Press.

Berelson, Bernard, Lazarsfeld, Paul and McPhee, William (1966) *Voting*, Chicago, IL: University of Chicago Press.

Beristain, Carlos Martin (1998) "Guatemala: Never Again," *Forced Migration Review*, www.fmreview.org/text/FMR/03/06.htm.

Berman, Paul (2005) "The Philosopher of Islamic Terror," *NYT Magazine*, March 23.

Beveridge, Andrew and Oberschall, Anthony (1979) *African Businessmen and Development in Zambia*, Princeton, NJ: Princeton University Press.

Block, Robert (1993) "Killers," *NYRB*, October 21.

Boal, F. W. (2002) "Belfast: Walls Within," *Political Geography*, 21: 687–94.

Bollens, Scott (1998) *Urban Peace Building in Divided Societies*, Boulder, CO: Westview Press.

Bonn International Center for Conversion (2004) "Exchanging Guns for Tools," Brief 29, April 24.

Bose, Sumantra (2002) *Bosnia after Dayton*, London: Hurst.

—— (2005) "The Bosnian State a Decade after Dayton," *International Peacekeeping*, 12(3): 322–35.

Bowden, Mark (2003) "The Dark Art of Interrogation," *Atlantic Monthly*, October, 51–74.

Boyle, Kevin and Hadden, Tom (1994) *Northern Ireland: The Choice*, London: Penguin.

Brams, Steven and Taylor, Alan (1999) *The Win–Win Solution: Guaranteeing Fair Shares to Everybody*, New York: Norton.

Bremer, Thomas, Popov, Nebojsa and Stobbe, Heinz-Guenther (eds.) (1998) *Serbiens Weg in den Krieg*, Berlin: Arno Spitz.

Bringa, Tone (2005) "Reconciliation in Bosnia-Hercegovina," in Elm Skaar, Siri Gloppen and Astri Suhrke (eds.) (2005) *Roads to Reconciliation*, New York: Lexington Books, chapter 9.

Brown, Michael (ed.) (1993) *Ethnic Conflict and International Security*, Princeton, NJ: Princeton University Press.

Brugnola, Orlanda, Fein, Helen and Spirer, Louise (eds.) (1998) Panel 4, "Considering an International Rapid Reaction Force to Deter and Stop Genocide," in *Ever Again: Evaluating the UN Genocide Convention on its 50th Anniversary*, New York: Institute for the Study of Genocide.

Bryan, Dominic (2001) "Parade Disputes in the Peace Process," *Peace Review*, 13(1): 43–9.

Brynam, Rex (2000) *A Very Political Economy*, Washington, DC: United States Institute of Peace.

B'tselem (1998) "A Decade of Human Rights Violations," Information sheet, January, www.btselem.org.

—— (2002) "Total Casualties," www.btselem.org/English/statistics.

—— (2006) "Fatalities," www.btselem.org/English/statistics/casualties.asp.

Byrne, D., Nelson, D. and Reeves, K. (1966) "Effects of Consensual Validation and Invalidation on Attraction as a Function of Verifiability," *Journal of Experimental and Social Psychology*, 2: 98–107.

Callahan, David (2002) *The Enduring Challenge: Self Determination and Ethnic Conflict in the Twenty-First Century*, New York: Carnegie Corporation.

Carnegie Endowment for International Peace (2003) "From Victory to Success: Afterwar Policy in Iraq," *Foreign Policy*, 117 (special issue) (July–August): 49–73.

Carothers, Tom and Lacina, Bethany (2003) "Quick Transformation for Democratic Middle East is a Fantasy," *Seattle Post-Intelligencer*, March 13, www.ceip.org/files/Publications.

Carruthers, Susan (2000) *The Media at War*, New York: St. Martin's.

CEH (Commission for Historical Clarification) (1998) "Guatemala: Memorial of Silence," www.shr.aaas.org/guatemala/ceh/report/english/toc.html.

Chandler, David (1999) *Bosnia: Faking Democracy after Dayton*, London: Pluto.

Chirot, Daniel and Seligman, Martin (eds.) (2001) *Ethnopolitical Warfare*, Washington, DC: American Psychological Association.

Chollet, Derek (1997) *The Road to Dayton: U.S. Diplomacy and the Bosnian Peace Process, May to December, 1995*, Washington, DC: US State Department.

Clinton, Bill (2004) *My Life*, New York: Knopf.

Cohen, Abner (1969) *Custom and Politics in Urban Africa*, Berkeley and Los Angeles: University of California Press.

Cohen, Roger (1998) *Hearts Grown Brutal*, New York: Norton.

Cohen, Stanley (2001) *States of Denial*, Malden, MA: Polity Press.

Coleman, James (1969) "Race Relations and Social Change," in Patricia Gurin and Irwin Katz (eds.), *Race in the Social Sciences*, New York: Basic Books, chapter 6.

—— (1990) *Foundations of Social Theory*, Cambridge, MA: Harvard University Press.

Collier, Paul, Elliott, V. L., Hegre, Havard, Hoeffler, Anke, Reynal-Querol, Marta and Sambanis, Nicholas (2003) *Breaking the Conflict Trap*, Oxford and Washington, DC: Oxford University Press/World Bank.

Colovic, Ivan (1998) "Fussbal, Hooligans, und Krieg," in Thomas Bremer, Nebojsa Popov and Heinz-Guenther Stobbe (eds.), *Serbiens Weg in den Krieg*, Berlin: Arno Spitz, 261–76.

Corkalo, Dinka, Ajdukovic, Dean, Weinstein, Harvey, Stover, Eric, Djipa, Dino and

Biro, Miklos (2004) "Neighbors Again?" in Eric Stover and Harvey Weinstein (eds.), *My Neighbor, My Enemy*, New York: Cambridge University Press, chapter 7.

Coser, Lewis (1956) *The Functions of Social Conflict*, New York and Glencoe, IL: Free Press.

Crane, Conrad (2006) "The New Army–USMC Counterinsurgency Manual," presented at the Casualties and Warfare Conference, Duke University, Durham, NC, February 17–18.

—— and Terrill, Andrew (2003) *Reconstructing Iraq: Insights, Challenges, and Missions for Military Forces in a Post-conflict Scenario*, Carlisle, PA: Strategic Studies Institute, US War College (February).

Crocker, Chester, Osler, Fen and Mampson, Pamel Aal (2001) *Turbulent Peace: The Challenge of International Conflict Management*, Washington, DC: United States Institute of Peace.

CRPC (Commission for Real Property Claims) (2003) *End of Mandate Report 1996–2003*, www.crpc.org.ba.

Danner, Mark (2004a) "The Logic of Torture," *NYRB*, June 24, 70–4.

—— (ed.) (2004b) *Torture and Truth: America, Abu Ghraib, and the War on Terror*, New York: New York Review of Books.

—— (2005) "Reply," *NYRB*, February 10, 44–6.

Darby, John (2006a) "Post-accord Problems during Peace Processes," in John Darby (ed.), *Violence and Reconstruction*, South Bend, IN: University of Notre Dame Press, 143–60.

—— (ed.) (2006b) *Violence and Reconstruction*, South Bend, IN: University of Notre Dame Press.

—— and Rae, James (1999) "Peace Processes from 1988–1998," *Ethnic Studies Report*, 27(1) (January): 45–57.

—— and Mac Ginty, Roger (eds.) (2000) *The Management of Peace Processes*, New York: Palgrave.

Del Ponte, Carla (2001) "Case against Milosevic Is Not Simple to Prove," *NYT*, July 2.

Denitch, Bogdan (1996) *Ethnic Nationalism*, Minneapolis: Minnesota University Press.

—— (1999) "A Botched Just War," *Dissent*, Summer, 7–10.

Derrienic, J.-P. (2002) *Les guerres civiles*, Paris: Presses des Science Po.

Deutsch, John (2005) "Exiting Iraq," *Harvard Magazine*, September/October, 26–87.

Devlin, Patrick (1968) *The Enforcement of Morals*, Oxford: Oxford University Press.

Dicht, Robert (1984) "Die Versoehnung ist kein Grund zur Selbstzufriedenheit," in Klaus Manfrass (ed.), *Paris–Bonn: eine dauerhafte Bindung schwieriger Partner*, Sigmaringen: Jan Thorbecke Verlag.

Dimitrijevic, Vojin (1996) "The War Crimes Tribunal in the Yugoslav Context," *East European Constitutional Review*, Fall, 85–92.

Djilas, Aleksa (1995) "Fear Thy Neighbor," in Charles Kupchan (ed.), *Nationalism and Nationalities in the New Europe*, Ithaca, NY: Cornell University Press.

Downs, George and Steadman, Stephen (2002) "Implementation Strategies," in Stephen Steadman, Donald Rothchild and Elisabeth Cousins (eds.), *Ending Civil Wars*, Boulder, CO: Lynne Rienner, chapter 2.

Doyle, Michael and Sambanis, Nicholas (2000) "International Peacebuilding: A Theoretical and Empirical Analysis," *American Political Science Review*, 94(4): 779–807.

du Toit, Pierre (2000) "South Africa: In Search of Post-Settlement Peace," in John Darby and Roger Mac Ginty (eds.), *The Management of Peace Processes*, New York: Palgrave, 16–60.

Elliott, Sydney and Flackes, W. D. (1999) *Northern Ireland: A Political Directory 1969–1999*, Belfast: Blackstaff Press.

Ellison, Graham and Smyth, Jim (2000) *The Crowned Harp*, London: Pluto Press.

Elon, Amos (2002) "No Exit," *NYRB*, May 23, 15–20.

—— (2004) "War without End," *NYRB*, July 15, 26–9.

Elon, Benny (2001) "Interview: Right Road to Peace," *Haaretz*, November 1.

Enderlin, Charles (2003) *Shattered Dreams: The Failure of the Peace Process in the Middle East 1995–2002*, New York: Other Press.

ESI (European Stabilization Initiative) (2004) "Making Federalism Work – A Radical Proposal for Practical Reform," www.esiweb.org/reports/bosnia/.

Ezrahi, Yaron (1997) *Rubber Bullets*, New York: Farrar, Straus & Giroux.

Fearon, James (2003) "Why Do Some Civil Wars Last Much Longer than Others?" unpublished paper, Political Science Department, Stanford University, Palo Alto, CA.

—— and Laitin, David (2003) "Ethnicity, Insurgency, Civil War," *American Political Science Review*, 97(1): 75–90.

Fein, Helen (1979) *Accounting for Genocide*, New York: Free Press.

—— (ed.) (1994) "The Prevention of Genocide: Rwanda and Yugoslavia Reconsidered," Working Paper of the Institute for the Study of Genocide, New York.

Ferry, Stephen (2003) *The Morning After*, Belfast: Alliance Party.

Filkins, Dexter (2005) "The Fall of the Warrior King," *NYT Magazine*, October 23.

Fisher, Roger (1971) "Fractionating Conflict," in Clagett Smith (ed.), *Conflict Resolution*, South Bend, IN: University of Notre Dame Press.

Foundation for Middle East Peace (2002) "Report on Israeli Settlements in the Occupied Territories/Settlement Database," www.fmep.org/reports.

Frank, Robert (1985) *Choosing the Right Pond*, New York: Oxford University Press.

Gagnon, V. P. (1994/5) "Ethnic Nationalism and International Conflict," *International Security*, 19(3): 130–66.

Gamba, Virginia (2006) "Post-Agreement Demobilization, Disarmament, and Reconstruction," in John Darby (ed.), *Violence and Reconstruction*, South Bend, IN: University of Notre Dame Press, 53–76.

Gamson, William and Modigliani, André (1987) "The Changing Culture of Affirmative Action," *Research in Political Sociology*, 3: 138–78.

Garraway, Charles (2002) "Training: The Whys and Wherefores," *Social Research*, 69(4): 949–62.

Gelpi, Christopher (2003) *The Power of Legitimacy: Assessing the Role of Norms in Crisis Bargaining*, Princeton, NJ: Princeton University Press.

—— (2006) "The Cost of War: How Many Casualties Will Americans Tolerate?" *Foreign Affairs*, 85 (January/February): 139–42.

Geneva Accord (2004) Chicago: Brit Tzedek v'Shalom.

Giles, Michael (1978) "White Enrollment Stability and School Desegregation: A Two-Level Analysis," *American Review of Sociology*, 42 (December): 848–64.

Glazer, Nathan and Moynihan, Daniel Patrick (1963) *Beyond the Melting Pot*, Cambridge, MA: MIT Press.

Goati, Vladimir (2000) *Elections in the Federal Republic of Yugoslavia (FRY) from 1990 to 1998*, Belgrade: CeSID.

Goldberg, Jeffrey (2004) "Among the Settlers," *New Yorker*, May 31, 47–9.

Goldstone, Richard (1997) Foreword to *Between Vengeance and Forgiveness*, by Martha Minow, Boston, MA: Beacon, ix–x.

—— (2000) *For Humanity*, New Haven, CT: Yale University Press.

Graham, H. D. and Gurr, T. R. (eds.) (1969) *Violence in America: Historical and Comparative Perspectives*, Washington, DC: US Government Printing Office.

Gudjousson, Gisli (1999) *The Psychology of Interrogations, Confessions, and Testimony*, New York: Wiley.

Gupta, Sanjeev, Clemens, Benedict, Bhattacharya, Rina and Chakaravarti, Shamit (2002) "The Elusive Peace Dividend," *Finance and Development*, 39(4): 49–51.

Gurr, Ted Robert and Khosla, Deepa (2000) "Domestic and Transnational Strategies for Managing Separatist Conflicts: Four Asian Cases," in Sean Byrne and Cynthia Irvin (eds.), *Reconciling Differences: Turning Points in Ethnopolitical Conflict*, West Hartford, CT: Kumarian Press, 240–87.

Hadden, Tom, Irwin, Colin and Boal, Fred (1996) *Separation or Sharing?* Belfast: Fortnight Education Trust.

Hamber, Brandon (2001) "Who Pays for Peace? Implications of the Negotiated Settlement in a Post-Apartheid South Africa," in Daniel Chirot and Martin Seligman (eds.), *Ethnopolitical Warfare*, Washington, DC: American Psychological Association, 235–58.

Harff, Barbara and Gurr, Ted R. (1998) "Systematic Early Warning in Humanitarian Emergencies," *Journal of Peace Research*, 35(5): 551–79.

Hartle, Col. Anthony (2002) "Atrocities in War: Dirty Hands and Noncombatants," *Social Research*, 69(4): 963–80.

Hayden, Robert (1998) "Bosnia: The Contradictions of 'Democracy without Consent,'" *East European Constitutional Review*, Spring, 45–50.

—— (1999) "Humanitarian Hypocrisy," *East European Constitutional Review*, Summer: 91–6.

Heath, Edward (1998) *The Course of My Life*, London: Hodder & Stoughton.

Hegland, Corinne (2006) "Who Is at Guantanamo Bay?" *National Journal*, February 8.

Heidenrich, John (2001) *How to Prevent Genocide*, Westport, CT: Praeger.

Heimerl, Daniela (2005) "The Return of Refugees and IDPs: From Coercion to Sustainability," *International Peacekeeping*, 12(3): 377–90.

Hersch, Seymour (2004a) "Chain of Command," *New Yorker*, May 24, 38–42.

—— (2004b) "The Gray Zone," *New Yorker*, May 17, 38–44.

Herzberg, Arthur (1990) "Impasse over Israel," *NYRB*, October 25, 41–6.

Hewstone, Miles and Cairns, Ed (2001) "Social Psychology and Inter-Group Conflict," in Daniel Chirot and Martin Seligman (eds.), *Ethnopolitical Warfare*, Washington, DC: American Psychological Association, 319–42.

Hills, Alice (2004) *Future War in Cities*, London: Frank Cass.

Hinde, Robert (1997) "The Psychological Bases of War," www.unc.edu/depts/diplomat/AD Issues/amdipl_7/hinde.html.

Hirsch, Fred (1976) *Social Limits to Growth*, Cambridge, MA: Harvard University Press.

Holbrooke, Richard (1998) *To End a War*, New York: Random House.

Hollis, Rosemary (2000) "Still Waiting," *World Today*, 56(6): 20–2.

Horowitz, Donald (1985) *Ethnic Groups in Conflict*, Berkeley and Los Angeles: University of California Press.

—— (1990) "Making Moderation Pay," in Joseph Montville (ed.), *Conflict and Peacemaking in Multiethnic Societies*, Lexington, MA: Heath, 451–76.

—— (2000) *Ethnic Groups in Conflict*, 2nd edn., Berkeley and Los Angeles: University of California Press.

—— (2001) *The Deadly Ethnic Riot*, Berkeley and Los Angeles: University of California Press.

—— (2002) "Explaining the Northern Ireland Agreement," *British Journal of Politics*, 32: 193–220.

Hovland, Carl, Janis, Irving and Kelley, Harold (1963) *Communication and Persuasion*, New Haven, CT: Yale University Press.

Hughes, Jane and Donnelly, Caitlin (2003) "Community Relations in Northern Ireland: A Shift in Attitudes?" unpublished paper, School of Policy Studies, University of Ulster at Jordanstown.

Human Rights Watch (2002) "Jenin: IDF Military Operations," *Human Rights Watch*, 14(3) (May).

—— (2003) "Hearts and Minds: Post-war Civilian Casualties in Baghdad by U.S. Forces," hrw.org/English/docs/2003/10/21/Iraq6467.htm.

—— (2005) "Leadership Failure: Firsthand Accounts of Torture of Iraqi Detainees," September 24.

Human Rights Watch/Middle East (1994a) *Israel's Interrogation of Palestinians from the Occupied Territories, Treatment and Ill Treatment*, New York: Human Rights Watch.

—— (1994b) *Torture and Ill Treatment*, New York: Human Rights Watch.

Human Security Centre (2005) *Human Security Report 2005: War and Peace in the 21st Century*, www.humansecuritycentre.org.

Hutchins, Christopher (1989) *Hostage to History*, New York: Farrar, Straus & Giroux.

ICG (International Crisis Group) (1998) "The Changing Logic of Bosnian Politics," March 10.

—— (2002) "A Time to Lead: The International Community and the Palestinian Conflict," www.crisisweb.org/projects.

—— (2006) "To Save Darfur," Africa Report no. 105, March 17.

ICTJ (International Center for Transitional Justice) (2004) "Bosnia and Hercegovina: Selected Developments in Transitional Justice" (October).

ICTY (UN International Criminal Tribunal for the Former Yugoslavia) (2003) Tenth Annual Report, www.un.org/icty.

Ignatieff, Michael (2004) *The Lesser Evil: Political Ethics in an Age of Terror*, Princeton, NJ: Princeton University Press.

Ingram, Mike (2002) "Sectarian Divisions Widen in Northern Ireland," www.wsws. org/articles/2002/jan2002/ire-j07_prn.shtml.

Institute for War and Peace Reporting (2005) "Balkan Crisis Report 564," July 6, www.iwpr.net.

International Commission of Inquiry on Darfur (2005) *Report to the UN Secretary General*, Geneva.

International Commission on Intervention and State Sovereignty (2001) Report, December.

Irwin, Colin (2003) "Devolution and the State of the Northern Ireland Peace Process," *Global Review of Ethnopolitics*, 2(3) (March): 1–21.

Jaksic, Bozidar (1999) *From a Balkan Perspective*, Belgrade: Institute of Philosophy and Social Theory, July 20.

Jaszi, Oscar (1961) *The Dissolution of the Habsburg Monarchy*, Chicago, IL: University of Chicago Press.

Jean, François and Ruffin, Jean-Christophe (eds.) (1996) *Économie des guerres civiles*, Paris: Hachette Pluriel.

Jeff, Dennis (2000) *Why Peacekeeping Fails*, New York: St. Martin's.

Judah, Tim (1997) *The Serbs: History, Myth, and the Destruction of Yugoslavia*, New Haven, CT: Yale University Press.

—— (2000) *Kosovo: War and Revenge*, New Haven, CT: Yale University Press.

—— (2003) "The Fog of Justice," *NYRB*, January 15, 23–7.

—— (2005) "The Stakes in Darfur," *NYRB*, January 13, 12–16.

Kaldor, Mary (2001) *New and Old Wars: Organized Violence in a Global Era*, Stanford, CA: Stanford University Press.

Kaplan, Robert (1994) "The Coming Anarchy," *Atlantic Monthly*, 273(2): 44–76.

Kaufman, Stuart (2001) *Modern Hatreds: The Symbolic Politics of Ethnic Wars*, Ithaca, NY: Cornell University Press.

Kaufmann, Chaim (1996) "Possible and Impossible Solutions to Ethnic Civil Wars," *International Security*, 20(4): 136–75.

Kelsen, Hans (1957) *What Is Justice?* Berkeley and Los Angeles: University of California Press.

Kepel, Gilles (2002) *Jihad: The Trail of Political Islam*, Cambridge, MA: Harvard University Press.

King, Charles (1997) *Ending Civil Wars*, Adelphi Paper 308, London: International Institute of Strategic Studies.

Kinzer, Stephen (2001) "The Unfinished Peace," *NYRB*, June 11, 61–3.

Kuran, Timur (1998) "Ethnic Norms and their Transformation through Reputational Cascades," *Journal of Legal Studies*, 27 (June): 623–59.

Kurspahic, Kemal (2003) *Prime Time Crime: Balkan Media in War and Peace*, Washington, DC: United States Institute of Peace.

Lake, David and Rothchild, Donald (1998) *The International Spread of Ethnic Conflict*, Princeton, NJ: Princeton University Press.

Lea, David (ed.) (2002) *A Survey of Arab–Israeli Relations, 1947–2001*, London: Europa Publishers.

Lerner, Melvin (1980) *The Belief in a Just World: A Fundamental Delusion*, New York: Plenum.

Lewis, Bernard (2002) *What Went Wrong: The Clash between Islam and Modernity in the Middle East*, New York: HarperCollins.

Licklider, Roy (1995) "The Consequences of Negotiated Settlements in Civil Wars, 1945–1993," *American Political Science Review*, 89(3): 681–91.

Ligthart, G. Jan (2005) Letter to the editor, *NYRB*, February 10, 43–4.

Lijphart, Arend (1990) "The Power Sharing Approach," in Joseph Montville (ed.), *Conflict and Peacemaking in Multiethnic Societies*, Lexington, MA: Heath, 491–509.

Lindblom, Charles (1990) *Inquiry and Change*, New Haven, CT: Yale University Press.

Linder, Doug (2006) "An Introduction to the My Lai Courts-martial," www.law.umkc.edu/faculty/projects/ftrials/mylai.

Linz, Juan and Stepan, Alfred (1992) "Political Identities and Electoral Sequences: Spain, the Soviet Union, and Yugoslavia," *Daedalus*, 121(2): 123–37.

—— and —— (1996) "Towards Consolidated Democracies," *Journal of Democracy*, 7(2): 14–33.

Lustick, Ian (1993) *Unsettled Lands, Disputed Borders*, Ithaca, NY: Cornell University Press.

Maas, Peter (1995) *Love Thy Neighbor: A Story of War*, New York: Knopf.

McGarry, John and O'Leary, Brendan (2005) "Federation as a Method of Ethnic Conflict Regulation," in Sid Noel (ed.), *From Power Sharing to Democracy: Post-conflict Institutions in Ethnically Divided Societies*, Montreal: McGill-Queen's University Press, 263–96.

Mac Ginty, Roger and Darby, John (2002) *Guns and Government*, New York: Palgrave.

Magas, Branka and Zanic, Ivo (2001) *The War in Croatia and Bosnia-Hercegovina, 1991–1995*, London: Frank Cass.

Makiya, Kanan and Mneimneh, Hassan (2002) "Manual for a Raid," *NYRB*, January 17.

Malcolm, Noel (1999) *Kosovo: A Short History*, New York: HarperCollins.

Mallie, Eamon and McKittrick, David (2001) *Endgame in Northern Ireland*, London: Hodder & Stoughton.

Malloy, Trove and Soyan, Tankut (2004) *The Cyprus Annan Plan*, ECMI Report 52, European Centre for Minority Issues, October.

Mann, Michael (2005) *The Dark Side of Democracy: Explaining Ethnic Cleansing*, Cambridge: Cambridge University Press.

Mansergh, Martin (2000) "The Background to the Irish Peace Process," in Michael Cox, Adrian Guelke and Fiona Stephen (eds.), *A Farewell to Arms? From Long War to Long Peace in Northern Ireland*, Manchester: Manchester University Press.

Mansfield, Edward and Snyder, Jack (2005/6) "Prone to Violence," *National Interest*, Winter, 1–5.

Margalit, Avishai (2001) "Settling Scores," *NYRB*, September 20, 20–4.

—— (2003) "The Suicide Bombers," *NYRB*, January 16, 36–40.

Markovic, Mira (1996) *Answers*, Kingston, Ontario: Quarry Press.

Marks, Susan Collin (2000) *Watching the Wind: Conflict Resolution during South Africa's Transition to Democracy*, Washington, DC: United States Institute of Peace.

Marshall, Monty (2003) "Global Trends in Democratization," in Monty Marshall and Ted Robert Gurr, *Peace and Conflict*, College Park: University of Maryland, Center for International Development and Conflict Management, 12–16.

—— and Gurr, Ted Robert (2003) *Peace and Conflict*, College Park: University of Maryland, Center for International Development and Conflict Management.

Marshall, T. H. (1965) *Class, Citizenship and Social Development*, New York: Doubleday Anchor.

Mason, Chris (2005) "Losing Our Way at an Afghan Crossroads," *Los Angeles Times*, April 11.

Mauro, Paul (1995) "Corruption and Growth," *Quarterly Journal of Economics*, 110 (August): 681–711.

Mayer, Jane (2005) "The Experiment," *New Yorker*, July 11/18, 60–70.

Mendlovitz, Saul (1999) "Considering an International Rapid Reaction Force," *Institute for the Study of Genocide Newsletter*, 22 (Winter): 2–24.

Mertus, Julie (1999) *Kosovo: How Myths and Truths Started a War*, Berkeley and Los Angeles: University of California Press.

Miller, Greg, Mazzetti, Mark and Meyer, Josh (2006) "Documents Reveal the Stories of Prisoners at Guantanamo Bay," *Los Angeles Times*, March 4.

Mishra, Pankaj (2005) "The Real Afghanistan," *NYRB*, March 10, 44–8.

Mitchell, George (1999) *Making Peace*, New York: Knopf.

—— (2002) "Soul of India," PBS, September 20, www.pbs.org/wnet/wideangle/shows/media/transcript2.html.

Monnesland, Svein (1997) *Land ohne Wiederkehr: ex Jugoslavien, Wurzeln des Krieges*, Klagenfurt: Wieser.

Montville, Joseph (ed.) (1990) *Conflict and Peacemaking in Multiethnic Societies*, Lexington, MA: Heath.

Muscat, Robert (2002) *Investing in Peace: How Development Aid Can Prevent or Promote Conflict*, Armonk, NY: M. E. Sharpe.

Naimark, Norman (2001) *Fires of Hatred: Ethnic Cleansing in Twentieth-Century Europe*, Cambridge, MA: Harvard University Press.

Neier, Arjeh (1998) *War Crimes*, New York: Random House.

"New Survey Shows Whites Resist Integration" (1979) *ISR Newsletter*, Institute for Social Research, University of Michigan, Summer, 4–5.

NILT (Northern Ireland Life and Times) (2002) "Module: Community Relations," www.ark.uk/nilt.

—— (2005) "In Search of the Middle Ground: Integrated Education and Northern Ireland Politics," www.ark.uk/nilt.

Noel, Sid (ed.) (2005) *From Power Sharing to Democracy: Post-conflict Institutions in Ethnically Divided Societies*, Montreal: McGill-Queen's University Press.

Oberschall, Anthony (1973) *Social Conflict and Social Movements*, Englewood Cliffs, NJ: Prentice Hall.

—— (1989) "Opportunities and Framing in the East European Revolutions in 1989," in Doug McAdam, Mayer Zald and John McCarthy (eds.), *Comparative Perspectives in Social Movements*, New York: Cambridge University Press, 93–121.

—— (1993) *Social Movements, Ideologies, Interests, and Identities*, New Brunswick: Transaction Books.

—— (2000) "The Manipulation of Ethnicity: From Ethnic Cooperation to Violence and War in Yugoslavia," *Ethnic and Racial Studies*, 23(6): 982–1001.

—— and Kim, Hyojoung (1996) "Identity and Action," *Mobilization*, 1(1): 63–85.

O'Connor, Walker (1978) "A Nation Is a Nation, Is a State, Is an Ethnic Group...," *Ethnic and Racial Studies*, 1(4): 329–98.

O'Flynn, Ian and Russell, David (eds.) (2005) *Power Sharing: New Challenges for Divided Societies*, London: Pluto Press.

Ogata, Sadako (2005) *The Turbulent Decade: Confronting the Refugee Crises of the 1990s*, New York: Norton.

OHR (Office of High Representative) (2003) Twenty-fourth Annual Report, www.ohr.int/other-doc/hr-reports/, p. 2.

Olcutt, Martha Brill and Babajanov, Bakhtiyar (2003) "The Terrorist Notebooks," *Foreign Policy*, 135 (March/April): 31–40.

Olson, Mancur, Jr. (1968) *The Logic of Collective Action*, New York: Schocken Books.

—— (1976) "Exchange, Integration, and Grants: A Critical View," in Martin Pfaff (ed.), *Frontiers in Social Thought*, Amsterdam: North Holland Publishing Co.

—— (1993) "Dictatorship, Democracy, and Development," *American Political Science Review*, 87(3) (September): 567–75.

Olzak, Susan (1966) "A Competition Model of Ethnic Collective Action in American Cities, 1877–1889," in Susan Olzak and Joane Nagel (eds.), *Competitive Ethnic Relations*, New York: Academic Press.

OSCE (Organization for Security and Cooperation in Europe) (2004) "War Crimes Proceedings in Croatia and Findings from Trial Monitoring," www.osce.org/croatia.

O'Toole, Fintan (2002) "Guns in the Family," *NYRB*, April 11, 30–2.

Ottaway, Marina (2002) "Nation Building," *Foreign Policy*, 132 (September/October): 16–24.

—— (2003) "The Post-War Puzzle," Carnegie Endowment for International Peace, www.ceip.org/Publications.

O Tuathail, Geroid and Dahlman, Carl (2004) "Displacement and Return in BiH," in Wendy Larner and William Walters (eds.), *Global Governmentality*, London: Routledge.

Paris, Roland (2004) *At War's End: Building Peace after Civil Conflict*, Cambridge: Cambridge University Press.

Patten, Chris (2003) "Democracy Does Not Flow from the Barrel of a Gun," *Foreign Affairs*, 138 (September/October): 40–4.

"Peace Index" (2003) Tami Steinmetz Center for Peace Research, www.tau.ac.il/peaceindex.

"Peacekeeping" (2002) in *The Greenwood Encyclopedia of International Relations*, Westport, CT: Greenwood Press.

Pearlman, Wendy (2001) "Why the Checkpoint Ordeals?" *International Herald Tribune*, June 15.

Perkins, Dale (2000) "Law, Family Ties, and the Asian Way of Doing Business," in Lawrence Harrison and Samuel Huntington (eds.), *Culture Matters: How Values Shape Human Progress*, New York, Basic Books, 232–43.

Pillar, Paul (2006) "Intelligence, Policy, and the War in Iraq," *Foreign Affairs*, 85 (March/April): 15–28.

Poggi, Patricia, Muzur, Mirsada, Djpa, Dino and Kofic-Hasnagic, Snjezana (eds.) (2002) *Local Level Institutions and Social Capital*, Washington, DC: World Bank.

Popovic, Srdja, Jankovic, Ivan, Pesic, Vesna, Kandic, Natasa and Slapsak, Svetlana (1990) *Kosovski Cvor: Drestiti ili Seci*, Belgrade: Biblioteka Kronos.

Posen, Barry (1993) "The Security Dilemma and Ethnic Conflict," in Michael Brown (ed.), *Ethnic Conflict and International Security*, Princeton, NJ: Princeton University Press, 103–24.

Pratkanis, Anthony and Aronson, Eliot (2001) *The Art of Propaganda: The Everyday Use and Abuse of Persuasion*, New York: Freeman.

Press, Daryl G. and Valentino, Benjamin (2004) "A Victory, but Little Gained," Op-Ed, *NYT*, November 17.

Pressman, Jeremy (2003) "Visions and Collisions: What Happened at Camp David and Taba," *International Security*, 28(2): 5–43.

PRI (Penal Reform International) (2004) "From Camp to Hills: The Reintegration of Released Prisoners," *Gacaca Report VI*, May.

Quinn, David and Gurr, Ted Robert (2003) "Self-Determination Movements," in Monty Marshall and Ted Robert Gurr, *Peace and Conflict*, College Park: University of Maryland, Center for International Development and Conflict Management, 26–38.

Raban, Jonathan (2005) "The Truth about Terrorism," *NYRB*, January 13, 22–6.

Ramsbotham, Oliver and Woodhouse, Tom (1996) *Human Intervention in Contemporary Conflict*, Cambridge: Cambridge University Press.

—— and —— (eds.) (1999) "Overview," *Encyclopedia of International Peacekeeping Operations*, Santa Barbara, CA: ABC-Clio, 1–24.

RAND Palestinian State Study Team (2005) "Building a Successful Palestinian State" (MG-146-DCR), Santa Monica, CA: RAND Corporation.

Rashid, Ahmed (2001) *Taliban*, New Haven, CT: Yale University Press.

Renan, Ernest ([1882] 1996) "What Is a Nation?" in Geoff Eley and R. G. Suny (eds.), *Becoming National: A Reader*, New York: Oxford University Press.

Reynolds, Andrew (1999–2000) "Constitutional Pied Piper: The Northern Irish Good Friday Agreement," *Political Science Quarterly*, 114(4): 613–37.

—— (ed.) (2002) *The Architecture of Democracy*, New York: Oxford University Press.

Reyntjens, Filip and Vandeginste, Stef (2005) "Rwanda: An Atypical Transition," in Elm Skaar, Siri Gloppen and Astri Suhrke (eds.), *Roads to Reconciliation*, New York: Lexington Books, chapter 5.

Rieff, David (1995) *Slaughterhouse*, New York: Simon & Schuster.

—— (2004) "Kosovo: The End of an Era," in Fabrice Weissman (ed.), *In the Shadow of Just Wars: Violence, Politics, and Humanitarian Action*, Ithaca, NY: Cornell University Press, 286–96.

Ron, James (2003) *Frontiers and Ghettos: State Violence in Serbia and Israel*, Berkeley and Los Angeles: University of California Press.

Rose, Richard (1971) *Governing without Consensus: An Irish Perspective*, Boston, MA: Beacon Press.

Rosenberg, Cheryl (2003) *The Palestinians*, Boulder, CO: Lynne Rienner.

Rotberg, Robert (2003) *Cyprus after Annan: Next Steps toward a Solution*, World Peace Foundation Report no. 37, Cambridge, MA: World Peace Foundation.

Rotchild, Joseph (1981) *Ethnopolitics: A Conceptual Framework*, New York: Columbia University Press.

Roth, Kenneth (2004) "The Law of War in the War on Terror," *Foreign Affairs*, 83 (January/February): 2–7.

Rouleau, Eric (2002) "Trouble in the Kingdom," *Foreign Affairs*, 81 (July/August): 75–89.

Rumbach, R. and Fink, D. (1994) "Humanitarian Action in Current Armed Conflicts," *Medicine and Global Survival*, 1(4) (December): 1, 11.

Sambanis, Nicholas (2004) "What Is Civil War? Conceptual and Empirical Complexities of an Operational Definition," *Journal of Conflict Resolution*, 48(6) (December): 814–58.

Schelling, Thomas (1984) *Choices and Consequences*, Cambridge, MA: Harvard University Press.

Schiff, Ze'ev and Ya'ari, Ehud (1989) *Intifada*, New York: Simon & Schuster.

Schroeder, Paul (2001/2) "The Risks of Victory," *National Interest*, Winter: 28–36.

Segal, Jerome, Katz, Elihu, Levy, Shlomit and Izaat Sa'id, Nadar (2000) *Negotiating Jerusalem*, Albany, NY: SUNY Press.

Serbian Helsinki Committee on Human Rights (2001) "Media in Serbia," May, www.hrweb.org.

Seselj, Vojislav (1991–2001) *Collected Works*, vol. 41, Belgrade: Velika Serbia.

Shavit, Ari (2006) "The General," *New Yorker*, January 23 and 30.

Sherif, Muzafer (1966) *In Common Predicament: The Social Psychology of Intergroup Conflict and Cooperation*, Boston, MA: Houghton Mifflin.

Shikaki, Khalil (1998) "The Peace Process and Political Violence," *Meria Journal*, 2(1), March.

—— (2002) "Palestinians Divided," *Foreign Affairs*, 81(1): 89–104.

Shirlow, Peter (2003) "Who Fears to Speak: Fear, Mobility and Ethno-sectarianism in the Two Ardoynes," *Global Review of Ethnopolitics*, 3(1): 76–91.

Shlaim, Avi (2001) *The Iron Wall: Israel and the Arab World*, New York: Norton.

Simon, Herbert (1969) *The Sciences of the Artificial*, Cambridge, MA: MIT Press.

Sisk, Timothy (1996) *Power Sharing and International Mediation in Ethnic Conflicts*, Washington, DC: United States Institute of Peace.

Skaar, Elm, Gloppen, Siri and Suhrke, Astri (eds.) (2005) *Roads to Reconciliation*, New York: Lexington Books.

Smith, Anthony (1993) "Ethnic Sources of Nationalism," in Michael Brown (ed.), *Ethnic Conflict and International Security*, Princeton, NJ: Princeton University Press: 27–42.

Smucker, Philip (2004) "How bin Laden Got Away," *Christian Science Monitor*, March 4.

Snyder, Jack (2000) *From Voting to Violence: Democratization and Nationalist Conflict*, New York: Norton.

Sontag, Deborah (2000) "Mideast's Talking Heads Turn Downright Neighborly," *NYT*, July 13.

Spear, Joanna (2002) "Disarmament and Demobilization," in Stephen Steadman, Donald Rothchild and Elisabeth Cousins (eds.), *Ending Civil Wars*, Boulder, CO: Lynne Rienner, 164–5.

Staub, Ervin (1989) *The Roots of Evil: The Origins of Genocide and Other Group Violence*, New York: Cambridge University Press.

Steadman, Stephen, Rothchild, Donald and Cousins, Elisabeth (eds.) (2002) *Ending Civil Wars*, Boulder, CO: Lynne Rienner.

Stern, Jessica (2000) "Pakistan's Jihadi Culture," *Foreign Affairs*, 79(6) (November/ December): 115–26.

—— (2003) *Terror in the Name of God*, New York: HarperCollins.

Stiglitz, Joseph (2002) *Globalization and Its Discontents*, New York: Norton.

Stover, Eric (2004) "Witnesses and the Promise of Justice in The Hague," in Eric Stover and Harvey Weinstein (eds.), *My Neighbor, My Enemy*, New York: Cambridge University Press, chapter 5.

—— and Weinstein, Harvey (eds.) (2004) *My Neighbor, My Enemy*, New York: Cambridge University Press.

Sudetic, Chuck (1998) *Blood and Vengeance*, New York: Norton.

Sundkler, B. (1961) *Bantu Prophets in South Africa*, Oxford: Oxford University Press.

Suny, Ronald (1993) *The Revenge of the Past: Nationalism, Revolution and the Collapse of the Soviet Union*, Stanford, CA: Stanford University Press.

Taub, James (2004) "Nation Building," *NYT Magazine*, April 11.

Teitel, Rudi (1996) "Judgment at The Hague," *East European Constitutional Review*, Fall, 80–5.

—— (1999) "War Crimes: Brutality, Genocide, Terror and the Struggle for Justice," *East European Constitutional Review*, Winter/Spring, 110–12.

Thatcher, Margaret (1993) *The Downing Street Years*, New York: HarperCollins.

Thompson, Mark (1994) *Forging War: The Media in Serbia, Croatia and Bosnia-Hercegovina*, Avon: Bath Press.

Thompson, Robert (1966) *Defeating Communist Insurgency*, New York: Praeger.

Thucydides (1960) *History of the Peloponnesian War*, translated by Rex Warner, New York: Oxford University Press.

Tilly, Charles, Tilly, Richard and Tilly, Louise (1975) *The Rebellious Century 1830–1930*, Cambridge, MA: Harvard University Press.

Toft, Monica Duffy (2002/3) "Indivisible Territory, Geographic Concentration, and Ethnic War," *Security Studies*, 12(2): 82–119.

Tolnay, Stuart and Beck, E. M. (1995) *A Festival of Violence*, Urbana: University of Illinois Press.

TRC (Truth and Reconciliation Commission) (1998) *Truth and Reconciliation of South Africa Report*, 5 vols., Capetown: TRC, www.truth.org.za.

—— (2000) Amnesty Hearings and Decisions, January 11, Moringer, www.truth.org.za.

UNC-CH (University of North Carolina, Curriculum on Peace, War and Defense) (1999) "Bombing of Yugoslavia" panel, November 4.

UNDP (UN Development Program) (2003) "Millennium Development Goals."

UNHCR (UN High Commission on Refugees in Bosnia and Hercegovina) (2004) "Municipal Authorities, DP Associations and NGOs: Statistical Summary as of 31 August 2004."

van Creveld, Martin (1991) *The Transformation of War*, New York: Free Press.

Varshney, Ashutosh (2002) *Ethnic Conflict and Civic Life*, New Haven, CT: Yale University Press.

Wagley, Charles and Harris, Marvin (1958) *Minorities in the New World*, New York: Columbia University Press.

Wald, Patricia (2002) "Punishment of War Crimes by International Tribunals," *Social Research*, 69(4): 1119–34.

Wallensteen, Peter (2002) *Understanding Conflict Resolution*, Thousand Oaks, CA: Sage.

Walter, Barbara (1997) "The Critical Barrier to Civil War Settlement," *International Organization*, 51(3): 335–61.

Walzer, Michael (1997) *Just and Unjust Wars*, New York: Basic Books.

—— (1998) "Kosovo," *Dissent*, Summer: 5–7.

—— (2002) "The Triumph of Just War Theory," *Social Research*, 69(4) (Winter): 938–40.

Weber, Max ([1923] 1956) *Wirtschaft und Gesellschaft*, Johannes Winckelmann (ed.), vol. 1, Tübingen: Mohr.

—— (1958) *From Max Weber: Essays in Sociology*, Hans Gerth and C. Wright Mills (eds.), New York: Oxford University Press.

Welsh, David (1993) "Domestic Politics and Ethnic Conflicts," in Michael Brown (ed.), *Ethnic Conflict and International Security*, Princeton, NJ: Princeton University Press, 43–60.

Wieviorka, Michel (1993) *The Making of Terrorism*, Chicago, IL: Chicago University Press.

Williams, Paul (2006) "Military Response to Mass Killing: The African Union Mission in the Sudan," *International Peacekeeping*, 13(2): 168–83.

Winik, Jay (2003) "A Brief History of Resistance," Op-Ed, *NYT*, December 16.

Wood, Nicholas (2006) "Serbia Begins Prosecuting Some War Crimes Cases," *NYT*, January 8.

Woodward, Susan (1995) *Balkan Tragedy*, Washington, DC: Brookings.

World Bank, ECSSD (2001) "Local Level Institutions and Social Capital Study" (June), Washington, DC: World Bank.

Wright, Charles (1959) *Mass Communications*, New York: Random House.

Wright, Robin (2001) *Sacred Rage: The Wrath of Islam*, New York: Simon & Schuster.

Zartman, William (2001) *Preventive Negotiation: Avoiding Conflict Escalation*, Boulder, CO: Rowman & Littlefield.

Zinni, Gen. Anthony (2003) "A General's View," PBS *NewsHour*, September 30.

Index